NOV 1 3 2006

DATE DUE

The Jewish Enemy

The JEWISH
ENEMY

NAZI PROPAGANDA
DURING WORLD WAR II
AND THE HOLOCAUST

Jeffrey Herf

The Belknap Press of
Harvard University Press

Cambridge, Massachusetts
London, England
2006

In memory of
George L. Mosse (1918–1999)
and
for Walter Laqueur

Copyright © 2006 by the President and Fellows of Harvard College
All rights reserved
Printed in the United States of America

Library of Congress Cataloging-in-Publication Data
Herf, Jeffrey, 1947–
    The Jewish enemy : Nazi propaganda during World War II and the
Holocaust / Jeffrey Herf.
        p. cm.
    Includes bibliographical references and index.
    ISBN 0-674-02175-4
    1. World War, 1939–1945—Propaganda. 2. Nazi propaganda—Ger-
many—History—20th century. 3. Antisemitism—Germany—History—
20th century. 4. Holocaust, Jewish (1939–1945). 5. Germany—Politics
and government—1933–1945. I. Title.
D810.P7G337 2006
940.53'181—dc22   2005056279

Contents

Preface

Why did European, especially German, anti-Semitism, which had never led to an effort to murder all of Europe's Jews before, do so between 1941 and 1945 in the midst of World War II? What changed to make anti-Semitism a rationale for mass murder rather than for a continuation of centuries-old patterns of persecution? The answer lies in what Hitler and his leading propagandists and ideologists had to say about the "Jewish question" in the midst of the war and the Holocaust and in their efforts to shape the narrative of events through propaganda in the controlled press. Rather surprisingly, in view of the vast literature on the subject, *The Jewish Enemy* is the first book to examine in depth the Nazis' paranoid anti-Semitic account of the world war. Their story of an innocent Germany besieged by international Jewry intent on its "extermination" served as both the public announcement of and the justification for the Final Solution.

In the jargon of historians, this is a work of modified intentionalism. That is, it examines the ideological intentions of key political actors in the historical conjuncture that was World War II. The Holocaust, however, was not the inevitable outcome of the continuities of German, or of European, history. The long tradition of elite and popular anti-Semitism created a climate of indifference in which the murderers could operate but did not per se inspire a policy of mass murder. The historians' search for ideological origins has taken us toward but not to the Final Solution. For it was only in the historically specific circumstances of the war that the most radical and paranoid current of European and especially German anti-Semitism, which Hitler had adopted from the beginning of his political activities, became the key to the German dictatorship's explanation of ongoing events and thus a causal factor in the evolution of the Holocaust. Hitler and his associates had long believed that anti-Semitism offered *the* explanatory framework for world history. First in 1939, then still more in 1941, and on up through the last days of the Nazi regime, he and his leading propagandists argued that it was necessary to "exterminate" the Jews before they were able to exterminate Germany and the Germans.

Historians of a previous generation enlightened and inspired me and many others with their work and personal encouragement. Karl Bracher's analysis of the Nazi regime and of Europe's century of ideologies has been an exemplar of historical explanation and moral clarity. François Furet's examination of the intersection of ideas, events, and circumstances surrounding the Terror in the French Revolution served as a model for integrating radical ideological currents into the narrative of political history and as an antidote to historical determinism. Thomas Nipperdey examined anti-Semitism as one of the "multiple continuities" of German, and European, history. The deaths of Furet and Nipperdey leave an intellectual and personal void.

Bracher, Furet, and Nipperdey are part of a rich scholarly tradition of examining the intersection of ideas and politics. George Mosse and Walter Laqueur also worked in this tradition. Together they founded and edited the *Journal of Contemporary History*, in which much important work on Nazism and Fascism has been published. Laqueur made essential contributions to the history of the Holocaust, stimulated my interest in the mixture of secrecy and blunt talk in Nazi anti-Semitic propaganda, and encouraged me over the years. Mosse led the historical search for the Holocaust's ideological origins and illuminated in many ways how various components of European culture contributed to a climate in which the Holocaust became possible. He was an inspiring teacher, example, and friend for three decades.

However much I resisted it, *the Jew* is in every respect the center of the language of the Third Reich, indeed of its whole view of the epoch.

—Victor Klemperer, *I Will Bear Witness, 1942–1945,* July 20, 1944, Dresden

What is characteristic of Nazi propaganda is less the lie than the imposition of a paranoiac pattern on world events.

—E. H. Gombrich, *Myth and Reality in German Wartime Broadcasts,* London, 1969

1 The Jews, the War, and the Holocaust

The texts and images of wartime ideology and propaganda of Nazism are a rich and revelatory means of understanding why European, and in particular German, anti-Semitism, the source of centuries of persecution, led between 1941 and 1945 to the Holocaust. From 1919 to January 30, 1939, Hitler hurled terrible abuse and threats of violence at the Jews. In a speech to the Reichstag when he was making plans to begin a second European war, he publicly threatened to "exterminate" all the Jews of Europe if they provoked such a war.[1] In their public statements, the Nazis repeatedly asserted that the connection between World War II and the Jews was causal and necessary and thus by implication not an accident of timing and geography. Though Hitler had long planned to launch the war at a time and place of his choosing, he and his propagandists insisted that the "extermination" of the Jews was a justified response to a war launched against Germany by "international Jewry." A blend of hatred, self-righteous indignation, and paranoia was at the core of the Nazi justification of genocide. Nazi propaganda presented Germany's war against the Allies and its intention to "exterminate" the Jews of Europe as part of one overarching war of retaliation and defense. This escalation of Nazi policy from persecution to extermination was accompanied and prefigured by a radicalization of Nazi Germany's public language about the Jews.

1

The Jewish Enemy

There was, of course, an abyss between Nazi propaganda that presented the Third Reich as the innocent victim of others' malice and the reality of Hitler's long-planned policy of expansion and aggression. This gap tempted contemporaries to assume that the propaganda was merely a manipulative means used by cynics who were fully aware that it reversed the chronology of events that their own aggressive plans had set in motion. Yet some contemporary observers concluded that the Nazis believed their own paranoid logic. The literary scholar and diarist Viktor Klemperer wrote in his diary in 1944, soon after D-day: "However much I resisted it, *the Jew* is in every respect the center of the language of the Third Reich, indeed *of its whole view of the epoch.*"[2] Klemperer recognized that anti-Semitism was not only a set of prejudices and hatreds but also an explanatory framework for historical events. The young E. H. Gombrich, who subsequently gained fame as an art historian, worked at the British Broadcasting Corporation (BBC) translating and analyzing German wartime propaganda. A quarter century later, Gombrich wrote that Nazi propaganda had created a mythic world by "transforming the political universe into a conflict of persons and personifications" in which a virtuous young Germany fought manfully against evil schemers, above all the Jews. The Jews were the cement for this myth, first in the political battles within Germany and then on the international plane. It was "this gigantic persecution mania, this paranoiac myth that [held] the various strands of German propaganda together." Gombrich concluded that what characterized Nazi propaganda was "less the lie than the imposition of a paranoiac pattern on world events."[3] During World War II, the propaganda of the Nazi regime repeatedly asserted that an actual political subject, an actor called Jewry or international Jewry, was "guilty" of starting and prolonging the war and that a Jewish international conspiracy was intent on exterminating Germany and the Germans. These statements rested on a paranoia inherent in the Nazis' radical anti-Semitism. In the context of World War II, these beliefs transformed the centuries-old European anti-Semitism from a justification for traditional forms of persecution into what the historian Norman Cohn called a "warrant for genocide."[4]

2

Faced with expressions of such views by Nazi Germany's national political leaders, most contemporary Marxists, liberals, and conservatives of the time, as well as a good number of postwar scholars, were skeptical that the Nazis truly believed their own propaganda. And yet an examination of modern political culture draws attention to the causal significance of many irrational and illusory ideological perspectives. In the case of Nazi Germany, historians have amply documented what Saul Friedlander has called Hitler's early "redemptive anti-Semitism," which combined paranoid fantasy about an all-powerful international Jewry with promises of redeeming and saving Germany from that pernicious influence.[5] Ian Kershaw notes "the all-devouring manic obsession with the Jews" that Hitler displayed in his beer hall tirades in Munich just after World War I.[6] This obsession is evident in a speech to a Nazi party meeting of April 6, 1920, when Hitler said, "We don't want to be emotional anti-Semites who seek to create a mood for pogroms. Rather, we are driven by a pitiless and fierce determination to attack the evil at its roots and to exterminate it root and branch. Every means is justified to reach our goal, even if it means we must make a pact with the devil."[7]

In the early years, Hitler denounced the Jews as an element alien to the German nation, and the cause of Germany's problems, from military defeat to the Depression. Not until January 30, 1939, however, did he publicly threaten to exterminate the Jews. Between 1920 and 1939, often in the most vicious terms, he called for the "removal of the Jews from the midst of our people."[8] Toward the end of *Mein Kampf,* he wrote, "If at the beginning of the war and during the war twelve or fifteen thousand of these Hebrew corrupters of the people had been held under poison gas, as happened to hundreds of thousands of our very best German soldiers in the field, the sacrifice of millions would not have been in vain."[9] Yet however vicious his language or profound his hatred, between April 1920 and January 1939 he did not repeat the threat to kill all the Jews in Germany or in the rest of Europe. Rather, he spoke of "world" or "international Jewry" as an actually existing political subject with vast power that was hostile to Germany.[10] This subject had played a role in Germany's defeat in World War I, he claimed, and had helped bring about the Bolshevik Revolution, Germany's postwar inflation, and the economic crisis of 1929. Between 1933 and 1939, international Jewry had been responsible for the criticism leveled by the European powers and the United States at Nazi Germany's domestic policies, including but not limited to its anti-Semitism. Before 1939 Hitler made no secret of his violent hatred of the Jews and of his determination to drive them out of public life, the professions, and the economy, deprive them of German citizenship, and then, by force if need be, drive them out of Germany. Indeed, during the era of anti-Jewish persecution between 1933 and 1939, the Nazi regime through its Transfer (Haavarah) Agreement with some Jewish organizations, encouraged and allowed the movement of sixty thousand German Jews and about a hundred million marks from Germany to Palestine.[11] Hitler justified every escalation of persecution against the Jews as a response to what he alleged was a prior act of aggression by international Jewry. Yet from January 1933 to January 1939, through six years of escalating anti-Semitic persecution, boycotts, arbitrary arrests, theft, purges, and the pogrom of November 1938, Hitler, without declaring war against the Jews, repeated his assertion about the threat international Jewry posed to Germany.[12] In January 1939, however, he struck a distinctly more radical and murderous tone.

While proclaiming Jewry's threat to Nazi Germany, Hitler prepared to launch a war for Lebensraum in the East. Such a military action would provide Germany with raw materials and food supplies safe from an Anglo-American blockade and would lay the groundwork for a subsequent bid for world domination and an attack on the United States.[13] Hitler presented himself publicly as a man of peace and as a provincial, albeit radical, German nationalist who sought merely to apply to the German-speaking peoples of Central Europe the League of Nations principle of the right of national self-determination.[14] In fact, his strategy for victory entailed preparation for a series of short wars against isolated enemies, in which victory would offer resources that would facilitate further expansion, on the path to world domination. Waging war sooner rather than later would exploit Nazi Germany's head start in armaments. Delay would undermine its initial advantage.[15]

Hitler was the central, decisive historical actor driving events toward the war and the Holocaust. Yet the propaganda of the Nazi party and Nazi regime presented Hitler and Germany as merely responding to the initiatives, injustices, and threats of others. It was a propaganda that trumpeted innocence and self-righteous indignation and turned the power relations between Germany and the Jews upside down: Germany was the innocent victim; Jewry was all powerful. From 1933 to 1939, the translation of anti-Semitic ideology into a policy of persecution was presented as a justified response to what the Jews had done to Germany and the Germans. On January 30, 1939, a distinct shift occurred, as Hitler depicted the war that he was preparing to launch as the last in a long series of acts of aggression by international Jewry against Germany. According to Hitler's paranoid logic, the Jews had launched the war so that the Nazis would be compelled to wage a war of retaliation against the Jews of Europe. In his speech to the Reichstag on January 30, Hitler made his first unequivocal public threat to exterminate (that is, murder)—not merely to remove, deport, or defeat— "the Jewish race in Europe" in the event that "international finance Jewry inside and outside Europe" brought about a new world war. He publicly repeated the genocidal prophecy on at least six subsequent occasions between January 30, 1939, and February 24, 1943.[16] In contrast to his public practice between 1919 and 1939, in the ensuing years Hitler spoke and wrote with unprecedented clarity, bluntness, and frequency about acting on his threats to exterminate the Jews of Europe. He cast himself in the role of the prophet: the outbreak of World War II was further proof that international Jewry had indeed been out to destroy Germany and the Germans.

Hitler and his leading propagandists were able to entertain completely contradictory versions of events simultaneously, one rooted in the grandiose idea of a master race and world domination, the other in the self-pitying paranoia of the innocent, beleaguered victim.[17] Grandiosity and paranoia were two poles of one fanatical ideology.[18] The Nazis projected their own aggressive and murderous intentions and policies onto their victims, the Jews most of all. Max Horkheimer and Theodor Adorno captured this aspect of Nazism when they wrote in 1944 that the "blind murderer has always seen his victim as a persecutor against whom he must defend himself."[19] From beginning to end, the narrative of paranoia displayed in the propaganda accompanied and justified the Nazi regime's grandiose war of aggression and its genocidal policies.

The radical anti-Semitism of Nazi Germany's wartime propaganda also constituted an interpretive prism through which Nazi leaders viewed and misconstrued events as they unfolded. Indeed, the misperceptions of reality deriving from the anti-Semitic agenda contributed to major blunders and eventually to the Allies' ability to defeat the Nazis, albeit at horrendous cost. In *The Jewish Enemy,* I examine the process of translating anti-Semitic ideology into a narrative and tailoring the weekly and daily news to fit that narrative.[20] Like other practitioners of paranoid politics before and after, the Nazis believed they had uncovered deep secrets of modern history and politics, secrets that the great mass of humanity, mired in events, failed to grasp. At the same time that they entered an utterly mythic world, they convinced themselves and millions of others that their Ministry for Public Enlightenment and Propaganda (Reichsministerium für Volksaufklärung und Propaganda) was educating the masses about the people behind the scenes and the realities that were the driving force behind events.[21] Within the "delirious discourse" of radical anti-Semitism, all riddles were solved, all historical contingency was eliminated, and everything became explicable.[22]

Historians of anti-Semitism and the origins of the Holocaust have fully documented its extent and depth in European, and especially German and Austrian, society and culture. With particular insight, they have explained the roots of "the era of persecution."[23] This impressive body of scholarship explains the path to an anti-Semitic "consensus," which led by the mid- and late 1930s to the Nuremberg race laws, denial of citizenship, economic impoverishment, and imprisonment of Jews.[24] George Mosse, the pioneering historian of fascism and racism, boldly claimed that the racism of bodily stereotypes and countertypes "was the catalyst which pushed German nationalism over the edge, from discrimination to mass extermination."[25] Yet however despicable this consensus was or however odious the familiar caricatures of supposed Aryan and Jewish bodies, neither had led to a policy of mass murder. Reference to the long-term history of anti-Semitism leaves unanswered the question of why mass murder took place between 1941 and 1945 and not earlier.[26] The answer to this question lies in the efforts by the radical anti-Semites at the head of the Nazi regime to make sense and nonsense of the role of international Jewry in the outbreak and unfolding of World War II. The Nazi leaders believed that the unfolding events of the war confirmed the truth of their radical anti-Semitic ideology and reinforced the need to eliminate Jews from the face of the earth.

Radical anti-Semitism rested on the belief that the Jews were a cohesive, politically active subject—that is, a group united on a global scale by racial bonds that transcended any allegiance to nation-states. In the Nazi view, this powerful and autonomous entity, international Jewry, controlled assorted stooges and accomplices who served its evil interests. One way in which this view of a Jewish global conspiracy was distinct from less radical, and nongenocidal, forms of Jew hatred was the relative lack of importance it attached to Jews' presumed physical appearance. Indeed, the Nazis claimed that the Jews were experts at camouflage and that as a result a massive effort at "public enlightenment" was needed to expose them and their aim of world domination. If not identified and destroyed, the Nazi propagandists feared, Jewry would annihilate the German people. As a result, Hitler and his associates publicly declared on numerous occasions that they would "exterminate" Jews before the Jews could exterminate the Germans. The idea of a Jewish a conspiracy was popularized by the mass publication of *The Protocols of the Elders of Zion* in the decades preceding the Nazis' arrival in power. The accomplishment of the Nazi propagandists was to bring the idea of this conspiracy up to date and to flesh it out with the names and faces of recognizable prominent figures in mid-twentieth-century Europe and the United States. The theory of an international Jewish conspiracy supplied answers to such seemingly difficult questions as, Why did Britain fight on in 1940 rather than negotiate? Why was it likely that the Soviet regime would collapse like a house of cards following the German invasion of June 1941? Why did Franklin Roosevelt oppose Hitler? Why did the anti-Hitler coalition remain intact as the Red Army continued to push toward Central Europe after spring 1943? In the idea of a vastly powerful international Jewish conspiracy operating behind the scenes Nazi leaders believed they had found the answer to these and many other riddles of modern history.

Though there exists an excellent group of works on Nazi propaganda, none has focused on the translation of radical anti-Semitism into the texts and visual images of wartime propaganda.[27] *The Jewish Enemy* draws on numerous sources to trace that translation process: relevant speeches by Adolf Hitler; speeches, essays, and the multivolume diary of Joseph Goebbels, head of the Ministry for Public Enlightenment and Propaganda; selections from the thousands of daily and weekly press directives that Reich press chief Otto Dietrich and his staff gave to newspaper and periodical editors at press conferences in Berlin; front-page articles and headlines in government-controlled newspapers; and the relevant anti-Semitic wall newspapers and posters, black and white or in color, which intruded on the everyday visual experience of millions of Germans during the Third Reich. Some of these texts and images are well known. Others were familiar at the time but have been given short shrift even in the scholarship on Nazi propaganda. The vitally important press directives, *Word of the Day (Die Parole des Tages),* came to light in Otto Dietrich's postwar trial in Nuremberg but have been oddly underutilized. The brightly colored anti-Semitic political wall newspapers have also attracted little scrutiny.[28] Drawing on this wealth of material, I will argue that Nazi Germany's radical anti-Semitic

8

propaganda during World War II was integral to Nazi motivation and to the launching of the war and perpetration of the Final Solution.

What does "the war against the Jews" mean? For Lucy Dawidowicz, who made the phrase famous in her pioneering work, it meant the Holocaust, the Final Solution of the Jewish question in Europe.[29] With the ensuing explosion of scholarship about the Holocaust, two scholarly communities emerged. One, composed of military historians, continued to focus on the conventional battlefield narratives of World War II, while the second examined the history of the Holocaust in more detail. While the military historians wrote about Stalingrad and D-day, the others examined the Wannsee Conference and Auschwitz-Birkenau and other extermination camps. Although this dichotomy gave way to an attempt to connect World War II and the Holocaust in time, space, and ideological inspiration, Dawidowicz's phrase "the war against the Jews" still evokes in our minds specifically the mass murder of European Jewry.[30] The time has come to reach a more inclusive understanding of "the war against the Jews," one in which World War II plays a critical role.

When the Nazi leaders, in private conversations, office memos, or public statements, drew a connection between the Jews and World War II, they were referring to World War II and the Holocaust taken together as one apocalyptic battle. They did not limit the meaning of their war against what they called international Jewry to the Final Solution. Instead, they viewed the Final Solution, the details of which they never discussed in public, as a necessary campaign of retaliation in the context of a broader war of defense waged by Nazi Germany against international Jewry, world Jewry, and less frequently "the Jews." In the minds and public assertions of the Nazi leaders, they were fighting a single war that pitted Germany and its allies against a colossal international conspiracy of nonequals driven by Jewish figures working behind the scenes, while their non-Jewish accomplices, primarily the Allies, were the enemy's public facade. The Nazi narrative attributed enormous autonomy and power to the Jews, while denying those attributes to the nominal leaders of the most powerful nations in the world, Franklin Roosevelt, Winston Churchill, and Joseph Stalin, whom it identified as the Jews' puppets, accomplices, stooges, and servants.

Nazi Germany saw its enemy as a conspiracy of nonequals. International Jewry stood at its center, pulling the wires that controlled their stooges, the leaders of the Soviet Union, Great Britain, and the United States. From the months preceding the beginning of the war in September 1939 up until Hitler's last days in the bunker in Berlin, the Nazi narrative presented World War II and the intent to exterminate European Jewry as components of a war of defense against an act of aggression launched, escalated, and then carried to a victorious conclusion by an immensely powerful international Jewish conspiracy. The radicalism and extremism of Nazi anti-Semitism did not lie only in the familiar and disgusting racist caricatures of the Jews' physical appearance or of their alleged sexual proclivities. These prejudices and phobias had been commonplaces of European anti-Semitism long before the Third Reich. Indeed, it was because Nazi leaders were so worried about what they regarded as the ability of Jews to camouflage themselves as non-Jews that they restored the medieval custom of forcing Jews into the open through the compulsory wearing of the identifying yellow Star of David. It was the conspiratorial aspects of modern anti-Semitism that were most important in fostering its radical, genocidal implications. The desire for a Final Solution to the Jewish question was inseparable from the Nazis' view of the Jews as an internationally organized political power that was playing a decisive role in the events of World War II.

With too few exceptions, Hitler's bitterest opponents found it difficult to believe that he actually meant what he said concerning the extermination and annihilation of the Jews. Here I shall stress the similarity between publicly declared intentions and actual policy.[31] We need to revise conventional wisdom regarding the role of euphemism and clarity in the public language of the Nazi regime. In fact, when its leaders spoke publicly after 1938 about what they intended to do to Europe's

Jews, they were remarkably blunt and unambiguous about their intention to exterminate or annihilate—that is, to murder—all the Jews of Europe. George Orwell famously wrote that the language and propaganda of totalitarian dictatorship is that of "euphemism, question begging and sheer cloudy vagueness." In efforts to "defend the indefensible," he argued that totalitarian regimes substitute clinical abstractions for straightforward proper nouns and visceral verbs that refer directly to the violent and criminal acts committed.[32] Orwell's argument applies well to the internal office memos of the Reich Security Main Office, the agency of the Nazi regime that carried out the genocide of European Jewry, to its famous name for the Holocaust itself, the Final Solution, and of course to the vicious deceptions that the officials engaged in the mass murder used to obscure from their intended victims their awful fate.[33] Yet public language in Nazi Germany was not limited to these now infamous euphemisms. As Hannah Arendt noted in her classic work *The Origins of Totalitarianism,* "in order not to overestimate the importance of the propaganda lies one should recall the much more numerous instances in which Hitler was completely sincere and brutally unequivocal in the definition of the movement's true aims, but they were simply not acknowledged by a public unprepared for such consistency."[34] In fact, the public language of the Nazi regime combined complete suppression of any facts about the Final Solution with a brutal, sometimes crude declaration of murderous intent. Two key verbs and nouns in the German language were at the core of this language of mass murder: *vernichten* and *ausrotten.* These translate as "annihilate," "exterminate," "totally destroy," and "kill," and the nouns *Vernichtung* and *Ausrottung* as "annihilation," "extermination," "total destruction," and "killing."[35] Whether taken on their own from the dictionary meaning or placed in the context of the speeches, paragraphs, and sentences in which they were uttered, their meaning was clear. When Hitler and other Nazi leaders and propagandists uttered them to describe what they intended to do to the Jews, they almost always did so after claiming that it was the Jews who were intending to exterminate or annihilate not only the Nazi regime, the Nazi party, and the German armies but the German people as a whole. When the Nazis projected a policy of *Vernichtung* or *Ausrottung* onto international Jewry, the clear meaning in that context was that the Jews were supporting a genocidal policy aimed at Germany. By summer and fall of 1941, Hitler and Goebbels were saying publicly that the threatened extermination of the Jews was now a part of ongoing official policy.

The extraordinary meaning of these words was clear to German listeners and readers.[36] To the ears of military men, the term *Vernichtungschlacht*, "battle of annihilation," had a familiar, Clausewitzian ring and denoted complete defeat of the enemy armies. In describing the Jewish people as a whole as Nazi Germany's enemy, the Nazi narrative was an attempt to situate the threats to annihilate and exterminate within the normal or at least known language of warfare. In so doing, it went far beyond Clausewitzian orthodoxy. For those who remembered Germany's episode of colonialism in Africa, *Vernichtung* may have evoked memories of the German "war of extermination" in Namibia in the first decade of the century.[37] The blurring of distinctions between soldiers and civilians in Belgium and France during the first months of World War I may have offered a precedent to conducting a war against peoples instead of armies.[38] Yet as historians of the ideology of Hitler's war on the eastern front have demonstrated, German generals understood that this was not going to be a *Vernichtungschlacht* in the conventional Clausewitzian sense of the term but a *Vernichtungskrieg*, that is, a leap into an abyss beyond any European precedent.[39] From 1941 to 1945, the ordinary and daily experience of all Germans included exposure to radical anti-Semitic propaganda whose unambiguous intent was to justify mass murder of Jews. "Ordinary" men and women saw and heard a kind of radical anti-Semitism that was extraordinary even against the background of centuries of anti-Jewish hatred. The Nazi regime strove to assimilate extraordinary and genocidal language into a seemingly ordinary or more conventional narrative of war.[40] In the words and images the Nazis disseminated, the Jews of Europe were not anyone's innocent victim but were the party chiefly guilty for World War II. Therefore, exterminating the Jews did not obliterate the distinction between civilians and combatants: as the Nazi leadership saw it, *all* Jews were at war with Nazi Germany. The task of translating ideology into a coherent narrative of events for the news took place in the Propaganda Ministry, and especially in Dietrich's Reich Press Office. On a daily and weekly basis, this was the office that gave orders to the press about how to narrate ongoing events.[41] Although the thousands of orders given to the controlled press came to light at Otto Dietrich's trial in Nuremberg after the war, they have played only a modest role in scholarly accounts. Yet the directives illustrate how the propagandists drew on radical anti-Semitism to explain the course of events. Though Goebbels obviously played a central role in the history of Nazi propaganda, he did *not* play the key role in the purging and control of the daily and periodical press. As the abundant and fascinating evidence presented at his trial in Nuremberg in 1947 and 1948 made clear, that task was carried out by the Reich press chief, Otto Dietrich. Dietrich, unlike Goebbels, worked in Hitler's office every day and gave the Führer a summary of international news every morning. Dietrich then conveyed to his staff in Berlin Hitler's suggestions and wishes about what the German press should write or not write. During the course of the war, tens of thousands of confidential "press directives" were communicated orally and in written form at a daily press conference in Berlin. These orders—compliance with which was compulsory—were then conveyed to several thousand newspapers and periodicals. Through Dietrich and his staff, Hitler had a more important and direct impact than has previously been acknowledged on the chronicle of events that ran in German newspapers and periodicals. In the realm of propaganda and control of the press, the regime displayed coordination and efficiency, even in the face of internal personality conflicts and organizational disputes, and presented a united front on its core policy aims. In Ian Kershaw's words, Goebbels and Dietrich were both "working towards the Führer." Yet Dietrich, with his daily rather than periodic access to Hitler, did not have to make educated guesses about what his desires were. Hitler simply told him.[42]

Another important dimension of Nazi propaganda concerns the mix of text, imagery, and photographs evident in the *Parole der Woche Wandzeitungen* (*Word of the Week* wall newspapers). Distributed by the tens and sometimes hundreds of thousands of copies on a weekly basis, they were the most ubiquitous and intrusive aspect of Nazism's visual offensive in the new era of mechanical reproduction of illustrations, whether black and white or in color. German wall newspapers were a unique combination of newspaper editorial, political leaflet, political poster, and tabloid journalism, employing modern techniques of reproduction and directed at a society whose daily rhythms were characterized by walking and mass transit. Some visual aspects of Nazism—the Nuremberg rallies, torchlight parades, the gates to Auschwitz-Birkenau, Albert Speer's buildings, *Triumph of the Will* (Leni Riefenstahl's documentary on the Nuremberg rallies), and such notorious anti-Semitic films as *Der ewige Jude* (*The Eternal Jew*) and *Jud Süss*—have long been familiar icons of modern consciousness and memory of the Nazi era. Yet aside from the weekly newsreels, no form of Nazi visual propaganda made so crucial a contribution to the regime's presentation of ongoing events as did the *Word of the Week*.[43] One could, after all, decide not to go to the movies and weekly newsreels. By contrast, one could not avoid the *Word of the Week*. Every week from 1937 to spring 1943, an estimated 125,000 copies of black-and-white or color wall newspapers were displayed in the nooks and crannies of everyday life. Issues of the *Word of the Week* were posted in German and Austrian market squares, metro stations, bus stops, payroll offices, hospital waiting rooms, factory cafeterias, hotels, restaurants, post offices, train stations, schools, and street kiosks. In densely populated Germany, where people got around primarily on foot or by mass transit, political wall newspapers, strategically situated at nodal points where the "masses" converged and dispersed in the course of any given day, were the most effective means of intruding on the visual field of millions of individuals. Indeed, using the techniques of modern advertising and mechanical and photographic reproduction, and the organizational weapon of the Nazi regime and party, Nazi propagandists made political wall newspapers into an effective method of diffusing political propaganda on a mass scale. Each week, hundreds of Nazi party activists, members of the German Labor Front, and front organizations of hotel and guesthouse owners, gardeners, physicians, war veterans, and landowners distributed and posted them.[44] A powerful link between the leaders' views and aims and the everyday experience of millions of German pedestrians and strap-hangers, these extraordinary texts and images deserve to be moved from the periphery to the center of historical writing and reflection. They reinforced and elaborated on the message conveyed by government-controlled papers, such as the *Der Völkische Beobachter*.

The evidence and argument in the following pages detail what the Nazi regime told Germans, not what "ordinary" Germans, or "most" Germans, made of it. The record of Nazi pronouncements is far more extensive and detailed than is that on popular consciousness. The regime's efforts to assess public opinion were tainted by the unrepresentative and unscientific manner of collection and reporting used. Postwar evidence was subject to the distorting influences of memory and political self-interest.[45] Though the evidence presented here cannot resolve the issue of what most Germans believed, it does demonstrate, in greater detail than previously, the extent to which Hitler and his associates *told* the German population on numerous occasions that his government was following a policy of exterminating and annihilating Europe's Jews. If a person could understand German, read a major newspaper, listen to the radio news with some regularity, and view the ubiquitous Nazi political wall newspapers, he or she would know this basic fact. That person would know of the German government's insistence that current events could be understood only in reference to the power of international Jewry and that the Jews were conspiring to destroy the Nazi regime and murder the German people. The existing evidence plausibly suggests that a fanatical but not meager minority embedded both in the Nazi party and in its front organizations believed this message to be the truth, and that its members disseminated it to a society in which milder forms of anti-Semitism had become commonplace. In shifting the focus from what ordinary Germans thought to the texts and images of the Nazi dictatorship itself, I seek in this book to address the as yet unanswered question concerning why in 1941, for the first time in the grim history of Europe's longest-standing hatred, anti-Semitism assumed an unprecedented degree of radicalism and was used to justify a policy of continentwide mass murder.[46]

2 Building the Anti-Semitic Consensus

The Nazi assumption of power in January 1933 brought with it two elements of decisive significance for the anti-Semitic campaigns that would accompany World War II and the Holocaust. First, Hitler and some of his closest associates constituted an experienced core of anti-Semitic propagandists. Second, the Nazis created a large new institution, the Reich Ministry for Public Enlightenment and Propaganda, known by its German initials as the RMVP. The Nazi party itself became the instrument for diffusing the regime's message from the ministry and from party headquarters throughout German society. During the Weimar years, Nazi propagandists learned how to translate fundamental ideological postulates into a continuous narrative of events, a heavily slanted story of good and evil, easily accessible to mass audiences.[1] Hitler remained the key storyteller and propagandist. His speeches were printed in the press, broadcast over the radio, and excerpted on hundreds of thousands of posters. Though anti-Semitism had been only one of several sources of Nazi voting strength, after 1933 Hitler placed anti-Semitic ideologues, the most important of whom were Joseph Goebbels, Otto Dietrich, and Alfred Rosenberg, at the top of the key opinion-shaping institutions. In a dictatorship resting on the "leadership principle," Hitler's anti-Semitic convictions defined policy.

Shaping popular opinion began with destruction of the free press. In the weeks and months following January 30, 1933, about two thousand German journalists, including Jews, liberals, conservatives, apolitical writers, Social Democrats, and Communists, were driven from their jobs, arrested, or driven into exile, and sometimes all three. The great majority of journalists remained in their jobs. Control of the press entailed both the expulsion and repression of suspected dissenters, which opened jobs for Nazi party members, and opportunistic adaptation by journalists who made common cause with conservative elites under the new regime.[2] In all, two hundred Social Democratic papers and thirty-five Communist papers, with a total combined circulation of about two million, were closed. In July 1933, the papers of the Mosse publishing firm, including one of the flagships of German liberalism, the *Berliner Tageblatt,* succumbed to *Gleichschaltung,* or "coordination," the Nazi term for the purging, incorporation, and control of the various institutions of German society, politics, economics, and culture.[3] On October 4, 1933, the Editorial Control Law formulated by Reich press chief Otto Dietrich placed all remaining newspaper and periodical editors under government control, thereby ending any pretense of freedom of the press. Editors had to be "Aryan" and could not be married to a non-Aryan. The law thus banned Jews and those married to Jews from the practice of journalism. All editors were required to be members of the Reich League of the German Press (Reichsverband der Deutschen Presse), of which Dietrich was the chairman. The law established courts run by the league that could punish and purge editors deemed to have violated the law's requirements.[4] On December 12, 1933, major German press services were merged to form the official German News Agency (Deutsches Nachrichtenbüro, or DNB), which in turn was placed under the supervision of Dietrich's Press Office in Propaganda Ministry. The German press had become a state monopoly.

The Nazi regime also gained control of the press by buying various newspapers and periodicals, often at bargain-basement prices. A key player in this process was Max Amann (1891–1957), a publisher who had gained Hitler's favor by helping make *Mein Kampf* a commercial success, and Hitler a wealthy man. After 1933, Hitler appointed Amann president of the Reich Press Chamber and chair of the German Association of Newspaper and Periodical Publishers. Under his direction, Nazi ownership of the German press expanded dramatically, from 2.5 percent of all newspaper publishing houses, producing about 120 dailies and weeklies with a combined circulation of about one million in 1933, to 1,500 publishing houses and more than 2,000 newspapers by 1939. By 1945, the Nazi-controlled press accounted for 82.5 percent of the total circulation.[5] By 1939, the Nazi-controlled Franz Eher publishing house alone controlled about 200 newspapers with a circulation of 13.2 million and constituted the world's largest publishing company. The 2,200 newspapers that were still privately owned were nonetheless subject to a detailed system of orders from the political authorities.[6]

The Nazi party played a central role in the regime's propaganda operations *after* January 1933 through its powerful hierarchy. In 1928, the NSDAP had 96,918 members. By January 1933, in the wake of the Depression and political crises of the Weimar Republic, membership had increased eightfold, to 849,009. After 1933, membership dramatically increased, to 2,493,890 in 1935, 5,339,567 in 1939, 7.1 million in 1941, 7.3 million in 1943, and more than 8 million in May 1945.[7] At the apex of the party stood Hitler, surrounded in various cabinet positions by deputies and loyalists, such as Martin Bormann, Joseph Goebbels, Otto Dietrich, Heinrich Himmler, Robert Ley, Hans Frank, and Alfred Rosenberg. Subordinate to the national leaders were the *Gauleiter,* gauleiters, or regional leaders, responsible for territories coinciding with the German states; the *Kreisleiter,* responsible for whole cities or metropolitan areas; and the *Ortsgruppenleiter* and *Stützpunkleiter,* or local leaders, responsible for parts of cities or small towns, respectively. At the most local level were the *Zellenleiter,* or cell leaders, and finally the *Blockleiter,* neighborhood or block leaders.[8] As of 1936, there existed 33 *Gaue,* 772 *Kreise,* and 21,041 *Ortsgruppen* and

Stützpunkten. Six more *Gaue* were added after the annexation of Austria and the Sudetenland in 1938.[9] By 1939, 6 more regional offices had been added.[10] By 1943, according to the party's updated *Organisationsbuch,* the numbers had increased to 43 *Gaue,* 869 *Kreise,* 26,103 *Ortsgruppen,* and 106,168 *Zellen,* and 559,020 block and neighborhood groups, seeking to reach a population of about 80 million.[11] As the territory dominated by the Nazi regime expanded through the force of German arms, new offices of the RMVP were opened in Eastern and Western Europe. The 1943 map of the *Gau* districts of the Nazi party organization illustrates its expansion into occupied Polish and Czech territories.[12] Working in conjunction with these officials were the Security Service (Sicherheitsdienst, or SD), which regularly reported to Berlin on the popular mood and the public's response to policies and propaganda.[13] This vast organizational weapon played the decisive role in the diffusion of Nazism's messages into many areas of German society.

In March 1933, Hitler appointed Goebbels head of the newly created Propaganda Ministry. Goebbels was the party's leading propagandist and inciter of anti-Semitic hatred. He had received a doctorate in German literature from the University of Heidelberg and had come to public prominence as editor of the Nazi weekly *Der Angriff* (The Attack) in the Weimar years.[14] As director of the Propaganda Ministry, in charge of a staff that grew to 1,300 people, he became the public face of Nazi propaganda. By 1939, his ministry included departments for propaganda, the domestic press, the foreign press, the periodical press, radio, film, writers, theater, fine arts, music, and popular culture.[15] Its budget almost doubled from 1937 to 1942.[16] Every day he held a conference at which he conveyed orders to the organs of propaganda in the government and party. At his first press conference, on March 16, 1933, he said that propaganda's essence was "simplicity, force, and concentration." Objectivity was a myth. "Nothing in the world exists without a tendency . . . There is no such thing as absolute objectivity."[17] Only power could resolve issues of truth and falsehood, and power was now concentrated in the Nazi party-state.

Goebbels's power and position reflected the intertwining of party and state in Nazi Germany. He was the gauleiter of Berlin, the minister of the RMVP, and the head of the of the Nazi party's Reich Propaganda Directorate (Reichspropagandaleitung, or RPL). The Reichspropagandaleitung included divisions for press, speaker training, mass meetings, culture, film, and radio and the Office of Active Propaganda, which coordinated speakers, oversaw the writing of pamphlets, and produced posters. Many of these offices existed at the party's regional (*Gau*), city (*Kreis*), and in some instances at local (*Ort*) levels.[18] If posters needed to be distributed, meetings organized, texts of Hitler or Goebbels brought to the attention of "the masses," this party and governmental organizational weapon was ready to carry out the task.[19]

Goebbels was prolific. His personal diary covering the period from the mid-1920s to April 1945 takes up more than forty volumes of six hundred pages each. Although in the 1930s his articles appeared with some regularity on the first page of *Der Völkische Beobachter (VB)*, Goebbels also sought to have a weekly political and cultural journal on a sophisticated level, aimed at an intellectual readership in Germany and abroad. He found the answer in *Das Reich*, which appeared weekly from May 26, 1940, to April 15, 1945. Circulation of the journal grew from 500,000 in October 1940 to 800,000 in 1941 and finally to more than 1,400,000 by 1944.[20] Beginning in 1941, he wrote the editorials in the journal almost every week until April 1945, for which he was paid 2,000 Reichsmarks each (slightly less than a third of a skilled worker's annual salary).[21] He or others then read them on national radio.[22] *Das Reich* became the single most important journal read by the Nazified German political and intellectual establishment. It was a bellwether of Nazi policy and offered the propaganda minister a weekly platform from which he could reach both the Nazi faithful and a more sophisticated and politically astute readership than that of mass-circulation newspapers.

Though few of his 218 editorials in *Das Reich* focused exclusively on the Jews, anti-Semitic motifs were ubiquitous. Some, such as "Mimikry" (July 20, 1941), "Die Juden sind Schuld" (November 16, 1941), and

"Der Krieg und die Juden" (May 9, 1942), set forth at some length views that for the remainder of the war appeared more briefly in scores of other essays and radio addresses.[23] These anti-Semitic themes bolstered key arguments or appeared strategically in editorials dealing with England, the United States, the Soviet Union, the Allied bombing of German cities, the Western alliance with the Soviet Union, the origins of the war, the need for national unity in "total war" to the bitter end, and Germany's victories and reverses. The more literate readership of *Das Reich,* as well as regular listeners to Goebbels's editorials on the radio, absorbed a consistent story, a construction of events in which radical anti-Semitism played a central role.

A less famous figure of the Nazi regime's anti-Semitic narrative, but critical nevertheless, was Otto Dietrich (1897–1952), Reich press chief from 1937 to 1945. The relatively minor role Dietrich has been accorded in relation to Goebbels in historical scholarship stands in striking contrast to the significance attributed to him by the American prosecution team in the so-called Ministries Trial in Nuremberg that ended in 1949. One member of that team, Alexander Hardy, went so far as to call him "by far the most important" of the Nazi leaders, including Goebbels, involved in propaganda.[24] Largely on the documentary basis of the daily press directives issued by Dietrich during the war and the Holocaust, the court convicted him on charges of war crimes and crimes against humanity.[25] The court's judgment read in part:

It is thus clear that a well thought-out, oft-repeated, persistent campaign to *arouse the hatred* of the German people against Jews was fostered and directed by the press department and its press chief, Dietrich. That part or much of this may have been inspired by Goebbels is undoubtedly true, but Dietrich approved and authorized every release . . . The campaign's only rationale was to blunt the sensibilities of the people regarding the campaign of persecution and murder which was being carried out . . . These press and periodical directives were not mere political polemics, they were not aimless expression of anti-Semitism, and they were not designed only to unite the German people in the war effort . . . Their clear and expressed purpose was to enrage Germans against the Jews, to justify the measures taken and to be taken against them, and to subdue any doubts which might arise as to the justice of measures of racial persecution to which Jews were to be subjected . . . By them Dietrich consciously implemented and, by furnishing the excuses and justifications, participated in the crimes against humanity regarding Jews.[26]

Goebbels was crucial to the anti-Semitic campaigns in many ways, but he did not control the press. That was Dietrich's task. Addressing Dietrich's role in daily operations of the Nazi propaganda offensives draws attention to oddly underexamined evidence that came to light in Nuremberg, as well as to the significant role that Hitler himself played in shaping the German press.

With Goebbels and Hitler conveniently dead, Dietrich's lawyer sought to place Goebbels at the center of press control and to minimize his client's involvement. Unfortunately for Dietrich, he had left an extensive paper trail of speeches and books extolling his close and important relationship with Hitler and elaborating on the tasks of the press under Nazism.[27] Even more crucial, the secret daily and weekly orders that went out from his office to the press came to light in the course of his postwar trial. Dietrich's path to the apex of the Nazi regime was a familiar one. After serving in the German army during World War I, he studied political science at the universities in Munich, Frankfurt am Main, and Freiburg, where he completed a doctorate, paradoxically, on the work of the sociologist Georg Simmel, a German Jew. After working as a research assistant at the Essen chamber of commerce, he turned to journalism. In 1928, he became head of the business section of the conservative *Münchener-Augsburger Zeitung*. In 1931, he became the associate editor of the *Essener Nationale Zeitung*. He joined the Nazi party in 1929 and became Hitler's personal press adviser and a conduit to Ruhr coal and iron executives. Hitler appointed him director of the Reich Press Office of the Nazi party in 1931, a position in which he managed Hitler's election campaigns. In 1932, he joined the SS, and Hitler named him a *Reichsleiter* in the Nazi party. In 1933, as the vice-president of the Reich Press Chamber, he took an active role in purging the German press of political opponents. In 1937, Hitler appointed him state secretary, formally under Goebbels in the Propaganda Ministry with direct responsibility for the offices that dealt with the German press, foreign press, and periodicals. From 1938 to March 1945, Dietrich was the Reich press chief, state secretary of the Press Division in the Propaganda Ministry, and president of the Reich Press Chamber.[28]

Dietrich's impact was due to his connection to Hitler. He worked in Hitler's office on a daily basis, first before the war when Hitler worked in Berlin, and then during the war years in Hitler's East Prussian war compound. Every working morning, he delivered to Hitler "Führer material" consisting of selections from the foreign press. These daily briefings influenced Hitler's understanding of events abroad and were evidence of his trust in Dietrich's judgment. According to trial testimony by Paul Karl Schmidt, the director of the Press Division of the German Foreign Office, the "Führer material" selected by Dietrich was "the foundation for the detailed propaganda directives which were given almost daily by Hitler to Dr. Dietrich for the releases in the German Press and to Goebbels for the general propaganda to foreign countries."[29] Dietrich and his staff in Berlin then transformed Hitler's broad suggestions into daily and weekly press directives. Bringing Dietrich back into the history of Nazi propaganda thus reinserts Hitler into the day-to-day construction of the story the Nazi regime told Germans and the world on a daily and weekly basis.

The central institution for control of the press was a daily noon press conference in the Propaganda Ministry attended by about 150 journalists. Between 1933 and 1945, the Press Office conveyed more than seventy-five thousand secret *Presseanweisungen* (press directives), also called *Die Parole des Tages (Word of the Day),* on every conceivable political subject. They told the press which stories it should cover, how it should present them, what language to use, and what sources of information to draw on. From 1938 to 1945, Dietrich and his staff controlled their content. Occasionally, Dietrich himself, wearing his SS uniform, conducted the press conference, after being hailed with the Hitler salute. Normally though, members of his staff—Helmut Sündermann, Alfred Ingemar Berndt, or Hans Fritzsche—did so.[30] No probing questions were allowed. Violation of rules regarding publication of classified materials was regarded as treason and treated accordingly. Immediately following the conferences, the Press Office sent the directives over teletype to the *Gau* press offices and propaganda offices. They in turn distributed the directives to their district newspapers, thereby ensuring their timely arrival under localized modes of press control and surveillance. The *Word of the Day* directives went out to more than three thousand German newspapers a day. Each week the office of the Reich Press Chief also issued the *Zeitschriften-Dienst (Periodical Service)* directives to periodicals. They were also available to editors of the daily press.[31] The number of periodicals receiving the orders ran from four thousand to six thousand with a circulation of between seventy and ninety million readers.[32] Both daily and weekly directives were at the center of the regime's anti-Semitic propaganda campaigns. In his capacity as Reich press chief, Dietrich stood at the apex of Nazi hierarchy of offices at the *Gau, Kreis,* and *Ort* levels that diffused Hitler's general take on the events of the day, including the propaganda offensive against the Jews, to every newspaper and periodical in Germany.

Goebbels was displeased with Dietrich's control of the press conference and tried to gain control of it or supplant it with his own daily Minister's Conference held one hour earlier. Drawing partly on interviews with Goebbels's former associates, the historian Jay Baird concluded that "the relationship between Goebbels and Dietrich was hostile in the extreme."[33] By the summer of 1942, the conflict over control of the press directives became so intense that Hitler himself issued the "Order of the Führer of August 23, 1942 for Securing Cooperation between the Reich Propaganda Minister and the Reich Press Chief." It required Goebbels to issue directives to the press only through Dietrich and confirmed that Dietrich and his representatives at the daily noon conference in Berlin were Hitler's sole official conduit to the assembled press.[34] In supporting Dietrich's prerogative, Hitler was defending his own control over the government's instructions to the German press.[35]

Der Völkische Beobachter, the national official daily paper of the Nazi party and regime, was a key organ in the regime's anti-Semitic campaigns. Its bold red and black headlines and front-page stories conveyed the core propaganda themes emanating from Dietrich's press conferences. The VB was founded in 1920. In 1923, Alfred Rosenberg, known as one of the leading anti-Semitic ideologues in the Nazi party, became its editor. He remained in that position until 1938. His pseudoscholarly 1930 work Der Mythos des 20. Jahrhunderts conveyed a mélange of racist, anti-Semitic, and mystical ideas. Under his leadership, the VB's circulation grew to 330,000 by 1933. It exceeded 1 million by 1940 and sold about 1.7 million copies a day in 1944.[36] It was a paper by and for Nazi believers and for anyone who wanted to know what the regime's official policy was.[37] Rosenberg's successor at the VB was Wilhelm Weiß (1892–1950). He remained editor of the VB until it ceased publication in April 1945. In that capacity, he dutifully and consistently transformed the daily press directives into bold red and black headlines and front-page stories that were central elements in the regime's anti-Semitic campaigns and in the translation of Nazi ideology into an ongoing anti-Semitic narrative of events.[38] Anti-Semitic themes constituted a modest percentage of the first-page lead stories in the VB during the war. From September 1939 to April 1945, eighty-four of the more than 2,100 daily editions carried headline stories inspired by the regime's radical anti-Semitism. The rest dealt with denunciations of and attacks on Nazi Germany's enemies, conventionally understood, as well as celebrations of the regime's successes.

The anti-Semitic headlines came in a series of concentrated barrages. There were two such headlines in 1939; none in 1940; seventeen in 1941; four in 1942; fifty in 1943; ten in 1944 and two in spring of 1945. Four periods accounted for most of the front-page stories: July–August 1941 (seven); April–July 1943 (twenty-six); October–November 1943 (thirteen); and May–June 1944 (nine). Twenty-six anti-Semitic headlines appeared at other times during the war and Holocaust.

Within the Office of Active Propaganda of the Propaganda Ministry, the Antikomintern office directed by Eberhard Taubert produced much of the anti-Semitic propaganda aimed at Eastern Europe and the Soviet Union. It also supplied anti-Semitic materials to other offices in the Propaganda Ministry, the Foreign Office, the military high commands, and the administrative offices in the occupied territories.[39] In November 1939, following the signing of the Hitler-Stalin nonaggression pact and the resulting cessation of anti-Soviet propaganda, the budget for the office was cut by 30 percent and twenty staff members were dismissed.[40] Yet it continued to produce anti-Semitic propaganda. In December 1940, it had about forty staff members.[41]

A second important gathering point for anti-Semitic propagandists in the Office of Active Propaganda was the Institut zum Studium der Judenfrage (Institute for the Study of the Jewish Question).[42] Alfred Rosenberg was its founder. Beginning in 1939, he oversaw the theft of books, archives, and treasured objects from Jewish libraries and religious institutions in Nazi-occupied Europe. In November 1939, after the signing of the nonaggression pact, an office of Antisemitische Aktion (Antisemitic Action) was formed that drew staff from Taubert's office as well as Rosenberg's. It was in the offices of Antisemitische Aktion that *Die Judenfrage* (The Jewish Question), a biweekly journal of some importance to the anti-Semitic campaigns, was edited and published. Its 1,200 subscribers were to be found in the Propaganda Ministry, the Nazi party, the anti-Semitic think tanks, some universities, and among editors of newspapers and periodicals. With offices on 95 Wilmersdorfer Straße in Berlin's fashionable Charlottenberg/Wilmersdorf district, the journal and its associated press clipping archive and library offered a pleasant, centrally located gathering point for an anti-Semitic intelligentsia that wrote for this high-profile, small-circulation journal directed at officials of the Nazi regime and members of the Nazi party. It was published from 1937 to 1943 under slightly different names.[43]

As its first issue asserted, the journal would focus on the following topics: the Jews as a race; the national and international impact of the Jews on the economic, political, and cultural life of modern nations; the task of awakening "critical opposition against the alien element of the Jews" and fostering anti-Semitism among German and foreign opinion makers; the "solution of the Jewish question in the new Germany"; and the effort of the Jews themselves to "solve the Jewish question" by founding their own state.[44] Reich Press Office directives, which regularly drew attention to articles and authors that appeared in *Die Judenfrage,* provided the address and phone number of the office in case editors sought additional assistance in publication of anti-Semitic articles. That around nine of some forty contributors to the journal held doctorates from German universities imparted a patina of prestige and scholarship to it.

The last of the core institutions from which the anti-Semitic campaigns derived was the office in the Active Propaganda Division in the Propaganda Ministry responsible for visual propaganda in the form of political posters. However effective films were in conveying fundamental stereotypes and fanning elemental hatreds, they did not provide an explanatory narrative of events. The weekly newsreels contributed to that effort.[45] As mentioned earlier, the regime's weekly *Word of the Week* wall newspaper was the most intrusive and pervasive form of visual propaganda in everyday life in Nazi Germany from 1937 to 1943. Its images were literally everywhere.[46] Making effective use of color and graphics, the *Wandzeitungen* graced walls, specially designed glass-fronted viewing boxes, and kiosks in every imaginable public place. To paraphrase Walter Benjamin, the *Word of the Week* wall newspapers were stunning examples of the work of propaganda in the era of mechanical reproduction. For reasons connected with the organization of movement and space in the Germany of the 1930s and 1940s, visual presentation of propaganda in wall newspapers was of great importance. The vast majority of Germans did not get around by private car. In fact, the predominant forms of daily transportation were walking, bicycling, and public conveyance—trains, streetcars, the underground metro, and buses. In 1939, there were only 25 motor vehicles in Germany per 1,000 people, or 1 for 40 people; car ownership was less than a tenth of that in the United States (227 cars per 1,000, or 1 for 4.4 people). Car ownership in Germany was lower than in France (54 cars per 1,000, or 1 for 18.5 people) or Britain (51 per 1,000, or 1 for per 19.6 people).[47] Of the world's largest cities, only in London and New York did more people ride street cars every day than in Berlin.[48] Notwithstanding the public images of mechanized speed and fascination with aviation, the Third Reich was overwhelmingly a nation of pedestrians. The rhythms of daily life brought the "masses" together in central public places, as people entered and exited various forms of transport. There bystanders could spend a minute or two to observe the colorful and striking *Word of the Week* papers.

In 1936 Hitler appointed the graphic artist Hans Schweitzer (known as Mjölnir) to the post of Reich representative for the creation of artistic form. He was charged with translating Nazi ideology into "artistic form" and distinctive style in various arenas—uniforms, stamps, flags, and posters.[49] Schweitzer had established a name as the leading Nazi poster artist in the 1920s with images celebrating Hitler, depicting Germany's economic crises, and demonizing and denouncing Jews. In these years he had also worked closely with Goebbels, who became one of his admirers. In October 1937 they and other visual artists and journalists in the Reich Propaganda Directorate (Reichspropagandaleitung) began to publish and distribute the *Word of the Week. Unser Wille und Weg,* the RPL's monthly internal journal, informed regional and local officials that "the *Word of the Week* must not be absent anywhere! It is the only official party wall newspaper of the NSDAP. It presents the unified words published by the Reich Propaganda Directorate that refer to the most important prevailing political events . . . The *Word of the Week* must penetrate every last community in the nation." The first edition was distributed on March 16, 1936. By January 1941, eight million copies had been distributed, approximately 125,000 a week.[50] Each was clearly marked as *Die Parole der Woche: Parteiamtliche Wandzeitung der NSDAP (The Word of the Week: Official Party Wall Newspaper of the NSDAP)*.

The posters were 100 centimeters high and 212 centimeters wide. They were printed in large, bold type and were meant to be read from a distance of a few feet or less. Several people could read one at the same time, so a small, shared public reading and viewing experience was created. The posters were designed "not only to slow the stride of the passerby but also to compel him to read" them. Their efficient distribution was an important task for propagandists. A new poster appeared each week. Wherever party officials decided to post the wall newspapers, "the key thing," as one official in the Reich Propaganda Directorate wrote, "was that they should always be in the pedestrian's field of vision."[51] Wall newspaper distribution and maintenance became a form of Nazi political activism. Each week, the old poster needed to be taken down and a new one put up. The poster boxes in which they were displayed had to be kept in good repair. If the glass was broken, it needed to be replaced. Any critical graffiti that appeared (though this was rare) had to be erased. According to one commentator, the effort was a success. The posters, he wrote, comprised "what we all heard and read every day."[52] Their aesthetics were conventional compared to modernist poster aesthetics of mid-twentieth century Europe. Yet with their striking colors, bold type, and technical modernity, they caught the eye of German passersby who had been warned against the "degenerate art" of Expressionism, the Bauhaus, Dada, and other modernist aesthetics. Between 1936 and 1940, anti-Semitic themes were infrequent. In 1940, only three of the wall newspapers broached them. From 1941 to winter 1943, by contrast, about a quarter of wall posters included attacks on the Jews.[53] The *Parole der Woche* was an important visual component of the regime's anti-Semitic propaganda during the Holocaust. Moreover, of the twenty-seven posters produced from January 1942 to July 1942, at a time when all the extermination camps had begun full operation, twelve posters were devoted partly or wholly to anti-Semitic attacks.

■

On September 23, 1939, several weeks after Hitler began World War II with the invasion of Poland, Goebbels sent a memo titled "Guidelines for the Implementation of Propaganda of the NSDAP" to all gauleiters and to Gau propaganda officials.[54] He wrote that the party's political propaganda would include meetings, speakers, and film.[55] Yet he devoted more space to posters than to anything else. The RPL would distribute to the regional offices "above all the *Word of the Week,*" dealing with ongoing events. "Everywhere in the Reich where there is dense traffic, poster boards of the Nazi party are to be set up." Local party groups were to maintain them in good condition and immediately put up new posters when delivered. "All means of transport (railroad, streetcars, subways, buses, and so on) will receive posters, which are to be placed in every wagon, on the train platforms, in the ticket windows, as well as in the entrances to these forms of public transport. If means of public transport (city buses) are now displaying commercial advertising, these are also to be covered with photo posters." The party should display posters "above all in market squares, as well as in the windows of businesses . . . Factories will also receive posters for poster boards, cafeterias, corridors, and other waiting rooms. Likewise, posters will be made available to all public service offices of the state, cities, the party, banks, payroll offices, welfare offices, post offices, and other offices of public services as well."[56]

A report from the RPL files for April and May 1940 offers more insight into channels of diffusion that linked the propaganda issuing from above to everyday experience. Its contents are summarized in the chart "Subscription Orders for the *Word of the Week* in Spring/Summer 1940."[57] It records 63,121 orders from various organizations for subscriptions to the weekly *Word of the Week*. Of these, more than half, 34,635, came from regional and local offices of the Deutsche Arbeitsfront (DAF, the German Labor Front), whose leader, Robert Ley, was well known for his violent anti-Semitic rhetoric. A striking number of orders, 10,940, came from physicians' organizations. 5,960 orders came from organizations of owners of restaurants, the numerous family-owned inns *(Pensionen),* bars, and hotels. Mayors, organizations devoted to gardening, and Nazi organizations of war veterans also put in orders. Another 1940 memo from the files of the Reichspropagandaleitung referred to 149,422 requests in spring and summer for posters. They came from mayors' offices, the German Labor Front, organizations of physicians, gardeners, restaurateurs, innkeepers, hoteliers, and home owners; veterans welfare organizations; chambers of commerce; Nazi student associations; and of course the regional offices of Nazi party propaganda officials.[58]

To facilitate the effectiveness of the *Word of the Week* program, the Nazis supported research of sorts into the political posters of the Weimar era. In 1938 and 1939, the Reichspropagandaleitung published the first and second editions of Erwin Schockel's *Das Politische Plakat: Eine psychologische Betrachtung* (The Political Poster: A Psychological Assessment) as the first in a series of instructional works intended for use only by propagandists of the Nazi party.[59] The work surveyed the political posters of all the major political parties of the Weimar period. Schockel praised several of Hans Schweitzer's works of the 1920s, including one of his early anti-Semitic works, "Nieder mit der Finanzversklavung! Wählt Nationalsozialist!" ("Down with Finance Enslavement! Vote National Socialist!"), dating from 1924. In it, a Jewish man, fat, bald, in formal wear and top hat, wielding a whip and a cane, was caricatured standing on the shoulders of a large, muscular male figure in chains labeled "the Dawes Plan." The small physical stature of the Jew unaccustomed to physical labor presents a contrast to the enslaved man of the people who, however, looks with hope and determination toward the swastika in the upper left-hand corner of the poster. Schockel also drew attention to "Der Drahtzieher" ("The Wire Puller"), another poster from the 1924 election. The overweight Jewish man in the caricature holds the strings that control the subordinate masses. The poster, with factory smokestacks in the background, evokes leftist posters of the era that depict a complacent capitalist class' exploiting the working class. "Der Drahtzieher," however, transformed class conflict between capital and labor into a national and racial battle between Jews and the German masses. The image of the wire puller would be reproduced widely in wartime propaganda. Schockel concluded that there were "no new understandings" regarding poster propaganda: Hitler had already grasped the possibilities in *Mein Kampf*. All that remained was to translate his insights into general practice.[60]

In 1941, Friedrich Madebach's *Das Kampfplakat: Aufgabe, Wesen und Gesetzmäßigkeit des Politischen Plakats, nachgewiesen an den Plakaten der Kampfjahre von 1918–1933* (The Fighting Poster: Mission, Essence, and Rules of the Political Poster, with Reference to the Posters of the Years of Struggle 1918–1933) was published.[61] Madebach articulated the continuing importance of the poster in an era of radio, film, and newspaper. Posted on walls in streets and public squares, posters would be noticed "whether or not one wanted to see them." Other means of propaganda depended on the decisions of viewers and listeners. But the poster, placed in public spaces where people lived their daily lives, compelled them to confront and respond to its contents.[62] In contrast to newspapers, the political poster expressed an opinion in concentrated form. Madebach drew on *Mein Kampf* to arrive at "basic laws" of mass influence: intellectual simplification, limitation to a few key points, repetition of those points, focus on one subjective standpoint to the exclusion of others, and appeal to the emotions and to stark contrasts between good and bad or truth and lies, rather than to nuance or shades of gray. The graphic design of posters should be simple, suited to the "limited artistic visual abilities" of the masses; distinctive but not monotonous; and able to arouse the emotions. "Form and color must correspond to the primitive emotions of the masses." No refined or modulated use of color was called for. Rather, clear colors were preferred that would have a simple emotional impact (red and white, red and black, yellow and black, and so forth). The lines must express a similarly "simple emotional rhythm."[63]

Artistic mediocrity was not an issue. Proliferation was the key. An appeal published in *Unser Wille und Weg* of April 1940 conveys the scope and spirit of poster diffusion. Alongside two posters, one proclaiming "With Our Flags Comes Victory!" and the other "Attention, Spies, Take Care in Conversations," the text urges "Officials! Propagandists! You yourselves should find the best places to display these posters! In streets and squares, hotel halls, restaurants, cafes, cinemas, theaters, factories, businesses, cafeterias, train stations, and post offices . . . they must dominate the street scenes all over Germany. They cannot be missing anywhere, whether in the city or country. They must be in dominant places that are easily seen, so that they are always before the *Volksgenossen* (people's comrades) to strengthen their will toward victory and remind them of their duty."[64] By January 1941, the Propaganda Ministry claimed to have produced and distributed "more than" seven million posters, two million pamphlets, sixty million periodicals and wall newspapers, and sixty-seven million leaflets. Party propagandists had conducted about thirty thousand slide shows and forty-five thousand film evenings every month (!) and had organized about two hundred thousand meetings and demonstrations. More than sixty thousand radios had been distributed to the troops. Twelve hundred slide shows had been shown to more than a hundred thirty thousand soldiers and "about thirty million" soldiers had seen movies for relaxation and entertainment, obviously including repeat attendees.[65] The Nazi party propaganda offices also sent out quite detailed instructions about how propaganda work should be carried out, down to the details of how to run an effective evening program.[66]

The essays, books, and weekly posters coming from the Propaganda Ministry, press directives from Dietrich's Reich Press Office, *Der Völkische Beobachter,* speeches by Hitler and other leaders published in the press and broadcast on radio, essays by Goebbels, and articles in small-circulation anti-Semitic journals and think tanks were the core elements of the anti-Semitic campaigns aimed at Germans and Austrians at home and in the armed forces. To be sure, Julius Streicher's viciously anti-Semitic newspaper *Der Stürmer* made a contribution as well, but its circulation of four hundred thousand was modest by comparison with the operations run by Goebbels and Dietrich. Despite the famous personal rivalries and bureaucratic confusion, coordination and cooperation among a variety of offices and personalities were effective. Time and again, Nazi officials drew favorable attention to one another's efforts, thereby multiplying the impact of each book, essay, article, and visual image diffused via the Nazi party's massive organizations.

As this massive propaganda apparatus was devoted to denouncing vast Jewish power in Germany, the following facts about the social, economic, and political circumstances of the six hundred thousand German Jews in the Weimar Republic should be kept in mind.[67] The percentage of Jews in the German population had declined from its peak of just over 1 percent in 1880 to .76 percent in 1933.[68] Owing to that declining birth rate, Jewish enrollment in German universities dropped from 9.4 percent in 1894–1895 to 4.7 percent in 1932–1933.[69] This small and diminishing minority was concentrated in Germany's largest cities, and in forms of commerce and professional work that lent it social visibility out of proportion to its numbers. In 1933, 54.5 percent of all German Jews lived in cities with populations of 500,000 or more. Out of all German Jews, 160,000, or 32.1 percent, lived in Berlin, a fact of considerable importance for Joseph Goebbels before and after 1933. Almost three-quarters of German Jews made their living from trade, commerce, or banking, with strong concentrations in sales, white-collar jobs, and office work.[70] Anti-Semitic prejudice had kept to a minimum the numbers of Jews in the judiciary, civil service, diplomatic corps, and to a large degree corporations before 1918. With a few exceptions, Jews had no influence on boards of directors and leading executive positions in German big business. Hence, a disproportionate number went into law and medicine, both professions open to Jews.

Nazis focused on the supposed Jewish domination of German professional life, despite the conflicting reality. In 1933, according to German official statistics, Jews made up 10.9 percent of Germany's doctors and 8.6 percent of dentists, 16.3 percent of lawyers and 2.8 percent of judges and district attorneys, 2.6 percent of university professors, and 0.7 percent of engineers. In the cultural and intellectual professions that anti-Semites claimed were dominated by Jews, the same official statistics of 1933 reveal similarly small proportions. Jews accounted for 2 percent of German musicians, 5.1 percent of editors and writers, 3 percent of dancers and actors, 2.4 percent of visual artists, 1.6 percent of photographers and motion picture camera operators, and 5.6 percent of directors and producers.[71] In the central forum of political representation, the Reichstag, Jews were significantly underrepresented. Of the 577 members of parliament elected on September 14, 1930, 17 were of Jewish origin, and of the 608 members elected on July 31, 1932, 14 were of Jewish origin.[72] The conspiratorial notion of vast Jewish power had no factual basis, although Jews had made professional advances, which were especially noticeable in Berlin. In 1925 in Prussia, the state in which Berlin was situated and where Goebbels was active as a leader of the Nazi party, Jews made up 26.6 percent of all lawyers and 15.5 percent of the doctors. In 1930, the 2,138 Jewish doctors practicing in Berlin constituted between a third and a half of all doctors in the city.[73] In 1933, 48.5 percent of the lawyers in metropolitan Berlin, 45.3 percent in Frankfurt am Main, and 35.6 percent in Breslau were Jews.[74] For a non-Jewish lawyer or doctor in Berlin or Frankfurt, the Nazi anti-Semitism promised to eliminate a great deal of competition.

Jews had made economic and social advances for which there were plausible commonsense explanations that had nothing to do with conspiracy. The Nazis rejected the plausible in favor of the paranoid. As conspiracy theorists had done in blaming the Jews during the Weimar Republic, Nazis propagandists convinced themselves and their followers that commonsense explanations for developments were deceptive and illusory. The Jews' small numbers, economic vulnerability, and lack of political influence were mere surface phenomena. The truth was that a small number of unseen conspirators controlled the course of national and international events from the shadows of the wings. The speed and ease with which the Nazis' blizzard of anti-Semitic legislation destroyed the economic and social position of Jews in Germany did not change the Nazis' view of Jewish power.[75] By the end of 1933, 37,000 of the 525,000 Jews in Germany had already left the country.[76] To anyone not imbued with Nazi ideology, it was obvious that the Nazi regime had launched a campaign of persecution against a small minority that had no access to the instruments necessary to wage "war" against Nazi Germany or any other nation-state.

From the foundation of the Nazi party to Hitler's rantings in a Berlin bunker in 1945, the key themes in the regime's anti-Semitic story line were righteous indignation about victimization at the hands of a powerful and evil foe, promises of retaliation, and projection of aggressive genocidal intention onto others. The core of Hitler's attacks on the Jews in *Mein Kampf* and of Goebbels's diatribes in *Der Angriff* in the late 1920s did not focus on racist biology. To be sure, a great deal of sarcasm was directed at the stereotyped Jewish body. But the core of the assault concerned what "the Jew" or "Jewry," identified as one political actor, had allegedly done to Germany.[77] The list of sins was long. In July 1927, Goebbels wrote that Germany had become "an exploitation colony of international Jewry," which controlled its railroads, economy, and currency. Three million Germans were unemployed as a result of the "murderous economic war" waged by the Jews against "German discipline and German work."[78] "The Jew" was connected with capitalist exploitation as well as with communism. He "lives from the collapse of nations, whether he cloaks himself in the form of interest capitalism or Bolshevism." The

Jew was dangerous as he sought to "annihilate" peoples, "destroy" races, "turn blood comrade against blood comrade." Nazism was a national struggle for freedom and against the "chains of slavery" imposed by Jewry.[79] Following Hitler, Goebbels presented the struggle between Germans and "the Jew" as one in which no middle ground existed. "One was either a servant of the Jews (*Judenknecht*) or an enemy of the Jews (*Judengegner*)." Quoting Musssolini, he said that taking such people "out of circulation" was not terror but "social hygiene," just as "a doctor takes a bacillus out of circulation."[80]

Goebbels summarized his Jew hatred in one of his better-known essays, "Why Are We Enemies of the Jews," published in *Der Angriff* on July 30, 1928. "The Jew" was "the cause and the beneficiary of our enslavement," divided the country, and thus was "the real cause for the loss of the Great War" and the 1918–1919 postwar revolution. Jewry had broken Germany's power. "It is because of the Jew that we are pariahs in the whole world." As of the late 1920s, the Jew had "triumphed over us and over our future." The Nazis as nationalists were enemies of the Jews because "nationalism is the doctrine of blood and race," while "the Jew is enemy and destroyer of blood-based unity, the conscious destroyer of our race . . . the eternal enemy of our national honor and our national freedom." As members of the German nation, the National Socialists are enemies of the Jews. "The Jew is the greatest source of our unhappiness." The Jew was also "the World Enemy," given Jewish control of "international high finance."[81] Only the Nazi party had not undergone a "shameful capitulation in the face of the world enemy's hunger for power."[82] As Germany was in a "state of permanent emergency, . . . every means [was] justified to defeat the enemy." Though a radicalization of Nazi anti-Semitism occurred in 1939 and in 1941, this hysterical tone and the perception that the conflict with "the Jew" was literally an issue of life and death formed a constant in Nazi anti-Semitism.

The pattern of justifying each new anti-Jewish measure as a response to a previous act of Jewish aggression was set in the first months of the regime. Though Hitler did not repeat his public threats of 1920 to murder the Jews, he repeatedly described "international Jewry" as an actual political force that was responsible for a host of catastrophes including World War I, the Bolshevik Revolution, the postwar inflation, and the Great Depression.[83] As chancellor, on March 29, 1933, Hitler announced and justified a boycott of Jewish businesses as a "defensive measure against Jewish atrocity propaganda abroad . . . Jewry must recognize that a Jewish war against Germany will lead to sharp measures against Jewry in Germany."[84] Two days later, Goebbels followed suit in a speech in Berlin advocating the boycott of Jewish businesses on April 1, 1933. In "Against the Atrocity Campaign of World Jewry," broadcast on German radio, he referred to "the last power, that of international Jewry, which because it has branched out and is dispersed throughout the world, can represent a danger" to the new regime. The Jews were mistaken if they believed "they could call upon an international world power" to strengthen their moral position within Germany. Jews in Germany would be held accountable for criticism of Germany by Jews in England and the United States. Without specifying what it was that Jews abroad were saying about events in Germany, Goebbels denounced the "campaign of lies and tales of atrocity." In fact, the German government "had not touched a hair" on the head of any Jew. "The thanks we get for this is that in London and New York they [the Jews] launch a boycott campaign and incite the world press against Germany." Previously the government had been "too mild" but now "they [the Jews] issue challenges and incite to battle." The Jews abroad had conveyed "a false picture of Germany." If the Jewish "atrocity campaign" ceased, Germany would return to "normal circumstances, . . . but if not, then the boycott [of German Jewish businesses] will be undertaken in a manner designed to destroy German Jewry!"[85] The source of tension was therefore foreign criticism of the regime's anti-Semitic policies, not the policies themselves, which established that Jewish businesses should be boycotted, Jews hauled off to concentration camps, and the windows of Jewish stores, synagogues, and meetinghouses smashed.[86] Goebbels's broadcast "Against the Jewish Atrocity

Campaign" contained enduring Nazi themes that linked the Jewish question to matters of war and peace. The Nazi regime maintained that it wanted peace with all countries; however, peace was precluded because "international Jewry" threatened Germany. Proof of Jewish power lay in the protests and critical editorials in the press in London and New York. If the Jews in Germany refused to tell their associates abroad to cease their anti-German activities, the German government would defend itself and "destroy" the German branch of the international Jewish conspiracy. Once the direction of causality and chronology had been reversed, Goebbels presented the party's plans to boycott Jewish businesses as the response to a worldwide campaign of lies by the Jews, and "atrocity stories" that remained unspecified in content and form.[87]

From 1933 on, attacks on the alleged power of Jews in the United States, and in particular in New York City, increased. According to articles in *Der Völkische Beobachter,* New York was, along with Moscow and London, one of the centers of "anti-German" agitation in the world.[88] In 1937, following a warning by Fiorello LaGuardia, the Italian Catholic mayor of New York, about the global danger of Nazism, the *VB* ran an article under the headline "New York's Jewish Mayor as Political Gangster." LaGuardia, according to the voice of the regime, was "a sworn enemy of world peace and understanding among peoples . . . The Jew LaGuardia" was both "Moscow's tool" and a "businessman of death." A "criminal like LaGuardia would be rendered harmless in a state governed in a modern way."[89] This attack on LaGuardia and the assertion that he was Jewish reflected an enduring aspect of the Nazi narrative: adversaries of the regime either were Jews or were dominated and controlled by Jews. Opposition by non-Jews, or a "half-Jew" such as the Italian Catholic LaGuardia (whose mother was Jewish) was further proof of Jewish control from behind the scenes.

Goebbels repeated the themes of innocence and projection on the international stage in "The Race Question and World Propaganda," his speech of September 2, 1933, delivered at the first Nuremberg Party Rally following the Nazi seizure of power. In the speech that was broadcast over national radio, he described Nazi anti-Semitic policy as a set of defensive measures against an alleged "Jewish danger . . . Jewry . . . was trying to mobilize the world against us in the secretly nourished hope that it could thereby reconquer the terrain it had lost" in Germany as a result of Nazi policy since January 1933.[90] These efforts would only bring more danger to the Jews. Goebbels then proffered a series of completely false assertions about the extent to which the Jews had supposedly overwhelmed German intellectual and cultural life with foreign influences and had dominated German medicine, law, and the universities. To reverse this terrible situation, "which no self-respecting people could tolerate for any length of time, . . . was only an act of German reawakening."[91]

The Nazi party Nuremberg Rallies of the 1930s, shown in weekly newsreels and captured in Leni Riefenstahl's cinematic images in *Triumph of the Will,* are often remembered more for the visual spectacle of totalitarian coordination they present than for the content of the speeches from the podium.[92] Yet Hitler and the other Nazi party leaders used the rallies to reiterate and expand on points of Nazi ideology and to announce policies that flowed from it. On September 15, 1935, at the "Party Rally against Bolshevism" in Nuremberg, Hitler laid the basis for the Nuremberg race laws. It was, he said, "exclusively Jewish elements that emerge as agitators of conflicts between peoples and of their inner disintegration." Protests from the United States and calls to boycott German goods merely confirmed the correctness of National Socialist anti-Jewish policies and the need for new anti-Jewish legislation.[93] Goebbels's speech, reprinted under the title "Communism without a Mask," grounded the Nazis' anti-Bolshevism in anti-Semitism and elaborated on the threat posed by Bolshevism and the Jews.[94] Bolshevism, he said, was the Jews' "declaration of war" against culture. It would bring about "the absolute destruction" of the accomplishments of the West in the interest of a "rootless and nomadic international clique of conspirators." A small Jewish cabal had come to dominate the Soviet Union.[95] The mission of National Socialism was to prevent the "Bolshevization of the world." In fact, "the Bolshevik International" was "a Jewish international."[96] Eradicating Bolshevism meant attacking its supposed roots, which lay in Jewish culture. Hitler had saved Germany and Europe by establishing a "dam" against the threat of Bolshevism. He bemoaned the "incomprehension" of West European intellectuals regarding Communism in the Soviet Union, a benightedness due to Jewry's "mastery of the art of deception." Nazi enlightenment amounted to tearing away the mask of Communism to reveal a Soviet Union dominated by "a small, terrorist, mostly Jewish minority."[97]

This effort at unmasking was central to National Socialism's "world mission" of preventing the "international Bolshevization of the world." Goebbels posed the Bolshevik threat as one of life and death. The Bolsheviks were openly planning "the extermination of peoples and states" as well as the "destruction" of the bourgeois world. In 1935, Goebbels accustomed his listeners to hearing the words "extermination" and "destruction" applied to the goals of the "Judo-Marxist domination by force" in Moscow.[98] The propaganda minister asked who the "men [were] behind the effort to poison the world." His answer was that the Bolshevik International was "in reality a Jewish International." Bolshevik materialism was waging a "battle against Western culture" in the interest of "international Jewry."[99] The Nazis were defending Western culture from "complete destruction."[100] In Nuremberg Goebbels associated National Socialism with the salvation, not the destruction, of Europe, and indeed of the West as a whole. Nazi Germany claimed the mantle of defender of the West.

The theme of the Nuremberg Party Rally of 1936 was the "World Danger of Bolshevism." In his speech of September 9, Hitler said, "We all know that Bolshevism's goal is to exterminate (*auszurotten*) the existing blood- and organically rooted peoples' leadership and to replace it with Jewish elements alien to the Aryan peoples." This constituted the "international" dimension of the problem. Hitler asserted that 98 percent of the leaders of the workers and peasants' state in the Soviet

Union were Jews, whom he called "overrefined, parasitic world intellectuals." While in Spain, Jewish emigrants were seeking to "exterminate" Spain's indigenous leaders.[101] Goebbels repeated these themes
in his address. Bolshevism had been created and directed by the Jews
who now planned the "extermination," or "destruction" of "Europe's
peoples of culture." Extermination would be followed by the "establishment of an international Jewish world domination over Europe." It was
the Nazis' mission to convince their fellow Germans of the "parasitic
danger of this race" and to open the eyes of the world to the true nature
of Jewry and of Bolshevism. Therefore, the Nazi regime would never
tire of publicly asserting, "The Jews are guilty! The Jews are guilty!"
Goebbels presented Nazi Germany as a David courageously standing
up to the Goliath of Jewish power. Because the Jews aimed at world
domination, the struggle against them was "in the truest sense of the
word a global battle." Germany did not seek European or world domination but was merely engaged in a justified defense against an already
existing Jewish campaign in pursuit of the same goal. Indeed, Hitler
and the Germans were now "the best Europeans . . . an outpost of European culture" and defenders of "a better, defendable, noble, and hap-
pier Europe."[102]

In his speech at the Nuremberg Rally of September 13, 1937, Hitler
returned to the supposedly dominant influence of the Jews on politics
and economics. It was the Jews' striving for "a certain economic influence" that had brought about the reaction by "guest peoples." This "natural defense" had led Jewry to seek by assimilation to gain a "direct and
political influence." On the other hand, Jews made up the "avant-garde
of Jewish world revolution." He repeated his false assertion that Jews
occupied "98 percent of leading positions" in the Soviet Union. Therefore, not the proletariat but the race associated with the Star of David
had become the symbol of the "so-called proletarian state." Who, he
asked, had been the leaders of the Bavarian council republic, the
Spartacist League, and the Communist party in Germany? In each case
it was the Jews, even though the press and democratic leaders could

not bring themselves to say so publicly. It was the Jews who were responsible for bringing about unemployment for seven million Germans, in hopes of fomenting a revolution and "thereby exterminating the national intelligentsia of our people."[103]

Faced with the consolidation of the Nazi dictatorship and Hitler's program of expansion and rearmament, Hitler's potential adversaries remained divided and indecisive. In March 1938, Nazi Germany annexed Austria. In Munich, at the end of September 1938, appeasement of the regime reached its peak, as Britain and France agreed to Hitler's demands that the Sudetenland be handed over to the Third Reich, contrary to the wishes of the Czech government. Hitler's belief in his genius, along with popular acceptance of his infallibility, grew in the post-Munich atmosphere of political success. Foreign policy victories fed Hitler's determination to proceed with an escalation of the campaign against the Jews at home. The nationwide anti-Jewish pogrom of the evening of November 9–10, 1938, was presented as retaliation for an alleged Jewish international conspiracy. On November 7, 1938, Herschel Grynszpan, a seventeen-year-old Polish Jewish refugee in Paris seeking to avenge the persecution of his family languishing on the German-Polish border, shot Ernst von Rath, a career diplomat in the German embassy. A few hours after the shots had been fired, the German News Agency instructed German editors to give the greatest prominence to the item. "In your commentaries you will point out that the Jewish plot must have the most unfortunate results for the Jews as well as for the foreign Jews in Germany."[104] On November 8, pogroms, including burning of synagogues, destruction of Jewish property, and mistreatment of individual Jews, were instigated by local Nazi party leaders. On November 9, the day the Nazis gathered in Munich in honor of the abortive Beer Hall Putsch of November 1923, von Rath died of his wounds. Contrary to his usual custom, Hitler did not speak to the party veterans assembled in the Old Town Hall and, after a whispered exchange with Goebbels, left the meeting. Goebbels then informed the Nazis gathered there of the diplomat's death and delivered a tirade denouncing "international Jewry." Without explicitly saying so, he made it clear that the party should organize and carry out "demonstrations" against the Jews throughout the country.[105] Goebbels wrote in his diary: "I go to the party reception in the Old Town Hall. Huge tumult. I explain the matter to the Führer. He decides: Let the demonstrations continue. Pull back the police. The Jews should for once feel the anger of the people. That's right. I immediately give the corresponding directives to the policy and party. Then I speak for a short time in that vein to the party leadership. Storms of applause. All tear straight off to the telephone. Now the people will act."[106]

A confidential report issued later by the Supreme Court of the Nazi party showed that Goebbels's speech was interpreted by party leaders "to mean outwardly that the party was not to give the appearance of having provoked the demonstrations, while in reality it was to organize and carry them out."[107] The results of the pogrom are familiar: destruction of around a hundred synagogues, the burning of several hundred others, the destruction of at least eight thousand Jewish businesses, and the vandalizing and wrecking of countless apartments and homes. A hundred or so Jews were murdered, many more beaten and mistreated. Thirty thousand male Jews were arrested and sent to Dachau, Buchenwald, and Sachsenhausen concentration camps. In an article in *Der Völkische Beobachter* of November 12, 1938, Goebbels denied that the government had anything to do with the pogrom and that it had been a spontaneous outburst of an enraged nation.[108] A confidential report of the Nazis' Supreme Party Court concluded, however, that it was obvious that the party had carried out the action.[109] Goebbels's denials failed to convince foreign correspondents who had been eyewitnesses to the violence.[110] On November 25, two weeks after the pogrom, Goebbels spoke to the fifth annual conference of the Reich Chamber of Culture and the Strength through Joy organization at the opera house in Berlin. The regime had broken the Jews' hold over German politics, economics, and culture. "The German press was written by Jews. German film was made by Jews. A theater without Jews was inconceivable.

Writing had only Jews as its leading representatives. Musical creation and music criticism were completely in the hands of international and foreign Jews." But now that the Nazis had eliminated the Jews from German cultural life, it "could really blossom."[111]

The evening after the pogrom, Hitler spoke in Munich to publishers and leading editors. Drawing on racial analysis to explain the international situation, he made the case, for those able to read between the lines, that conditions were favorable for launching the war that the Munich agreement had just postponed.[112] Hitler had built a party that was "fanatically" behind him. Now it was time to bring "the whole German people" along. For that to happen, it was necessary that "the press blindly accept the notion that the Führer has acted correctly!" and that it "always stress the correctness of the leadership," in order to create a unified nation. His racial analysis of world politics led to an optimistic assessment of the global balance of power. Hitler said that the German racial composition was the best that had ever existed. If one subtracted Germans, Italians, Negroes, and Jews from the total American population, there remained only sixty million Anglo-Saxons. Russia had only fifty-five or fifty-six million Great Russians. The British Empire had only forty-six million English, while France had only thirty-seven million "real Frenchmen." Italy had more than forty million Italians, and Poland only seventeen million Poles. But in 1938 Germany had "eighty million people of one race and almost eight million people living around us who really belong to us racially. Whoever doesn't believe in the future of this great block of humanity is himself just a weakling. I believe unconditionally in this future."[113] If race was the driving force of history, as Hitler believed, then the Great Russians, Americans, French, and English would have had no motive to go to war against their presumed racial allies in Berlin.

Yet Franklin D. Roosevelt's opposition to Hitler's domestic and foreign policy was apparent from the earliest days of the Third Reich. Nazi attitudes towards FDR and the United States went from dubious assertions of common interests, during the New Deal, to growing hostility and then rage as time went on. Initially, *Der Völkische Beobachter* published articles underscoring the points in common between the New Deal and National Socialism. Both, according to the Nazi press, favored a strong state, public welfare over self-interest, and even authoritarian rule by a strong national leader to overcome the shortcomings of the market.[114] In 1934 and 1935, however, the German press focused on the success of the Nazi economic recovery in comparison to the continuing unemployment and strikes in the United States. These, in turn, were due to Roosevelt's support for liberal democracy and the resulting weakness of state power, by contrast with that of the Hitler regime. The disparity between the economic recovery in Nazi Germany and the unalleviated unemployment in the United States during the early years of the New Deal became an important element in the Nazi attack on American democratic institutions. The Nazi press stressed the supposed obsolescence and economic disadvantages of liberal democratic institutions.[115] Whereas in the 1920s some German conservatives had presented the United States as the model of a productivist future, by 1936 and 1937, *Der Völkische Beobachter* laced its anti-American articles with warnings about Bolshevism and radicalism in the United States and noted that such problems had been erased in National Socialist Germany.[116]

Disdain and contempt for the United States, heavily tinged with anti-Semitism, came to the fore. Academic and popular authors sympathetic to the regime distinguished between a "bad" (that is, Jewish-dominated) America, and the "Germanic-Celtic" majority.[117] Following Roosevelt's "Quarantine the Aggressors" speech in Chicago in October 1937, German propaganda adopted a tone of unambiguous hostility toward Roosevelt and the United States. German propagandists as well as German diplomats in Washington, including the ambassador Hans Diekhoff, explained the depiction of Japan, Italy, and Germany as "enemies of peace" as an effort by Roosevelt to divert attention from the domestic economic, social, and political problems in the United States and to defend himself against criticism that he was seeking dictatorial powers by pointing the finger at dictators abroad.[118] In his speech to the Reichstag of April 28, 1938, Hitler sarcastically gave his "answer" to Roosevelt's plea that he not attack the independent nations of Europe.[119] Hitler presented himself as a man of peace seeking to overcome the presumed injustices of the Versailles treaty. Pointing to the Monroe Doctrine and Roosevelt's questions about German intentions in Europe, Hitler claimed that he was not trying to start a war, but simply to right past wrongs and defend the national interest, just as Britain, France, and America did in their foreign policies. The problem in Europe was not German aggression but Germany's encirclement by potential adversaries that opposed justified revisions to the territorial provisions of the Versailles treaty.[120] Although the Roosevelt administration had not placed the persecution of the Jews at the center of its policy toward Germany, from 1938 on anti-Semitism became increasingly important to the Nazi view of the United States.[121] A memo from the German Foreign Office of January 1939, "The Jewish Question as a Factor in Foreign Policy in 1938," described the United States as the "headquarters" of "world Jewry" and asserted that Roosevelt had surrounded himself with Jewish advisers.[122] In his State of the Union Message of January 4, 1939, Roosevelt warned of the threats posed to peace and the danger of indifference and neutrality on the part of the democracies in the face of acts of aggression.[123] In winter and spring 1939 *Der Völkische Beobachter* ran stories under the following headlines: "The Hebrew Posters for F. D. Roosevelt" and "USA under Jewish Dictatorship."[124] According to the German press, Roosevelt was a servant of the Jews and was resisting German policy in order to divert attention from domestic problems.

Hitler was always the key figure in German propaganda, either through his own words or through the messages he sent to his associates. During the mid-1930s, he held this rhetorical violence somewhat in check as he sought to present himself at home and abroad as a man of peace. Beginning with the Nuremberg Party Rally of September 1937, this relative moderation gave way to a return to and then escalation of his anti-

Jewish threats. There he said for the first time in a major public setting that "Jewry" was intent on "exterminating" Germany's "national intelligentsia."[125] At the Nuremberg Rally in 1938, he accused "the Jewish world enemy" of the attempted "annihilation of the Aryan states."[126] By January 1939, the Nazi regime had flooded the Third Reich with anti-Semitic propaganda and legislation. As a result, an anti-Semitic consensus had become widespread in German and Austrian society in favor of revoking citizenship rights for Jews, destroying their economic prospects, purging them from the professions, confiscating their property, and subjecting them to arbitrary arrest and expulsion from Germany and then from the rest of Europe. According to this consensus, "destruction" of German and Austrian Jewry amounted to elimination of its alleged power and, if possible, deportation to some other part of the globe. It was not a consensus in support of mass murder. It was only in the months preceding World War II that Hitler, and consequently Nazi propaganda, began to make the case for mass murder should the war that he was planning to start take place. The anti-Semitic consensus shaped in the 1930s created an indispensable reservoir of public hatred, contempt, and indifference toward the Jews that made it possible for the Third Reich to move on to a Final Solution.[127] Buried within that consensus was another, more radical anti-Semitism, which Hitler brought to the fore on January 30, 1939.

3 "International Jewry" and the Origins of World War II

In the era of appeasement in the West and the nonaggression pact with the Soviet Union in the East, Hitler and the core Nazi leaders asserted that a powerful international Jewish conspiracy was mobilizing against the Third Reich. It is a terrible historical irony that Nazi paranoia came into its own precisely in the late 1930s, characterized as they were by an absence of international anti-Nazi solidarity and by Jewish political weakness. If international Jewry had organized an effective anti-German political conspiracy, why had it been incapable of placing any effective deterrent in the way of Hitler's plans? Why had the League of Nations been so feckless? Why did Britain and France pursue a policy of appeasement and turn a cold shoulder to Soviet suggestions for a "popular front against fascism"? Why did the United States, which the Nazis claimed was dominated by the Jews, fail to intervene in European affairs more vigorously to stop Hitler early on? Why, finally, did Nazi Germany's archenemy, the Soviet Union, which Hitler and Goebbels had described as a dictatorship of Jewry, sign a nonaggression pact with the Nazi regime in August 1939? Were the Jews were so devilishly clever that they supported peace through appeasement, in order to conserve their strength to fight later on? In any case, Nazi propaganda never accused "international Jewry" of supporting peace in the short run to favor Allied success in the long run. There were no facts that could refute the assertions of the anti-Semitic conspiracy theory.

In accordance with his strategy to initiate an early offensive against isolated, unprepared countries, Hitler had decided on war in the winter of 1938–1939, following its supposed postponement at the Munich conference. On January 30, 1939, in his annual speech to the Reichstag and eight months before he invaded Poland, he presented what became the core Nazi narrative of the coming conflict. He accused international Jewry of planning to exterminate—that is, to kill—all the German people. Hitler was at the peak of his power and popularity in Germany at that moment. The intellectual, cultural, economic, and industrial elites had supported or adapted to his rule. After his apparent success at Munich, the last skeptics in the diplomatic and military establishment fell into line. Political opposition, a free press, an independent judiciary, and the rule of law had been crushed. Economic recovery fueled by military spending and huge public works projects established a base of popular support that extended well beyond the Nazi party. Half of Germany's Jews had fled into exile, leaving behind an impoverished and powerless minority surrounded by a largely hostile or indifferent Christian majority. All the instruments of police power and legal coercion were in the hands of the Nazi regime, and of Hitler and Himmler in particular. The Propaganda Ministry extolled the infallibility of Hitler. Britain and France had acceded to his desire to annex the Sudetenland and had assured him that there would be no war if he expanded no further.

Halfway through the more than two-hour Reichstag address, Hitler mentioned "the Jewish world enemy" that had been defeated "within Germany" but now confronted it from abroad. Assertions about Germany's aggressive intentions were an "outrageous slander" due to "sick hysteria, . . . lies, . . . the interests of amoral businessmen," and "above

all, international Jewry," which hoped to "satisfy its desire for revenge
and hunger for profit." He repeated the litany of suffering for which he
held the Jews responsible: the German defeat in World War I, widespread hunger in the postwar era, and the inflation and economic crisis
of the 1920s.[1] He warned that if "Jewry," by using the "press, film, radio,
propaganda, theater, and literature, which are in its hands, . . . should
again succeed in agitating and driving millions among the masses of
people into a conflict that is utterly senseless for them and serves only
Jewish interests," Germany's policy toward the Jews would have reper-
cussions elsewhere. "The peoples no longer want to die on the killing
fields, so that this rootless international race can make money off the
business of war and satisfy its Old Testament desire for revenge. A
higher knowledge" would rise above "the Jewish words 'Proletarians of
all nations, unite'—namely: 'Productive members of all nations, recognize your common enemy!'" Following this by now familiar tale of German suffering at the hands of international Jewry, Hitler returned for
the first time since 1920 to an open threat of mass murder.

> I have very often in my lifetime been a prophet and have been
> mostly derided. At the time of my struggle for power it was in the
> first instance the Jewish people who only greeted with laughter
> my prophecies that I would someday take over the leadership of
> the state and of the entire people of Germany and then, among
> other things, also bring the Jewish problem to its solution. I be-
> lieve that this hollow laughter of Jewry in Germany has already
> stuck in its throat. I want today to be a prophet again: if interna-
> tional finance Jewry inside and outside Europe should succeed
> in plunging the nations once more into a world war, the result
> will be not the Bolshevization of the earth and thereby the vic-
> tory of Jewry, but the annihilation of the Jewish race in Europe![2]

In at least four subsequent speeches broadcast on radio and published
in the German and world press, Hitler repeated the prophecy. As was

mentioned earlier, he did so twice more, in speeches to Nazi party officials read in his absence on February 15, 1942, and February 24, 1943.[3] By "international Jewry," Hitler had in mind an international conspiracy operating behind the scenes and dominating government policy in the Soviet Union, England, and the United States. Invisible to those lacking the insight provided by Nazi ideology, this conspiracy was perceived by Hitler and his henchmen as the driving force of modern history. When the major powers opposed Nazi Germany, they were doing so as *Judenknechte,* or servants of the Jews.

Hitler's "prophecy" of January 30, 1939, postulated an existing historical subject called international Jewry, a threat as real to him and the rest of the Nazi elite as the nation-states of the Soviet Union, Britain, France, and the United States. For the Nazis it was Jewry, present both "inside and outside Europe," that had as its war aim the extermination of the German people. Should a war begin, it would necessarily be due to an act of aggression by international Jewry. Hitler promised, however, that the result of such a war would be the extermination of the Jewish race in Europe. This result would be achieved because the "propagandistic defenselessness of the non-Jewish peoples" was a thing of the past, for National Socialist Germany and Fascist Italy now had the intent and the ability to enlighten the world about the Jews. An internationalism based on class would be replaced by one based on race composed of the Aryan, productive members of the societies of both Europe and the United States.

On March 14, 1939, in violation of the agreement he had signed less than six months earlier in Munich, Hitler ordered the German armed forces to invade and occupy the remainder of Czechoslovakia. As a result, it became obvious to leaders in Paris and London that they had erred in assuming that Hitler's goals were limited to the incorporation of German-speaking territories such as Austria and the Sudetenland. After the invasion of Czechoslovakia, Britain and France declared their willingness to defend Poland, should Nazi Germany invade it as well. Hitler's invasion brought the era of appeasement to an end and enhanced the credibility of Churchill and others who had earlier warned of the expansionist nature of the German threat.

The Nazi regime's anti-Semitic intellectuals interpreted the invasion of Czechoslovakia rather differently. In the March 21, 1939, issue of *Die Judenfrage,* the lead article by a Dr. Rudolf Urban, titled "Jewish Domination of Central Europe Ended," blamed the invasion on "world Jewry" and the "Beneš clique" in Prague, which Jewry supported. German intervention had turned a Jewish threat "into a decisive Jewish defeat, which deprived world Jewry of its last base in Central Europe." Germany could not tolerate a "stronghold of Jewry and Bolshevism" on its borders. The Czechoslovak government under Jewish influence had "completely failed" to crush the threat of Bolshevism and Jewry. Urban surveyed with dismay the Czech newspapers and periodicals that expressed support and sympathy for the Jews, and the Czech government's arrests of members of "anti-Jewish organizations" (that is, Nazi front groups) that had attacked Jewish businesses and synagogues. "Hence, we again see that those who get involved with the Jews are soon delivered up to them." The Czechs had the Jews to blame for their fate.[4]

In "Who Wants War?"—an essay published ten days after the German invasion of Czechoslovakia—Goebbels blamed the prospect of more widespread war on a "war psychosis" being fostered in Paris, London, and New York. The "average citizen" of England or France did not care if the Sudetenland returned to Germany and did not even know where the place was. Talk of war emanated from "cliques and circles that have an interest in war." The general war psychosis, he asserted, had also received a powerful impetus from the United States: it was "an open secret" that Roosevelt had "gathered around him a great number of Jewish advisers. One can just imagine what they are blaring into his ear. But what does this have to do with the American people?" As there was no reason for the United States to care about German borders, the war fever there must have another explanation. "There must be an anonymous power that is standing behind everything . . . It is the same power that confronted us National Socialists at the time of the battles (*die Kampfzeit*) in Weimar in Germany . . . The Jews are guilty! If in a dark hour war should one day break out in Europe, this cry must resound over our whole part of the earth. The Jews are guilty! They want war, and they are doing everything in their power to drive the peoples into it. They believe they will be not the victims, but rather the beneficiaries, of such a war. Therefore, all over the world, they foster this infernal campaign and witch hunt against Germany and Italy and call for a fighting bloc of democratic against authoritarian states." The Jews (and the Freemasons) wanted the war because it would allow them to "regain their old positions of power in Germany and Italy."[5] On May 20, 1939, in his essay "The Encircler," Goebbels denounced a coalition of feudal lords, working-class leaders, dandies, fat lawyers, "sordid" Jews, and "revenge-seeking emigrants" in London.[6] The "London encirclers" spoke of a German aggression "that is not present and is not planned." The following week, Goebbels described the English as the ultimate cynics, whose disingenuousness was evident in their willingness to include the Soviet dictatorship in the "ring of encirclement" around Germany, despite the huge discrepancies between London and Moscow in worldview and institutions.[7]

No single event refuted the notion of either an international Jewish conspiracy or Jewish domination of the Soviet Union more dramatically than the Ribbentrop-Molotov nonaggression pact of August 1939. None seemed to suggest more clearly the depth of Hitler's cynicism or the disdain with which he regarded ideological principle, in his search of power. In fact, it was an example of his ability to combine tactical flexibility with long-term ideological consistency.[8] Stalin, through a similar mixture of cynicism and ideology, signed the pact. Blinded by Communist orthodoxy, he assumed that the "imperialist" states would, as they had in World War I, bleed each other white, radicalize the Continent, and create an opening for the nonbelligerent Soviet Union, patiently waiting to pick up the pieces.[9] In taking this stance, Stalin delivered a devastating blow to Jews all over Europe. He turned his back on the Communist antifascism of the Popular Front era of 1935 to 1939 and made it possible for Hitler to launch World War II without having to worry about fighting battles on the eastern and western fronts simultaneously. Moreover, Stalin agreed to sign a nonaggression pact only eight months after Hitler had uttered his murderous anti-Jewish prophecy for the first time in public. Signing the pact was stunning confirmation of the lack of Jewish influence within the Soviet government and Communist party. The turning point was clear for all to see in Stalin's decision to replace his Jewish foreign minister, an advocate of the popular front against fascism, Maxim Litvinov, with Vyacheslav Molotov.[10] As Churchill put it, Litvinov, "the eminent Jew, the target of German antagonism, was flung aside for the time like a broken tool . . . The dismissal of Litvinov marked the end of an epoch. It registered the abandonment by the Kremlin of all faith in a security pact with the Western Powers and in the possibility of organizing an Eastern Front against Germany . . . The Jew Litvinov was gone, and Hitler's dominant prejudice was placated."[11] Litvinov's dismissal was both part of a dramatic foreign policy shift and the beginning of a purge of Jewish officials from the Soviet Foreign Ministry and from other positions in the party and government.[12]

The collapse of collective security that culminated in the nonaggression pact made it far easier for Hitler to launch and quickly win wars against Poland, the Low Countries, and France in 1939 and 1940, while the Soviet Union looked on without intervening. If the Jews were the power behind the scenes, they could not have arranged a more tragic scenario. If Jews were in charge, why would they have put their faith in Hitler's promises to uphold the nonaggression pact, left the Soviet armed forces so unprepared, or refused to heed warnings coming from around the world about an impending attack of which they would be the principal target?[13] Part of the Nazi answer was to point to Jewish incompetence and still more insistently to Hitler's genius. The Nazis did not recognize Germany's incredible good luck in finding itself confronted with years of disarray, disunity, blunders, and underestimation of its strength on the part of its major adversaries. Rather, the Nazi leaders saw themselves as brilliant and bold in thwarting the clever plans of international Jewry. If Hitler's followers had asked why "Jewry" had allowed Hitler to attack Poland without any fear of retaliation from the Soviet Union, Goebbels would have answered that Hitler was a political genius who had outwitted the Jews. As powerful as the Jews were, he had shown that they were not invincible. The now familiar story of buck-passing, mutual mistrust, failure to stop German expansion, and the collapse of deterrence could not dent the Nazi narrative of a powerful Jewish conspiracy.[14] The Jews were powerless to stop the Reich Press Office from describing the pact as a "sensational turning point in the relations between these peoples" that continued "the traditional commonalities of German-Russian politics."[15]

Hitler initiated World War II with an act of unprovoked aggression, bolstered by projection and lies concerning a border incident the regime had fabricated. It followed months of propaganda blaming Poland for the war Hitler was planning to start. Hitler claimed that Polish troops had engaged in an unprovoked armed assault on a German radio station at Gleiwitz in Upper Silesia. In fact, the faked "attack" was carried out by SS troops; the bodies of Polish concentration camp prisoners who had been killed by lethal injection and then shot were left lying at the site.[16] Later that day, Hitler declared, "Last night Poland fired on our territory with regular soldiers. Since 5:45 the fire has been returned. And from now on bomb will be met with bomb."[17] On September 1, 1939, as German troops invaded Poland, the Reich Press Office directives referred to "Polish attacks on Germans in Poland."[18] On that day as well, the *Periodical Service* in the Reich Press Office informed editors that they were not to use the word "war" to refer to the German invasion. Rather, there had been a German "response to the Polish attack."[19] Dietrich's staff instructed the press that Hitler's speech to the Reichstag on September 1, 1939, which placed the entire blame for the outbreak of the war on Poland, England, and France, was to serve as "the foundation of all considerations of the current situation."[20] Two days later, after England declared war on Germany, Hitler informed members of the Nazi party, "Our Jewish-democratic world enemy succeeded in inciting the English people to a state of war against Germany."[21] A *Periodical Service* directive several weeks later instructed editors to hold Jews, with their incitement, responsible for the English declaration of war. Poland was not the cause but merely the pretext for England's declaration of war against Germany. "English and Jewish philistines had a common political and economic interest in working against the process of liberation that Germany was leading against English-Jewish capitalist domination." At this early point in the war, editors should avoid attacks on the English people as a whole. German periodicals were ordered to associate English opponents of appeasement, such as Duff Cooper, Anthony Eden, Leslie Hore-Belisha, and of course Winston Churchill, with the Jews. This supposed link accounted for their otherwise inexplicable anti-Nazism.[22] The tone of the directives conveyed deep conviction.

Similarities existed between Nazi racism directed at Nazi Germany's assorted national enemies and that directed at the Jews. For one thing, Nazi anti-Polish propaganda stressed Polish inferiority. On October 23, 1939, a *Periodical Service* directive declared that the Poles had contributed little to European culture, and directed German periodicals to associate the words "Pole," "Poland," and "Polish" with objectionable and sloppy behavior. "The common equation in Germany of Poles and Jews must be encouraged." The Poles were "by nature servants and should be handled that way."[23] Two weeks later, apparently responding to reports of fraternization between German soldiers and Polish women, the November 3, 1939, directive stated, "Every blood-linked mixture between Germans and Poles leads to racial decline in German blood." The magazines ought to inform German men, women, and children that "any connection with people of Polish extraction" was dangerous. The Poles were to be viewed as "on the same level as Jews and Gypsies." The overall goal was to establish a "distance between Germans and Poles."[24] Yet Nazi propaganda did make a distinction between Poles and Jews, too: this "same level" did not extend to viewing Poles or Gypsies as part of a powerful, international conspiracy. The Nazis restricted that accusation to the Jews.

In the first years of the war, the Nazi party was a beehive of propagandistic activity, even though many party members had been called into the armed forces.[25] According to figures, of almost comical precision, offered by the Propaganda Ministry, in the first sixteen months of the war, the Nazi party organized about 200,000 political meetings. From September 1939 to October 1, 1940, the Nazi party Propaganda Directorate (RPL) produced nine slide shows (including "Our Führer," "Germany's Racial Policies," "Plutocracy and Jewry," "World Pirate England," and "On the Road to Victory"). The forty-one *Gau* offices organized 29,674 slide show evenings with a total attendance of 4.3 million. Nine to ten million people saw the *Wochenschau* (German Weekly Newsreel) each week. The output of printed matter was no less daunting. From the beginning of the war, the RPL produced 1.9 million copies of *Unser Wille und Weg,* 2.3 million copies of informational material for party speakers, 32.5 million copies of the NSDAP Weekly Quotation, and 65 million leaflets. Text posters were printed in editions of between four hundred thousand and five hundred thousand. Picture posters might appear in editions of 300,000 ("Take Cover from Flak"), 650,000 ("Our Flag is Victory"), and even 1,000,000 ("Down with Germany's Enemies"). By the end of 1940, 700,000 photos of Hitler had been produced and distributed; 23,000 color posters were produced to accompany the film *The Eternal Jew.*[26]

On September 3, 1939, Otto Dietrich informed the press assembled in Berlin that the tasks of the German journalist had changed with the outbreak of the war. The newsman was no longer to be "only a reporter . . . We are . . . the soldiers of the German people. Today we build a West wall of the soul and constitute the power that stands behind our troops fighting now in the East in Poland." It was, he continued, the mission of the press to convey Hitler's will and determination to the whole people. Dietrich announced that he would be working at Hitler's headquarters but would stay in regular contact with the press. He expected "above all that every day the German press will have editorials and leading articles that will strengthen the home front with the arguments you know, and which will be made available to you" from the offices of the state and the Nazi party. The press, he continued, needed to change its reporting of international news. It could not "debate every speech of our enemies" or convey their arguments. That would "amount to doing the enemy's business." The Press Office would publish an overview of international political developments. The press was to "give the reader the feeling that he will be [as a result] informed about the factual developments taking place in the world."[27] In other words, the press was not to print, for example, Churchill's or Roosevelt's speeches, the Atlantic Charter, the Allied declarations offering specifics about German war crimes, or the Allied communiqués from the conferences in Casablanca, Tehran, and Yalta. Rather, the press was to present the Nazi regime's take on events. Dietrich's order forbidding publication of statements by foreign leaders became crucial to suppressing information about the Final Solution. Press directives were to be kept secret. Their loss or communication of their contents to unauthorized persons was a crime punishable by loss of employment or a prison sentence. Editors in chief were personally responsible for preserving the confidentiality of directives and were ordered to burn or shred them within six months of receiving them. A written record of the documents' destruction was to be preserved.[28] With varying degrees of ideological agreement, opportunism, and fear, German editors and reporters complied. There was little factual reporting in the press in Nazi Germany.

The fact that Neville Chamberlain, the advocate of appeasement, remained British prime minister until May 1940 did not stop the Reich Press Office from incorporating anti-Semitic arguments into its anti-British propaganda. A directive of September 1939 stated, "The force of our argument must be directed against England, but not against the British people as such but rather against those eternal warmongers who act on behalf of Jewry, international capitalism, and the democracies and plutocracies." Just as British propaganda sought in its statements to separate the German government from the German people, so the German press was directed that it must "clearly stress the difference between the English government and the misled and deceived English people." The English ruling circles "wanted a world war!"[29] In articles about the United States, the press was to take care to avoid undermining the opposition to Roosevelt. A press directive of September 23, 1939, ordered "the greatest discretion and reserve" regarding the American domestic debate over neutrality. Everything must be done to avoid adding to suspicions that the American isolationists were "agents of Hitler." "Each of our friendly positions on their behalf will be immediately attacked by the Jewish press." As it appeared that the isolationists would lose the 1940 elections in the United States, "we must not be identified with them, so that their defeat will not be interpreted as a German defeat. *This language rule is to be treated with particular confidentiality.*"[30]

In the tense days preceding the German attack on Poland, Chaim Weizmann, president of the World Zionist Organization and a British citizen, asserted that Jews stood on the side of Britain and of democracy and against Nazi Germany. In view of the Nazi regime's anti-Semitic policies, it was an obvious thing for any Jewish leader to say, though Weizmann was in no position to speak for Jews in general. Yet that was how the Nazi propagandists viewed his statement. The lead article, by Wolff Heinrichsdorff in *Die Judenfrage* of September 18, 1939, "The Jewish Decision: The Jews on England's Side," viewed support for England by Weizmann, and also by Albert Einstein, as confirmation of the anti-Semitic narrative. "The Führer's clear assertion that international and plutocratic Jewry is guilty for the outbreak of the war has been confirmed very quickly. Immediately after England's entry into the war, the Jewish world organizations have placed themselves at its disposal. Chaim Weizmann thinks it right and necessary to again assure England of the sympathy and support of 'Alljudas.' This decision does not surprise us. Rather it confirms our experience and knowledge. Everyone has the

The Jewish Enemy

allies he deserves. England has the Jews on its side. We don't envy it."[31] The author noted that Zionists, who had criticized England for its policies in Palestine, nevertheless firmly supported it in the war. The decision was "not only understandable but obvious in light of the strong Jewification (Verjudung) of the English upper strata . . . Today we know whom we are facing in England: the world enemy number 1: international Jews and the power-hungry, hate-filled world Jewry."[32]

The Nazi anti-Semitic barrage against England constituted an important chapter in its wartime propaganda offensive; however, it is important to note, as one historian has put it, that there was "little to celebrate in . . . British policy towards the Jews of Europe between 1939 and 1945." The British government took the lead in barring escape routes from Europe for Jewish refugees. It permitted fewer than the seventy-five thousand emigrants to Palestine allowed under the White Paper. It did not offer safe haven in the vast British Empire outside Palestine for Jewish refugees, even though Zionists were willing to cooperate in the diversion of refugees to safe destinations. Though Britain gave aid to non-Jewish resistance movements in Europe, such as the Warsaw rising of the Polish Home Army in 1944, none was forthcoming for the Jews, such as those in the Warsaw Ghetto in 1943. Despite Churchill's sympathy for the Jews, officials in the British Foreign Office at times viewed them as a nuisance, given England's concerns about Arab support during the war.[33] At no time did Jews in Britain or anywhere else influence British wartime policy. Had the Jews had any of the power and influence attributed to them by Nazi propaganda, Britain's policy toward refugees might well have been modified, Jewish resistance in Europe might have been greater, and the death camps and the railways leading to them would possibly have been bombed.

None of this mattered to the Nazis. What did matter was that Britain was at war with the Third Reich. From the regime's anti-Semitic perspective, the only reason for this otherwise incomprehensible decision was the undue power of the Jews. The Reich Press Office directive of

October 23, 1939, on "the Jews in England" included clear instructions about how anti-Semitism could serve to undermine public support for the war in England.

> Goal: Contradiction between the English people and the English upper class, influenced and descended as it is by and from the Jews. Command posts of Jewry in public life in England. Jews as inspirers and beneficiaries of English policy aimed at world domination.
>
> Organization: Emphasize: Misuse of Parliament and the press for Jewish interests. Voices hostile to the Jews (Mosley followers in concentration camps, protest against émigré doctors, protest against art trade). Cultural affinity between the English (Puritans) and Jews. English-Jewish community of interest despite Palestine conflict. Social misery.
>
> Avoid: Claim of Jewish origin if it cannot be clearly proven. (Proof in most cases very difficult!) Attacks against the English people.[34]

Such directives illustrated the diffusion of ideas from Nazi think tanks to the government and then to the press, thereby offering evidence of effective coordination among various government offices in support of shared goals. The *Periodical Service* indicated that the source for all of these insights into England and the Jews encompassed the full panoply of a firmly established anti-Semitic intellectual establishment: the Institute for the Study of the Jewish Question, in the so-called Office of Anti-Semitic Action of the Propaganda Ministry in Berlin; the Nazi Party Institute for the Study of the Jewish Question, in Frankfurt am Main, founded by Alfred Rosenberg; the Press Office of the Foreign Office; and the press archive of the Hochschule für Politik in Berlin. Their addresses and phone numbers were given in the directives, to assist editors who sought further information, as were the titles of a host of ostensibly scholarly works, including *Die Juden und das Wirtschaft-sleben* (The Jews and Economic Life), by Werner Sombart, and his essay dating from World War I *Handler und Helden* (Merchants and Heroes); a work by Heinrich Hest (whose real name was Hermann Erich Seifert), *Palästina: Judenstaat?* (Palestine: Jewish State?); and articles by Wolf Meyer-Christian about "the English-Jewish alliance" published in the journal *Die Judenfrage* in fall 1939.[35]

The assertion of an elective affinity between the Jews and the English was an enduring wartime theme. Some of the more prominent works to make the claim were the prolific Nazi propagandist Peter Aldag's two-volume 1939 work *Juden in England* (Jews in England), comprising *Juden erobern England* (Jews Conquer England) and *Juden beherrschen England* (Jews Dominate England). Aldag offered an anti-Semitic interpretation of English history, with extensive footnotes citing apparently scholarly works. The history covered the ancient world, the first Jewish migrations to England, the expulsion of the Jews in 1290, and their return, which Aldag identified with Oliver Cromwell and the Glorious Revolution of 1688. Thereafter, he discerned a growing bond between Jews, the Church of England, and the monarchy, as well as an intellectual and theological bond between Puritanism and Judaism rooted in the Puritan self-conception of being a chosen people that had God's blessing.[36]

In his annual New Year's address to the nation on January 1, 1940, Hitler again asserted that there was a connection between the outbreak of the war and a Jewish plan to exterminate Germany and the Germans. He warned: "The Jewish-capitalist world enemy that confronts us has only one goal: to exterminate Germany and the German people." Hitler claimed that he had sought a peaceful solution with Poland and an agreement with England; "however, the Jewish and reactionary warmongers in the capitalist democracies had waited for years for this moment. They were ready for it and were not willing to abandon their plans to exterminate Germany."[37] Though the German language had perfectly suitable terms for "defeat" or "vanquish," Hitler chose his words carefully as he projected his own lethal aims onto his enemy. The imputation of genocidal war aims to Nazi Germany's enemies, especially the Jews, remained a core element of wartime propaganda.

Inconvenient facts had little effect on Nazi propaganda. England and France began their supposed campaign to exterminate Germany by refraining from engaging in any military offensives at all in the fall and winter of 1939 and 1940. Poland fought alone and was defeated within six weeks. The French remained behind their defensive fortification the Maginot Line. Britain's efforts were focused on desperate measures to protect shipping from attack by German submarines. In the same month that Hitler repeated that the Jews were plotting to exterminate Germany, Chamberlain removed his Jewish secretary of state for war, Leslie Hore-Belisha. Hore-Belisha had made enemies on the right wing of the Conservative Party because he was a strong proponent of rearmament, opposed appeasement, and broadly agreed with Churchill's assessment of Germany. The Reich Press Office confidential press directive of January 8, 1940, distorted the Hore-Belisha story by referring to "the resignation" of "the Jewish war minister Hore-Belisha as a clever deception maneuver." It claimed that the real grounds for his departure were the "revelation of his Jewish-Moroccan origins," which had made his continuation in office "intolerable." Further, "international Jewry" had counted on a short war and quick victory and thus was willing to have a Jew serve as secretary of state for war. Now that England was in a difficult fight, "this Jewry was no longer willing to leave the responsibility for the war in the hands of a Jew." Moreover, the officer corps feared the spread of anti-Semitism among the troops. Hore-Belisha's departure from the cabinet was thus "a clever move by Jewry," motivated primarily by "a desire to hide Jewish influence." In fact, Hore-Belisha had been born in London. The Reich Press Office directive transformed Chamberlain's decision to remove his Jewish secretary of state for war over policy disagreements into a clever ruse by Jewish forces operating behind the scenes. The Hore-Belisha story demonstrated a crucial aspect of the anti-Semitic conspiracy theory: it was a closed system, immune to refutation or falsification. If Hore-Belisha had remained as secretary of state for war, or if Maxim Litvinov had remained as Soviet foreign minister, Nazi propaganda would have pointed to them as examples of the power of international Jewry.[38] That they were dismissed was evidence of Jewish cleverness at work behind the scenes. In fact, it was plausible to view the firings of Litvinov and Hore-Belisha as setbacks for the Jews and concessions to anti-Semitism. For the Nazis, such an interpretation demonstrated the superficiality of common sense and how easily it could be led astray by appearances. It was only the radical anti-Semites who understood the truth lurking in the shadows.

Though England and France did not move into the offensive in winter and spring 1940, they refused to accept Hitler's demands for a negotiated settlement on his terms. In a speech delivered in Münster on February 28, 1940, titled "Let Us Praise What Makes Us Hard," Goebbels asserted that their refusal to sign a peace agreement with Germany was due to the influence of Jews and "plutocrats." The Jews, he said, had not learned from the catastrophe that befell them in Germany in 1933. They had become the "intellectual leaders . . . of the plutocratic war that England and France have launched against the Reich." He proceeded to denounce "plutocracy . . . a numerically small Western ruling stratum that owns the earth" and that was trying to prevent "the striving young peoples from finding a place in the sun." Though the English talked about humanity and civilization, they actually wanted to defeat Hitlerism "in order to annihilate the German people" and return the country to the divided and fragmented state left in the wake of the Peace of Westphalia.[39] This was no time for illusions. "If English plutocracy was successful, it would not hesitate for a moment to exterminate the German people in its totality."[40] Even at this early point in the war, before Britain or France had launched any attacks on the German armed forces or had bombed any German cities, Goebbels used the verb "exterminate" (*vernichten*) to describe British war aims. These war aims had been hatched by Jewish journalists who had fled Nazi Germany and were now "the intellectual leaders of the plutocratic war against Germany." But the Jews and plutocrats in England were wasting their time, for there would be no second collapse of the home front, such as he asserted had taken place at the end of World War I. Moreover, this most vehement of anticommunists noted that Germany now had the "most populous and largest world power on the earth" on its side—namely, the Soviet Union. Hence, it could focus exclusively on the war in the West. With Hitler's brilliant leadership and a national spirit of sacrifice, Germany's war prospects were excellent.[41]

In the first years of the war, even before the predictions of a quick collapse of "Jewish Bolshevism" in Moscow in summer and fall 1941, anti-Semitism was the basis for a confident belief in victory. In a June 16, 1940, radio speech "Die Zeit ohne Beispiel" (The Time without Parallel), Goebbels promised German listeners that the war would not be a repetition of the two-front war of 1914–1918.[42] Not only had Hitler's diplomatic genius produced the nonaggression pact with the Soviet Union; by ascribing all criticism of Nazi policy in Britain, the United States, and the Soviet Union to the Jews, Goebbels hoped that existing anti-Semitism would undermine support for their fight against the Third Reich. Presentation of the World War II as a "Jewish war"—that is, as one between Germany, on the one hand, and international Jewry on the other—would, he hoped, turn non-Jewish majorities everywhere against the war effort against the Third Reich.[43] In April 1940, an announcement of a slide show and lecture in *Unser Wille und Weg* asserted, "In this war we are dealing exclusively with the world enemy *Juda,*" one that sees "the existence" of Hitler's Germany as precluding "realization of the old Jewish dream of a world state and of Jewish domination." Germany was not confronted "with two separate enemy fronts." Rather, the "plutocracy of the Jewish Reich was largely identical with that of political Jewry."[44] The equation of international Jewry with the governments at war with Nazi Germany remained a component of Nazi wartime propaganda, as did the use of the word *Juda.*

Defamation of the French played a more modest role in Nazi wartime propaganda, primarily because France was defeated in six weeks and replaced by the accommodating Vichy regime.[45] Here too, recognition of the subversive role of the Jews contributed to an understanding of why France had been defeated. A *Periodical Service* directive of July 26, 1940, asserted that France's defeat was unavoidable because "the French had placed leadership in the hands of the Jews," who in turn had become "France's gravediggers."[46] The directive included a compressed anti-Semitic history of the supposed emergence of Jewish power over France in the nineteenth and twentieth centuries, and references to works supporting this narrative. German propaganda was expected to describe France's defeat as a "definitive end to France's insane policies" and to assert that the Jews were responsible for the war; however, German periodicals should avoid attacking "the clerical, church-linked anti-Jewish movements in France."[47] Following German victories in the Low Countries and in France in summer 1940, as Jews were fleeing or attempting to flee Nazi-dominated Western Europe, a *Periodical Service* directive spoke of "the liberation of Europe from Jewish domination."[48]

Winston Churchill became British prime minister on May 10, 1940. From then until the end of the war, Goebbels and Dietrich directed a steady stream of abuse at him. They found in the Nazi anti-Semitic narrative an explanation for British antagonism. Hitler's strategy to win the world war was to win a series of short, decisive campaigns against politically isolated opponents in Europe before the United States could intervene effectively.[49] He had argued in his unpublished Second Book of 1928 that Germany should focus on *Lebensraum* to the east and seek rapprochement with England, while it established a Continental empire. There was, he wrote, "no reason for the perpetuation of the English animosity toward Germany." If such animosity had reemerged, it was because "world Jewry . . . also exerts a controlling influence in England." Though the English could "overcome the war psychosis" toward Germany, "it is just as certain that world Jewry will leave nothing undone to keep the old enmities alive," prevent peace in Europe, and foster Bolshevik tendencies. "One cannot," he concluded, "speak of world politics without taking this most terrible power into account."[50] This "terrible power" became a key element in the Nazi propaganda directed against England and Churchill during World War II.

Hitler's racial thinking had obscured the fact that England had always opposed any power seeking to establish hegemony on the Continent and eliminate the system of independent states. In this tradition, Churchill argued in his correspondence with Franklin D. Roosevelt and in his major speeches that if defeat could be avoided in the short run, England would find a way to win the war in the long run. If Hitler's initial strategy of quick victory over unprepared and isolated adversaries could be thwarted, time would be on the side of his enemies. The ferocity of Nazi propaganda aimed at Churchill followed from the anti-Semitic explanation Hitler had offered. Goebbels unleashed his first wartime attack on Churchill with bitter sarcasm in "On the Godliness of the English" on June 16, 1940, five weeks after Churchill had replaced Chamberlain and three weeks after British and French forces were evacuated from Dunkirk. He poured out a comprehensive list of insults and stereotypes. The English plutocrats were alien to Europe, snobbish, uneducated, intellectually lazy lords of a colonial empire that they held together through cunning, tricks, lies, and violence. Indeed, in their mix of "brutality, lying, pious hypocrisy, and pietistic godliness, they are the Jews among Aryans and belong to that group of men who must first be smashed in the teeth before one can hope to speak rationally with them."[51] In his denunciation of these "Jews among Aryans," Goebbels was incorporating into mass propaganda the arguments that had issued from the regime's anti-Semitic writers working in think tanks, on journals, and at the universities. The supposed Jewishness of the English became another enduring theme of Nazi wartime propaganda.

At his Minister's Conference of July 24, Goebbels was still instructing the Propaganda Ministry officials to attack "British plutocracy alone . . . and not the British people as a whole . . . Our official propaganda media must make it clear to the British people that the plutocratic clique ruling them has nothing in common with them nor does it feel any ties with them."[52] Given that Jewish domination had contributed to France's defeat, it was indeed fortunate for the Reich that England too was dominated by Jews. Yet by August 1940 a shift had taken place in anti-British propaganda. In the midst of the Battle of Britain, the Reich Press Office *Periodical Service* of August 16, 1940, asserted that England was "to a considerable extent in the hands of the Jews." Given that it was clear the Jews bore the "guilt for the racial collapse" of peoples on the Continent and that England had become the "center of world Jewry," it had thus sown the seeds of its coming collapse as well. Yet "Jewification" had gone further in England than in France. In England, the Jews had "penetrated the plutocracy," and society at large as well. The directive ordered editors not to place the blame for English policy only on the Jews and their friends among royalty, gentry, and official-dom. "The people are also guilty."[53] The directive included a summary of books and essays published by government presses that revealed the supposed emergence of Jewish domination over English politics, education, the economy, culture, and entertainment. It claimed that the Jews dominated film, theater, music, radio, and the press, along with the faculties of the universities in Cambridge, London, and Birmingham.[54] The anti-Semitic analysis was now a source of optimism for the Nazis. If Jewish domination had contributed to the collapse of one country after another in the face of the Nazi onslaught, was not victory over the presumably more Jewified English a matter of a rather short time? What further proof did one need of the burden Jews placed on any nation's struggle to resist German expansion and of the rosy prospects for German success?

Yet the English were not collapsing in August 1940; they were in the midst of what Churchill called their finest hour. Why were they so stubborn? There were a host of plausible reasons accounting for British resistance, having to do with mundane and not so mundane factors like the English Channel, the equipment and training of the Royal Air Force, and a widespread sense that Hitler was indeed a threat to everything England stood for. The Nazis' distinctive anti-Semitic explanation of the finest hour appeared in a *Periodical Service* directive of October 14, 1940, about "the English-Jewish alliance." It drew heavily on a book of the same title by Wolf Meyer-Christian, an anti-Semitic author, and offered evidence of coordination between Dietrich's Reich Press Office and the Office of Anti-Semitic Action within Goebbels's Propaganda Ministry.[55] This directive included the address and phone number of the Propaganda Ministry's Office of Anti-Semitic Action and referred editors to other works by anti-Semitic authors favored by the Propaganda Ministry, including Jens Lornsen's *Britain: The Hinterland of World Jewry* and Aldag's *Jews Dominate England* and *Jews Conquer England*.[56] The Reich Press Office regarded the latter book as an "extraordinarily important contribution" to the propaganda effort against England, and an "excellent reference work" for journalists.[57]

The October 14 directive asserted that the war had originated with English and Jewish "dominant circles" that sought the "annihilation" of Germany's political and economic power. German periodicals were to explain "the real essence of our principal enemy (the British-Jewish alliance)" and the "inner Jewification of English politics." It was important to stress that the "Jewish-English commonality of interest" was no mere propaganda assertion. It penetrated the English essence to its core. No important English decisions were conceivable any longer without the influence of Jewry. England's "policy of world domination" was interwoven with the interests of Jewry. It was important for editors to understand that the roots of the English-Jewish alliance of 1940 lay deep in English history and culture, particularly in English Puritanism. Like Judaism, Puritanism rested on the Old Testament. Puritan "this-worldliness" and acceptance of wealth as a sign of God's blessing displayed elective affinities with the Jews. Indeed, "the Old Testament united Englishmen and the Jews."[58] In the November 8, 1940, *Periodical Service* directive, the Reich Press Office requested that "all periodicals that reviewed political" publications "should review Meyer-Christian's *Die Englisch-jüdische Allianz*" (The English-Jewish alliance). The directive informed editors that "the book shows the wide-ranging identification between the English and the Jews and presents the essential presuppositions for understanding the deeper reasons for the current war, one that is simultaneously an English and a Jewish war." Moreover, the book offered an "intellectual framework for the definitive confrontation with the English-Jewish world power."[59]

Meyer-Christian asked why England and the English upper class were seemingly so Jewified. To answer that question, he placed England's opposition to Nazi Germany in 1939, as well as its support for a Jewish homeland, in the context of an anti-Semitic interpretation of four centuries of English history. The English upper class he pronounced "as English as it is Jewish and Jewish as it is English!" Whereas Jews in Germany were critics and opponents of the status quo, in England Jewry was "an inseparable part" of the upper class. The Jewish question in Europe and in Germany could be solved only "if the alliance between the traditional English upper class and the leadership of world Jewry" was "broken once and for all."[60] The key to the advent of the English-Jewish alliance lay in "Puritanism, the specific English form of Christianity." The alliance between the Jews and the English upper class would not have come about without "the fundamental preexisting similarity of both peoples, consisting in the capitalist way of thinking and the claim to world domination." Indeed, "none other than the Christian dictator Oliver Cromwell first recognized this and made it the foundation of his politics." His decision to recall to England the Jews previously expelled had "ensured their assistance in the founding of today's British Empire." The "degeneration of the English upper stratum" was not the result of "accidental bonds of love" or careless individualism. Rather, it was due to a carefully planned effort by the Jews who "made the British aristocracy a fifth column of world Jewry."[61]

That effort succeeded because there was an elective affinity between Puritanism and the Jews in England and the "close connection between English Christianity and the Jewish religion." Both are outspokenly "capitalist religions. They affirm the accumulation of wealth as God's command. Both are religiously articulated egoism." Both "rest on the idea of a chosen people. Among Jews and the English, political superiority and unscrupulousness are grounded in this kind of religion."[62] Meyer-Christian's interpretation of the links between the Jews and capitalism drew directly on Werner Sombart's *Die Juden und das Wirtschaftsleben*.[63] English imperialism derived its power and lack of scruples from its Puritan religious origins, which were in turn "Jewish." In its orientation toward the Old Testament, Calvinism had distanced itself from true Christianity and opted instead for a this-worldly life, in accord with the rules stipulated by Judaism. "Puritanism and Judaism are identical." Political England in 1939 was "nothing other than a modernized Jewry" harboring "within itself the will to dominate the world." The urgent conclusion "for the whole world must therefore be the equating of hostility toward the Jews with hostility toward England. Only if this is done can Europe be freed from the English-Jewish alliance."[64]

English support for Zionism offered further evidence of the philo-Semitic essence of English Puritanism.[65] Meyer-Christian argued that the English-Jewish alliance had led to England's support for a Jewish state in Palestine.[66] National Socialism opposed a Jewish state because it would be "nothing other than an international center of power over non-Jewish peoples, a state whose citizens did not live within its borders but rather were all over the world."[67] It would be a "power center" and "a key base for world Jewry," a group that would enjoy citizenship in the new state without giving up citizenship rights in the nations of Europe or the United States. Most of the Jews would remain in other states and would "in cooperation with the false state help strengthen the power of Jewry as a world power."[68] Meyer-Christian viewed Jewish disputes with Britain about immigration to Palestine in the 1930s as further evidence that the Jews were becoming or had become a world power. For him and for the officials at the Reich Press Office in fall 1940, English resistance to Nazism and support for a Jewish state in Palestine seemed to confirm the validity of their ideological outlook. The "same clique" in Britain linked to "world Jewry" was waging war against Germany and was supporting the Zionists. In one of the earliest of Nazi references to a "Jewish war," Meyer-Christian wrote, "The English war is a Jewish war, a preventive war of the English-Jewish upper strata against the strengthening Reich and the *völkisch* idea to which the Reich owes its strength. For the Arabs, Germany is the second common enemy of the English-Jewish alliance."[69] Meyer-Christian took Chaim Weizmann's statement in support of Britain in the war, as well as British cabinet minister Duff Cooper's speech of January 6, 1940, in Washington, D.C., in support of the Jews in Palestine, as further evidence of the English-Jewish alliance.

Meyer-Christian was only one of a number of Nazi publicists who denounced Zionism during the early phases of the war. At one level, this seems an obvious result of an anti-Semitic outlook. Yet in view of subsequent allegations by the Soviet Union and Arab states of wartime collaboration between Nazi Germany and Zionist leaders in Palestine, it is important to recall that Nazi Germany was opposed to the establishment of a Jewish state in Palestine or anywhere else.[70] Between 1933 and 1939, sixty thousand German Jews were able to emigrate to Palestine under the terms of the Haavarah (Transfer) Agreement. Though it allowed for Jews to transfer some one hundred million Reichsmarks to Palestine, it did not signify support for creation of a Jewish state. The agreement came to an end when the war broke out.[71] Opposition to creation of a Jewish state drew on the belief that it would only aggravate the danger of global domination by an international Jewish conspiracy, aiming to exterminate Germany and the Germans. The conspiracy theory came to overshadow the idea of Palestine as a place to which Germany's Jews could be deported. As war approached, and Nazi Germany had eleven million Jews within its grasp, the issue of deportation became moot. In the Nazi view, Zionism remained within the context of a conspiracy. Hitler himself presented an early version of this view in Mein Kampf, when he contemptuously rejected the "lie" that Zionism was primarily a movement focused on creation of a homeland for the Jews in Palestine. "For while the Zionists try to make the rest of the world believe that the national consciousness of the Jew finds its satisfaction in the creation of a Palestinian state, the Jews again slyly dupe the dumb goyim. It doesn't even enter their heads to build up a Jewish state in Palestine for the purpose of living there; all they want is a central organization for their international world swindle, endowed with its sovereign right and removed from the intervention of other states: a haven for convicted scoundrels and a university for budding crooks."[72] For Hitler and the Nazi regime, Jewish immigration to Palestine could never be part of a "solution," final or otherwise, to "the Jewish question" in Europe. Nazi opposition to a Jewish state was rooted in the core ideological conviction that a Jewish state in Palestine would become a component, or perhaps the very headquarters, of "international Jewry's" efforts to dominate the globe.

Alfred Rosenberg, though also convinced of the existence of a Jewish conspiracy, showed less alarm about Zionism in his essays of the 1920s and 1930s than Hitler did.[73] Rosenberg's key text on the subject was *Der Staatsfeindliche Zionismus* (Zionism hostile to the state), which he initially published in 1921 and which the main Nazi publishing house brought out again in 1938. In it he argued that the Jews were incapable of statecraft. If a Jewish state in Palestine were to be established, it would collapse and the Jews would again become an "international nation." Zionism was "the ineffectual effort of an incapable people to engage in productive activity. Mostly it was a means for ambitious speculators to establish a new arena for receiving usurious interest on a global scale."[74] In the midst of World War II, Hitler's view that a Jewish state would provide another base for the international Jewish conspiracy displaced Rosenberg's contemptuous dismissal and fostered a convergence of anti-Semitism and anti-Zionism.[75]

Giselher Wirsing's *Engländer, Juden, Araber in Palästina* (The English, the Jews and the Arabs in Palestine), published in 1939 (in four editions and ten thousand copies) defined the Zionist goal as the "establishment of a Vatican of world Jewry. A firm base is to be built on which in later years Jewish world policy can rest."[76] Wirsing argued that a Jewish state would foster cooperation between the Jews in Palestine and the assimilated Jews who worked in finance and banking in Western Europe and the United States, thereby strengthening their existing political and economic power.[77] Opposition to Zionist aims made Nazi propagandists pay attention to what they viewed as Arab sensibilities. The *Periodical Service* directive of June 13, 1939, instructed editors not to use the term "anti-Semitism" because doing so offended Arabs. The proper terms to describe Nazi policy were "defense against the Jews" or "hostility to the Jews" (*Judengegnerschaft*).[78] Five years later, the Press Office again voiced concern that the term "anti-Semitism . . . could destroy our relationships with non-Jewish Semites—namely, the pan-Arab world that is so important to us." Therefore, the press was to replace the word "anti-Semitism" with such expressions as "opposition to Jews," "hostility toward Jews," or "anti-Judaism," and the word "anti-Semitic" with "antagonistic to Jews" or "anti-Jewish."[79]

In the summer and fall of 1940, England's "finest hour" brought victory in the air in the Battle of Britain, an emerging alliance with the United States, and the first defeat for Hitler's strategy of winning a short war.[80] This first act of effective resistance to Hitler left the Nazi leaders enraged at Churchill yet still confident of victory. On December 12, 1940, in a speech to a sympathetic audience of Nazi gauleiters, Hitler expressed confidence saying, "The war is as good as won, militarily." England was isolated and would gradually be defeated.[81] Yet Britain refused to accept defeat—this despite severe setbacks in the Battle of the Atlantic, as German submarines exacted a terrible toll on merchant shipping. In his essays of winter and spring 1941, Goebbels hurled personal insults—"fat cynic . . . friend of the Jews and plutocrats . . . political and military dilettante . . . unteachable boob"—at Churchill, but they did nothing to bring victory within Hitler's grasp.[82] On February 5, 1941, the lead article in the *Der Völkische Beobachter* trumpeted, "Churchill Promises Germany to Jews as Plunder; Solidarity of World Parasite Renewed."[83]

In his speech to the Reichstag of January 30, 1941, Hitler suggested that his past threats had led international Jewry to pressure the Western powers into taking an accommodating stance toward Germany. So his renewed threats in 1941 would lead to Jewish pressure on England to make peace with Germany, in order to save European Jewry. With this bizarre combination of a gangster's mentality with fantasies about Jewish power to influence British policy, he repeated his prophecy about the war and the Jews in his annual speech to the Reichstag. As if to underscore the link in his own mind between the war and his policies toward the Jews, he erroneously dated the first utterance of the prophecy as September 1, 1939, the day he ordered the invasion of Poland.

> Not to be forgotten is the comment I've already made in the Reichstag, on September 1, 1939 [actually January 30, 1939], that if the world were to be pushed by Jewry into a general war, the role of the whole of Jewry in Europe would be finished . . . Today, they [the Jews] may still be laughing about [that statement], just as they laughed earlier about my prophecies. Now our racial knowledge is spreading from people to people. I hope that those who still are our antagonists will one day recognize the greater domestic enemy and will then make common cause with us: against the international Jewish exploitation and the corruption of nations![84]

The text of the entire speech was published in the German and translated in the international press. The response the following day by the editors of the *New York Times,* who in the minds of the Nazi leaders were the leaders of "the Jewish press" in the United States, illustrated the difficulty that even the most sophisticated and informed observers had in understanding Hitler. They wrote that "inside Germany or outside, no one in the world expects truth from Adolf Hitler. For eight years he has wielded absolute power over a people whose voice is submerged, as it was yesterday at the Sportpalast by the mechanical clamor of the Party claque. In all that time there is not a single precedent to prove that he will either keep a promise or fulfill a threat. If there is any guarantee in his record, in fact, it is that the one thing he will not do is the thing he says he will do. For eight years he has been the sole and uncontradicted spokesman for Germany—and today the word of Germany is worthless."[85] The *Times* editors found it difficult, as had many of Hitler's adversaries before them, to imagine that such an accomplished and cynical liar was also a fanatical ideologue who would make good on his threats.

In an essay two weeks later in *Das Reich,* Goebbels assured his readers that the British were not so clever as they believed. Many Germans had made the mistake of exaggerating the cleverness of the Jews in Germany. "What remains of the famous cleverness of the [German] Jews?" In the past, the German petit bourgeois was a coward in the face of the Jews. After the Nazis took the problem in hand, it became clear that the Jews' "intellectual superiority was only appearance, and accordingly their power fell apart . . . The same thing applies to the English. It is not for nothing that one calls them the Jews among the Aryans." When the British are confronted, it will become apparent that they are "a colossus with feet of clay." Where Hitler had been playing "the right cards," Churchill had only been overseeing one defeat after another. Germany represented the future, England the past. Its leader was becoming the "laughing stock" of the world. Just as the Nazis, facing enormous odds, had "defeated" the Jews in Germany, they would do the same to the Jews in England.

In his editorials of winter and spring 1941 in *Das Reich,* Goebbels repeatedly imputed to the British dire, even genocidal, war aims. If Churchill had the power, he wrote in an essay of February 23, 1941, he would "wipe Germany out" and divide it into about forty small states governed by "plutocratic cliques," which would dance to the tunes of their English masters.[86] To add to the horror scenario, "the Jews would naturally be restored to their old rights—that is, they would again dominate politics, economics, finance, and culture." A parliament would be restored, to give English dominance a legal facade, while the Germans would again be allowed to write novels, compose symphonies, paint, write poetry, and think while enduring a standard of living reduced to a minimum.[87] In "Britannia Rules the Waves," published in *Das Reich* on March 30, 1941, Goebbels wrote that "if he could, he [Churchill] would annihilate Germany *(Deutschland ausrotten),* exterminate our people *(unser Volk vernichten),* and raze the Reich to rubble and ashes."[88]

The Nazi leaders understood that American aid to Britain was crucial for keeping Britain in the war. As a result, they intensified their propaganda attacks on Franklin D. Roosevelt. In American society and politics in the 1930s and during World War II, Jews were a marginal ethnic group with modest political influence, living in a society still riven by powerful anti-Semitism. In view of their small numbers, it was not surprising that their influence on American foreign and military policy was negligible. Following four decades of immigration, the 4.8 million American Jews made up 3.7 percent of the American population. Though widely distributed around the country, almost half lived in the state of New York, mostly in or around the city of New York.[89] Of the six Jews in the United States House of Representatives, Seventy-sixth Congress, in 1940–1941, four came from New York City, and one each from Chicago and Philadelphia. There were no Jews in the United States Senate. New York's governor, Herbert Lehman, elected in 1932 and reelected in 1934 and 1936, was Jewish.[90]

Although New York's Jews were among Roosevelt's earliest and most loyal supporters, there were no Jews in the top positions in the key government departments of the Roosevelt administration dealing with foreign and military affairs. Cordell Hull, Roosevelt's secretary of state from 1933 to 1945, and Henry Stimson, the secretary of war from 1940 to 1945, were members in good standing of the WASP establishment.

None of the Joint Chiefs of Staff of the United States military were Jews. Anti-Semitism remained a force in the U.S. officer corps. Roosevelt's Jewish secretary of the treasury, Henry Morgenthau, lobbied with little success against resistance from the Department of State to expanding Jewish emigration to the United States.[91] Indeed, citing domestic anti-Semitism, and displaying some of their own, State Department officials avoided any focus on the persecution of the Jews, so as not to intensify already considerable domestic opposition to American intervention in the war in Europe. Some Jewish leaders agreed, fearing that raising the issue would only add to American anti-Semitism.[92] Though Franklin D. Roosevelt despised the Nazi regime from the outset and found its anti-Semitic policies repulsive, the president's public case for resisting Hitler's Germany did not focus on anti-Jewish persecution. Rather, he argued that Nazi Germany posed a threat to American national security as conventionally understood. Should Hitler defeat Britain, dominate the European Continent, and achieve naval dominance in the Atlantic, FDR believed that Germany would pose a direct threat to the United States. On this score he expressed a view shared by the American political and military establishment, especially the leadership of the Navy.[93] American Jews in and outside government were unable to convince the administration to lift immigration quotas to aid Jews seeking to escape from Germany.

Drawing on a tradition of respect for learning, American Jews had made significant advances in the professional world. While the Sulzberger family made the *New York Times* into the nation's paper of record, most of the American press was dominated by conservative publishers, some of whom supported isolationism in the 1930s.[94] In the medical and legal professions and in the universities a small number of talented Jews emerged, even in the face of continuing anti-Semitic discrimination. In the 1920s and 1930s, Harvard, Yale, and Princeton established quotas limiting the number of Jews who were admitted, quotas that remained in place well into the postwar era.[95] Despite some advances in the legal profession, the highest-paying and most powerful and prestigious corporate and Wall Street law firms remained largely closed to Jews.[96] In the corporate world, as the editors of *Fortune* magazine stated in 1936, there was "no basis whatever for the suggestion that Jews monopolize U.S. business and industry." Their review of directors of leading banks indicated that Jews were underrepresented in leading institutions of finance and banking and had even less of a presence in heavy industry, transportation, power utilities, communication, and agriculture. With regard to politics, the editors disputed the anti-Semitic notion that "the New Deal is the Jew Deal." In fact, "Jewish influence in Mr. Roosevelt's Washington is minor."[97]

That the editors of *Fortune* devoted an entire issue to the subject of the Jews in America was also evidence of the persistence of anti-Semitism in the business establishment, most notably anti-Semitism financed and supported by the auto magnate, Henry Ford. He supported the publication of the infamous anti-Semitic forgery *The Protocols of the Elders of Zion*. His articles in the *Dearborn Independent* attacking American Jews fanned the fires of anti-Semitism in American life. They provided material for a transatlantic echo in Nazi propaganda.[98] In the late 1930s, Charles Lindbergh and members of the America First Committee argued that it was the Jews who were driving the United States to intervene in European affairs.[99] Four surveys of the Opinion Research Corporation (ORC) from 1939–1941 found that about a third of the American population answered yes when asked whether "the Jews in this country would like to get the United States into the European war." The most striking finding of the wartime surveys was that anti-Semitism actually increased in American society during World War II. According to one series of polls, it reached its high point in spring 1944, during the Allied invasion of Normandy. In fourteen polls between 1938 and 1946, the ORC asked, "Do you think the Jews have too much power in the United States?" The number of those answering yes increased from 41 percent in March 1938 to 42 percent in August 1940, 47 percent in February 1942, 56 percent in May 1944, and 58 percent in June 1945.[100] Beginning in August 1940, the ORC asked,

"What nationality, religious or racial groups in this country are a menace to America?" and received sobering responses. Of the eight polls conducted from August 1940 to June 1945, Jews were regarded as the greatest menace to the country in every one except those of February and December 1942, when the Japanese replaced them, followed by the Germans in February 1942 (when German submarines were sinking American ships off the Atlantic coast). When American forces stormed the beaches of Normandy, the percentage of Americans who viewed Jews as a menace to the United States peaked.[101] In no small measure because of Roosevelt's leadership, anti-Semitism was relegated to the fringes of American politics before and during the war. Yet as has been well documented, official indifference, the small numbers of Jews in the United States and their modest political influence, popular anti-Semitism, and fear of an anti-Semitic backlash all contributed to keeping discussion of the persecution and then the mass murder of European Jewry on the margins of American governmental policy and public discourse during the war.[102]

Nazi ideologists and propagandists ignored these inconvenient facts about the marginal political and economic influence Jews had in American society. On March 28, 1941, the Institute for Research on the Jewish Question opened in Frankfurt am Main. In his speech to commemorate the opening, broadcast on radio and printed the following day on the front page of *Der Völkische Beobachter* and in other major papers, Alfred Rosenberg gave a speech titled "The Jewish Question as a World Problem."[103] He began, before turning to Jews in the United States, with an attack on the "encirclement policy of Jewish-British high finance" in World War I. Although the "Jewish domination had been broken" in Germany, the Jews had expanded their power in the United States. Here Rosenberg linked actual facts and increasingly famous names with exaggerations about Jewish professional and political gains in the United States. It was true that Felix Frankfurter was a Supreme Court justice; Samuel Rosenman had become a member of the New York State Supreme Court and was an adviser to President Roosevelt; Henry Morgenthau was secretary of the treasury in the Roosevelt administration. Despite the successes of Marcus Loew, Adolph Zukor, Samuel Goldwyn, and Louis Mayer, however, the American film industry was not "100 percent owned by Jews." This did not stop Rosenberg, a self-proclaimed expert on the subject of the Jews, from asserting that "these people own all film production. There is practically no American film [industry], but rather only a Jewish one."[104]

Anti-Semitic arguments played an important role in Nazi anti-American propaganda in 1941. In April 1941, following the publication of a series of Theodor Seibert's articles in *Der Völkische Beobachter,* the Nazi party's Franz Eher Verlag published his book *Das amerikanische Rätsel: Die Kriegspolitik der USA in der Ära Roosevelt* (The American Riddle: The War Policy of the USA in the Roosevelt Era).[105] The riddle to be solved was why the United States supported Britain and opposed Nazi Germany. Seibert found the answer in Franklin Roosevelt's character and in the power of the Jews in the United States. Roosevelt's "inner essence is un-American, New Hollandish, and English." He was also a New Yorker. New York, Seibert wrote, was an "alien body in the American being," a city of wealth and of not yet Americanized emigrants, of Harlem's Negro section and above all "a great Jewish city, the largest Jewish city in the world." In this, it stood in contrast to London and Paris as capitals of their respective countries. Nowhere were the Jews so powerful as in New York. Roosevelt's Brain Trust, including Henry Morgenthau, Felix Frankfurter, and Samuel Rosenman, had gathered around him in New York and had accompanied him to Washington.[106] Those who remembered Weimar, he wrote, could see that in New York and on the American East Coast in general, "the numerical, financial, and political influence of the Hebrews is many times greater" than in pre-Nazi Germany.[107] Roosevelt's "senseless" path of intervention was explicable only by reference to "a very powerful clique of political and financial power holders" who wanted to "save Jewish, Anglo-Saxon democracy." With this analysis of the determinants of American foreign policy, Seibert declared, "Roosevelt's policy is no longer a riddle."[108]

In late May 1941, in his essay "Aus dem Lande der unbegrenzten Möglichkeiten," (From the Land of Unlimited Opportunities), Goebbels described the leading voices of American intervention as Jews, capitalists, industrialists, bankers, and newspaper owners seeking to maneuver the United States with "cunning and deception." These cliques hated Nazi Germany "because it took away the privileges of their racial and religious comrades." They sought American intervention into the war in order to restore these privileges, a ploy, of course, that "had nothing to do with USA interests" and was instead "a pure ghetto project."[109] The anti-Semitic framework explained why a scion of the WASP establishment such as Franklin Roosevelt was such an unwavering opponent of Hitler and Nazism.[110] On May 30, 1941, in "Message from the United States," Goebbels rebutted Roosevelt's warnings about Nazi plans for expansion into the Atlantic and the threat that posed to North and South America. In fact, Goebbels wrote, the Germans had no such plans but were merely countering British control of the sea. Roosevelt's "Jewish advisers" were a key force urging Roosevelt to intervene.[111] That same evening, Goebbels confided to his diary that though "the New York Jewish press tried to push him further," Roosevelt had limited himself for the time being to his neutrality policy.[112]

The identical themes emerging from the anti-Semitic think tanks and the Office of Active Propaganda in the Propaganda Ministry under Goebbels's control were evident in the daily and weekly press directives issued by Dietrich and his staff in the Reich Press office in Berlin. The *Periodical Service* directives of May 30, 1941, and June 6, 1941, on "Jews in the USA" were particularly telling.[113]

Why relevant now:

England ultimately ruled by Jewry; same is true of the USA; accordingly, English–North American plans for conquering the world serve Judas's plan to use, deracinate, and in this way generally exterminate all non-Jews of all peoples. What is at first the for us incomprehensible, hostile stance of the USA towards Germany becomes understandable as soon as one recognizes the degree to which the non-Jewish citizens of USA are already in the hands of warmongering Jews.

Goal:

Clarity about the aim of Jews in the USA at any price to destroy and exterminate Germany, which grasped the Jewish danger in time.

Framework:

Emphasize: In the USA, even more than in England, there is a Jewish parallel government alongside the official U.S. government. The latter becomes ever less important, the more it is filled with Jews selected from the parallel government. Today, this process can be seen as having already been completed.[114]

The article continued by saying that the Jews in the United States spread falsehoods about Germany and were pushing America into a war of revenge from which they would benefit financially. The periodicals should "avoid injuring or mocking non-Jewish USA citizens, owing to their apparent acceptance of enslavement by Jewry or their cowardice in the fight against Jewry and its slaves." Nor should German periodicals suggest that in spring 1941 it was "too late" to break the oppression of the Jews in the United States.[115]

The May 30 directive drew attention to Hitler's claims in *Mein Kampf* that the Jews were responsible for American entry into World War I. The current "warmongering" was therefore the second Jewish anti-German campaign. The directive asserted that Franklin D. Roosevelt had "Jewish blood" traceable to Dutch Jewish ancestors in seventeenth-century Holland. However, Nazi wartime propaganda focused more on Roosevelt as a servant of the Jews than as a Jew himself. The directive listed his Jewish friends and advisers as the banker Bernard Baruch; secretary of the treasury Henry Morgenthau; the governor of New York, Herbert Lehman; the mayor of New York, and "half-Jew," Fiorello LaGuardia, described as a "well-known agitator against Germany"; "Jew professor" and member of the Supreme Court Felix Frankfurter; Benjamin Cohen, a White House adviser; New York State Supreme Court justice Samuel Rosenman; and secretary of state Cordell Hull, who was married to a Jewish woman. These people remained among the core group of villains, the names and faces of the American branch of the international Jewish conspiracy, in the Nazi wartime imagination. Yet the problem went beyond these few. The directive made the claim that most of the members of the then overwhelmingly WASP State Department were Jews. The directive supplied the institutional location and the personal identity of the Jews striving for power in the United States, in an impressive list of Jewish organizations in the United States that included the American Jewish Committee, the American Jewish Congress, the Zionist Organization of America, the Union of American-Hebrew Congregations, the Union of Orthodox Jewish Congregations, the Anti-Nazi League, Hadassah, and the National Organization of Christians and Jews. The goal of this last organization was nothing less than the "establishment of Jewish world domination."[116]

The following week more material on the "Jews in the USA" was disseminated from the Office of Anti-Semitic Action and the "archive" of the Propaganda Ministry. Again, to facilitate contact, the new directive provided editors with addresses and phone numbers for the ministry offices.[117] Drawing extensively on the *American Jewish Year Book,* it combined factual statements about the number and location of Jews in the United States with distortions about Jewish influence on mass culture, law, and finance, as well as about the absence of Jews in the classic "productive" industries (mining, transportation, heavy industry, forestry, and construction). The directive informed German editors that in New York, non-Jews "know that when facing a Jewish lawyer they have hardly any rights in financial conflicts." Despite admonitions not to label non-

Jews as Jews, this directive informed German editors: "Today the king of USA banking and stock exchanges is the Jew J. P. Morgan." Morgan was of course not Jewish, but the Nazis found Jews in many places of power.

> The Jews in the USA hold power with the help of the Jewish government, bleed the people white, and oppress them . . . *The Jews in the USA have treated the non-Jews [there] exactly as the* "Protocols of the Elders of Zion" *prescribed.* The Jew is on the way to destroying and annihilating the USA, that is, the USA of non-Jewish people and things. In the process and until his final victory, he uses a modest number of non-Jewish creatures (for the purpose of more effective camouflage). The non-Jewish residents of the USA face extermination by the Jews. The Jews want to speed up progress toward their goal by trying to push the USA into the war. If so, the American (that is, non-Jewish) people must make great economic, cultural, and physical sacrifices, while the Jew benefits through huge war profits. The Jew also gains as a result of the general impoverishment, owing to participation in the war, which makes it possible for him to buy the property and business of non-Jews at low prices.[118]

Not only were the Jews threatening to "annihilate" Germany—they were also intending to "annihilate" non-Jewish Americans.

Such directives, bringing the arcane arguments of the *Protocols* up to date, were distributed to several thousand newspapers and periodicals. The Nazi propagandists could now point to Jewish names and faces in public places. In this way, the press directives of May and June 1941 brought radical anti-Semitic paranoia to the fore. They turned the abstraction of an international conspiracy into proper names, places, and organizations. Here was a simple explanation of why the United States was giving aid to Britain and was led by a president who opposed Nazism. Henry Morgenthau and Felix Frankfurter *were* friends and political supporters of Roosevelt. As governor of New York, Franklin D. Roosevelt *did* forge strong bonds with the city's and the state's Jewish communities and voters. New York's Italian Catholic mayor, Fiorello LaGuardia, was indeed a fierce and vocal opponent of Nazism and Italian fascism. For anyone who understood the workings of politics and ethnicity in the United States, these relationships were perfectly normal and legitimate expressions of democratic life in a multiethnic society. They had nothing to do with a conspiracy of any kind.

The tenuous position of Jews in American politics and policy making was apparent in Roosevelt's unwillingness to make the persecution and extermination of Europe's Jews a major rationale for American entry into the war. Before Pearl Harbor and Hitler's declaration of war on the United States, Roosevelt focused instead on the danger for the United States that Nazi Germany would pose should it defeat Britain and then seize control of shipping in the Atlantic Ocean. Nazi propagandists, aware of the existence of anti-Semitism in American society, always associated advocates of American intervention in Europe with the Jews and hoped thereby to weaken support for that policy. In so doing, they displayed a characteristic blend of belief and calculation. The press directives are evidence that high-ranking officials of the Nazi regime believed—or gave every indication that they believed—that Jews were driving the United States into war in Europe. Moreover, neither in the thousands of wartime memos nor in more private documents, such as the Goebbels diaries, does one find evidence that Hitler, Goebbels, Dietrich, or their staffs disbelieved what they were writing or viewed their anti-Semitic assertions as a cynical stratagem to fool the gullible masses. However intelligent or clever these men were, they were in the grip of an obsession that profoundly distorted their understanding of reality. The extent and reach of Jewish power that they imagined were a projection of the extent and reach of their own power.

The Nazi leaders did not understand, nor could they appreciate, the realities of Jewish political weakness and marginality, the crosscurrents of American politics, the variety of pressure groups at work within the

Roosevelt administration, and the Atlanticist definitions of national security that were emerging within the American defense establishment. Ideologically induced perceptions about the United States, Britain, and the Soviet Union contributed to the escalating series of miscalculations and underestimations by the Nazi regime of its enemies in World War II. Nazism's rise was attributable in part to the underestimation of its enemies. The failures to grasp reality that were a hallmark of Nazi ideology with its radical anti-Semitism made their own contributions to the defeat of the Nazi regime.

Goebbels's diary entries of April, May, and June 1941 illustrate the sincerity of his views about the United States. Goebbels worked out ideas in private before developing them more fully in public. In his diary he acknowledged that it was difficult to disseminate Nazi propaganda successfully in the United States. The American debate over intervention was intensifying. "We are agitating as best we can, but in the face of the overwhelming Jewish chorus we can hardly be heard."[119] Before American entry into the war, Goebbels wanted to make sure that criticism of Roosevelt and the interventionists was not accompanied by open praise for advocates of isolationism in the United States, such as Charles Lindbergh. He confided to his diary that the famous pilot was "a brave youngster!" to oppose American intervention. "We respond with reserve, in order not to harm Lindbergh . . . Roosevelt is a bit restrained. He cannot act any longer with gusto but must take public opinion into account."[120] Goebbels expressed confidence that the United States would not be prepared for war for "four years." In light of England's merchant shipping losses to German submarines in the Atlantic, England would have to "capitulate this coming fall."[121] In his June 8, 1941, entry, speaking of articles in the American press, Goebbels wrote, "These Jews want war. One day, they will suffocate from that wish."[122] To their enormous frustration, the Nazis were unable to defeat Britain or compel the British to negotiate. The anti-Semitic explanation was that Roosevelt and his Jewish advisers operating behind the scenes had saved the English from defeat.

In the weeks preceding Hitler's momentous wartime decision to invade the Soviet Union, Goebbels began to redirect the vast propaganda apparatus back toward its accustomed themes linking anti-Semitism and anti-Bolshevism. The focus would be on "Stalin and his Jewish men behind the scenes."[123] Goebbels was certain that the Soviet Union would be defeated quickly. "Actually no one any longer thinks there is going to be serious resistance" to a German invasion.[124] On June 16, 1941, Goebbels met with Hitler in the Reich chancellery. The latter estimated that victory would be theirs in four months. Goebbels thought it would be sooner than that. "Bolshevism would collapse like a house of cards. We stand before an unparalleled victorious campaign." An intact Soviet Union was tying down 150 German divisions, which were needed on the western front. With the collapse of the Soviet Union, England would lose its last hope on the Continent and thus agree to a compromise peace with Nazi Germany.[125] At the same meeting on June 16, Goebbels heard comments from Hans Frank, the head of Germany's General Government in Poland. Frank looked forward to being "able to get rid of the Jews. Jewry in Poland was gradually going to rack and ruin. This was a just punishment for inflaming the peoples and instigating this war. The Führer prophesied that this would be what would happen to the Jews."[126]

In his "Proclamation to the German People" announcing the German invasion of the Soviet Union on June 22, 1941, Hitler placed the blame for his decision to invade on the "Jewish Bolsheviks" who held power in Moscow. They had been involved in an "encirclement policy" with England. A "familiar conspiracy between Jews and democrats, Bolsheviks and reactionaries" had emerged at the international level that recapitulated the fault lines of Weimar politics. Its purpose had been to prevent the emergence of a German national state and, once that aim failed, and to render that state powerless.[127] With the invasion and the beginnings of the anti-Hitler coalition between the Soviet Union and Britain, Nazi propagandists had a new set of events that called for explanation. As they had before, they turned to the anti-Semitic framework to illustrate how "international Jewry" was organizing and leading the increasingly international war against the Third Reich. In summer and fall of 1941, Nazi propaganda focused on the link that the leaders imagined existed between "international Jewry" and World War II. Propaganda did so at the same time that Nazi policy moved from the era of persecution to that of extermination.

4 At War against the Alliance of Bolshevism and Plutocracy

After a temporary suspension during the period of the nonaggression pact, the Nazi propaganda assault on "Jewish Bolshevism" resumed in full force when Germany invaded the Soviet Union on June 22, 1941. The rapid reversal of alliances offered a welcome return to the blend of anti-Semitism and anti-Bolshevism that were core elements of Nazi ideological orthodoxy. The course of events seemed again to confirm the fundamental hypothesis of Nazi racial ideology, that an international Jewish conspiracy was seeking world domination. The summer of 1941 brought the first of the wartime anti-Semitic verbal barrages of the Nazi propaganda apparatus, along with increased diffusion of anti-Semitic visual propaganda through the medium of posters. The summer of 1941 also coincided with and contributed to Hitler's greatest miscalculation of the war—namely, that the Soviet regime was a house of cards that would quickly collapse. The propaganda of outraged innocence and no less angry projection attained unprecedented levels of mendacity and viciousness. In summer and fall of 1941, Nazism's anti-Semitic propaganda assumed its wartime role as a public justification for mass murder.

With righteous indignation, Hitler claimed that the invasion was a defensive war that had prevented an imminent Soviet attack. In fact,

Operation Barbarossa came as a total surprise to Stalin, who had steadfastly refused to believe the tidal wave of reports from his own and foreign intelligence services accurately predicting the coming invasion. From August 1939 to June 22, 1941, the Soviets had shipped massive amounts of oil and other strategic raw materials and agricultural goods to Nazi Germany. Indeed, the last train of goods carrying Soviet raw materials and foodstuffs bound for Germany crossed the Soviet border a few hours before the invasion began.[1] While the nonaggression pact was in force, Stalin put an end to all antifascist propaganda and carried out large-scale dismissals of Jews working in Soviet foreign policy institutions and in the press. The replacement of the Jewish foreign minister Maxim Litvinov by Vycheslav Molotov had signaled the end of Soviet support for popular-front antifascism. As the historians of the Soviet Union Mikhail Heller and Alexander Nekrich put it, "for the first time since the founding of the Soviet state anti-Semitism was becoming official policy."[2] In the first weeks and months of the invasion, Soviet armed forces were so badly prepared that by fall 1941 more than three million soldiers had been taken prisoner. Nothing in Stalin's actions before the German attack or in the course of events in summer and fall 1941 supported the Nazi claim of an imminent Soviet attack.

These facts caused no problem for the regime's anti-Semitic interpretation of the course of events and did not deter Hitler—or, consequently, Goebbels and Dietrich—from repeating the falsehood that the Nazi attack was an example of preventive war. At his Minister's Conference on June 22, 1941, Goebbels noted, "National Socialism started as a movement in the struggle against Bolshevism." That struggle had been set aside for two years, until Hitler "unmasked the treachery of the Bolshevik rulers." Goebbels said: "National Socialism and the German people are reverting to the principles that first impelled them—the struggle against plutocracy and Bolshevism." While Hitler estimated that the war on the eastern front would take three months, Goebbels told his staff, "It will take only eight weeks."[3] In this early phase of the war in the East, the anti-Semitic argument placed less emphasis on the Jews' power and more on the supposed incompetence of the "Jewish Bolshevik" regime, which would collapse under the onslaught of the German armies.

In the weeks preceding the German invasion, reports from British intelligence warned Stalin about the imminence of an invasion. Indeed, the absence of a unified anti-Hitler coalition made it vastly easier for Hitler to start the war in 1939 and then to attack the Soviet Union in June 1941. Now, however, Winston Churchill, long a harsh critic of the Bolsheviks, immediately offered to ally Britain with the Soviet Union.[4] Speaking on the BBC on the evening of June 22, 1941, he described the Nazi regime as "indistinguishable from the worst features of Communism," adding, "It excels all forms of human wickedness in the efficiency of its cruelty and ferocious aggression." He would not retract any of his harsh criticisms of Communism. Even as the Nazis claimed to be confronting a unified international Jewish conspiracy, Churchill made a plea to end the disunity among Hitler's adversaries. With the misjudgments of the recent past in mind, he said, the "past, with its crimes, its follies, and its tragedies, flashes away."[5] The British government, he continued, had "but one aim and one single, irrevocable purpose. We are resolved to destroy Hitler and every vestige of the Nazi regime." England would never negotiate with Hitler. "Any man or state who fights on against Nazidom will have our aid. Any man or state who marches with Hitler is our foe . . . That is our policy and that is our declaration. It follows, therefore, that we shall give whatever help we can to Russia and the Russian people." Churchill noted that Hitler hoped that "the process of destroying his enemies one by one by which he has so long thrived and prospered" would continue until he dominated the Western hemisphere. "The Russian danger is, therefore, our danger, and the danger of the United States, just as the cause of any Russian fighting for his hearth and home is the cause of free men and free peoples in every quarter of the globe. Let us learn the lessons already taught by such cruel experience. Let us redouble our exertions, and strike with united strength while life and power remain."[6] Hitler had benefited from the disunity of his adversaries. This state must now be replaced by unified resistance.

In his Minister's Conference on June 24, Goebbels said that Germany's propaganda task lay in "uncovering the English-Russian conspiracy." He saw Churchill's BBC speech two days earlier as "the best proof" of the existence of that conspiracy.[7] The following day Goebbels told his staff that "the old well-known front of capitalism and Bolshevism now reemerged in foreign policy," as Britain and the United States indicated support for the Soviet Union.[8] German propaganda should exploit existing anticommunist sentiment in Western Europe and the United States.[9] On June 25, a confidential directive to the press from the Propaganda Ministry instructed its readers that the German invasion was no "isolated battle" but instead represented "the uniting of all European peoples against Bolshevism" and should be mentioned in connection with the war against England. "The treasonous cooperation of Jewish plutocracy with the Bolsheviks should always be mentioned."[10] In his editorial in *Das Reich,* "Die alte Front" (The Old Front), on June 26, 1941, Goebbels focused on the formation of the anti-Hitler coalition between Great Britain and the Soviet Union. The "Moscow-London conspiracy against the Reich caught now between plutocracy and Bolshevism" confirmed for him "the old suspicion" that the Nazis had never abandoned during the era of the nonaggression pact.[11] He claimed that the Soviet Union had used that period to prepare for a long war, that cooperation between Britain and the Soviet Union had existed before June 1941, and that the Nazi invasion was in fact a preemptive strike in the face of a planned Soviet attack.[12]

Given Nazi claims about "Jewish Bolshevism," it is important to take note of the actual role of Jews in Soviet political life. Drawing on data gathered at the annual party congresses of the Communist Party of the Soviet Union, the historian Benjamin Pinkus has assessed the statistical and organizational representation of Jews within the power institutions of the party—the Central Committee, Politburo, Secretariat, and government bureaucracies. He concludes that there was "no historical basis" for claims that the Bolshevik regime was the work of the Jews.[13] As of 1917, roughly 1,000, or about 5 percent, of the 23,000 members of the Bolshevik party were Jewish.[14] By August 1917, 6 of 21 members of the Central Committee were Jews: Lev Kamenev, Grigory Sokolnikov, Jakov Sverdlov, Grigory Zinoviev, Leon Trotsky, and Moisei Uritsky. The party census of 1922 showed 19,564 Jewish members, 5.21 percent of the total. By 1927, the 49,627 Jewish members comprised 4.34 percent of all party members. Pinkus estimated the percentage of Jewish members of the party in 1940 at 4.3 percent or less. By 1939, only 10 percent of the Central Committee was composed of Jews. After Trotsky, Kamenev, and Zinoviev had been ousted from the leadership in 1926, no Jews remained in the Politburo. In the Stalin era in the 1930s, Lazar Kaganovich became the only Jewish member of the Politburo—the exception that proved the rule.[15] Of the 417 people who constituted the ruling elite of the Soviet Union in the mid-1920s (members of the Central Executive Committee, the party Central Committee, the Presidium of the Executive of the Soviets of the USSR and the Russian Republic, the ministers, and the chairman of the Executive Committee), 27, or 6 percent, were Jewish. This proportion decreased radically in the 1930s, partly owing to the purge trials, which had strong anti-Semitic overtones.[16] During the Holocaust, the Stalin regime said very little about Nazi policies aimed specifically at Jews. By fall 1943, and perhaps earlier, the Nazi death camps were within range of the Soviet air force. Yet Stalin did not order it to destroy the gas chambers and crematoria.[17] Thus, Nazi propaganda about Jewish domination of the Soviet regime had no basis in reality. It was a complete fantasy.

Dietrich's and Goebbels's staffs worked together to bring to the attention of the press the latest propaganda brochures emerging from the now combined forces of the offices of Anti-Semitic Action, Anti-Comintern, and the journal *Die Judenfrage*. On June 27, 1941, the *Periodical Service* directive recommended the pamphlet *Why War with Stalin?* produced by the ministry's anti-Comintern office. The directive stated: "Treatment of the Jewish question is the best starting point for the ideological confrontation" with the Soviet Union.[18] After 1939, it continued, the German government expected a reduction in Jewish influence in the leadership of the Soviet Union, but the Soviets were not willing "to break or limit the absolute Jewish domination of the Soviet Union." To make sure Jews could not avoid scrutiny, the Press Office set out clear rules about how Jews were to be named. The name Finkelstein was to be added before the last name of Jewish leaders in the Soviet Union. Hence Maxim Litvinov became "Finkelstein-Litvinov." The directive used this protocol when it claimed that the removal of "Finkelstein-Litvinov" as foreign minister in 1939 was not a change in policy, because he continued to work in the Foreign Affairs Division of the Central Committee. "A few Jews disappeared, but the most important remain and occupy new key positions. The Soviet Union created by the Jews is still today ruled by Jews," including the clique around Stalin organized by "the Jew Kaganovich." The army, according to the directive, was dominated by a "Jewish leadership clique" and its attendant political commissars. The economy, press, cultural and scholarly life, and the Comintern had all been "Jewified."[19] On July 14, another directive to the press asserted, "The public reemergence of the Jew Finkelstein-Litvinov, who has been kept in the background for two years for purposes of deception, offers a special opportunity to point to the Jewish leadership of the Soviet state."[20] The August 1, 1941, issue of *Die Judenfrage* led with a front-page article summarizing its arguments and recommending that subscribers read *Warum Krieg mit Stalin?* (Why War with Stalin?)[21] All relevant press and propaganda offices cooperated effectively to incorporate the attack on the Soviet Union into the enduring anti-Semitic consensus.

Warum Krieg mit Stalin? repeated the argument that the Nazi attack on the Soviet Union was a preemptive war that was essential to prevent the extermination of Germany, of the rest of Europe, and indeed of humanity. It referred to the "hate-filled encirclement" of Germany organized by a "conspiracy of Jews and democrats, Bolsheviks and reactionaries" whose goal was to plunge Germany into "powerlessness and suffering."[22] The pamphlet quoted Hitler's assertions that England and the Soviet Union had formed a coalition before June 1941. It referred to "the common roots of the war in the West and the East" and denounced Churchill and Roosevelt as warmongers, despite the fact that the United States had not yet entered the war. It directly addressed the puzzle of the emerging Soviet-British alliance.

"How is this possible?" Were the new allies not "by their nature enemies"? Was this not an alliance of convenience that "would be abandoned with relief at the first opportunity"? The answer was an emphatic No! If the comrades could recall the alliances of the Weimar era, then they would know that *this alliance is the most natural one in the world. Regarded superficially, plutocracy and proletarian dictatorship are as different as fire and water. In fact, they are two sides of the same coin. Their common denominator is the Jews.*"[23] British and American wealth, based as it presumably was on the exploitation of colonies, was threatened by National Socialism. "Therefore, the plutocrats in Great Britain and the plutocrats in the USA decided as early as 1933 to wage war against the Reich." They found that the Reich, "which has overcome classes," had to be "destroyed and annihilated," to prevent its example from unleashing "a storm among all the oppressed and exploited peoples in the whole world, which would have destroyed and dispensed with the Jewish exploiters in the plutocracies. That is the deepest cause of the war in the West."[24] The idea that Germany was waging a war of defense against Western aggression, the deployment of the discourse of antiimperialism and anticolonialism, and the assertion that the Jews were "the common denominator" in the anti-Hitler coalition remained enduring features of wartime propaganda.

The pamphlet made light of the setbacks endured by Soviet Jews during the purges and the Hitler-Stalin pact. The Soviet system was a sort of reverse plutocracy that produced slavery and misery for millions and whose "only beneficiaries were the Jewish power holders." The few non-Jews in leading positions were "advertising goys whose only task lay in hiding from the outside world the thoroughness of Jewish domination." Litvinov's dismissal in spring 1939 was merely part of a campaign of deception whose purpose was to obscure the continuity of Soviet aggressive designs on Europe. "A few Jews disappeared," but others, such as Lazar Kaganovich, Solomon Losovsky, and the Soviet ambassador to London, Ivan Maisky, still dominated the party and the state. The pamphlet then listed names of Jews in the party, Central Committee, army, economy, press, and intellectual life, in support of the claim of Jewish domination.[25] Indeed, it continued, "the finance Jews" in the United States and Great Britain envied "their Jewish colleagues at the pinnacle of the Soviet trusts" because they did not have to contend with working-class organizations still tolerated in the West. Jewish rule in Moscow was "the absolute ideal of the Jews" seeking "world domination resting on exploitation and terror." The defeat of the Western plutocrats would be "no less but no more a defeat of Jewry" than would the defeat of Bolshevism. That was why two such seemingly distinct systems "stuck together through thick and thin" and that was why "they both hated a single enemy," Nazi Germany and its emerging *Volksgemeinschaft.*[26] In propaganda and policy, Nazism was returning to its core beliefs.

As the invasion of the Soviet Union was a surprise attack, it had not been preceded by an anti-Soviet propaganda offensive. After the invasion, the propaganda offices sent out directives to officials around the country about how to present the dramatic reversal of policy in the East. On July 21, 1941, the party Reich Propaganda Directorate (RPL) Office of Enlightenment and Speaker Information Materials distributed a pamphlet entitled *Germany Has Entered the Fight to the Finish with the Jewish-Bolshevik System of Murder,* to guide local Nazi party speakers, propagandists, and officials in relevant propaganda offices around the country.[27] Propagandists were to first stress the Bolshevik's "treasonous double game" and "the secret cooperation between England and the Bolsheviks." Once the Reich had destroyed Bolshevism, it would also deliver a heavy blow against England. Second, officials and party speakers were to present the war as part of Germany's "great struggle for freedom," which must destroy "a conspiracy among Jews, democrats, Bolsheviks, and reactionaries." The invasion had brought clarity. "Now we recognize our old enemy, world Jewry. After being defeated within Germany, it now is embodied in Anglo-Saxon plutocracy and Bolshevik state capitalism and tries to attain its goal from abroad." In summer 1941, the "final confrontation" of "German socialism with world capitalism" that dominated England and America, as well as the Soviet Union, was at hand. Nazi party propagandists, now freed from the taboos imposed by the Hitler-Stalin nonaggression pact, could return to "our familiar anti-Bolshevik propaganda" and to attacks on the "Jewish-Bolshevik instigators of the world conflagration" who were seeking to dominate Germany and Europe. The concluding sentence of Hitler's proclamation to the troops of June 22, 1941, was especially important. The invasion was designed not only to win the war but "to save European civilization and culture." Party speakers at the *Gau,* *Kreis,* and *Ort* levels were to convey these themes at meetings and by "word-of-mouth propaganda."[28]

Operation Barbarossa represented a return to orthodoxy in two ways. It brought a renewal both of Nazism's the long-standing hatred of "Jewish Bolshevism" and of its argument that an international Jewish plot against Germany was evident in the unfolding events of the war. The pamphlet described Bolshevism as "a system of Jewish criminals and their accomplices whose purpose is the exploitation and enslavement of humanity."[29] England's decision to ally with the Soviet Union was "a new piece of evidence of the absolute identity of plutocracy and Bolshevism." Speakers needed to answer the "oft-posed question"—"How it is possible that very wealthy English plutocrats and the moneybag dynasties of America are going hand in hand with the (supposedly) anticapitalist Soviet power holders, for Moscow's victory would mean the end of these wealthy people and strata."[30] Nazi propaganda directly addressed this central paradox of the war with the assertion "Plutocracy and Bolshevism have one master, the Jews! . . . The answer to this question [why the Soviets, British, and Americans were allied] is found in the idea that both plutocracy and Bolshevism are led by a power whose representatives shape the fate of the people in the same way in all three countries and subject them to its will. That power is international Jewry. These all-powerful forces include, to name only a few, the following names: in America, Schiff, Warburg, Guggenheim, Morgenthau, Goldman, Baruch, Bullit, Untermeyer, and so on; in England, Hore-Belisha, Salmon, Stern, Reading, Green, Isaacs, and so on; in the Soviet state, Kaganovich, Bermann, Schwernik, Mechlis, Maisky, and so on. The bank Jew Schiff who lives in America . . . financed the Bolshevik revolution against the tsar. The English press indicates how the English think about Soviet Jews, whose trial balloons they publish. Here, you can say only that all of Israel sticks together."[31]

The phrase "Juda wants world domination" appeared in the margin alongside the succeeding section about a possible Jewish state in Palestine. None of the Jews really wanted to go to Palestine: "These parasites don't want to work and don't need a national state of their own. They want world domination and to live at the cost of other peoples who have to work for them."[32] Bolshevism and Marxism, founded by "Karl Marx-Mordechai" were the Jews' instrument to achieve this goal.

> This system of chaos, extermination and terror was conceived and led by Jews. It is the action of the Jewish race. Through subversion and propaganda, world Jewry attempts to gather the uprooted and racially inferior elements of all peoples together in order to lead an extermination battle [*Vernichtungskampf*] against everything positive, against native customs and the nation, against religion and culture, against order and morals. The goal is the introduction of chaos through world revolution and the establishment of a Jewish state under Jewish leadership.[33]

The pamphlet then proceeded to employ an important and oft repeated tool of Nazi propaganda: the highly detailed falsehood. The document discussed Jewish-sounding names of members of the Soviet regime and referred to detailed and preposterous links between Foreign Minister

Molotov's Jewish wife and the American Jewish banker Jacob Schiff. Notwithstanding the well-known demotion and jailing of thousands of Jewish members of the Soviet Communist Party in Stalin's purges of the late 1930s and the Hitler-Stalin pact itself, the writers claimed that the Communist party leadership, the Politburo, and the Central Committee were all dominated by Jews.[34]

The long and detailed list of names was a staple of Nazi propaganda. If opponents ignored such lists completely, the Nazis interpreted the silence as confirming the validity of their representations. Conversely, if they spent time trying to refute them, controversy would focus on the issues which the Nazis were framing, from the broad accusation that the Jews sought to rule the world to arguments about specifics of the real or imagined connection between Molotov's Jewish wife (whom Stalin had sent to the Gulag) and Jacob Schiff. Even skeptics had to admit that Lazar Kaganovich was Jewish, that Churchill was allied with Stalin, that Roosevelt was going to send military supplies to Moscow, and that Felix Frankfurter was a Supreme Court justice and a friend of the president. What more did one need to know?

The increased pace of anti-Semitic denunciation in the *Word of the Week* series was evident in the edition of the week of July 23, 1941, "Sie sind gerichtet!" (They are ordered!), which showed a photo said to be of Baltic and Ukrainian citizens murdered by the "Jewish-Bolshevik system" and discovered by the "victorious German army." It referred to "the shared responsibility of the plutocratic-Bolshevik Jews and servants of the Jews (*Judenknechte*) for the horrible atrocities that the world has witnessed."[35] The *Word of the Week* for the following week, July 30, 1941, "Das ist der jüdische Bolschewismus . . ." (That is Jewish Bolshevism . . .) showed a larger photo of corpses in a field and proclaimed, "That is the Jewish Bolshevism with which Churchill and the British plutocratic clique are fighting a war against Germany! The German people thank the Führer for protecting them from the deadly threat of Bolshevism."[36]

A desperate Soviet Union sent its first request for aid to the United States on July 1, 1941. In his July 4 address to the nation, President Roosevelt remarked, "The United States will never survive as a happy and prosperous oasis in the midst of a desert of dictatorship." Freedom was endangered by tyranny, and Americans must be ready, if necessary, to give their lives to defend it.[37] By July 11, 1941, Roosevelt responded to an Independence Day greeting from Soviet president Mikhail Kalinin by "observing with sympathy and admiration the valiant struggle which the Russian people are waging at the present time in self-defense."[38] Extensive American military assistance to the Soviet Union began soon after. Roosevelt's hope was that American aid to Britain and the Soviet Union would be sufficient to defeat Nazi Germany without American entry into the war or, failing that, at least would prevent a Nazi victory before the United States had to enter the conflict. He, like Churchill, found the Nazi regime's persecution of the Jews repugnant. Yet he did not make it a primary reason for American intervention in the war in Europe. Roosevelt believed that Nazi control of all of Europe's natural and economic resources and defeat of the British Navy as well would present a dire and direct threat to American national security defined in conventional terms.[39]

In accord with his position as minister of propaganda and public enlightenment, Goebbels entitled his weekly editorial of July 6, 1941, in *Das Reich,* "Der Schleier fällt" (The Veil Falls Away). This was one of many instances in which Nazi propaganda boasted of having revealed and unveiled unsolved mysteries. Goebbels now claimed that it had solved the one about the Soviet Union.[40] He was sure that the "Jewish company" around Churchill had "eased his path to finding the Kremlin."[41] As the Nazi war on the eastern front began and the *Einsatzgruppen* and Order Police *(Ordnungspolizei)* began mass shooting behind the lines, Goebbels described Germany's war in the East as one of "ethical humanity as a whole against the collapse of the soul, the collapse of public morality, and intellectual and physical terror and criminal terror." German soldiers were "the saviors of European culture and civilization against the threat from a political underworld."[42] In defending Nazi Germany as "the new Europe," he returned to the themes of his speeches at the Nuremberg Party Rallies against Bolshevism of 1935 and 1936.[43]

Following the German invasion, the Soviet regime returned to the policies of the popular-front years abroad. Stalin appealed to Russian patriotism and turned to the Russian Orthodox churches for support.[44] In his diary entry of July 10, 1941, Goebbels called this Soviet interest in religion a "swindle. The Bolshevik Jews, as they always have in such situations, engage in mimicry"—that is, they adapt to the changing European situation.[45] After Stalin had Maxim Litvinov reappear in public to appeal for aid from England, Goebbels wrote, "Apparently, he [Litvinov] only stood pro forma in the background so that he wouldn't serve as a red flag in our faces. Now [that the Soviets] no longer need to worry about offending us, they no longer need to keep the Jews . . . in the background and to conceal them. They can again act openly on the stage. Naturally, we bring this to the attention of the German public."[46] Public enlightenment in Nazi Germany meant unveiling public appearances to reveal the Jewish secret behind the facade. *Der Völkische Beobachter* for July 10, 1941, led with "Bolshevism Reveals Its Jewish Face; Litvinov-Finkelstein Emerges from Behind the Scenes."[47] In his diary entry of July 11, Goebbels noted that London radio was broadcasting Soviet reports of atrocities committed by the *Einsatzgruppen*.[48] The broadcasts offered yet further evidence of the international Jewish conspiracy. "The Jews are extraordinarily active on both wings [east and west]."[49] Broaching "the Jewish question," he noted with pleasure, "has been especially effective in all the occupied territories [on the eastern front]. It is very important to me that the treatment of the Jewish question not be raised separately from the assessment of the political situation. Rather, the impact of Jewry within the plutocratic-Bolshevik front should be presented."[50]

Reports of German atrocities began to appear in the foreign press in the summer of 1941. Goebbels and Dietrich either ignored them completely or, if they mentioned them, did so only to denounce them as lies and further evidence of the work of the Jews. By never mentioning the contents of the accusations, the leaders kept them out of the German press. Nazi officials never denied that the *Einsatzgruppen* were murdering tens of thousands of Jews behind the eastern front. Rather, they said that the Soviet or the British press was again printing lies about Germany—without mentioning what the "lies" were.[51] In his diary entry of September 17, 1941, Goebbels noted that the reports of Solomon Lozovsky, deputy commissar in the Soviet Foreign Ministry and vice-chairman of the Soviet Information Bureau with responsibility for dealing with the Western press, were clever but so marked by "exaggerations and really unbelievable numbers" that they were "discredited in the whole world and only good for use at home."[52] The press purges carried out by the Nazis in the 1930s had silenced any journalists who might have been able and willing to ask unwelcome questions about the content of the unspecified "lies" emanating from Allied capitals.

In a meeting on July 14, Hitler encouraged Goebbels to stoke the flames of anti-Semitism ever more intensely. That evening, Goebbels wrote in his diary, "The conspiracy between Bolshevism and plutocracy is revealed. The enemies of 1932 confront us again, and they will collapse now just as they did in January 1933 inside Germany." Hitler had offered a "sober and realistic judgment" that "the war in the East was essentially already won."[53] They both agreed that it was again important to unleash anti-Bolshevik "resentments." The [Nazi] party was happy that the "evil compromise" of the nonaggression pact was over. The propaganda line for the regime was now clear: "We must again uncover the cooperation between Bolshevism and the plutocracy and now also underline ever more the Jewish character of this front. In a few days, slowly at first, the anti-Semitic campaign will get started, and I am firmly convinced that in this way we will be able to bring more and more of world public opinion over to our side."[54]

Hitler presumably gave identical orders to Otto Dietrich. The directive of the *Periodical Service* for July 18, 1941, stated that the emerging cooperation among the Soviet Union, Britain, and the United States was due to "the commands of a master, world Jewry." In its service, Roosevelt, Churchill, and Stalin "had conspired against the peoples of Europe, the home of all human culture . . . All efforts at camouflage are pointless. Europe recognizes and is fighting against world Jewry in both of its surface forms—Bolshevism and plutocracy."[55] In tune with this campaign, the lead story on July 23, 1941 in *Der Völkische Beobachter* was "Roosevelt Main Tool of Jewish Freemasonry; Sensational Document Reveals Connections of the Warmonger with the International Clique; Where Roosevelt's Hebraic Hatred of Germany Comes From."[56] The article breathlessly reported on a "secret photo" of Roosevelt and his sons in the company of Masons, which was said to prove that he was "a tool of the Jewish world conspiracy." The photo was thought to confirm what the *VB* had been saying all along—namely, that Roosevelt's policies were a "betrayal" of the American people and were understandable only as the product of advice from people such as Morgenthau, LaGuardia, Frankfurter, Untermayer, Bloom, Cohen, and Rosenman.[57] The following day, the ministry sent a confidential directive to the press about the "sensational" photo, to emphasize that Roosevelt's membership in the Freemasons was important not merely in itself but because it underscored his identity as a "Freemason warmonger."[58]

In an essay entitled "Mimicry," published in *Das Reich* of July 20, 1941, Goebbels wrote one of his most important and extended attacks on the Jews.[59] He offered an anti-Semitic analysis of the political events of summer 1941. The Jews, he wrote, are masters at learning to "adapt to their surroundings without losing their essence. They practice mimicry." One had to be a "student of the Jews" (*Judenkenner*) to "unmask them," for "the Jew is the master of the lie."[60] Jewish chutzpah had paralyzed a whole people intellectually and emotionally, and thus made it defenseless in the face of Bolshevism, that "most devilish infection that Jewry can bring to a people." Bolshevism was a means to achieve "total Jewish domination over a people. The crassest plutocracy uses socialism to establish the crassest dictatorship of money." The spread of Bolshevism from the Soviet Union would end in "the domination of the world by Jewry." National Socialism had been dealing a "mortal blow against this effort," and was continuing to do so. When "the leading circles of international Jewry" had realized that Bolshevization could not be brought about through "political agitation," they had seized on the "great opportunity of a coming war" and sought to make the war last "as long as possible." They hoped that they could then "attack a Europe that was exhausted, bled white, and powerless and Bolshevize it with violence and terror."[61]

The denial of historical contingency that characterizes all conspiratorial thinking was on full display in "Mimicry." Jewish plotting would remain unrecognized by superficial minds focused on the welter of contingencies and chronological sequences in which actual events take place. Yet once the Nazis revealed the conspiracy, everything became clear and explicable. Moscow's tactics in the war, Goebbels continued, were based on plans to attack Nazi Germany when it was unable to bring a rapid end to the war in the West. Hitler's decision to attack the Soviet Union on June 22, 1941, "tore this finespun net of lies and intrigue to pieces with the blow of the German sword." Until the moment of the invasion, he continued, the Soviets had cleverly kept Jewish leaders, such as Litvinov and Kaganovich, in the background, "probably in the mistaken assumption that [the Soviets] could thereby deceive us." The Jews continued to work in an "all the more sinister manner behind the scenes and tried to give us the impression that the Jewish Bolsheviks in Moscow and the Jewish plutocrats in London and Washington were bitter enemies. Secretly, however, they moved ever closer to each other, in order to make the encircling grip with which they wished to crush us ever stronger. All of this becomes clear from the fact that in the very moment when this devilish scheme was unmasked, they were reconciled in each other's arms."[62]

Though Goebbels restated the idea that the Nazi attack was a preventive war, the key theme of the essay was his accusation against the Jews. "Above all it is the same Jews, on both sides, whether out in the open or camouflaged, who establish the tone and establish the line. When they pray in Moscow and go to London to sing the International, they are doing what they have done for ages. They practice mimicry."[63] They adapt, hide, and blend in. So of course the Jews were furious with the Nazis, who could claim, "We unmask them," and this anger made the Jews lose their balance.[64] When the Soviet press and the Western press printed detailed articles about German atrocities, German propaganda interpreted the reports as further evidence of international Jewry at work. As Goebbels put it, "the Moscow Jews invent the lies and atrocity stories, and the London Jews quote and spread them."[65] The Germans were not guilty of anything. Rather, "'the Jews are guilty! The Jews are guilty!' The punishment that will break over them will be frightful. Just as the fist of an awakened Germany once slammed down on this racial rubbish, one day the fist of an awakened Europe will do likewise. Then the Jews' mimicry will be useless . . . That will be the day of people's justice over the source of their ruin and downfall. The blow will be delivered without pity and without mercy. The world's enemy [*Weltfeind*] will collapse, and Europe will have its peace."

With the publication of "Mimicry," the Nazi leadership was, in the summer of 1941, publicly declaring that it was already "without pity and without mercy" meting out justice to this "world enemy."[66] Goebbels's story was one of Jewish crime and German punishment. In declaring Jewry guilty of starting and then prolonging World War II, Goebbels was elaborating on Hitler's famous prophecy. The propaganda campaigns that followed established a causal and temporal connection between the start and expansion of the war and a shift in Nazi policy from the persecution to the mass murder of European Jewry. Having found the Jews guilty, Goebbels justified blows against them that would bring about their "ruin and downfall."

In addition to dire threats, "Mimicry" offered an explanation for either possible success or failure in the war itself. If the Soviet Union was a house of cards, it was so because it was "Jewish Bolshevism." The persistence of Soviet resistance while Britain stayed in the war proved that "international Jewry" was indeed as powerful as the Nazis claimed it was. In either case, "Mimicry" connected the beginning and expansion of World War II to a determination to "retaliate" against "Jewry." In another display of effective synergy among different components of the propaganda apparatus, the Propaganda Ministry offered striking visual aids to elaborate on the meaning of mimicry.

In his anti-Semitic photo collection, *Juden in USA (Jews in the USA)*, 420,000 copies of which were published in 1939 and 1941 by the Nazi Eher Verlag, Hans Diebow included two photographic juxtapositions that supposedly supplied visual evidence of Jewish efforts at camouflage and mimicry.[67] The first contrasts a campaign poster of New York's Governor Herbert Lehman with the photo of a smiling Lehman on his election night victory.[68] Diebow describes Lehman's election poster as a "characteristic example of Jewry's deception maneuvers" because it shows Lehman as a "100 percent American whom one could place physiognomically in the ranks of the best presidents." Yet the election night photo reveals the real Lehman, an "orthodox Jew" among smiling Jews. A second contrasted two photos of the industrial magnate and banker Charles Schwab. Diebow claimed that the photos were "an interesting example of Jewish mimicry." The large photo of a smiling Schwab "whose face revealed . . . Jewish elements" contrasted with an earlier shot in the lower left of "a completely un-Jewish . . . Yankee mask."[69] Schwab was not Jewish. Yet given that Jews were such masters of camouflage, how could one ever really be sure who was and who was not Jewish? "International Jewry" could hide behind such deceptive physical traits as blond hair, blue eyes, upright posture, or a six-foot frame. Who, indeed, could be certain that the now infamous physical racial stereotypes really were the key to revealing the Jews?[70]

The pace at which anti-Semitic messages appeared in *Word of the Week* wall newspaper series quickened. An edition of summer or fall 1941, "Die Juden haben den Krieg gewollt!" ("The Jews Wanted the War!") focused on England and the Jews and drew murderous implications from the editors' interpretation of the origins of the war. In bold yellow letters against a blue background, the text made striking assertions.[71] Not only did the Jews want the war. The wall newspaper accustomed the reader or viewer to the idea that "world Jewry" was, through its proxies, conducting the war against Germany, so Germany would conduct a war against Jewry until it was "exterminated":

> In order to subject the world to domination by Jewish money and blood, Churchill, Roosevelt, and Stalin, as instruments of world Jewry, have opted for war. They have received war in return! The German army has already delivered decisive blows against its enemies and will not rest until it has achieved final victory and the Jew has been exterminated. Now the richly deserved fate of Jewry will be pitilessly realized. It will perish according to its own law, "An eye for an eye, a tooth for a tooth" along with those who do its business. Mr. Churchill belongs in the family tree![72]

This was the first time that the wall newspaper series had put on display the regime's intention to exterminate the Jews.

That summer the Nazi propaganda assault on Franklin D. Roosevelt and the United States intensified. Anti-Semitism lay at the heart of the attacks. Over time, FDR joined the Jews as Nazism's primary hate object. The August 19, 1941, *VB* led with the article "Roosevelt's Goal is the World Domination by the Jews." Its publication came in the wake of Roosevelt and Churchill's signing of the Atlantic Charter in July as well as of FDR's warnings against Nazi Germany's efforts to expand its influence in Latin and Central America.[73] On July 24, 1941, the *VB* headline announced: "An Enormous Jewish Annihilation Program (*Vernichtungsprogramm*); Roosevelt Demands Sterilization of the German People; The Germans are Supposed to Be Exterminated in Two Generations." The author of *Germany Must Perish,* a book advocating a plan to "exterminate" the German people, was one "Jew Theodore Kaufman" described as the president of the American Federation of Peace.[74] Kaufman, the *VB* continued, was a "close associate of the New York Jew Samuel Rosenman" who was an adviser to President Roosevelt. In

"Jewish-literary circles in New York, it was an open secret . . . that Roosevelt himself inspired the main theses of the book and had personally dictated the most important parts of this shameful work."[75] The plan called for sterilizing German prisoners of war, sending them to labor camps to work on postwar reconstruction of other countries, sterilizing the remainder of the German population so that the Germans would die out in two generations, and then dividing up German territory among the neighboring countries. Official American policy, it was averred, called for an "enormous program of annihilation." This story about Kaufman's book was carried in other German papers, such as *Die Frankfurter Zeitung, Münchener Neuesten Nachrichten,* and Julius Streicher's *Der Stürmer,* as well as the supposedly high-toned weekly *Das Reich.*[76]

■

Although Kaufman and his book did exist, he was not the influential figure depicted by Nazi propaganda. According to a *Time* magazine article, *Germany Must Perish!* was the real Theodore Kaufman's first and only book. No American publisher would publish it. Kaufman founded Argyle Press and printed and distributed the book himself through the U.S. Post Office rather than through bookstores. The book received only a few reviews, highly unsympathetic. Though sales figures are not available, its mode of distribution suggests they were minimal. There was no such organization as the American Federation of Peace, nor was Kaufman known to be involved in any other American Jewish organizations, whether major or peripheral, or connected in any way to the Roosevelt administration.[77] He was an independent, understandably very angry Jewish writer who published his own book. But his book had no importance in American politics or intellectual life, inside or outside the Roosevelt administration.

Goebbels, however, leaped at the chance to assign another name, face, and text to the abstraction of the international Jewish conspiracy and its alleged plans to exterminate the Germans. In his diary entry of July 24, 1941, he linked Kaufman with American policy. In so doing, he made a telling mistake in the title of the book. "In the United States a book by the Jew Kaufman has just been published under the title, *Germany Must Be Annihilated!* which clearly prophesies what threatens . . . The book seriously makes the proposal to exterminate the entire German population by sterilization. As stupid and absurd as this project is, it shows the mentality of our enemy."[78] Goebbels had transformed Kaufman, the independent writer from New Jersey, into the quintessential representation of the mentality of "the enemy." After reading Kaufman's book in English, Goebbels confided to his diary on August 3, "He really could not have done it better and more advantageously for us if he had written the book to order. I will have this book distributed in millions of copies in Germany, above all on the front, and will write a preface and afterword myself. It will be most instructive for every German man and for every German woman to see what would happen to the German people if, as in November 1918, a sign of weakness were given."[79]

In an August 19, 1941, conversation with Hitler, Goebbels brought up the idea of German publication of fragments of Kaufman's book. Hitler approved.[80] Goebbels then assigned Wolfgang Diewerge, director of the radio division in the Propaganda Ministry, to edit and comment on Kaufman's *Germany Must Perish!*[81] He thought Diewerge's work "excellent" and wrote the afterword for it. He would have it published in a print run of five million copies. "Above all," he wrote, "this brochure will finally and definitively do away with the last remnants of a still-existing softness. In reading this brochure, even the stupidest idiot can figure out what threatens us if we become weak."[82] In yet another example of the coordination of effort between Goebbels's and Dietrich's daily and weekly press directives, the September 5, 1941, *Periodical Service* directive, "Judas Satanical Murder Plan," referred to "Jewish plans for extermination of the Germans" and repeated the accusation that the plan was "encouraged," and even had some of its "key sections personally dictated, by President Roosevelt." The service urged editors to bring the offending passages from Kaufman's book to their readers' attention.[83]

In September 1941, the Propaganda Ministry published Wolfgang Diewerge's pamphlet under the title *The War Aim of World Plutocracy: Documentary Publication of the Book of the President of the American Peace Society, Theodore Kaufman, 'Germany Must Perish.'*[84] The front-cover collage, done by Hans Schweitzer himself, stands as one of the defining anti-Semitic visual images of the era of the war and Holocaust. It displays a photo of a middle-aged man wearing glasses, vest, and tie and working at a typewriter. One assumes it is Kaufman himself. In the lower right is a photo of Franklin D. Roosevelt, Winston Churchill, and military leaders, perhaps singing "Onward Christian Soldiers" during their meeting off Newfoundland during the ceremonies surrounding the signing of the Atlantic Charter. The collage depicts a key anti-Semitic trope: the Jewish brain, safely at home behind the scenes, writes the lines sung by witless non-Jewish front men. Lines from the edition of the book in English (including the underlined phrase "Germany must perish forever from this earth!") are evident in the center and right of the image. The thirty-two-page pamphlet interspersed quotations from Kaufman's book with Diewerge's comments, which "revealed" the book's message concerning "the extermination of the German people, including women and children and the division of Greater Germany among its neighbors." This plan was to be accomplished by disarming Germany and carrying out "the sterilization of all men, women, and children able to procreate."[85] In view of the thousands of forced sterilizations the Nazi regime had already done and was continuing to do, this was a particularly grotesque case of projection of the sins of the perpetrators onto the victims.[86]

Diewerge claimed that Kaufman's book was further proof that "world Jewry in New York, Moscow, and London agrees on demanding the complete extermination of the German people."[87] He described Kaufman as an advocate of "Jewish genocide." He had "openly uttered what world Jewry wished and hoped for: the murder of the German people."[88] Germany now faced a choice: "victory or death." By 1941 the Germans understood that "the international Jew" stood behind the war aims of "world plutocracy and warmongers all over the world." Yet the Germans were determined not to perish. "Who should die, the Germans or the Jews?" There were "about twenty million Jews in the world. What would happen if instead of eighty million Germans, twenty million Jews were treated according to the proposals of their racial comrade Kaufman? Then peace would be secured. For all over the world the Jew is the one who causes trouble and who destroys peace."[89] Goebbels wrote in the unsigned afterword, "You know what your eternal enemy and opponent intends for you. There is only one instrument against his plans for annihilation [*Vernichtungspläne*]: Victory! Reading this Jewish plan for murder will steel you and only strengthen your will for victory."[90] Stark fear of mass death at the hands of Germany's archenemy and other enemies remained an enduring leitmotif of Nazi propaganda and a key public justification for its murderous policy toward the Jews. Indeed, as the tide of the war turned against the Third Reich, the great fear deepened. It contributed to terrible self-fulfilling prophecies as well as to stiffening German resistance to the Allied war effort. Theodore Kaufman became a familiar face in Nazi anti-Semitic propaganda. A full-page photo of a man said to be Kaufman appeared in Diebow's *Jews in the USA*.[91] The caption read: "He Demands the Complete Extermination of the German People."[92] The wall newspaper for October 10, 1941, also focused on Kaufman. "Immer das gleiche Ziel: Deutschland muß vernichtet werden!" ("Always the Same Goal: Germany Must Be Exterminated!") juxtaposed a quote from Hitler with quotations from the *London Daily Mail* and from "the Jew Kaufman, one of the close advisers to the Freemason Roosevelt."[93]

The directive from the Reich Press Office *Periodical Service* for the week of August 8, 1941, continued the anti-Semitic propaganda offensive. "Fight World Jewry!" described World War II as a

struggle driven by world Jewry's immeasurable hatred against Aryan people as such, against their spirit, worldview, and culture. The Jewish wire pullers in London, in New York, and not least in

Moscow planned and prepared this war with shameless campaigns of agitation . . . so that nations would take up arms against the Aryan powers of the earth. World Jewry intentionally expanded the war in hopes of winning as a result of the exhaustion of the Aryan adversary.

World Jewry entered this pitiless battle in three forms: first as a Jew; second as plutocrat descended from Jews; and third as a Jewish Bolshevik. The Aryan resistance is concentrated primarily in the Axis Powers, Germany, Italy, and Japan.

What does world Jewry seek? For thousands of years, it has aimed at nothing but Jewish world domination. This goal was already present in the Old Testament of the Jews, religiously hidden but clearly evident. Repeatedly over the centuries the Jew appeared close to his goal, but then again and again the Aryan peoples put the Jews in their place. Today Jewry again seeks world domination. That British and American plutocrats on the one hand and Bolsheviks on the other appear with apparently distinct political goals is only Jewish camouflage. The Jew strives for world domination in order to rob and plunder the world for his exclusive benefit, without distraction or hindrance.[94]

It was the responsibility of German periodical editors to set forth the grounds for the war, to explain how to recognize the "Jewish spirit," and to convince other Europeans that it was in their interest as well that Germany and Italy were fighting the war. The press was to stress that the form in which Jewry appeared as plutocrats around Churchill, as Communists in Moscow, or as a "warmonger in the form of imperialism like the Freemason Roosevelt" was irrelevant. Aryan men would strike back in any case.[95]

Goebbels left hints in his diaries that Hitler was keeping him informed, at a minimum, that the mass murder of the Jews was under way. Goebbels diary entry of August 19, 1941, reported, "The Führer believes that his past prophecy in the Reichstag is being confirmed, that if Jewry succeeded in again provoking a world war, it would end with the annihilation of the Jews. It is coming to pass in these weeks and months with an almost eerily graceful certainty. In the East, the Jews are paying for it. In Germany, they have already in part paid for it, and in the future they will have to pay still more." The Jews will "not have much to laugh about in the coming world." Encouraged by his conversation with Hitler the day before, Goebbels was pleased that Hitler approved introduction of the yellow star for Jews, their exclusion from city centers, and deportation of Jews from Berlin. "Berlin," he continued, "must become a Jew-free city . . . We have to approach this problem without sentimentality. One has to imagine what the Jews would do with us if they had the power in order to know what to do now that we have the power."[96] The above entry indicates that Hitler and Goebbels had drawn a causal connection between the mass murder of European Jews and the expansion of World War II. Hitler had told Goebbels, in terms they both understood, that mass murder had begun following the German invasion of the Soviet Union.

Goebbels's primary contribution to the Final Solution was to offer ideological justifications for mass murder. Yet he also played a practical role in the deportation of Berlin's Jews, whose presence in wartime he found "unbearable."[97] In late September 1941, Goebbels met with Reinhard Heydrich, Himmler's main deputy in the Reich Security Main Office (the bureaucracy that was implementing the Final Solution), to discuss "a few important things regarding the Jewish question." The Jews were to be "evacuated from Berlin as soon as possible . . . as soon as we resolve the military questions in the East. They should all be transported in the end to the camps built by the Bolsheviks."[98] The unusually indiscreet diary entry of October 19, 1941, refers to "reports of huge shootings of Jews in the Ukraine." Goebbels's response was to increase anti-Semitic propaganda in the occupied territories. "Bolshevism has gradually weakened the anti-Semitic instincts of the peoples of the Soviet Union. We must, so to speak, start over from the beginning."[99] In late October he noted that the regime had begun expelling Jews from Berlin "to the East." It was "a bit uncomfortable at the moment to discuss this issue before a broader world public," but the main point was that Berlin would be free of Jews, and he would "not rest until this goal [was] completely attained."[100] It defies belief that officials as politically astute, as ideologically driven, and as close to Hitler as Goebbels and Dietrich did not know or surmise that the mass murder of Jews was taking place in the East beginning in summer 1941. They had identified the Jews as key actors in the war against the Third Reich, and *all* the Nazis' anti-Semitic propaganda served as a justification for a policy that went beyond persecution to the waging of "war" against the Jews.

Though the United States had not entered the war in Europe, the Nazi leaders understood that Roosevelt's support for Britain and then the Soviet Union was crucial in thwarting Nazi hopes of an early victory. In an effort to take advantage of existing American anti-Semitism, Nazi propaganda sought to contrast Roosevelt, his supposed Jewish brain trust and powers behind the scenes, and the power of New York (and to a lesser extent Hollywood), with the "real," that is, non-Jewish, American people. Charles Lindbergh, who had expressed his admiration for Hitler's Germany and opposed American entry into the European war was, in Goebbels's opinion, "a splendid fellow." Lindbergh was "of great use to us, above all because we take no notice at all of his activities in our press. That way he is much more independent and does not have to confront the objection that he is a member of a fifth column."[101]

Lindbergh's best efforts notwithstanding, Goebbels feared that the isolationists would not prevent Roosevelt from intervening. Roosevelt, he wrote in the September 14, 1941, entry, "is the one who really is prolonging the war. If he were not there, England would presumably have capitulated long ago." It was unfortunate, he wrote, that the anti-interventionists lacked a "superb leader! Lindbergh has a good character and means well and brings forth good arguments. But he is naturally not equal in intelligence to the red chorus of Jews, businessmen, and corrupt plutocrats."[102] By September 1941, Goebbels—and thus presumably Hitler as well—thought American entry into the war was simply a matter of time. "If we can't prevent Roosevelt from drawing the USA into the war, so certainly under all circumstances we want to prevent him from putting the blame on us."[103] If the European war was to become a world war, then Roosevelt, not Hitler, would be responsible. With increasing rage, frustration, and hatred, Nazi propaganda denounced Churchill and Roosevelt, and the Jews allegedly controlling them, for preventing Nazi Germany from winning the early victory that had once seemed within reach.

In late October 1941, after Roosevelt warned that Nazi Germany had plans to expand beyond Europe into Central and South America, Dietrich's daily press directive ordered the German press to "denounce Roosevelt's speech as the speech of a liar and falsifier and as the product of Jewish demagoguery and hysterical warmongering."[104] Though Nazi propaganda generally did not claim that Roosevelt was himself Jewish, this directive referred to him as "Judenstämmling Roosevelt" (Roosevelt of Jewish stock). It was pointless to "engage in a serious political debate with the speech of this fool." Instead, the press was to use "all our polemical methods" to "confront Mr. Roosevelt and thus the spirit of Jewish falsification, with which Mr. Roosevelt must be identified."[105] That same week, in accord with the coordinated assault on Roosevelt from both the Goebbels and the Dietrich wings of the Propaganda Ministry, Peter Aldag, writing in *Die Judenfrage,* imputed to Roosevelt "plans for world domination." According to Aldag, FDR's policy toward Europe was due to advice from "a small group" devoted to the Old Testament and more interested in "the interests of international Jewry" and their own financial gain than in those of the United States.[106]

Following the spectacular successes of the summer and the capture of more than three million Soviet prisoners of war, Hitler and his generals believed that the war on the eastern front was won. Otto Dietrich himself, in his SS uniform, conveyed the news in a press conference in October. On October 10, 1942, a *VB* front-page headline in bold black and red letters announced: "The Military End of Bolshevism, the Eastern Campaign Has Been Decided . . . Incomparable Masterstroke of Strategy." The article asserted that the blitzkrieg had realized its aims, having delivered "deadly blows" from which the Soviet Union "could never recover."[107] As a result of German success in the East, Nazi Germany would now be able to count on secure oil supplies and to withdraw much of its air force from the eastern front to deploy against England. Now that nights in the Atlantic were growing longer, German submarines would have even more success in sinking Allied ships. Even if the United States did enter the war, it was too late to make any difference. Thanks to Nazi control over the industrial and agricultural sectors in the East, Germany was immune to British and American naval blockade. The tension between American and English public opinion was growing, while Roosevelt's expressions of support for the Soviet Union were causing him political difficulty at home.

The lead article of *Die Judenfrage* of October 15, 1941, "The War Guilt of the Jews," repeated the increasingly familiar accusation and offered a typical example of how the Nazi propagandists used evidence to support the charge.[108] The unnamed author strung together quotes from an array of Jewish leaders and advocates in the mid- and late 1930s calling for struggle against Nazi Germany. He took them as evidence that "international Jewry" was driving Europe toward war. A speech of one Jew or a selection of seemingly prominent Jewish figures was enough to make assertions about all Jews. Working as "men behind the scenes and wire pullers" (*Hintermänner und Drahtzieher*) of non-Jewish political leaders, the author offered a list of now familiar last names: "Litvinov-Finkelstein and Kaganovich in the Soviet Union, Hore-Belisha, Lord Samuel, Lord Melchett, Lord Rothschild in England, Léon Blum, George Mandel in France, Baruch, Frankfurter, Morgenthau, Rabbi Wise in North America." The author's grasp of chronology left something to be desired. He credited French prime minister Léon Blum, the British secretary of war, Leslie Hore-Belisha, and Soviet foreign minister Maxim Litvinov with creating the anti-Hitler coalition that had emerged after the Nazi invasion of the Soviet Union in June 1941. This was an impossibility. Edouard Daladier had replaced Léon

Blum as French prime minister in 1938. Neville Chamberlain removed Hore-Belisha as British secretary of war in January 1940. Stalin removed Litvinov as foreign minister in May 1939, during the negotiations that led to the Hitler-Stalin pact. Undeterred by facts and chronology that undermined its key thesis, the author stressed that the Jews and their allies were on the run. France had been defeated and occupied. "The power of Bolshevism has collapsed. The English island anxiously ponders its fate. Will the Jews of North America be able to undertake a final attempt to realize the Jewish goal?" The author concluded by quoting Hitler's prophetic threat of January 30, 1939, concerning the "extermination of the Jewish race in Europe" if "international finance Jewry" should start another war. In his diary entry of October 9, 1941, Goebbels dismissed American refutations of Nazi propaganda about Jewish power based on the small number of Jews serving in the Roosevelt administration. "The Jews," he wrote, "don't need to sit in the government to preserve and build their position of power. They remain in the background in order to pull from there the strings that make their puppets dance."[109] Faced either with Jewish presence or with Jewish absence, Goebbels in his anti-Semitic indictment came to the identical conclusion.

In his annual address of November 1941, to Nazi party members in Munich to commemorate the Beer Hall Putsch, Hitler delivered a by now familiar denunciation of the Jews as the instigators of World War II and as creators of the coalition between Britain and the Soviet Union.[110] He emphasized that "the international Jew" was "the real firebrand and instigator behind all world events." Thanks to scientific analysis of the race question, he "knew above all that the Jew was the driving force behind events." The Jew could always find "straw men who were ready to work for him, partly without character, partly paid off, people who wanted to do business, who were and are ready to do business every time blood is flowing." He told his comrades that "this enemy" had been the driving force against the Nazis in the Weimar era and that the Nazis had defeated their enemy within Germany. "Following the defeat in Germany, the same enemy naturally confronts us from out-side the country. He [the Jew] was the inspirer of the world coalition against the German people and against the German Reich. Once he used Poland, then later forced France, Belgium, Holland, and Norway into his service. From the beginning, England was a driving force. It was obvious that one day the power would advance against us which the Jewish spirit most clearly dominates: for the greatest servant of Jewry is the Soviet Union."[111] Some wondered, he continued, whether "the na-tional tendency" in the Soviet Union would win out over that of the "enormous organization of Jewish commissars." In fact, the leader of the state "was nothing other than an instrument in the hands of all-powerful Jewry. When Stalin stands on the stage or in front of the cur-tain, behind him stand Kaganovich and all the Jews who in tens of thousands of ramifications lead this powerful government from top to bottom."[112] With this address, Hitler expressed confidence that the in-terpretation of events he had adopted since the 1920s remained the key to unlocking the complexities of international events in 1941. His deeply provincial application of an ideologically distorted interpretation of the past to the events of the war years endured to end of the regime.

By early fall 1941, Hitler had ordered Himmler to expand the mass shootings of Jews on the eastern front into a Continental program to mur-der all of Europe's Jews.[113] In late October, Goebbels traveled to the east-ern front and to the Jewish ghetto in Vilna. His sentiments expressed in the diary entry of November 2, 1941, conveyed the genocidal consen-sus that had emerged at the top of the Nazi regime.[114] "Here," he wrote, "the Jews crouch among one another, horrible forms to see, not to men-tion touch . . . The Jews are the lice of civilized humanity. They have to be exterminated somehow; otherwise, they will again play their tor-menting and annoying role. Only if one proceeds against them with the necessary brutality will we be finished with them. When you spare them, you subsequently become their victim."[115] Goebbels's anti-Jewish ha-tred and his public support for mass murder burst forth in even greater detail than in "Mimicry" on November 16, 1941, in the pages of *Das*

121

Reich and on German radio in his important essay "Die Juden sind Schuld," (The Jews Are Guilty).[116] The essay marked the first time that a leading official of the Nazi regime publicly announced that the "extermination" of European Jewry had shifted from hypothetical notion or the threat included in Hitler's famous prophecy to ongoing action. Three weeks before the Japanese attacked Pearl Harbor, Goebbels said, "The historical guilt of world Jewry for the outbreak and expansion of this war has been so extensively demonstrated that there is no need to waste any more words on it. The Jews wanted their war, and now they have it."[117] Goebbels depicted an active subject, "international Jewry" on the offensive against an innocent, victimized German object. Nazi Germany was waging a war of national self-defense that grew in intensity and ruthlessness in response to the war the Jews were presumably waging against Germany. But the Jews had miscalculated:

In unleashing this war, world Jewry completely misjudged the forces at its disposal. Now it is suffering a gradual process of extermination that it had intended for us and that it would have unleashed against us without hesitation if it had the power to do so. It is now perishing as a result of its own law: An eye for an eye, a tooth for a tooth . . . In this historical dispute every Jew is our enemy, whether he vegetates in a Polish ghetto or scrapes out his parasitic existence in Berlin or Hamburg or blows war trumpets in New York or Washington. Owing to their birth and race, all Jews belong to an international conspiracy against National Socialist Germany. They wish for its defeat and annihilation and do everything in their power to help to bring it about.[118]

Publication of "The Jews Are Guilty" ended the period of threats. The Jews had started the war. They were now suffering a "gradual process of extermination," one they had originally intended to inflict on Germany. Goebbels concluded with a ten-point indictment of the Jews. They had started the war and wanted to "exterminate" the German

Reich and people. All Jews, without exception, were "sworn enemies" of the German people. The death of every German soldier "shows up as a debt in the account book of the Jews. They have him on their conscience and therefore must pay for it." Because the Jews bore the guilt for starting the war, the treatment the Germans were meting out to them was not unjust. "They have more than deserved it." Thus, it was "the government's policy to finish once and for all" with the Jews.[119]

"The Jews are Guilty" was a paradigm of Nazi anti-Semitic propaganda. It was blunt and noneuphemistic about general policy. Yet the extremist language went along with a total absence of revealing details about where, when, and how this mass murder was taking place. This was extraordinary language, embedded in a more ordinary narrative of war. It was so monstrous that many of Goebbels's contemporaries found it impossible to believe that it had anything to do with the actual policy of the German dictatorship.[120] The essay simultaneously displayed verbal brutality and calculated ambiguity. What, after all, could the reference to a "gradual" process of extermination actually mean, except mass murder? Perfectly adequate German nouns existed to denote impoverishment, discrimination, deportation, and illness. Yet Goebbels and Hitler repeatedly referred to "extermination." Skeptics noted that Goebbels was an accomplished liar and was, after all, the minister of propaganda. Was he lying about this too? The case was compelling for imposing the most radical interpretation of Goebbels's remarks, but his formulations left enough ambiguity and absence of detail to promote plausible deniability among an indifferent or incredulous mass audience. That evening, the propaganda minister repeated in the privacy of his diary what he had conveyed to a mass audience. "The current fate that the Jews are now suffering is not an injustice. Rather, it merely returns to them what they had intended to do to us. My Jewish essay is quoted in all the world press . . . Anti-Semitism is growing in Europe, and the longer the war lasts, the stronger it will become."[121] As World War II continued, victory proved elusive, military casualties mounted, and German cities endured Allied bombing. The Nazis hoped and expected that the idea that the Jews were guilty for the war and its pro-longation would lead to an increase of anti-Semitism in all of the countries at war. The German leaders sought to present World War II as "the Jewish war," in hopes that doing so would inflame mass opinion inside and outside Nazi-occupied Europe, and bolster the will to fight on among the Germans, while eroding the enemies' will to continue the battle.

With his doctorate from the University of Heidelberg, Dr. Goebbels, as he preferred to be called, was well equipped to convey Nazi propaganda to German elites. In a formal lecture delivered to the Deutsche Akademie (German Academy) on December 1, 1941, in the new main lecture hall of the Friedrich-Wilhelm University in Berlin, he elaborated on the anti-Semitic themes he had broached in the summer and fall. The Reich Press Office directive that day instructed editors to publish the text of the speech as a front-page story.[122] The lead story in the following day's Berlin's *Deutsche Allgemeine Zeitung* in Berlin described a "large number of generals and other officers, including many holders of medals of honor, other officers, leading personalities of the [Nazi] party and its offices, members of the police and the German Labor Service, as well as many diplomats, along with their wives, and leading figures in German scholarship and art, the economy, and the domestic and international press" attending the lecture.[123]

Adopting a scholarly tone, Goebbels promised to present "fundamentals and theses" beyond the rush of daily political polemics.[124] He expressed confidence about the war, which he again described as necessary, in view of an imminent threat of the "ruthless extermination of the Reich" by the Soviet Union.[125] It was "clear," he continued, that "the first task" of Soviet soldiers would have been "the extermination of the national intelligentsia and cultural leadership of the nation."[126] The war in the East was therefore a matter of national survival. However, he thought the overall military situation looked quite favorable. German submarines were sinking numerous ships going to and from England. The threat of an Allied naval blockade against Germany had been averted. An English return to the Continent appeared to be "in the present situation completely out of the question." American aid was not a cause for alarm. "The offensive power of the Soviet Union was . . . smashed" and England was "on the path to defeat." Contrary to Churchill's claims, time was on Nazi Germany's side.[127] Even though Roosevelt had been able to keep England in the war, Goebbels expressed confidence that American weapons and supplies would have difficulty getting to England across the dangerous Atlantic. Germany, by contrast, had established secure internal lines of communication and transportation throughout Europe. Furthermore, whereas the anti-German coalition was based on cynical opportunism and leading to a pact between between capitalism and communism, the alliance between Nazi Germany and Italian Fascism was grounded in shared "worldviews and morality."

Goebbels then turned to the origins of the war and to "the Jewish question."

> The historic guilt of world Jewry for the outbreak and expansion of this war is so sufficiently proven that we don't need to waste any more words about it. The Jews wanted their war, and now they have it. But now the prophecy which the Führer expressed on January 30, 1939, in the German Reichstag is also proving true—namely, that if international finance Jewry should succeed in driving the peoples once again into a world war, the result would not be the Bolshevization of the earth and thus the victory of Jewry but rather the annihilation of the Jewish race in Europe.
>
> We are now experiencing the implementation of this prophecy. Jewry is thus now enduring a fate that is hard but is more than deserved. Sympathy or even regret is wholly out of place. World Jewry in unleashing this war made a completely false assessment of the forces at its disposal. It is now suffering a gradual process of extermination ["Es erleidet nun einen allmählichen Vernichtungsprozeß"] that it intended for us and that it would without question have carried out if it had the power to do so. It is now

perishing as a result of Jewry's own law: "An eye for an eye and a tooth for a tooth."[128]

Goebbels's vocabulary was not ambiguous. He referred to "a gradual process of" either "extermination" or "annihilation." When Goebbels justified the surprise attack on the Soviet Union, he used the noun *Vernichtung* (extermination) to refer to what the Soviet Union would do to the Germans if Hitler had not struck first. In that instance he meant that the Soviets would murder the German "national intelligentsia." Only a few minutes later, he used the same words to mean the same thing about German policy toward the Jews. Perhaps some in his audience thought the addition of the adjective "gradual" before "process of extermination" may have meant slow starvation or death by exposure, a sort of German version of the Soviet camps, rather than sudden death by shooting or gassing in the not yet fully functioning death camps. Both text and context, however, suggest that Goebbels meant that the Nazi regime was at that moment carrying out Hitler's "prophecy"—that is, it was engaging in the mass murder of "the Jewish race in Europe." This was not the language of euphemism, bureaucratic avoidance, or banality. It was extraordinary and blunt discourse. Goebbels was telling this sophisticated and well-connected audience in language it could understand that the German government had begun to murder the Jews of Europe.

Goebbels repeated the accusations he had made in "The Jews Are Guilty." He said: "In this historic confrontation, every Jew is our enemy, whether he is vegetating in a Polish ghetto or enjoying his parasitic existence in Berlin or Hamburg or blowing the trumpets of war in New York or Washington. Owing to their birth and their race, all Jews belong to an international conspiracy against National Socialist Germany. They wish for its defeat and annihilation and do all that is in their power to help bring that about."[129] In the main lecture hall of one of Germany's greatest universities, he lent further weight to the direst interpretation of his words. The most effective measures required "a pitiless, cold hardness against the corrupter of our people, against the instigator of this war . . . The Jews are guilty of causing this war. Therefore, they are suffering no injustice as a consequence of the treatment we are giving them. They have more than deserved it. The definitive solution of the Jewish question will be one of the first and most important tasks of the coming period." There would be no peace in Europe until it was "fully clarified" and Jewish "domination" of the Continent had ended.[130] Lest his audience avoid drawing the murderous conclusion that clearly flowed from his murderous pronouncements, Goebbels used a variety of gruesome verbs to describe the catastrophe that would descend upon Germany if the Jews were to win the war. Germany's enemies were united in believing that Germany "must be annihilated, exterminated, and wiped out."[131] Defeat would be worse than a second Versailles. The victors would unleash "Old Testament fantasies of revenge." Their "naked will to annihilation" would produce an "inferno." Faced with this possible catastrophe, the demands of elementary survival required that the Germans unite behind Hitler and the Nazi regime to prevent their own annihilation and extermination. As would be the case for the next four years, playing on fear was not separate from the anti-Semitic narrative. It was one of its necessary components.

Goebbels's presentation of the attack on the Jews as a preemptive strike—indeed, as an act of self-defense—demonstrated that denial of the dimensions of the Holocaust was an essential component of the act itself. Its perpetrators presented mass murder as a typical and common feature of the war in which Germany was now engaged—indeed, as a policy that its archenemy was intending to inflict on the Germans. The balance of justification for mass murder and silence about the details was characteristic of Nazi propaganda throughout the Holocaust. That evening, Goebbels wrote in his diary that he was "extraordinarily pleased with my appeal to the Berlin intelligentsia."[132] The following evening he added that the Deutsche Akademie had offered him and the Propaganda Ministry "a great podium from which we are able to speak to the intellectual world at home and abroad."[133]

Following the Japanese attack on Pearl Harbor, Hitler expressed his satisfaction to Goebbels with the turn of events. He thought that American energies would be drawn toward the Pacific and thus away from the European theater.[134] The Reich Press Office directive for December 7, 1941, declared that the war in "East Asia" was in fact "the work of the warmonger and world criminal Roosevelt, who has, as henchman of the Jews second only to Churchill, been pushing incessantly towards war. He has finally achieved his goal in the Far East."[135] The most important task for the press was to describe "the horror of the path taken by the American president," so that "every reader will be filled with disgust for this greatest hypocrite of all times and for his imperialist policies." The press was to depict Roosevelt as "a warmonger" linked to "Jewish plutocracy."[136]

On December 10, 1941, the day before Hitler declared war on the United States, the Propaganda Ministry sent its customary 125,000 copies of the *Word of the Week* to be posted in the familiar prime locations for the greatest visual impact around the country. "Das jüdische Komplott ("The Jewish Conspiracy") offered a detailed, indeed byzantine, diagram of the names and channels of influence of "the Jewish wire pullers" and their "stooges and accomplices" involved in the international Jewish plot.[137] Here, in black and yellow, the immense conspiracy was depicted for all to see. In its apparent exactitude about the names of particular individuals and their alleged connections to and influence on one another, the poster was a paradigmatic case of the paranoid vision of radical anti-Semitic propaganda. Appearing in yellow (a color associated in Nazi propaganda with the Jews) against a black background, the wall newspaper combined text and image to draw the eye first to an anti-Semitic caricature of a male face with oversized ears, nose, and lips, curly hair, heavy eyebrows, and a small growth of a beard—this was the Jew at the center of the plot. Wide arrows in striking yellow, showing direction of influence, issue from two Stars of David named for the two key figures in the international conspiracy, Bernard Baruch of the United States and "Mosessohn," a sarcastic reference to the Soviet Politburo member Lazar Kaganovitch. Baruch exerts direct influence on the non-Jews Roosevelt and Churchill and on the Jewish bankers Schiff, Warburg, Kahn, Karp, whose names are inscribed between two Stars of David. Baruch also has a direct link to "Roosevelt's intimates and leading advisers," identified as "Jews!": Henry Morgenthau, Felix Frankfurter, New York governor Herbert Lehman, Fiorello LaGuardia, Sol Bloom (chairman of the House Foreign Affairs Committee), and an unidentified Cohen. The arrows of influence stemming from "Mosessohn" Kaganovich extend to "Finkelstein-Wallach"—that is, former Soviet foreign minister Maxim Litvinov.[138] "Mosessohn" Kaganovich influences the non-Jew Stalin. The circle of influence is completed by a yellow line connecting Roosevelt, Churchill, and Stalin.

Once the curiosity of passersby had been aroused by the striking colors, the arrows, the caricatures, and the familiar-sounding Jewish names, the viewers' attention might turn to the text of the poster, which revealed the secrets of this vast and powerful conspiracy. To the left, the text identified Baruch, Mosessohn, Schiff, Finkelstein, and Maisky as Jews and asserted that they were in league with the non-Jews Roosevelt, Churchill, and Stalin. Below, text about the Jewish "wire pullers" ("die Jüdischen Drahtzieher") introduced four points identifying the images and the connections between them: for example, the "Jew . . . Baruch" was "one of the great warmongers and war profiteers of the world war [World War I], inventor of the Versailles tribute clauses, close friend and adviser to the Freemason Jewish hireling Roosevelt, personal friends with Churchill, called today by the Americans the unofficial president of the USA." LaGuardia, Morgenthau, Bloom, Frankfurter, Lehmann, Cohen, and Kaufman were "Roosevelt's intimates and associates." Kaganovich, or "Lazarus, son of Moses Kaganovich," was "Stalin's only trusted aid, most intimate adviser, deputy, and father-in-law." Maxim Litvinov and Ivan Maisky were both mentioned, as were such Jews active in English politics as Leslie Hore-Belisha and Lord Rothschild.

Among the millions of Germans who walked past this wall newspaper in that second week of December 1941, those who may have stopped long enough to read the text probably had no idea whether Roosevelt was really a Freemason, whether Churchill was a Jewish father-in-law (*Judenschwiegervater*), or whether Stalin had married Kaganovich's daughter. They would have had only a smattering of information about who Baruch, Kaganovich, and the others were; however, especially after Hitler declared war on the United States on December 11, they did know that Russia, England, and the United States were now at war with Nazi Germany. The image and text of the wall newspaper offered a seemingly compelling explanation of how the Jews, so few in number, could have been so successful in plotting against Germany. Perhaps the passerby would have been impressed by all the specific names and the graphic illustration of the arrows of influence, not to mention its technical expertise. For those immersed in the Nazi context, it could also convey the impression of a complex, well-researched and compelling causal explanation of why it was that three of the most powerful countries in the world were at war with Nazi Germany. Surely not all the names could be fictional. Surely some part of this conspiracy must exist. The Propaganda Ministry had not pulled Bernard Baruch and Lazar Kaganovich out of thin air. Of course, to people outside Nazi Germany the wall newspaper would have appeared, as it appears today, to be crackpot realism based on a combination of mental derangement, political fantasy, unjustified hatred, pathetically erroneous causal connections, and inferences—all of which amounted to a sick grotesque falsification. Yet the Germans gazing at this wall newspaper during that week of short, cold, mostly gray December days were within Nazism's grasp and thus had access to no alternative explanation of how political decisions were being made in Moscow, London, and Washington and how or whether Jews had any impact whatsoever on them. Some unknown number of pedestrians turned away from the wall newspaper in disgust and anger, appalled at the distortions of the criminals in charge of their government. Yet an equally unknown though larger group of passersby in all likelihood believed that "The Jewish Conspiracy" taught them a great deal about the world as it really was. As we shall see, in the year to come, Nazi propagandists drew on mass reproduction of photos in the press to add faces to the names and arrows of influence that had adorned the ubiquitous wall newspapers displayed in the fateful second week of December 1941. In the process, the international Jewish conspiracy became less of an abstraction and more a group of actual people.

On December 11, 1941, Hitler declared war on the United States in a speech to the Reichstag broadcast over German radio and printed in full in the German press.[139] He spoke for almost ninety minutes and reached a crescendo of hatred in his attack on Franklin D. Roosevelt and the Jews around him. His central point was that "a single man," Roosevelt, "and the forces driving him" were the cause of World War II.[140] "The brain trust that the new American president must serve consists of the members of the same people we fought in Germany as a parasitic appearance of humanity and which we began to push out of (German) public life."[141] Roosevelt, Hitler continued, sought to divert attention from the "collapse of his whole economic house of cards" through his foreign policy. The "circle of Jews surrounding him" encouraged his foreign policy initiatives. They were "motivated by Old Testament greed" and he was a man of "utterly satanic perfidy." This tactic of diversion was a key reason for Roosevelt's meddling in European affairs.[142]

Anti-Semitism was at the center of Hitler's attack on Roosevelt. "We know what powers stand behind Roosevelt. It is the eternal Jew who thinks his time has come to inflict on us what we shudder to see and must experience in Soviet Russia." It was, he continued, "Franklin Roosevelt's and the Jews' intention to destroy one state after another."[143] The war was a matter of the "existence or nonexistence" of nations. If given the opportunity, Roosevelt and the Jews "would now exterminate National Socialist Germany."[144] The United States under Roosevelt was striving for "unlimited world domination" and would deny Germany, Italy, and Japan the necessities of national survival. For the "National Socialists," he continued, it was "no surprise that the

Anglo-Saxon-Jewish-capitalist world [found] itself in a common front with Bolshevism." This was the anti-Nazi coalition of the Weimar era projected onto a world stage.[145]

Roosevelt and the United States had enraged Hitler from the beginning of the war, well before the United States had entered it. He was convinced that if Roosevelt had not supported Churchill, Britain would have agreed to a negotiated settlement following the German victories of 1939 and 1940. In the summer of 1941, Roosevelt's decision to offer assistance to the Soviet Union thwarted German hopes for a quick victory on the eastern front. By December 1941, Hitler, who had invaded and occupied most of the countries on the Continent, with the exception of neutral states and his own allies, blamed the war on the president of a country on the other side of the Atlantic. He and his propagandists presented Nazi Germany as the innocent victim of the aggression of others. Hitler never accepted any responsibility for the war that he, and he alone, had initiated and expanded.

On December 12, Hitler spoke to a gathering of Nazi political leaders.[146] Goebbels reported: "Regarding the Jewish question, the Führer is determined to settle the matter once and for all. He prophesied that if the Jews once again brought about a world war, they would experience their extermination. This was not an empty phrase. The world war is here. The extermination of the Jews must be its necessary consequence. ("Der Weltkrieg ist da. Die Vernichtung des Judentums muß die notwendige Folge sein.") This question must be viewed without any sentimentality. We are here not to express sympathy for the Jews, but only to express sympathy for our own German people. As the German people again has sacrificed 160,000 dead in the eastern campaign, so the originators of this conflict must pay [for these deaths] with their own lives."[147] Hitler again gave the war a causal and inherent, not a contingent or accidental, connection with his intent to exterminate the Jews. As the numbers of German soldiers dying in battle and of German civilians dying in Allied bombings increased, the more the Nazi leadership stressed the supposed connections between an international

Jewish conspiracy, the anti-Hitler coalition of the Soviet Union, Great Britain, and the United States, the death and suffering of the German people, and the consequent necessity of carrying out Hitler's prophecy. Nazi propaganda pointed its accusing finger at the Jews as the party guilty for every German death and injury. In so doing, propaganda provided a personal reason to "retaliate" against the Jews. In this way, for millions of Germans, the abstract slogan "The Jews are guilty" assumed direct emotional significance. For those who accepted this logic, Jew hatred would deepen as the numbers of Germans killed and wounded increased. The paranoid projections of Nazi propaganda seemed to emerge in actual experience. The more the *Allies* turned the tide against the German armed forces, the more Nazi propagandists asserted that the Jews were guilty and would pay for it.

Understandably, Japan and the war in the Pacific were not the most prominent aspect of the anti-Semitic narrative. Yet they fitted into the story in novel ways. "Japan's Battle against World Jewry," by "Gü," the lead article in the December 24, 1941, issue of *Die Judenfrage*, offered enlightenment to government and party propagandists on Asian matters.[148] Ever since Japan had sought Lebensraum and leadership in Asia, he wrote, it had had to face hostility from "the two neighboring Jewish states, . . . the Jewish-Bolshevik" Soviet Union and the "Jewish-plutocratic North America," as well as from Great Britain. All supported Chiang Kai-shek in China. Although the "German victory" in Europe had reduced the Soviet threat, the threat from the "Jewish plutocracy" of the United States and Great Britain and their "encirclement" policies had become all the more grave. Without mentioning the attack on Pearl Harbor, Gü noted that Japan had "exercised its duty for self-defense" against the "political representatives of international Jewry," who thought that they could crush Japan. Now Japan had entered "the freedom struggle of the young peoples, which is necessary to defeat the plutocratic world order." While Japan posed no threat to the United States or Britain, it was determined to defeat "Jewish finance capital" and Jewish circles in England and the United States that wanted to exploit China's economic potential.

Japan had "recognized" that Roosevelt was a tool of the Jews, that his was a "Jewish government" of aggressive imperialism guided by international Jewry and Freemasonry. While the Jewish threat within Japan was not yet "acute," the influence of the Jews in China was "unlimited." Chiang Kai-shek was, according to *Die Judenfrage,* also a Freemason who was receiving support from Jewish financial and industrial groups. "Jewish power in the Western democracies can rest in China on a firmly anchored and decisive Jewry"—that is, on the 37,000 Jews in China, mostly in Shanghai, who had escaped from Nazi-dominated Europe.[149] Japanese economic hegemony in Asia would undermine the "Jewish supremacy in China." The Japanese recognized that in "the imperialism of a Churchill, and above all Roosevelt, they were facing international Jewry's mania for domination." The article noted that the 1938 book *The Attack of the Jews against Japan* had pointed out, "The influence of Jewish finance capital in China is one of the main causes of the Japanese-Chinese conflict."[150] There seemed to be nothing that the anti-Semitic framework could not explain.

By the end of 1941, the blend of anti-Semitism and anti-Americanism staring out from *Word of the Week* and stressed in speeches by Hitler and in articles in the German press found a quieter echo in a flood of material, couched along the same lines, issuing from the Nazi publishing houses. *Powers behind Roosevelt,* by the prolific anti-Semite Johann von Leers, had gone into a third edition by 1942, with 28,000 copies in print.[151] Von Leers offered an anti-Semitic history of the United States focused on the growth of Jewish emigration since the 1890s and efforts by Jews to push the United States into war. "The Jewish newspaper the *New York Times,* of the Jew Adolf S. Ochs, was at the forefront of this agitation." Von Leers interpreted a 1925 speech by Ochs expressing gratitude for "the rights and privileges" Jews enjoyed in the United States as evidence of new-found power. "The same Jew," had spoken of bonds with European democracies. Like other Nazi propagandists, von Leers was obsessed with the possible Jewish identity of spouses. He made a great deal of the fact that the wife of U.S. Secretary of State Cordell Hull was Jewish, even though Hull had done little to raise the issue of Nazi persecution of the Jews. Americans meddling in European affairs were on the side of former French prime minister Léon Blum, former Soviet foreign minister Maxim Litvinov, and former British secretary of war Leslie Hore-Belisha, "three sons of Israel" constituting a "a trio of non-Aryans" united against Nazi Germany and seeking to "send Europe to annihilation!"[152]

Von Leers focused on the by now familiar suspects: Secretary of the Treasury Henry Morgenthau; the financier Bernard Baruch; Supreme Court justice Felix Frankfurter and the younger lawyers he had helped find positions under the New Deal (von Leers called it the Ju-Deal); labor leader Sidney Hillman; and Samuel J. Rosenman, "one of the most dangerous of the rising Jews in Roosevelt's circle" and a close adviser to Roosevelt. Von Leers concluded that the Jews dominated the U.S. Departments of the Treasury and Labor and had considerable influence in the Department of State. J. Edgar Hoover, the director of the FBI, was a Freemason of the thirty-second degree. Though Hoover was not Jewish, he was thus linked to a sinister international organization with ties to the Jews. Fiorello LaGuardia was a "Sicilian half-Jew." For von Leers, Roosevelt's expressions of friendship toward American Jews on Rosh Hashanah as early as 1933 clinched the argument. In 1933, FDR sent his "warm greetings to all those of Jewish faith in the USA. We are indebted to the Jews for many high ideals which enrich our nation and the world. May the coming year bring our Jewish fellow citizens happiness and prosperity."[153] With this quote von Leers ended a chapter, as if no further comment was needed. Roosevelt's kind words closed the case.

Von Leers appealed to "real" America, not New York, Washington's New Deal, or Hollywood films. Rather it was that vast non-Jewish heartland which would would put an end to the un-American policies of the Roosevelt administration. Von Leers was not a crazed street-corner orator but a member in good standing of the anti-Semitic intelligentsia whose work the major Nazi presses published. He and his bosses did not understand or simply refused to acknowledge that the American military and diplomatic establishment of the 1930s and 1940s remained overwhelmingly the preserve of white Anglo-Saxon Protestant men. If Nazi propagandists had been able to find Jewish faces from the State Department or the War Department to plaster over the pages of *Word of the Week,* they certainly would have put them there. The Nazis did not understand or believe that the American political, diplomatic, and military leadership had reasons to oppose Nazi domination and expansion that were totally unrelated to the fate of Europe's Jews.

American entry into the war and the consolidation of the anti-Hitler coalition between the United States, Britain, and the Soviet Union appeared to offer further proof that the anti-Semitic interpretation was correct and that Jewry was the driving force behind the anti-Hitler coalition. In his diary entry of December 31, 1941, Goebbels opined that the cooperation between "high capitalism and Bolshevism is now clear. Naturally, the international Jew, who is cleverly dealing the cards and convinced that he is now able to play his last trump, stands in the background."[154] The anti-Semitic framework divested the Nazi regime of responsibility for having brought about a hostile alliance of unlikely partners and at the same time offered an explanation of just why regimes with such contrasting principles would ally at all. By the end of 1941, a unified and coordinated narrative of events emerged from Hitler's speeches, Goebbels's editorials and speeches, the headlines and lead articles of thousands of newspapers and periodicals, the colorful and ubiquitous *Word of the Week* wall newspapers, books and pamphlets from Nazi presses, and the speeches at thousands of meetings at the regional and local level delivered by Nazi propagandists and officials. In the minds of the Nazi leaders and followers in the vast Nazi organization, the emergence of the anti-Hitler coalition between the Soviet Union on the one hand and Britain and the United States on the other was the most powerful piece of evidence that an anti-Semitic interpretation focused on the existence of an international Jewish conspiracy explained the actual course of events. Why else, if not for the behind-the-scenes maneuvers of the Jewish plotters, would such strange bedfellows be making common cause against the Third Reich? Was it not obvious that Roosevelt and the Jewish powers behind and around him had stood in the way of the early victory that had seemed so tantalizingly possible, thanks to Hitler's rearmament? Most terrifying of all, international Jewry had organized a massive international coalition and was, according to Hitler, Goebbels, and articles in the German press, intending to "exterminate"— that is, murder—all the Germans. By late 1941, Nazi propaganda had transformed the ancient hatreds of anti-Semitism into a public justification for mass murder. In 1942, Nazi propagandists hammered away at these points, repeating that the Jews were going to pay through their extermination and annihilation for their past and present sins and blunders.

5 Propaganda in the Shadow of the Death Camps

In the winter and spring of 1942 all six of the main Nazi extermination camps had begun operation. Their gas chambers and crematoria were operating at full capacity. Hitler repeated in several major speeches printed in the press and broadcast on radio his determination to "exterminate" and "annihilate" the Jews of Europe. At the same time, the number of anti-Semitic headlines and articles in the German press declined. They continued and even intensified, however, in the weekly wall newspapers distributed from June 1941 through December 1942.[1] The *Word of the Week* penetrated deeply into the daily life of German society, but its influence was much less visible to the world outside Germany. In winter and spring 1942, the regular German press featured a more conventional series of generally distorted, incomplete, and often false accounts of the battles of World War II. A daily press directive of January 7, 1942, from Dietrich's Reich Press Office ordered that nothing was to be reported about "the Jewish question in the occupied eastern territories."[2] In fact, from the beginning to the end of the Final Solution, Otto Dietrich, his staff in the Reich Press Office, and the purged and intimidated profession of German "journalism" cooperated so well that not a single fact about the genocide appeared in the pages of German newspapers and periodicals.

If German journalism worthy of the name had existed, the press would have been filled with the most astonishing story of Europe's twentieth century. In October and November 1941, 19,827 Jews were deported from Germany to the Lodz Ghetto in twenty rail transports.[3] In December 1941, the first death camp began to operate in Chelmno, Poland. By April 1943, between 150,000 and 300,000 Jews had been gassed and shot to death there. On January 20, 1942, at the Wannsee Conference, Reinhard Heydrich presented the plans for murdering eleven million European Jews to officials representing government ministries whose cooperation would be required. None leaked information to the press—or if they did, nothing appeared in print.

In March 1942, with the opening of the death camp in Belzec, Poland, Nazi officials opened a more extensive chapter in industrialized mass murder. Almost all the Belzec victims were Jews. Unlike Chelmno, which made use of mobile killing units, Belzec was equipped with permanent gas chambers—it was the first camp to have them. These had the capacity to kill 15,000 people a day. By November 1942, 600,000 Jews had been killed there. Their bodies were burned in open mass graves. In May 1942 the extermination camp in Sobibor, Poland, began its killing operations. By October 1943, 200,000 to 250,000 Jews had been murdered there. In August and September 1942, two provisional gas chambers were added to the concentration and extermination camp at Majdanek, Poland. By October 1942, three permanent gas chambers were functioning. It was at Majdanek, opened in October 1941, that the SS murdered thousands of Soviet prisoners of war. Of the 235,000 of its 300,000 inmates of fifty nationalities murdered from July 1942 to fall 1943, about 120,000 were Jews. In July 1942, the death camp at Treblinka, Poland began operation. From then until fall 1943, 750,000 to 800,000 Jews from central Poland, Germany, Austria, Czechoslovakia, the Netherlands, Belgium, and Greece were killed by gassing and their bodies incinerated on massive funeral pyres. In the spring of 1942, transports of Jews from all over Europe began to arrive at Auschwitz-Birkenau, the largest of the death camps. From then until 1945, between

1 and 1.5 million people, 90 percent of whom were Jews, were murdered in its gas chambers and their bodies cremated in its massive crematoria. In mid-July 1942, Heinrich Himmler ordered that the entire Jewish population of Poland's ghettos be killed by the end of the year. Most of the 350,000 inhabitants of the Warsaw Ghetto were murdered in the Treblinka extermination camp between July 22 and September 12.[4] In short, the Nazis murdered with breathtaking speed. By late fall 1943, 2 to 2.5 million Jews had been killed in the six death factories, five of which had completed their work and were closed. The gas chambers and crematoria in Auschwitz-Birkenau, which were operating at full capacity by spring 1942, continued to function.[5]

Not a word appeared in the German press about the death camps and mass shootings involving millions of victims, hundreds of high-ranking officials, tens of thousands of offenders, and an unknown number of bystanders who were witnesses, over the entire period. This absence of reports of any of the events of the Final Solution must be counted one of the major "accomplishments" of the Nazi leadership—of Dietrich, in particular, but also Goebbels. Instead, cheerleading and incitement came in the form of Hitler's occasional speeches, Goebbels's editorials in *Das Reich,* and the almost weekly doses of anti-Semitic hatred in the *Word of the Week* wall newspapers.[6] The regime not only hid the mass murder of millions of civilians but it suppressed the truth about the extent of German military losses. In December 1941, Hitler reported to a stunned Reichstag that 160,000 German soldiers had died since June 1941 on the eastern front. According to important recent research the actual figure by the end of November was 282,330. By the end of December 1941, the toll for the eight months since Operation Barbarossa had begun had risen to 324,528 deaths. The German home audience never heard these figures. They were 572,000 in 1942; 812,000 in 1943; 1,802,000 in 1944; and 1,540,000 from January to May 8, 1945.[7] In his diary entry of March 6, 1942, Goebbels offered the following casualty figures from the eastern front for the period from June 22, 1941, to February 20, 1942: 199,448 dead; 708,351 wounded; 44,342 missing.

Though these numbers represented significant undercounting, he wrote in his diary that it was "not opportune to give these numbers to the public. We'll wait for a more favorable moment. They will be published more usefully when we can show new military successes."[8] Silence and misinformation were of obvious importance for Goebbels's plans to sustain morale on the home front.

On January 1, 1942, Goebbels read Hitler's "New Year's Greeting" to the German people and the Wehrmacht on national radio. Hitler expressed confidence that the Axis powers and their new ally, Japan, would successfully resist "the Anglo-Saxon powers." He defended Japan's attack on Pearl Harbor. It was "understandable to us that Japan finally was fed up with the eternal blackmail and blatant threats from the most insane warmonger of all time [Franklin D. Roosevelt] and turned to self-defense. As a result, there now exists a powerful front of national states extending from the English Channel to East Asia fighting against the Jewish-capitalistic-Bolshevist world conspiracy."[9] Alluding to the German war on the eastern front, Hitler wrote that 1941 had included one of "the greatest victories of human history" and acknowledged the sacrifices it had entailed. The Germans, however, "had no idea of the horrible misfortune that would have broken over Germany and Europe if Jewish Bolshevism, in alliance with Churchill and Roosevelt, had gained victory. For Churchill and Roosevelt would have delivered Europe to Stalin!" Regarding the Jews, he abandoned hypothetical statements: "The Jew will not exterminate the peoples of Europe. Rather, he will be the victim of his own attack."[10] Hitler's New Year statement offered the public a briefer version of what he had expressed in greater detail to Nazi leaders earlier in December. The entry of the United States into the war on the side of Britain and the Soviet Union had brought into the open the existence of the international Jewish "world conspiracy." Hitler would now retaliate against "the Jew."

Retaliation against the Jews did not mean letting their supposed stooges off the hook. In his January 11, 1942, editorial in *Das Reich,* "We Build a Bridge," Goebbels attacked Britain and the United States for entering a coalition with the Soviet Union. Following paragraphs of personal insults and invective directed at Churchill and Roosevelt, he declared that Germany and its allies were "the last wall against the Mongol storm" threatening Europe. England had "betrayed" Europe, as it "sold itself to Moscow."[11] The *Word of the Week* of January 14, "They Wanted the War!!" attacked "Roosevelt and his Jewish inflammatory apostles" for wanting and causing the war. With his efforts to supply Britain across the Atlantic and his challenge to American neutrality laws, Roosevelt has driven the United States into the war. After Churchill, he was "warmonger number 1."[12] In a January 20, 1942, conversation with Goebbels, Hitler described Churchill as the "main criminal of this war."[13] Goebbels followed up in his front-page editorial in *Das Reich* of January 25, 1942, in which he denounced the "men behind the scenes" who were directing Churchill and Roosevelt and their repeatedly expressed supposed "will to annihilate the German people."[14]

The following week's *Word of the Week* elaborated on what would remain a key theme of Nazi propaganda: "Churchill's Betrayal of Europe."[15] It featured a 1920 quote from Churchill expressing his intense opposition to Russia's "world revolutionary fanatics." The article asserted that "since then," the Bolsheviks had worked towards "Europe's bloody extermination," and Stalin had transformed the Russians "into an enormous herd of depraved slaves of a Jewish-Bolshevik war of extermination against Europe's nations of culture." It went on, "This bloodthirsty son-in-law of the Jew Kaganovich has murdered more than thirty million people in cold blood, with a bullet to the head, hunger, and deportation." In 1941, with Europe facing "this second Genghis Khan" in a fight for its life, and Churchill leading the British people, "this war criminal [Churchill] betrays Europe to the Bolshevik murderers and sends weapons to them." The "young nations of Europe" would never forget the betrayal of the "whiskey-guzzling Churchill" and would pursue "only one goal: annihilation of the Bolshevik monster and annihilation of those who unscrupulously incited it against Europe: Churchill and his consorts!!"[16] When Churchill brought such left-leaning politicians as Stafford Cripps into his coalition government, Goebbels told his staff that this was evidence of Britain's Bolshevization.[17] He interpreted the emergence of coalition government in London, and to a certain extent that in Washington, as further evidence of the influence of both Communism and the Jews. In every instance, Nazi propaganda presented the anti-Hitler coalition as a conspiracy of nonequals in which the active though hidden subject, the real directing power, remained "international Jewry." By August 1942, Goebbels was calling Churchill a "Prisoner of the Kremlin," who had abandoned his anticommunist convictions for political expediency and thus had to "dance to the Soviets' tune."[18] The Propaganda Ministry published "Juden Komplott gegen Europa" ("Jewish Conspiracy against Europe"), a striking multicolored visual depiction of the source of the British-Soviet alliance formed in summer 1941. It shows stereotypical images of a Soviet commissar shaking hands with an overweight British bourgeois. They are standing on a map that places their handshake directly over Germany. Looking down from high above the earth, safely away from the action on the ground, is a caricatured Jewish head shown with an approving smile as the Soviets and British consolidate the plot. The male figure has a beard, nose, and lips intended to evoke a stereotypical, disembodied Jew.[19]

Though Hitler's public appearances became rarer, they remained the key agenda-setting documents of Nazi propaganda. In winter and spring 1943, Hitler delivered three virulent broadcast attacks on German radio against the Jews. The first and most widely noted he made on January 30, 1942, in his annual speech to the Reichstag commemorating his ascent to power. He worked himself into a rage, hurling insults at Churchill and the English, and dropped efforts to distinguish between the English ruling classes and the majority of the population. The English he now identified as "our irreconcilable enemies." Hitler continued, "They hate us, and so we therefore must hate them." He then turned his attention to the Jews and said:

We are clear that the war can come to an end only either with the extermination of the Aryan peoples or with the disappearance of the Jews from Europe. On September 1, 1939 [in fact, January 30, 1939], in the German Reichstag I already asserted—I do not engage in premature prophecies—that this war will not develop as the Jews imagined—namely, that the European-Aryan peoples will be exterminated. Rather, the result of this war will be the annihilation of Jewry. For the first time, the genuine old-Jewish law will be applied: An eye for an eye, a tooth for a tooth!

And the further this struggle expands, the more anti-Semitism will spread . . . It will find support in every prison camp, in every family that finally understands the cause of its suffering. The hour will come when the *most evil world enemy of all time at least in the last thousand years* will be finished off.[20]

Hitler again linked the grand historical narrative of a war between Aryan Europe and international Jewry with the biographies of countless individuals. Continuation of the war would spread anti-Semitism, because millions of individuals and families would blame the Jews for their own personal suffering and losses. This attribution of blame helps explain why, as Europe's Jews were being murdered, anti-Semitism actually became more virulent in Germany and in Nazi-occupied Europe. Goebbels thought that Hitler's speech would be extremely helpful in sustaining support for the war as hopes for an early victory evaporated.[21]

Two weeks later, Hitler launched into a tirade against the Jews in a one-on-one conversation with the propaganda minister. Bolshevism was "a doctrine of the devil . . . This Jewish terrorism must be eradicated root and branch from all of Europe. This is our historic task." To Goebbels he declared that he was "determined to ruthlessly get rid of the Jews in Europe." There was "no place here for sentimental impulses." The Jews deserved "the catastrophe that they are now experiencing. With the annihilation of our enemies they will also experience their own annihilation. We must accelerate this process with cold ruthlessness. In so doing, we are performing a service of incalculable proportions for a suffering humanity that has been tortured by Jewry for thousands of years. This clear anti-Jewish stance must also be conveyed and drummed into all the reluctant circles in our own people."[22] Following this conversation in Berlin, Hitler returned to his military headquarters in East Prussia. Goebbels regretted the move; he wished Hitler could stay in Berlin, "for these ongoing conversations with him are an eternally renewing source of power and inner security."[23] In conveying these anti-Semitic messages to Goebbels, Hitler knew that they would appear in the media under Goebbels's control, such as the *Word of the Week* and *Das Reich,* while the daily press directives issued by Dietrich's office would for the time being refrain from anti-Semitic campaigns, as the death camps began full operation. Probably Hitler did not want any concerted discussion of Nazi Jewish policy to appear in the German press while his unprecedented genocidal undertaking was moving into high gear.

The *Word of the Week* of February 11, 1942, offered a telling example of the continuing intensity of the anti-Semitic offensive by the Nazi party's Reich Propaganda Directorate, and one as well of the regime's ability to distort documents beyond recognition for consumption by a population that had no possibility of reading the originals.[24] On May 20, 1941, the *Washington Post* had reported that Gilbert Redfern, an American official working with former president Herbert Hoover in an extragovernmental capacity to reduce hunger in war-torn Europe, had asserted that Britain had made a "terrible blunder" in rejecting Hoover's proposal to feed destitute children and adults in Belgium. As a result, unnamed Belgians were accusing the United States of "trying to win the war by promoting pestilence and famine."[25] The *Word of the Week* attributed to Redfern, one of Roosevelt's "agitators," the following completely fictitious statement, falsely said to have appeared in the *Post* article: "The aim of this war is not to rescue democracy. Rather it is the subjugation of Germany and its allies with lice, rats, disease, and hunger and through the blockade in which the government of the USA is participating."[26] The wall poster then asserts that "the civilized

European world shook its head in disbelief over the formulation of plutocratic-Jewish war aims by an obvious career agitator." Redfern, it continued, had revealed the consequences of Roosevelt and Churchill's intention to deliver Europe to Bolshevism and thus to "world Jewry's sadistic lust for domination!!"[27] The wall newspaper transformed a quotation describing Nazi propaganda about British war aims into one in which an "agent" of Roosevelt himself supposedly advocated those aims. Despite the manipulations, one aspect of the message was clear: loss of the war would mean an absolute catastrophe for the Germans.

Goebbels wrote about three million words a year, including the weekly editorial for *Das Reich,* many speeches, and up to fifteen thousand words a night in his diary. Yet he never committed to paper any precise details about the Final Solution—although he left no doubt that he wanted the Jews of Europe dead. After reading a report by the Sicherheitsdienst about partisan warfare on the eastern front, he wrote on March 6, 1942, that "the Jews were active everywhere as inciters and agitators. That is why it is understandable that they must pay with their lives for that activity. Overall, I think that the more Jews that are liquidated during this war, the more consolidated the situation will be after the war. We cannot allow any false sentimentality. The Jews are Europe's misfortune. In one way or another, they must be done away with, for otherwise we run the danger of being done away with by them."[28] In the following day's diary entry, Goebbels reported reading an extensive memo from the SD about "the final solution of the Jewish question." The memo referred to "more than eleven million Jews" in Europe who "must first be concentrated in the East" and eventually, "after the war, be sent to an island," such as Madagascar. There would be no peace in Europe until the Jews were "excluded from the European territory." Even given "delicate questions" concerning half-Jews, relatives, and spouses, it noted, "the situation is now ready to introduce a definitive solution to the Jewish question. Later generations will no longer have the energy and also the alertness of instinct to do so. Therefore, it is important that we proceed radically and thoroughly. What is a burden for us today will be an advantage and source of happiness for our future generations."[29] Goebbels had earlier declared that in fall 1941 the Jews were undergoing a "gradual process of extermination." He would almost certainly have been informed about the decisions conveyed at the Wannsee Conference of January 20, 1942. Hence his reference to the period "after the war" and to Madagascar appear to be lies for posterity's sake. By March 1942, the Madagascar plan had been replaced by the Final Solution in Europe.

Hitler again attacked the Jews in a fifteen-minute speech he delivered in Berlin on March 15, 1942, on the occasion of a day to honor military heroes.[30] He placed the responsibility for Germany's troubles after World War I on England, France, and the United States. These "Jewish-capitalistic" states had proved unable to reduce unemployment in the Great Depression. Instead of learning from Nazi economic and social policies, the leaders of Germany's former enemies in World War I, "essentially directed by Jewish elements," had begun to attack the Nazi regime "immediately after" it came to power. "Today we know that already in 1935 and 1936 in England, France, and especially in America, the decision to wage a new war had already been taken by the really solely decisive Jewish circles and the political leadership strata belonging to them . . . We are only today recognizing the entire extent of the preparations of our enemies. Today we see the dispersion of cooperation among the Jewish wire pullers over a whole world. They unite democracy and Bolshevism into a community of interest engaged in a shared attack by a conspiracy that hopes to be able to annihilate all of Europe." That Germany was standing victorious against "this coalition of Jewish Marxism and capitalism" was due to the discipline and courage of the heroes who had withstood the hard tests of the past year.[31]

In reality, the Nazi regime had been criticized in Europe and the United States soon after it came to power because it had destroyed German democracy, jailed political opponents, destroyed the free press, and persecuted German Jews. All the rest of Hitler's statements were equally false. Far from deciding to wage war against Germany, Britain and France had appeased him, the United States had remained formally neutral and preoccupied at home, while the Soviet Union's mistrust of the Western democracies had become so deep that it had signed a nonaggression pact with Hitler. Indeed, Hitler's awareness of his enemies' disunity and lack of preparedness was a crucial element in his hope of winning quick and early victories over isolated and militarily inferior adversaries. Nowhere were the Jews in a position to push any government into war. To the believers, Hitler's anti-Semitic argument conveniently explained why a paradoxical coalition of opposites, capitalist democracies and Communist dictatorships, had joined forces against Germany. It was those ubiquitous Jewish wire pullers who behind the scenes had quietly organized this international conspiracy and unified this diverse coalition and its aims.

The following day, in another veiled reference to the Holocaust unfolding in the East, Goebbels alluded in his diary to an SD report on partisans in the occupied eastern territories whose leaders were said to be Communist political commissars, and "above all Jews." He concluded, "It is thus even more necessary to shoot Jews. There will be no order in these territories as long as the Jews remain active." He noted once more that "sentimentality" would be misplaced.[32] This equation of respect for elementary human rights with "sentimentality" was one of Goebbels's favorite turns of phrase. On March 20, 1942, following a conversation with Hitler in his Prussian headquarters, Goebbels recorded, regarding the Jews, "The Führer remains merciless. The Jews must be driven from Europe, if necessary by using the most brutal means."[33] With all the major death camps in operation, it was an obvious lie to write that Jews were being "driven from Europe"—that is, to another place. Rather, they were prevented from escaping from Europe and were being murdered there. Murder by machine gun continued but was now overshadowed by industrialized mass murder. And the mass killing had nothing to do with reactions to partisan warfare on the eastern front. Nazi policy toward the Jews was not a response to what they had done, but to what Hitler and his associates imagined that the Jews were doing. The mass shootings of Jews in the East were thus not acts of war.

In his diary entry of March 27, 1942, Goebbels went as far as he ever would in revealing on paper what he knew and felt about the details of the gas chambers and crematoria.

Beginning in Lublin, the Jews are being shipped to the East out of the General Government [in Poland]. A rather barbaric procedure, which I won't describe in more detail, is used. Not much is left of the Jews themselves. In all, 60 percent of the Jews must be liquidated, while only 40 percent can be put to work. The former gauleiter of Vienna, who is conducting this action, is doing it with circumspection and with a method that is inconspicuous. A punishment is being meted out to the Jews that is indeed barbaric but that they however completely deserve. The prophecy the Führer gave to them should they bring about a new world war is now beginning to be realized in the more frightful manner. One cannot allow any sentimentality in these matters. If we hadn't defended ourselves against them, the Jews would exterminate us. It is a battle of life and death between the Aryan race and the Jewish bacillus. No other government and no other regime could muster the power to solve this problem as a whole. Here as in other matters, the Führer is the steadfast champion and spokesman of a radical solution, which this situation demands and which therefore appears to be unavoidable. Thank God that now, during wartime, we have a whole series of opportunities that would be closed off to us in peacetime. Hence, we need to use them. The ghettos in the cities of the General Government that have been cleared [of Jews] will now be filled with Jews who have been expelled from the Reich, and there, after a while, the process will be repeated. Jewry has nothing to laugh about. Because the Jews' representatives today in England and in America are organizing and propagating the war against Germany, their representatives in Europe must pay a very high price, a price that really must be seen as a just one.[34]

The reference to a repeated process of expulsion, clearing, and re-filling of ghettos indicates that Goebbels was aware that the ghettos were not the endpoint of Jewish torment. In the privacy of his diary, he reiterated that because Jews were the driving force of the war in England and America, Europe's Jews would pay with their lives. This policy, far from being the result of a breakdown in normal government bureaucracy, was the "radical solution" that Hitler himself favored and implemented. The figure of 60 percent killed was false. The percentage of those killed at the death camps was often close to 100 percent. Even in his private reflections, Goebbels had mastered the art of manipulating the most delicate topics. Two days later, he wrote that Jews were being evacuated from Berlin at a rate of about a thousand each week and then sent to the East. They deserved "no other fate than the one they are now suffering. We have warned them for such a long time about continuing on their current path. They ignored our warnings and now they have to pay for what they are doing."[35] In August, Goebbels stopped in Warsaw and spoke to SS officials about the Warsaw Ghetto. His diary entry gave further veiled evidence that he was aware of the Final Solution in progress. "The Jews are evacuated in large numbers and sent to the East. This is taking place on a rather large scale. There the Jewish question is handled in the right place without sentimentality . . . It is the only way that the Jewish problem can be solved."[36] Goebbels noted in his diary comment of April 24, 1942, about the war, "Wherever one looks, international Jewry stands in the background as the power pulling the strings."[37] The master liar and cynical manipulator gave abundant evidence that he actually believed that an international Jewish conspiracy existed and was the driving force behind the enemy coalition.

These private reflections underscore the central point that the radical anti-Semitic ideology that justified and accompanied the mass murder of European Jewry was first and foremost *a paranoid political, rather than biological, conviction and narrative.* Nazism's genocidal policies were not due to anti-Semites' perception that Jews had ears and noses that were too large, or a body posture and shape they regarded as effeminate, or sexual appetites that posed a danger to German women and to the "Aryan race." To be sure, Julius Streicher's pornographic obsessions with the Jewish body and Jewish sexuality, along with the absurdities of Nazi racial science, contributed to the terrible toll. These prejudices, phobias, and obsessions were crucial justifications for Nazi policies of persecution, forced sterilization, and inhumane medical experiments. They certainly contributed to a generalized hatred of the Jews in Germany and Nazi-occupied Europe and offered an image of otherness to idealized Aryan physiques; however, by comparison with the potency of the political narrative of radical anti-Semitism, such representations were of secondary importance as causal factors contributing to genocide.[38] Hitler's repugnant attacks in *Mein Kampf* on the alleged physical appearance of East European Jews became world famous.

Yet the Nazi regime forced all Jews to wear the yellow Star of David precisely because its leading officials could not distinguish, strictly on the basis of physical appearance, who was and was not Jewish. They wanted to prevent Jews from passing as non-Jews, or in their terms, from practicing mimicry. (A *Word of the Week* of July 1, 1942, depicted the policy in word and image. In bold type alongside a yellow Star of David with *Jude* (Jew) printed in the middle, the poster declared, "Everyone knows that whoever wears this [yellow Jewish star] is an enemy of our people.")[39] Hitler and his associates decided to murder the Jews in Europe because of what they believed "international Jewry" *did,* far more than because of the way Jews were said to look. From the Nazis' perspective, it was the Jews' actions, not their bodies, that justified mass murder. If, as Goebbels put it on several occasions, all Jews by virtue of their race were members of an international conspiracy waging war against Germany and were thus Germany's enemies, then the distinction between Jews' identity and their actions disappeared.

Genocide was the Nazis' response to international Jewry, which they perceived as a unified, historically active, and above all *political subject* that was waging war against Germany. From the Nazi perspective, if the Jews had listened to Hitler's warnings, they would not have launched World War II. But they had refused to listen, made a strategic blunder, and started the war, and they were therefore receiving the punishment they had merited: death. It was not primarily disgust regarding Jewish bodies or fear of Jewish sexuality but the supposed "war" that the Jews were waging against Germany that stood at the center of the chain of logic that led to the Holocaust. It was because radical anti-Semitism was first and foremost a doctrine of *political* fanaticism, one that described those affiliated with Judaism as members of a racial group called Jewry with extraordinary powers of control and manipulation, that the doctrine produced genocide. The Nazis viewed Jewry as a political subject as real as and yet more powerful than the governments of the anti-Hitler coalition. This attack on the Jews as a political subject was fully in evidence in Hitler's third major rhetorical assault on them of April 1942, in a speech to the Reichstag, meeting in what turned out to be its last session. Its final act was to make Hitler's will the law, unanimously and without discussion.[40]

Parts of the speech, which was broadcast in full on the radio, were excerpted on the front page of *Die Judenfrage*. Because the National Socialists focused "on the essence of the race question, we have found the explanation for many processes that in themselves must appear incomprehensible," Hitler asserted. This revelation produced the following interpretation of recent history.[41]

The hidden powers who drove England in 1914 into World War I were *Jews*. The power that paralyzed us in that war and finally forced us to surrender, with the slogan that Germany may no longer carry its flag home in victory, was a Jewish one. *Jews* instigated the revolution [of 1918–19] and thereby robbed us of any further ability to resist. Since 1939, *Jews* have maneuvered the

British Empire into its most dangerous crisis. *Jews* were the carriers of the Bolshevik infection that once threatened to annihilate Europe. They were also at the same time, however, the warmongers among the plutocrats. A circle of *Jews,* acting only on the basis of Jewish-capitalistic perspectives, has driven America, against all its real interests, into this war. President *Roosevelt,* in a demonstration of his own lack of ability, has an intellectual brain trust whose leading men I don't have to mention by name: it is made up only of Jews."[42]

Jews around President Woodrow Wilson had been responsible for American entry into World War I.[43] The Jews favored the dictatorship of the proletariat and the "extermination of the national leadership and intelligentsia of nations."[44] Hitler continued by saying that anti-Semitism explained what at first seemed "incomprehensible"—namely, the alliance between the Soviet Union and the Western democracies. "Jewish capitalism" had joined forces with the Bolshevik state dominated by the Jews to fight against have-not nations like Germany and Japan seeking only freedom and independence.[45]

The wall newspaper of May 27, 1942, titled "Die Drahtzieher! Es sind nur Juden!" ("The Wire Pullers: They Are Only Jews!"), reproduced quotations from Hitler's April 26 speech about Roosevelt, the Jews in the United States, and "hidden powers" in England.[46] "Die Drahtzieher!" appeared at the top and "are only Jews" at the bottom in large bold type with the text in black against the customary yellow background. *Juden* and "Roosevelt" appeared in boldface type. This *Word of the Week* built on the representation of Jews as "wire pullers" that had been part of Nazi anti-Semitic visual images since the mid-1920s. The significance of this latest version lay in the use of photography. International Jewry ceased to be an artist's caricature or a mere list of names on a poster. At last, the actual faces of the enemy, the leading figures of the international conspiracy, were revealed for all passersby to see. On the right, prefaced by the boldface lead-in "the Jew," were photos of

Leslie Hore-Belisha, the former English minister of war; Walter Rathenau, former foreign minister of the Weimar Republic; and Kurt Eisner, leader of the Bavarian soviet during the revolution of 1918–19, who like Rathenau was murdered by right-wing assassins. On the left side were photos of "the Jew" Bernard Baruch, Felix Frankfurter, and Maxim Litvinov ("the Jew Litvinow-Finkelstein").[47] The wall newspaper certainly reinforced the beliefs of the party faithful and fellow travelers, while giving pause to the skeptics. After all, Baruch, Frankfurter, Rathenau, and others were not invented out of thin air. They were Jews. Perhaps a regime that had the technical competence to distribute 125,000 copies of such a poster, to virtually every visually arresting location in Germany, knew something about how the world worked and what these Jews were up to. In any case, no alternative explanation was available for why Germany was once again in a war with enemies to the east and west.

Robert Ley, the head of the German Labor Front, was another public advocate of radical anti-Semitism.[48] This crude and brutal man expressed his Jew hatred in a number of speeches to receptive audiences in the early years of the war and used his control of the German Labor Front to assist in the distribution of Nazi propaganda. At a meeting of local Nazi officials in Innsbruck, Austria, on September 5, 1939, he said, "The Jew cannot be annihilated only in our own country. Rather, we may not rest until the Jew is annihilated in the whole world."[49] In December 1939 in Lodz, Poland, at that time occupied by Germany, Ley warned that if England won the war, "the German people, man, woman, and child would be exterminated . . . The Jew would be wading in blood. Funeral pyres would be built on which the Jews would burn us." The Jews would do this in the name of God, but "we want to prevent this. Hence, it should rather be the Jews that fry, rather that they should burn—that they should starve, that they should be exterminated. Germany will live. That will be our slogan [strong applause, cries of Sieg Heil]."[50] On September 3, 1941, at a ceremony to award war service metals to women, Ley said that the war was a life-and-death struggle. There would be no Versailles peace at its end. If the Germans were defeated, the "German people would be exterminated root and branch, you and I, everyone, man and wife, children. The baby in the womb would be killed. The Jew would know no mercy or pity." Germany's cities would be turned into a "desert."[51]

On February 2, 1942, in a speech to employees of the Siemens corporation in the Berlin Sportpalast, Ley declared that *Juda* intended to exterminate and annihilate the Germans, "young and old, rich and poor." But thanks to Hitler's leadership, the Germans had seen that "humanity's enemy . . . *Juda* will and must be annihilated. That is our holy mission [applause]. That is what this war is about."[52] In May 1942, while in Amsterdam and the Hague, Ley delivered three speeches dealing with the Jews. To a meeting of German and Dutch workers in Amsterdam on May 10, broadcast on German radio, he described the war as one between peoples united by race, on the one hand, and *Juda* on the other. Toward the end of a speech interrupted often by applause and laughter, he said the following: "Comrades, believe me. I am not painting too grim a picture. It is bitter for me, bitterly serious. The Jew is the great danger to humanity. If we don't succeed in exterminating him, then we will lose the war. It is not enough to take him someplace. That would be as if one wanted to lock up a louse somewhere in a cage [laughter]. It would find a way out, and again it come out from underneath and make you itch again [laughter]. You have to annihilate them, you have to exterminate [them for what] they have done to humanity . . . [interrupted by ongoing applause]."[53]

Ley's Amsterdam speech went further in public than most Nazi leaders had, by asserting that moving the Jews from one place to another was not sufficient. The transcript conveys both Ley's call to murder the Jews and the audience's understanding and agreement. There is no hint of euphemism in these assertions, which the audience understood and cheered.

In the spring of 1942, under the direction of the newly appointed air marshal Arthur Harris, Britain intensified its bombing campaign against

German industrial centers, targeting factories and transportation, as well as the adjacent densely populated working-class neighborhoods. By forcing the German air force to concentrate aircraft on air defense, the air war over Germany in the next two and a half years significantly reduced the Luftwaffe's ability to operate on the eastern and western fronts and made a significant contribution to the Allied victory.[54] It also caused an estimated 500,000 German civilian deaths, disproportionately among women and children. The bombing became a key topic for Goebbels.[55] He offered the first of many comments in an editorial in *Das Reich* of June 14, 1942, entitled "The Air War and the War of Nerves." The essay denounced Churchill and the British bombing campaign, asserting, "Terror would not break German morale."

Toward the end of the essay, Goebbels shifted his focus away from Churchill and the British government and onto the Jews. They were "pursuing in this war a sacrilegious game, and they will pay for it with the extermination of their race in Europe and perhaps even beyond Europe as well."[56] The *Word of the Week* for October 21, 1942, entitled "The Man Who Invented the Bombing War against the Civilian Population," quoted from a speech in which Hitler attacked Churchill and the Allied bombing campaign, as well as Roosevelt, and promised German retaliation. Goebbels promised these "two general criminals of this war and their Jewish men behind the scenes" that "the end for England will be more terrible than the beginning!!!"[57] The wall newspaper, like Goebbels's essay, incorporated the anti-Semitic message into a tirade against the Allied air war, themes that would have resonance well beyond the ranks of the Nazi party.

On June 13 the *Washington Post* ran a story on page 12 with the headline "Nazis to Kill Jews in Reprisal for British Raids." The *Post* reported that German radio had broadcast the full version of the essay in which Goebbels "threatened extermination of Jews in reprisal for British air assaults upon Germany." On the same day, the *New York Times* ran a story on page 7 under the headline, "Nazis Blame Jews for Big Bombings; Goebbels Says 'Extermination of All in Europe and Perhaps

Beyond' Will Result." Both articles quoted Goebbels's speech citing the intention to exterminate European Jewry.[58] These articles, although they accurately reported the Nazis' murderous intentions, could be read as implying that the German threats came in response to Allied war measures and that halting these would prevent the announced "extermination." Yet in the context of the overall statements by Hitler and Goebbels about the Jews and the war, the proper reading of Goebbels's remarks was rather that the Jews bore responsibility for the war as a whole, of which the air war was only one component. The mass murder of the Jews had begun on June 22, 1941, long before the Allied air war over Germany. Nevertheless, the air war over Germany now assumed a special place in Nazi anti-Semitic propaganda. Germany's devastated cities and civilian deaths became a primary piece of evidence to support official claims that the Jews were indeed trying to exterminate the Germans.

Perhaps because anti-Soviet sentiment was already deeply rooted in Germany, Goebbels devoted fewer of his editorials to anti-Soviet than to anti-Western attacks. Still, neither he nor his ministry neglected anti-Soviet propaganda. Eight editions of *Word of the Week* from January to July 1942 included attacks on Russia, and two more followed in the fall. In July 1942, the Propaganda Ministry opened an exhibition, "The Soviet Paradise," that toured German cities, presumably revealing the truth behind the illusions of that paradise. On July 19, 1942, Goebbels's article "The So-Called Russian Soul" was published, in which he depicted the Soviet Union as a hybrid of Jewish brains and non-Jewish brawn. "There was no doubt," he wrote, that "in the silent and pliant human material of the East, international Jewry confronts us with the most dangerous adversary."[59] The "storm from the East" was a particular threat because it was "connected with Jewish intellectual strata, which are ruthlessly pursuing their infernal goals." It constituted a "deadly threat" to Germany and to "Western culture," because Jewry was making use of the "merely manual abilities of the human masses of the East," in order to create and use "the enormous storm of the armies of the Soviet system against Germany and thus against Europe." Defeat in the life-and-death struggle on the eastern front would "introduce the complete domination of Europe by international Jewry." The German people would "be delivered to the crude bestiality of a primitive race [the Russians], and the most valuable parts [of the German people] would succumb." Though he was confident that "the higher race" would be triumphant, he also believed that "Europe would be lost" if the Axis powers could not protect it.[60]

In the summer of 1942, North Africa became a major front in the war for Axis and Allied forces, as well as a larger focus of Nazi propaganda. In late May, General Erwin Rommel's Afrikakorps, driving eastward from Libya toward the Egyptian border, defeated the British Eighth Army at Tobruk and captured 28,000 soldiers. By the end of June, German forces had invaded Egypt and were within sixty miles of Alexandria. Following the disaster in Tobruk, the British changed military leaders, and the United States sped up delivery of new Sherman tanks to the front. In July a stalemate emerged at El Alamein, and General Bernard Montgomery assumed command of the Eighth Army, which in early September was able to repulse Rommel's attacks. In October 1942, the British Eighth Army crushed the Afrikakorps and pushed it back to Tripoli. The Nazi threat to the Jews in Palestine had been thwarted.[61] It did not, however, bring about a change in British policy as established in the White Paper of 1939 and maintained throughout the war. The White Paper had reversed the 1917 Balfour Declaration, which declared Britain's support for a national home for the Jewish people in Palestine. Instead it became the policy of the British government not to support the establishment of a Jewish state in Palestine and to limit Jewish immigration to 10,000 people a year, to amount to no more than a third of the population of Palestine. Though Churchill was sympathetic to Zionist aspirations and news of the Holocaust was public knowledge in Britain by fall 1942, these restrictions remained in place throughout the war and the Holocaust.[62]

In this context Nazi propaganda aimed at the Arab world shifted from pseudoacademic essays about England and the Middle East aimed at a

German and European audience to direct appeals to Arabs and Muslims in North Africa and the Middle East. In January 1942, the Office of Anti-Semitic Action in the Propaganda Ministry changed its name to the Office of Anti-Jewish Action. It did so in line with the general linguistic effort to avoid offending Arab and Islamic sensibilities through use of the term "anti-Semitic." Erroneously identifying the White Paper's permission for any Jews at all to emigrate to Palestine with support for the Balfour Declaration, Goebbels wrote in his diary of May 28, 1942, "The English are doing something very stupid" by promising Palestine to the Jews. He saw it as "wonderful news for us. We can make use of it in our propaganda aimed at the Arabs."[63] In fact, an alliance based on shared antagonism toward Britain and toward Zionism, as well on shared anti-Semitic ideology, had been emerging between the Nazis and the Grand Mufti of Jerusalem, Amin al-Husseini, since 1937. It was a bond that held strong throughout the period of World War II and the Holocaust.[64] From Berlin, where he was in exile after escaping arrest, following violent activities in Palestine in the 1930s and Iraq in 1941, the Grand Mufti broadcast radio addresses in support of the Nazi regime to the Arab world. On July 2, 1942, he addressed "the Egyptian people." He said that Rommel's initial victories in North Africa "filled all Arabs in the whole Orient with joy," because the Axis powers have "common enemies, the English and the Jews" and both were fighting against the Bolshevik danger. With the prospect of German occupation of Egypt, al-Husseini linked what he called the Egyptian struggle against British imperialism with the struggle of the Palestinians against the "concentrated British power and its alliance with the Jews."[65] As he noted in his diary of August 8, 1942, Goebbels was aware of English concerns that Jewish emigration to Palestine would antagonize the Arabs. In London, he remarked that there was "considerable fear of Muslims, a fact that is extraordinarily important for us and which we can use extensively in our propaganda directed at the world."[66]

The Propaganda Ministry extended its appeals not only to Arabs but to all Muslims. In the midst of the intense fighting in North Africa, the weekly *Periodical Service* directive stressed the need for deeper understanding of "the Islamic world as a cultural factor."[67] The service warned against "the danger" of underestimating the cultural contributions of the Orient. "Superficial discussions" due to "linguistic similarities between Arabs and Jews" had led to conflating the two groups. Much of the discussion of Islam in Germany was out of date or inspired by church polemics. German periodical editors needed to "strengthen and deepen existing [Nazi] sympathies in the Islamic world. We must draw this great cultural power, which in its essence is sharply anti-Bolshevik and anti-Jewish, closer to us. Through a friendly but not pandering presentation, we must convince the Muslims of the world that they have no better friend than the Germans. In the treatment of this theme, the words 'Semitism' and 'anti-Semitism' must be avoided."[68] As earlier directives had explained, Nazi policy should be described as hostile to the Jews rather than as anti-Semitic. Use of the latter term could undermine efforts to court support in the Arab world.

By August 1942, the tensions between Goebbels and Dietrich and their respective staffs had become sufficiently serious to warrant Hitler's intervention. At issue was control of the daily and weekly press directives and thus the power to control the press. Hitler supported Dietrich, who was thus assured full responsibility for and control over all the press divisions in the Propaganda Ministry, including the offices for the German press, foreign press, and periodicals.[69] The dispute did not represent any significant ideological difference of opinion. Rather, it demonstrated Hitler's determination to integrate daily and weekly instructions to the press with the military strategy that he was formulating. The best way for him to do so was to have directives conveyed by Dietrich, who worked in Hitler's headquarters daily and received orders or suggestions directly from him. Each morning, Dietrich provided Hitler with a digest of the international press. However much Hitler and Goebbels agreed on fundamentals, they did not see each other every day and were not working in the same place. Dietrich did; he thus became the conduit through which Hitler's wishes, hints, and suggestions were transmitted and elaborated into press directives. In an August memo, Hitler wrote that Dietrich was to deliver "the Führer's directives for the orientation of the press" to the divisions and staff members under him as well as to Goebbels, either by telex or by phone. He was to keep Goebbels informed of Hitler's views on matters of concern to the Propaganda Ministry. Goebbels was not allowed to give directives directly to the press but could relay them "only through the Reich Press Chief" or his representatives. In the event of differences of opinion between them, Dietrich was to discuss the matter with Goebbels directly, without, however, delaying dispersion of Hitler's directives. That is, Goebbels could not veto Dietrich's decisions, because they followed orders from Hitler. Hitler eliminated any doubt that it was Dietrich who was to control the daily press conference. "The Reich Press Chief represents the government before regular meetings of representatives of the press."[70]

Goebbels, however, remained in control of the *Word of the Week* and used it to produce a steady stream of anti-Semitic texts and images that summer. The issue for the week of August 8, "Ein weitblickender Engländer" ("A Farsighted Englishman") offered a blend of anti-Semitic and anti-American themes. The poster reproduced a series of drawings by an unnamed English artist, said to have been done in 1909, which offer a version of the history of the United States. An Uncle Sam figure comes up behind a Native American standing at the edge of a cliff. Uncle Sam then pushes the Indian off the cliff. A caricatured Jewish figure emerges from his hiding place behind a rock, pushes Uncle Sam over the cliff, and stands triumphant at the cliff's edge. The United States, having pushed aside the original inhabitants, has now been overrun in the late nineteenth and early twentieth century by a wave of Jewish immigrants, who have displaced traditional America. The poster quotes Heinrich Graetz, a nineteenth-century historian of the Jews, to the effect that the Jews will flourish in "the land of freedom and equality" and that "a large, powerful Jewry will emerge in the twentieth century." In large, bold letters the poster asserts, "This is exactly what has happened! The Jews have reached their goal in the United States. *Jews and comrades of the Jews are the real rulers in the USA.* They pushed the American people into the war in order to extend their power over Europe and the rest of the world. *We have taken up arms against them!* We will not lay down our arms until Jewry and its accomplices are defeated and its influence is finally destroyed. *The rule of Jewry will be brought to an end!*"[71]

The following week, the *Word of the Week* of August 19, 1942, pursued another anti-Semitic theme in again evoking the infamous Theodore Nathan Kaufman. "Der Jude Kaufman übertrumpft!" ("The Jew Kaufman Outdone!") showed the photo of "the Jew Theodore Nathan Kaufman" at his typewriter. It was the same photo that had adorned the cover of *The War Aim of World Plutocracy.* "*Buenos Aires Herald*" was superinscribed on it in red letters. To the right was a quote, lacking date or author, ostensibly taken from "the English newspaper" the *Buenos Aires Herald* in Argentina. The text imputed to the *Herald* the following sentiments: "The Germans are brutal beasts. They must be treated like devils. It would be madness when dealing with these creatures to distinguish between National Socialists and so-called Germans. *The only good German is a dead German.* Therefore, our motto should be: *The Germans must be exterminated!*" The text recalls Kaufman's plans to exterminate the Germans through sterilization in *Germany Must Perish!* "*We have all known for a long time what fate the Jews and plutocrats would like to inflict on us. That is why we are so determined to fight to victory this war that has been forced upon us.*"[72] What did a Jewish writer from New Jersey have to do with an editorial in a newspaper in Buenos Aires? Why would a newspaper in Argentina espouse such sentiments about a war in faraway Europe? If one accepted the assumption, implicit in the poster, that a unified, international subject called Jewry in alliance with "plutocrats" had expanded from the United States and England into South America, the mystery was solved. Again, the Ministry for Public Enlightenment and Propaganda revealed the deeper truth behind surface appearances. So Nathan Kaufman, who could not get any publisher in supposedly Jewish-dominated New York to publish *Germany Must Perish!* continued to serve as literally one of Nazi Germany's chief poster boys of the international Jewish conspiracy and its plans to obliterate Germany and exterminate the Germans.

The German press remained restrained in its attacks on the Jews in the early months of the death camp operations. On September 13, 1942, the front-page headline in *Der Völkische Beobachter* returned to anti-Semitic themes when it proclaimed: "Roosevelt and His Jews: Baruch Becomes the Economic Dictator of the USA." The article asserted that Roosevelt had appointed Bernard Baruch to direct all of American war production. With Baruch's "appointment," according to the *VB,* Jewry in the United States had finally achieved its goal: "the seizure of all power in the USA." Baruch, it asserted, was at the center of the "whole economic imperialist orientation of the Roosevelt circle."[73] The article fundamentally misconstrued the facts. In the summer of 1942, President Roosevelt had appointed Baruch, together with James B. Conant, president of Harvard University, and Karl Compton, president of the Massachusetts Institute of Technology, to lead a commission of technicians and engineers (subsequently known as the Baruch Committee) charged with recommending a solution for a possible wartime shortage of rubber. On September 11, 1942, after a more than monthlong examination, the Baruch Committee issued its recommendations. After stating that the United States faced the choice of "discomfort or defeat," the report recommended nationwide gasoline rationing and restrictions on automobile driving (including a thirty-five-mile-an-hour speed limit), to avoid "a civilian and military collapse."[74] After the attack on Pearl Harbor, 90 percent of America's rubber supply had been cut off, thereby causing an urgent need for both conservation and production of synthetic rubber. The Baruch Committee did not deal with issues relating to Jews. Baruch himself was an influential and highly respected figure in American public life but certainly no more so than the presidents of Harvard and MIT. The implication of the *VB* article was that Conant and Compton, two pillars of the WASP establishment, were part of a conspiracy to place Jews in control of the United States, did not understand or care that they were being used by the devilishly clever Baruch and his fellow Jews, and were traitors by virtue of having placed the interests of the Jews ahead of those of the "real" America.

Such assertions, however plausible they may have seemed to Nazi leaders and followers, presented a signal disadvantage when it came to non-Jewish Allied leaders and the English and American public: they constituted a sustained insult, in implying that the Allies lacked a mind or will of their own. As we have seen, a core theme of Nazi anti-Semitic propaganda was that of the conspiracy of nonequals. The propaganda endowed the Jews with supreme control and autonomy, while denying those attributes to their accomplices, stooges, and servants—including, in this case, presidents of two of America's most prestigious universities, and of course the president of the United States himself. According to this reasoning, James Conant and Karl Compton had not agreed to a thirty-five-mile-an-hour speed limit and gasoline rationing because they understood something about modern science, technology, and economics and wanted to contribute to the American war effort. Rather they, and the twenty-five engineers working for them, had sacrificed their professional integrity in order to aid a plan by the Jews to seize power. Nazi accusations that Roosevelt, Churchill, Stalin, or anyone else was a "tool" of the Jews had the same implication. The stooge in question lacked a mind of his own and had no motives for action other than those dictated by the Jews.

The governments of the United States, Great Britain, and the Soviet Union did not place Nazi extermination policies at the center of their rationale for fighting the German dictatorship.[75] Hitler's enemies went to great lengths to stress traditional reasons of state for their entry into the war—the Four Freedoms of the Atlantic Charter, freedom of the seas, the threat of aggression and territorial expansion, German attacks on American and British shipping after Pearl Harbor, the sheer evil of the Nazi regime itself, and in the case of the Soviet Union immediate survival following the German invasion. Nazi propaganda asserted that none of these were the real reasons for Allied policy and that Allied leaders were liars and hypocrites. To the extent that these leaders had popular support, Nazi propaganda constituted an ongoing insult to the citizens in democracies whom it accused, implicitly and then explicitly, of being at best naive or at worst duped by a small group of clever Jews. Despite surveys showing an increase in anti-Semitism in the United States during the war, however, the Nazis failed to undermine support for the war effort.[76]

The *Word of the Week* for September 30, 1942, followed up on the *VB* article about Baruch with "Die Maske fällt!" ("The Mask Falls!").[77] It erroneously claimed that American newspapers had reported that Roosevelt had appointed a new committee of personal advisers called the Brain Trust. The poster shows the boldfaced word *Jude* underneath photos of Bernard Baruch, Henry Morgenthau, Felix Frankfurter, and Representative Sol Bloom, mistakenly identified as a senator. (Bloom was the chairman of the Committee on Foreign Relations in the House of Representatives.) *Halbjude* (half-Jew) appeared beneath the photos of Fiorello LaGuardia. Secretary of State Cordell Hull was said to be "married to a Jewess." Large, boldfaced black letters against the telltale yellow background announced, "Here are the real rulers in the USA!" The text reads as follows:

What we have known for a long time has now been confirmed! In the service of his Jewish men behind the scenes, Roosevelt agitated for war and finally drove the American people into this hopeless war. In the service of world Jewry, the "defender of democracy" now demands unlimited dictatorial powers. *The appointment of the Jew Baruch to be economic director of the USA* shows where the path is leading . . . under servant of the Jews Roosevelt (*Judenknecht Roosevelt*). With this straw man at the top, Israel wants to establish Jewish world domination. The young peoples of Europe, united with their Japanese allies, will defeat this plan. *They will not lay down their arms until the enemy of humanity is annihilated.*[78]

Like the "Wire Pullers" wall newspaper of late May, "The Mask Falls!" used photography and its mass reproduction again to give faces to the now infamous names of the no longer secret or anonymous Jewish men behind the scenes. "Mimicry" had failed. The "mask" had been torn away. The Ministry for Public Enlightenment and Propaganda had focused the spotlight of publicity on the "wire pullers" and "men behind the scenes." For the Nazi party faithful and fellow travelers, and for German viewers who knew little or nothing about American politics and government and had no alternative sources of news, apart from the steady bombardment of statements about the international Jewish conspiracy, the sheer number of Jewish names and faces would have lent weight to the central Nazi thesis.

Responding to Goebbels's pleas to address a nation that yearned to see and hear him, Hitler spoke for an hour and ten minutes to a sympathetic audience in the Berlin Sportpalast on September 30, 1942. The speech was broadcast on national radio and to the armed forces, and prominently reported in the German press. He expressed confidence that Germany would bring about the "annihilation of the right arm of this international conspiracy of capitalism, plutocracy, and Bolshevism, which is the greatest danger ever to face the German people."[79] Germany's military capabilities were daunting, and its alliances impressive. It was now in possession of vast raw materials and agricultural resources in the occupied territories.[80] When Hitler spoke of the need for retaliation against the Allied bombing campaign, he again offered an incorrect date for his first uttering his prophecy about the Jews, and he repeated it as if the extermination of the Jews were an act of retaliation for the Allied bombing campaign. The following passage aroused great enthusiasm from the assembled listeners.

On September 1, 1939, in the meeting of the Reichstag I said two things. First, after we were forced into this war, neither the power of weapons nor the factor of time would defeat us; second, if Jewry unleashes an international world war in order to

"Down with Finance Enslavement! Vote National Socialist!" ("Nieder mit
der Finanzversklavung! Wählt National Sozialist!"), Nazi election poster
by Hans Schweitzer, 1924, in Erwin Schockel, *Das politische Plakat: Eine
psychologische Betrachtung* (Munich, Zentralverlag der NSDAP, 1939).

"The Wire Puller: Brain- and Manual Workers Vote for the People's Bloc" ("Der Drahtzeiher: Kopf- u. Handarbeiter wählt: Völkischen Bloc"), election poster, 1924, in Friedrich Arnold, *Anschläge: 220 politische Plakate als Dokumente der deutschen Geschichte, 1900–1980* (Ebenhausen: Langewiesche-Brandt, 1985).

Ein bezeichnendes Beispiel für die Tar-
nungsmanover des Judentums: das Plakat
für die Wahl zum Gouverneur des Staates
Neuyork zeigt einen 100prozentigen Ame-
rikaner, den man physiognomisch unter
die besten Präsidenten reihen könnte . . .

. . . Wenn man sich aber diesen Gouverneur, der ein enger Freund des Präsidenten Roosevelt ist,
einmal bei Lichte besieht, so findet man einen über seinen Wahlsieg triumphierend grinsenden Juden
mit Schnurrbart in den Nasenlöchern. Die orchideengeschmückte Sarah lächelt . . . Gouverneur Herbert H. Lehman, orthodoxer Jude, hat dank seiner Macht in zahlreichen Fällen Gangster begnadigt.

Photo of Governor Herbert H. Lehman in Hans Diebow, *Juden in USA* (Berlin:
Franz Eher Verlag, 1941), which claims to show and unmask an example of
Jewish "mimicry."

"The Jews Wanted the War!" ("Die Juden haben den Krieg gewollt!"), Ministry for Public Enlightenment and Propaganda, fall 1941. Bundesarchiv Koblenz, Koblenz, Germany, no. 003-020-023.

"The War Aim of World Plutocracy" ("Das Kriegsziel der Weltplutokratie"),
image by Hans Schweitzer, text by Wolfgang Diewerge, afterword by Joseph
Goebbels, Reich Ministry for Public Enlightenment and Propaganda, Berlin,
1941 (Berlin: Franz Eher Verlag, 1941).

Er fordert völlige Ausrottung des deutschen Volkes

Theodor Kaufman, Präsident der amerikanischen Friedensliga und engster Mitarbeiter des Rooseveltberaters Samuel Roseman (s. S. 13), hat ein Buch geschrieben, das unter dem Titel „Deutschland muß sterben" in großer Auflage herausgebracht worden ist. In jüdischen Literatenkreisen von Neuyork wird erzählt, daß Roosevelt die Hauptpunkte dieses Buches angeregt und wichtigste Teile selbst diktiert habe. In diesem Buch wird das Vernichtungsprogramm des deutschen Volkes entwickelt: „1. Die deutsche Wehrmacht wird gefangengenommen (!), sterilisiert und in Arbeitskommandos . . . verteilt. 2. Die deutsche Bevölkerung, und zwar Männer unter 60 Jahren und Frauen unter 45 Jahren, wird sterilisiert. Somit ist das Aussterben des deutschen Volkes innerhalb von 2 Generationen sichergestellt."

Photo of Nathan Kaufman in Hans Diebow, *Juden in USA* (Berlin: Franz Eher Verlag, 1941). Caption reads: "He Demands the Complete Extermination of the German People" ("Er fordert völlige Ausrottung des deutschen Volkes").

"Always the Same Goal: Germany Must Be Exterminated!" ("Immer das gleiche Ziel: Deutschland muss vernichtet werden!"), *Parole der Woche*, October 10, 1941, Reich Propaganda Directorate of the Nazi Party. Landeshauptarchiv Koblenz, Koblenz, Germany, no. 1717.

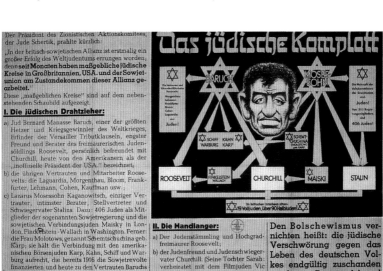

"The Jewish Conspiracy" ("Das Jüdische Komplott"), *Parole der Woche*, December 10, 1941, Reich Propaganda Directorate of the Nazi Party. Landeshauptarchiv Koblenz, no. 1709.

"Jewish Conspiracy against Europe" ("Juden Komplott gegen Europa"),
Reich Ministry for Propaganda and Public Enlightenment, summer 1941.
Imperial War Museum, London, PST 8395.

"The Wire Pullers: They Are Only Jews! ("Die Drahtzieher! Es sind nur Juden!"),
Parole der Woche, May 27, 1942, Reich Propaganda Directorate of the Nazi
Party. Landeshauptarchiv Koblenz, no. 1800.

Ein weitblickender Engländer

sah im Jahre 1909, also vor 33 Jahren, die Entwicklung der Vereinigten Staaten voraus, als er diese Zeichnung veröffentlichte.

Viel früher schon, nämlich im Jahre 1885, entschlüpfte dem bekannten jüdischen Historiker Heinrich Graetz in einem Vortrag in London folgendes bemerkenswerte Geständnis:

„Das jüdische Volk wird einst in Amerika, in dem Lande der Freiheit und Gleichheit, aufblühen. Ein großes, mächtiges Judentum wird entstehen im 20. Jahrhundert."

Genau so ist es gekommen!

In den Vereinigten Staaten haben die Juden ihr Ziel erreicht. Juden und Judengenossen sind die wahren Herren in USA. Sie haben das amerikanische Volk in den Krieg getrieben, um ihre Macht jetzt auch über Europa und die übrige Welt auszudehnen.

Dagegen setzen wir uns zur Wehr!

Wir werden die Waffen nicht eher niederlegen, bis das Judentum und seine Helfershelfer zu Boden geschlagen und sein Einfluß endgültig vernichtet ist.

Mit der Herrschaft des Judentums wird Schluß gemacht!

HISTORY OF THE UNITED STATES

"A Farsighted Englishman . . . . The Domination of the Jews Will Be Brought to an End!" ("Ein weitblickender Engländer: Mit der Herrschaft des Judentums wird Schluß gemacht!"), *Parole der Woche*, August 8, 1942, Reich Propaganda Directorate of the Nazi Party. Landeshauptarchiv Koblenz, Koblenz, Germany, no. 1722.

"The Jew Kaufman Outdone!" ("Der Jude Kaufman übertrumpft!"), *Parole der Woche*, Reich Propaganda Directorate of the Nazi Party, August 19, 1942. Landeshauptarchiv Koblenz, Koblenz, Germany, no. 1758.

"The Mask Falls! They Are the Real Rulers in the USA!" ("Die Maske fällt! Das sind die wahren Herren in USA.!"), *Parole der Woche*, September 30, 1942, Reich Propaganda Directorate of the Nazi Party. Landeshauptarchiv Koblenz, no. 1787.

"They Will Stop Laughing!!!" ("Das Lachen wird ihnen vergehen!!!"), *Parole der Woche*, Reich Propaganda Directorate of the Nazi Party, November/ December 1942. Hoover Institution Archives, GE 3848.

"Who Bears the Guilt for the War? Roosevelt, Churchill, and Stalin Bear the Responsibility for the War in the Eyes of History. Behind Them, However, Stands the Jew" ("Wer ist am Kriege schuld? Roosevelt, Churchill und Stalin tragen vor der Geschichte die Verantwortung für diesen Krieg. Hinter ihnen aber steht der Jude"), *Parole der Woche,* Reich Propaganda Directorate of the Nazi Party, November 18, 1942. Institut für Zeitungsforschung der Stadt Dortmund, Dortmund, Germany, *Parole der Woche,* Folge 47.

"Behind the Enemy Powers: The Jew" ("Hinter den Feindmächten: der Jude"),
Ministry for Public Enlightenment and Propaganda, spring/summer 1943.
Bundesarchiv Koblenz, Koblenz, Germany, no. 003-020-021.

"He Bears the Guilt for the War!" ("Der ist schuld am Kriege!"), Hans Schweitzer, Ministry for Public Enlightenment and Propaganda, spring/summer 1943. Bundesarchiv Koblenz, Koblenz, Germany, no. 003-020-020.

"The Jew: Instigator of the War, Prolonger of the War" ("Der Jude, Kriegsanstifter, Kriegsverlängerer"), Hans Schweitzer, Ministry for Public Enlightenment and Propaganda, spring/summer 1943. Bundesarchiv Koblenz, Koblenz, Germany, no. 003-020-022.

bring about the extermination *(Ausrottung)* of the Aryan peoples of Europe, then it will be not the Aryan peoples, but rather Jewry, that will be exterminated [long applause]. The wire pullers of the lunatic in the White House have dragged one people after another into the war. In the same measure, however, an anti-Semitic wave has flooded over the peoples. It will move further and seize one state after another that enters this war. Each will emerge from it one day as an anti-Semitic state. The Jews in Germany once laughed about my prophecies. I don't know if they are laughing today or if the laughter has already gone out of them. I can promise only one thing. They will stop laughing everywhere. And with this prophecy as well I will be proved right [vociferous expressions of agreement from the audience].[81]

The audience reaction in the Sportpalast suggests that the Nazi faithful understood that Hitler was telling them in language by then familiar that the Nazi regime was at that moment murdering the Jews. Moreover, the clear meaning of the noun "extermination" and the verb "exterminate" and the political and temporal context in which Hitler repeated them, as well as his insistence that he was a prophet, all indicated that he had ordered and was then implementing the destruction of the Jews. Despite his refusal to use the first-person pronoun, his reference to his own prophecy indicated that Hitler was then engaged in the mass murder of the Jews. Any benign interpretation of references to Jews' not "laughing any more" strains credulity. The inclination to view political statements as deceptions designed to hide real intentions, rather than as assertions in which word and meaning coincided, was a barrier to understanding what Hitler meant. His audience in Berlin appeared to suffer from no such handicap. Perhaps some wondered what Hitler meant by adding "everywhere" to his promise to end Jewish laughter. Perhaps they may have assumed that since the Jewish conspiracy was international, he was seeking to extend the Final Solution of the Jewish question in Europe to an act of global genocide against Jews everywhere. In any case, his listeners applauded.

Six weeks later the quotation reproduced earlier from Hitler's September 30 speech appeared on approximately 125,000 copies of the *Word of the Week* for the end of November 1942: "Das Lachen wird ihnen vergehen!!!" ("They Will Stop Laughing!!!") appeared in large white letters against a black background. The text is in bold type set against the usual telltale yellow background. The word *Judentum* in the key sentence referring to the extermination of Jewry appears in outsize boldface type, followed by an exclamation point. On the left, above "Jews around Roosevelt," are photos of a laughing Franklin Roosevelt and men in overcoats and fedoras. At the bottom, "They will stop laughing everywhere!!" appears in larger white type.[82] We do not know what readers and listeners made of the speech when they heard or read it, or what people thought about the combination of text and images they saw six weeks later when it was distributed and became the texture of German daily life; however, we do know that millions of people walked past this wall newspaper for a whole week and that thirty-four other issues of *Word of the Week* bearing more or less pronounced attacks on Jews were similarly displayed. We know that if people were not listening to the radio or reading the paper on September 30, 1942, they had a second opportunity to read this key passage from Hitler's speech.

There is no body of reliable evidence, whether in the form of police reports or memoirs, that tells us how many people had the intellectual curiosity, political acumen, and moral courage to conclude that this wall newspaper was an announcement of mass murder. All that we can conclude with confidence is that in late November 1942, the poster "They Will Stop Laughing!!!" became an extraordinary part of the experience of daily life for millions of literate, aware pedestrians walking around the villages, towns, and major cities of Nazi Germany.

On October 4, 1942, the director of the Four-Year Plan, chief of the Luftwaffe Hermann Göring, who had been designated Hitler's successor in 1934 and was generally regarded as the second most powerful figure in the Nazi regime, demonstrated that he too could recite the Nazi tale of wire pullers and marionettes. In the Berlin Sportpalast he warned: "If we lose the war, you [Germans] will be annihilated." The war was not a repeat of World War I. It was "a great race war . . . about whether the German and Aryan will survive or if the Jew will rule the world . . . that is why we are fighting abroad [applause]. We know the Jews! You can be sure that Churchill and Roosevelt . . . are all laughable little marionettes, drunken and mentally ill people, who dangle from the Jews' wires. The Jew may hide behind different faces, but his cucumberlike nose is still there. The Jew is behind everything, and it is he who has declared a fight to the death, and to ruin, against us."[83] He added that Germans must not delude themselves into thinking that Jews made distinctions among different kinds of Germans and would spare those who were not Nazis. Their "yearning for revenge encompasses the entire German people." They wanted to "annihilate everything that is German and racially pure."[84] So even during these months in which Hitler was expressing confidence that the war was going well, Göring fanned the flames of sheer and unrelenting terror among the populace at the prospect of mass murder of the Germans at the hands of the Jews. As the tide of war turned against Germany, the specter of international Jewry's alleged plans to exterminate all Germans remained a frequent element in Nazi propaganda.

On November 8, 1942, Hitler delivered his annual speech in Munich to the Nazi old guard in commemoration of the Beer Hall Putsch attempt of 1923. It was broadcast over the radio and printed in the press the following day. For the third time in 1942, he repeated his famous prophecy. The enemies of 1942 were the same as those of the Weimar era, except that they were now arrayed on the international plane, from "the chief of this international Freemason lodge, the half-Jew Roosevelt and his Jewish Brain Trust to Jewry in its purest expression in Marxist-Leninist Russia." It was "no accident that the same state [the United States] that then believed it could defeat Germany with a wave of lying propaganda now brings to the fore a man with the same mission. Then he was called Wilson. Today he is called Roosevelt." The old Germany—that is, the Kaiserreich—was "without any enlightenment about the problem of the Jewish question and the impact of the power of the Jews," and therefore it "fell victim to the [American] assault."

Another group, once very powerful in Germany, had since learned, "National Socialist prophecies are not empty phrases. This is the key power that is the source of all our misfortune: international Jewry. You will recall the Reichstag session in which I stated: If Jewry imagines itself to be able to lead an international world war to exterminate the European races, then the result will not be the extermination of the European races but rather the extermination of Jewry in Europe! [applause] The Jews always laughed at me as a prophet. Those who were laughing then are laughing no longer. Those who are still laughing will in a short time perhaps also no longer be laughing . . . [applause]."[85] While Wilson and the Jews had been able to defeat a Germany as yet unenlightened by anti-Semitism, the "half-Jew Roosevelt" would be defeated, just as the Nazis had defeated their opponents in the Weimar era. Again, the meaning of Hitler's words was clear. The Jews had intended to "exterminate"—that is, to kill—the Europeans. Instead, while yet again avoiding the first person and active verbs clearly linking subject and object, Hitler again let his audience know that the Nazi regime was in the process of exterminating—that is, killing—the Jews. The most plausible interpretation of the comment that the Jews were no longer laughing was that something of a catastrophic nature was being done to them. The applause with which his comment was greeted indicated that this audience approved of what it regarded as justified retaliation against Germany's greatest enemy.

Following Hitler's speech in Munich, Dietrich ordered an intensification of anti-Semitic themes in the newspaper and periodicals. The November 13, 1942, issue of the *Periodical Service* drew editors' attention to Hitler's Munich speech regarding the "gangster nature" of President Roosevelt. Next to Churchill, Roosevelt was "the main criminal of this war" and was acting "on behalf of international Jewry." Owing to the failure of his domestic economic program, Roosevelt had sharpened Germany's conflict with Poland, cooperated with "the war party in England," made empty promises of aid to France, and thereby driven Europe into war.[86] These accusations were a mix of half-truths and lies. To the extent possible, given the constraints imposed by neutrality laws, a reluctant Congress, and the 1940 Presidential election, Roosevelt had supported anti-Nazi forces in Europe and ordered the U.S. Navy to protect shipping in the Atlantic from German submarines beginning in 1939. He did so with the aims of deterring Hitler from starting a war, of preventing Britain's defeat, and of thwarting Hitler's hopes for a quick and decisive victory by 1942. Roosevelt had encouraged the French government to hold out. After Pearl Harbor, of course, American aid to Britain expanded significantly. In this sense, the war did continue in Europe in part because Roosevelt played a key role in preventing Hitler from ending it with an early victory. In late October and early November 1942, Montgomery's Eighth Army defeated Rommel's Afrikakorps. Shortly thereafter, American and British forces landed in Morocco and Algeria. In the Mediterranean, at least, the Allies had seized the initiative and placed the Axis powers on the defensive.[87] The Reich Press Office intensified its anti-American propaganda. The *Periodical Service* directive of November 20, 1942, included a note on "Gangsterism and Jewry in the USA." It referred to Roosevelt's "gangster methods" and his "close links with organized crime" and claimed that the Jews were the "most important" cause of organized crime in the United States.[88]

The *Word of the Week* for the week of November 18, 1942, "Wer ist am Kriege schuld?" ("Who Bears the Guilt for the War?") offers further evidence of the intensification of anti-Semitic propaganda.[89] A collage of Roosevelt, Churchill, and Stalin is striking because Roosevelt's image is the largest, followed by those of Churchill and Stalin, even though it was the Soviet Union that was bearing the brunt of the fighting. The text also assigns greatest blame to Roosevelt, exceeded only by that of the Jews:

Britain, in the service of the general warmonger Roosevelt, stirred up Poland against Germany, forced France to adopt the British declaration of war against Germany, then pushed Norway, Holland, Belgium, Greece, and Yugoslavia into the war, and finally allied with the utterly destructive force of Bolshevism. Churchill bears an enormous amount of guilt [for this war]. *Roosevelt, Churchill, and Stalin carry the responsibility for this war in the eyes of history. BEHIND THEM, HOWEVER, STANDS THE JEW.* International Jewry wanted this war, to realize its goal of world domination. Roosevelt, Churchill, and Stalin are the Jews' willing tools. *The guilty party for this war, for all the distress and suffering it has brought to the peoples, IS JEWRY.*[90]

The text stands the causal connections on their head. The poster presents World War II as the result of British and American aggression in the service "the Jew"—of the power behind the scenes—rather than as a series of wars of aggression launched by Nazi Germany, in response to which the other countries of Europe, in self-defense, allied themselves with Britain. Nazi propaganda never abandoned or qualified in the slightest its stance of utter innocence with regard to Nazi Germany's role in the outbreak and escalation of World War II or the projection of its own responsibility onto others.

On November 26, 1942, the Grand Mufti of Jerusalem again broadcast from Berlin a speech on German radio in Arabic to North African listeners. Al-Husseini's speech, attacking the United States in the aftermath of the American landings, was a striking example of the translation of Nazi propaganda into the idioms of the Arab world.

The strength of Jewish influence in America has clearly come to the fore in this war. Jews and capitalists have pushed the United States to expand this war, in order to expand their influence in new and wealthy areas. The North Africans know very well what unhappiness the Jews have brought to them. They know that the

Jews are the vanguard fighters of imperialism that mistreated North Africa for so long. They [North Africans] also know the extent to which the Jews served the imperialists as spies and agents and how they seek the energy resources of North African territories to expand their wealth . . . The American intervention in North Africa strengthens the power of the Jews, increases their influence, and doubles their misdeeds. America is the greatest agent of the Jews, and the Jews are rulers in America.[91]

Two weeks later, on December 11, 1942, al-Husseini again spoke over German radio to "the Arabs," this time about the value of martyrdom. Before World War II broke out, the Arabs had been fighting for twenty years against "the English and the Jews who were always hidden behind them."[92] The Arab peoples had shed "noble blood" for the freedom and independence of Palestine, Egypt, Syria, Iraq, and the Arabian peninsula. "The spilled blood of martyrs is the water of life. It has revived Arab heroism, as water revives dry ground. The martyr's death is the protective tree in whose shadows marvelous plants again bloom."[93] The goal of "English-Jewish policy" was to divide Palestine and to dominate the remainder of the Arab countries. "We Arabs," al-Husseini continued, those who have fought the English, "should clearly join the Axis powers and their allies in common struggle against the common enemy. Doing so for us means the continuation of the fight we have fought alone for the past twenty years. Today the powerful enemies of our enemies stand on our side."[94] Yet if England and her allies, "God forbid," were to win the war, "Israel would rule the whole world, the Arabian fatherland would suffer an unholy blow, and the Arab countries would be torn apart and turned into Jewish colonies." If England and her allies were defeated, "the Jewish danger" for the Arab countries would be defeated. Millions of Arabs would be freed, and millions more Muslims would be saved. The defeat of the Soviet Union would also liberate millions more Muslims suffering under Soviet rule. America, as it "was subject to Jewish will," offered nothing to the Arabs.[95] For al-Husseini, both short-term tactical considerations relating to shared enemies and longer-term ideological affinities argued in favor of Arab support for the Nazis.

Since summer 1941, reports of massive German atrocities against the Jewish population of Europe had been trickling out to Allied governments. In December 1942, the Allied governments finally spoke out loud and clear to denounce the extermination of Europe's Jewish population that was then in progress. On December 4, 63 United States senators and 181 members of the House of Representatives passed a joint congressional resolution declaring that Nazi anti-Jewish policy sought "to exterminate a whole people." The resolution expressed support for the United States' "declared and traditional policy" favoring a Jewish national homeland in Palestine. Senator Robert Wagner of New York declared: "We have been impelled to reiterate this position at this time by horrifying reports which have been pouring in concerning the mass slaughter of European Jews."[96] Those reports had been pouring in to other Allied governments in power and in exile as well. On December 17, 1942, the American, Belgian, Czechoslovak, Greek, Luxemburg, Dutch, Norwegian, Polish, Soviet, British, and Yugoslav governments, along with the French National Committee in London, simultaneously issued a joint declaration. The attention of these governments, it asserted,

has been drawn to numerous reports from Europe that the German authorities, not content with denying to persons of the Jewish race in all the territories over which their barbaric rule has been extended, the most elementary human rights, are now carrying into effect Hitler's oft-repeated intention to exterminate the Jewish people in Europe.

From all the occupied countries Jews are being transported in conditions of appalling horror and brutality to Eastern Europe. In Poland, which has been made the principal Nazi slaughterhouse, the ghettos established by the German invader are being systematically emptied of all Jews except for a few highly skilled workers required for war industries. None of those taken away is ever heard of again. The able-bodied are slowly worked to death in labor camps. The infirm are left to die of exposure and starvation or are deliberately massacred in mass executions. The number of victims of these bloody cruelties is reckoned in many hundreds of thousands of entirely innocent men, women and children.

The above-mentioned governments and the French National Committee condemn in the strongest terms this bestial policy of cold-blooded extermination. They declare that such events can only strengthen the resolve of all freedom-loving people to overthrow the barbarous Hitlerite tyranny. They reaffirm their solemn resolution to insure that those responsible for these crimes shall not escape retribution, and to press on with the necessary practical results to this end.[97]

The Allied declaration was a remarkable statement. Eleven governments now took Hitler's threats against the Jews seriously. Their declaration contained a considerable amount of accurate information regarding deportations, Poland as the site of mass murder, and exposure, starvation, and mass executions, as well as an estimate that "many hundreds of thousands" of innocent people had already been murdered. It did not include details about mass murder in the gas chambers, yet the key point, regarding the ongoing Nazi policy of mass murder, was correct. Moreover, the Allied governments were not willing to allow anti-Semitism in the Allied countries to stand in the way of a moral condemnation of Nazi Germany's genocidal policies. On the contrary, reports of atrocities against the Jews stiffened Allied determination to defeat the Nazi regime.

In London, on the same day, the members of the House of Commons stood in silence in memory of the Jews murdered by the Nazis, to protest what one member referred to as "this disgusting barbarism."

Foreign Minister Anthony Eden told Parliament that those responsible would be brought to justice, though at the moment Britain could do little to aid them. The House of Commons listened "in absolute silence" when J. A. E. de Rothschild said that there were many in Britain "who, but for the grace of God, might themselves be among the victims of Nazi tyranny at the present time. They might have been in those ghettos, those concentration camps, those slaughterhouses." He expressed the hope that the United Nations declaration would "percolate throughout German-infested countries and give some faint hope and courage to those unfortunate victims of insult, torment and degradation."[98] For the first time since the outbreak of the war, Britain's Political Warfare Executive, which conducted the propaganda war against Nazi Germany, made Nazi persecution of the Jews a central theme of British propaganda in Europe in its weekly directives of December 10 and 24.[99]

December 1942 marked a significant turning point in the propaganda war in World War II. So long as the facts about actual mass murder remained hidden or unacknowledged, Nazi anti-Semitic propaganda threatened to undermine Allied governments in these largely Christian societies through appeals to anti-Semitism. After mass murder became a public theme of Allied propaganda, however periodic or irregular a theme it may have been, Nazi barbarism, rather than the alleged evils of the Jews, became the subject of conversation in the Allied and occupied countries. Traditional anti-Semitism in the Allied countries was not a "warrant for genocide." Allied willingness to stress the issue of mass murder publicly revealed the limits of traditional anti-Semitism, which gradually ceased to work to the advantage of the Nazi regime. Reports of the Final Solution underscored the stark moral dichotomy between Nazi Germany and its allies, on the one hand, and the United Nations, on the other. They reinforced the Allies' conviction that this was a war between freedom and tyranny, good and evil, civilization and barbarism.

The response Goebbels made to these Allied statements was to dismiss them as false "atrocity stories." Never once did he, Dietrich, or any other Nazi official or propagandist mention the substance of such allegations, even if only to deny their veracity. Perhaps in response to the congressional resolution of December 4, Goebbels noted in his diary of December 9, "The Jews in the whole world are mobilizing against us. They report frightful atrocities that we have supposedly committed against the Jewish race in Poland" and threaten to bring the participants to justice after the war. These reports and warnings "cannot stop us from implementing a radical solution to the Jewish question. Moreover, the matter will rest with these threats. The Jews in Europe will probably never again have anything special to report."[100] On December 12 he wrote, "The atrocity campaign about Poland and the Jewish question is assuming enormous dimensions on the other side. I fear that over time we cannot master the issue with silence. We have to have some kind of answer . . . It is best to go over to the offensive and talk about English atrocities in India or in the Middle East. Perhaps that will get the English to keep quiet. In any case, by doing so, we change the subject and raise another issue."[101] Earlier that same day he informed officials at his daily Minister's Conference that it was time "to do something about" Britain's "propaganda campaign" regarding "alleged anti-Jewish atrocities in the East." The subject was "rather delicate." It was best "not to engage in polemics but instead give particular prominence to British atrocities in India, in Iran, and in Egypt. Our best weapon against this propaganda campaign is to go on the offensive" and to have the German press to feature such stories.[102]

In his diary entry of December 14, Goebbels wrote, "The English and Americans are glad that we are cleaning up the Jewish mob. But the Jews will put pressure on the British and American press. We do not want to get into this matter at all in public. Rather, I am ordering that we begin a propaganda campaign against the English concerning their treatment of colonial peoples . . . I hope that in this way we can succeed in getting the English to respond to our attacks. Then we will be not only the defender but also the attacker."[103] In a striking reaffirmation of the unity of private conviction and public propaganda, he said Jewish protests "would not help the Jews a bit. The Jewish race prepared this war. It is the intellectual root of all of the unhappiness that has broken over the world. Jewry must pay for its crime with the obliteration of the Jewish race in Europe and perhaps in the whole world, just as the Führer prophesied in his speech in the Reichstag."[104] At no time, either in public or in private, did Goebbels deny that the Nazi regime was murdering the Jews of Europe. Rather he called the accusations un-specified atrocity stories, offered justifications for actions whose details he and Dietrich were able to conceal, and then changed the subject.

At the same December 14 Minister's Conference, Goebbels again commented on the "worldwide Jewish propaganda campaign against Germany." He said, "This action . . . must at all costs be opposed by a German counter-action. There can be no question of a complete or practical refutation of the allegations of anti-Jewish atrocities, but merely a German campaign concerned with British and American atrocities throughout the world. There must be reports therefore about India, Iran, North Africa, and about acts of violence by Britain and America generally, and these extensive reports must be put out repeatedly and with the greatest emphasis." The reports, he added, should be diffused both at home and abroad.[105] At his Minister's Conference of December 16, he said he regarded creating a "general hullabaloo about atrocities [by the Allies] as our best chance of getting away from the embarrass-ing subject of the Jews. Things must be so arranged that each party ac-cuses every other of committing atrocities. The general hullabaloo will then eventually result in this subject disappearing from the agenda."[106] As noted earlier, denial of the uniqueness of the Holocaust, and its con-flation with other wartime "atrocity stories," were essential components of the propaganda that accompanied it.

Though the German people could not hear Anthony Eden's state-ment on December 17 in the House of Commons, Goebbels did. That evening he responded in his diary that the Jews were again talking about "supposed atrocities in Poland." He saw Eden's speech as evidence of the "strong influence of the Jews on English public opinion" but was not worried: "We have so many Jews as hostages in our hands that world Jewry will be careful not to engage in actions it knows will send us into a rage."[107] He noted that in the House of Commons, "Rothschild spoke and tearfully bemoaned the fate of Polish Jews," and that the Parliament rose and observed a moment of silence. This act, he added, was appropriate, given that "the Parliament is in reality a kind of Jewish stock exchange. The English really are Jews among the Aryans. The perfumed English foreign minister cuts a fine figure among these figures from the synagogue. His whole education and also his entire bearing can be characterized as thoroughly Jewish."[108]

The Allied declaration regarding the murder of Europe's Jews took place a day before the opening of the Islamic Institute in Berlin. Grand Mufti al-Husseini gave a speech at the event in which he argued that Arabs, and indeed all Muslims, should support the Nazi cause. By then he had held private meetings with Hitler and Himmler and had corresponded with Foreign Minister Joachim von Ribbentrop. With Goebbels in attendance, al-Husseini spoke from a text that had been approved by von Ribbentrop.[109] Before the event al-Husseini had written to Hitler to express his "friendship and sympathy to your excellency and to the German people. We are firmly convinced of the close cooperation between the millions of Mohammedans in the world, and Germany and its allies in the Three-Power Pact that is directed against the common enemies, Jews, Bolsheviks, and Anglo-Saxons and which, with God's help, will lead to a victorious outcome of this war for the Axis powers. This victory will bring happiness and good fortune to the Axis powers, the Muslims, and all of humanity."[110]

His speech included an extended attack on the Jews.[111] "The Jews were the bitterest enemies of the Muslims. They had always expressed their antagonism with cunning and deception. Every Muslim knows how, from the first days of young Islam, the Jews have assaulted him and his beliefs," and what "hatred . . . intrigues . . . [and] conspiracies" the Jews had directed at the Muslims. The Koran, he continued, was full of stories of Jewish lack of character, Jewish lies and deceptions. Just as they had been full of hatred against Muslims in the days of the Prophet, so they were in modern times. In Palestine they were trying to establish "a base from which to extend their power over neighboring Islamic countries."[112] The Jews were "a destructive element on earth" that had unleashed wars and played nations off against one another. Their "essence" was to keep the world in turbulence. Al-Husseini then misconstrued Chaim Weizmann as having said that World War II was a "Jewish war." The Jews dominated England and the United States and were the force behind "godless Communism." Jewry "drove the nations into this war of attrition" and dominated British policy. Together with the Allies, the Jews were "the Muslims' bitter enemies." Al-Husseini added that the Allied attacks in North Africa in fall 1942 demonstrated that the Jews, Americans, English, and Bolsheviks were all the "irreconcilable enemy of Islam" and had "oppressed and persecuted forty million Muslims . . . This war, which was unleashed by world Jewry," he continued, offered "Muslims the best opportunity to free themselves from these instances of persecution and oppression."[113] He concluded with a religious appeal to Muslims: God would help them to victory if they displayed sufficient willingness to sacrifice. The Reich Press Office directive for December 18 instructed that the Grand Mufti's speech be widely reported.[114]

The editors of Die Judenfrage joined in this coordinated campaign. The December 15 issue led with "Zionism's Postwar Program," which noted with regret that support for a Jewish national homeland had grown in the United States and England. As Die Judenfrage put it, with the help of the "plutocratic states, world Jewry" was preparing to "conquer Palestine for itself alone and thereby establish a position for world power in the future," from which it could "terrorize the Arab population."[115] More noteworthy, in the same issue was an essay, "Judaism and Islam as Opposites," by the now Professor Dr. Johann von Leers.[116] Von

Leers, who had previously displayed no particular expertise in the history of Islam, now presented a history of the Jews in the Arab and Islamic world marked by long-standing Islamic hostility toward the Jews. He noted that the Koran referred to the Jews as satanic. Arab political leaders had "paralyzed" Jewish activities, and the Jews had come to hate Islam. Even the Christian Crusades had been "to a not inconsiderable extent unleashed by Jewish agitation." Van Leers applauded what he depicted as Islam's long history of anti-Jewish sentiment and action. "Unquestionably, one result of Muhammad's hostility to the Jews was that oriental Jewry was completely paralyzed by Islam. Jewry's resistance was broken. Jewry in the Orient has not participated at all in Jewry's powerful climb to power in the last two centuries." Because of legally sanctioned discrimination, the despised Jews "vegetated" in narrow urban streets. In contrast to Europe, where the Jews were allowed to receive interest or engage in theft, the Arab and Islamic world kept the Jews in a state of fear. "If the rest of the world adopted a similar policy, we would not have a Jewish question today." Hence von Leers celebrated "the immortal contribution of the religion of Islam." It prevented the threatened domination of Arabia by the Jews. In so doing, Islam "opened the path to a higher culture [and] gave its adherents an education and human form that still today makes a Muslim who is serious about his faith one of the most noble phenomena in this confused and chaotic world."[117] Beyond the strategic and short-term tactical issues of the North African campaign of summer and fall 1942, von Leers pointed to apparent intellectual and moral foundations for an alliance between the Third Reich and radicalized Arabs and fundamentalist Muslims.

On the last night of 1942, faced with grim news from Stalingrad, Goebbels wrote in his diary that his primary mission in the coming weeks would be to prepare for "total war" on the home front.[118] With the turning of the tide in the war at Stalingrad in early 1943, Hitler ordered the most intense and sustained barrage of anti-Semitic broadcasts, headlines, and articles in the daily and periodical press of the entire period of World War II and the Holocaust. A rising river of anti-Semitic hatred in the period from June 1941 to late 1942 had accompanied Nazi military success and expansion, the murders by the *Einsatzgruppen* and *Ornungspolizei* units, and the start of full operations in the death camps. In 1943 the combined and coordinated efforts of Dietrich, Goebbels, and their staffs turned that river into a raging flood.

6 "The Jews Are Guilty of Everything"

The flood of radical anti-Semitic propaganda began in late winter 1943. The torrent continued in two intense bursts, in April through July, and in October and November. Between January 1939 and April 1945, eighty-four anti-Semitic lead stories appeared in the *Der Völkische Beobachter*. Between 50 and 60 percent of them appeared in 1943. In 1942 Goebbels, Schweitzer, and the graphic artists working on the *Word of the Week,* and the anti-Semitic intellectuals writing for *Die Judenfrage,* had done their best to keep the propaganda apparatus of the regime and party supplied with up-to-date attacks on the Jews. In 1943, their efforts were equaled and at times surpassed by the efforts of Otto Dietrich and his staff in the Reich Press Office. With daily orders from Hitler, they issued press directives calling for printing an unprecedented amount of anti-Semitic propaganda in the thousands of German newspapers and periodicals subject to the control of the Press Office.

As Dietrich had asserted in 1939, the press had become an arm of the state. It printed only the news that the government saw fit to print. Its sins of commission and omission were an important chapter in the history of the Final Solution. The stories the German press did not print in 1943 included those on the closing of the Chelmno death camp in November 1942, by which point between 150,000 and 300,000 Jews had

been murdered there; the operation of the other major death camps—
Majdanek, Sobibor, Belzec, Treblinka, and Auschwitz-Birkenau—at full
capacity in winter and spring 1943 (there were 15,000 murders a day at
Belzec alone); the deportations of Jews from Berlin, Hamburg, Cologne,
and Munich in February 1943; the movement of trains to places called
Auschwitz, Treblinka, and Sobibor; and deportations and mass shootings in eastern Galicia, the Balkans, Salonika in Greece, and numerous
small towns and cities in Poland. Needless to say, the first armed revolt
anywhere against Nazi occupation, the Warsaw Ghetto uprising, and
its suppression in April and May 1943 were also not news considered
fit to print in the Nazi-controlled press.[1]

Hitler's New Year's greeting to the nation on January 1, 1943, set the
tone for what did find its way into print. The current war was a matter
of "existence or nonexistence" for the Germans. The Germans would
not again make the mistake of believing in the good will of the United
States and England, as they had after World War I. "Therefore, when
the English and American Jews announce that it is the Allies' intention
to take the children away from the German people, slaughter millions
of young men, split Germany up, and turn it permanently into a defenseless object for exploitation under capitalist or Bolshevik auspices,
they don't have to tell us, because we already know it." National Socialist Germany would never capitulate or succumb to that fate.[2] In his
message to the armed forces on the same day, Hitler spoke of German
offensives on the eastern front and "from Norway to the Spanish border." An invasion of the Continent from the West would lead to the
enemy's "immediate annihilation." France was now totally occupied.
Germany and Italy were somehow in an improved position to fight in
North Africa. In the Atlantic, German submarines were devastating Allied shipping. Bombing of German cities by the Allies had intensified
hatred against them. The year 1943 would be difficult, but not more so
than the past year or the winter of 1941. Europe need no longer endure

"every twenty to twenty-five years the repeated efforts of the Jewish-capitalist hyenas to undermine the peaceful and above all social construction of a new world."[3]

The January 1, 1943, issue of *Die Judenfrage* contained an article by a regular contributor, Horst Seemann, "Roosevelt against Europe." The piece repeated and reminded readers of standard fare and offered an anti-Semitic outlook on recent events. It made the standard accusations that "world Jewry" had started the war to regain its position in Europe and finally "establish a Jewish world domination." Evidence cited for that claim was "a campaign of agitation and accusations of atrocities" fomented by "Jewish plutocrats" in the United States at rallies in Madison Square Garden in the 1930s, as well as Roosevelt's "Quarantine the Aggressors" speech of October 1937. "Had it not been for the early assurances of Roosevelt's Jewish Brain Trust, England would not have started a war." Clearly, "North American imperialism" and the associated economic interests had driven the United States into the war. Seemann noted with favor the Grand Mufti's recent speech at the opening of the Islamic Cultural Institute in Berlin, in which he had warned that French North Africa was becoming the "first bridge between Jewish centers in the USA and in Palestine." In every statement by Jewish organizations and writers expressing support for the United States and the Soviet Union, he found proof of the ubiquitous influence of world Jewry and of its determination to "exterminate" Germany by delivering it to Bolshevism. He recalled Kaufman's *Germany Must Perish!* and its threats to sterilize the Germans. He repeated as fact the falsehood that Churchill had approved a plan to remove all German children between the ages of two and six from their mothers. Without mentioning details of the Allied denunciations in December 1942 of German atrocities, Seemann referred only to "the infernal hate-filled declaration of England, the USA, and the Soviet Union in the English House of Commons in favor of world Jewry."[4] A month later, in the February 1, 1943, issue of *Die Judenfrage,* the editors published another of their biographical sketches of Jewish leaders, "Samuel Irving Rosenman, the Real

President of the USA." The article built on Walter Freund's 1942 work *The Great Unknown Men of American Foreign Policy*. Freund had "uncovered the Jewish world government," whose "most important branches" were the B'nai Brith, the American Jewish Congress, and the American Jewish Committee, at whose apex stood the three hundred men "who govern the world." One of them was New York judge Samuel Rosenman, FDR's adviser and speech writer.[5]

In the third week of January, Roosevelt and Churchill met in Casablanca at a war conference. At its conclusion they issued a joint statement asserting that peace was possible "only by the elimination of German and Japanese war power." This required "unconditional surrender by Germany and Japan . . . Unconditional surrender means not the destruction of the German populace, nor of the Japanese populace, but does mean the destruction of a philosophy in Germany and Japan which is based on the conquest of other peoples."[6] The two leaders were determined that World War II would have an unambiguous end, in contrast to World War I. They wanted to be sure that the German military would understand this time that it had been defeated on the battlefield and therefore that no second stab-in-the-back legend would emerge. The Casablanca statement was also meant to reassure the Soviets that the Western Allies did not intend to make a separate peace with Germany and did want to sustain the unity of the anti-Nazi coalition. Although the Allies sought to distinguish between the Nazi regime and the German people, Nazi propagandists suppressed these efforts and claimed that just the opposite was the case—namely that the Allies made no such distinctions.

Meanwhile, the Nazi leaders' attention was focused on the disaster unfolding at Stalingrad.[7] Hitler had refused Field Marshal Friedrich Paulus's request to be allowed to surrender to the surrounding Soviet forces. Between their encirclement in November 1942 and their defeat and surrender at the beginning of February 1943, most of the 250,000 men in the German Sixth Army died, from wounds, frostbite, and starvation. In the Soviet Union and around the world, the Soviet victory at

Stalingrad was seen as one of the turning points of the war, if not the decisive point, one that destroyed the aura of German military invincibility. The Germans at home, fed a steady diet of optimistic reports and appeals to heroism, were shocked at the news and appalled at the extent of the disaster.[8]

In the final days of the Battle of Stalingrad, Hitler remained in his East Prussian headquarters and had Goebbels read his annual January 30 speech to the nation. In it, Hitler again asserted that he and the Nazis had saved Germany from ruin at the hands of the Jews, that England and France had declared war on Germany without any good reason in 1939, and that the invasion of the Soviet Union in June 1941 had saved Europe from a devastating invasion by "barbaric hordes from the East." The war was the work of "agitators" who had rejected Hitler's peace proposals. "The conspiracy of international capitalism and Bolshevism is not at all a paradoxical or absurd phenomenon. Rather, it is a natural matter, because the driving force in both is that people which for thousands of years, driven by its hatred, has again and again slaughtered, divided, economically exploited, and politically destroyed humanity. Today, international Jewry is the ferment of the decomposition of peoples and states, just as it was in antiquity. It will remain that way as long as peoples do not find the strength to get rid of this virus."[9] Either Germany and its allies would be victorious, he continued, or Europe would be destroyed by a storm from the East. National Socialist Germany would continue the war with "fanaticism" because "in this war there will be no victors and vanquished, but only those who survived and those who were exterminated." The war, according to Hitler, had become a fight to the death between Germany and "international Jewry."

On the same day, Goebbels spoke to the nation from the Sportpalast in Berlin. The current battle lines in the war reproduced those of Weimar politics. "Just as in the battle for power [in the Weimar Republic], now too Jewry is besieging us from two sides of a gigantic circle. Bolshevism sends its mass armies, while plutocracy looses a barrage of lies and slanderous propaganda to hail down on us." The future of not only Germany, but all of Europe and "indeed the whole civilized West," hung in the balance.[10] Just as the Nazis had defeated a supposed pincer movement by plutocrats and Bolsheviks in Weimar, so they would defeat the facsimile of that coalition at the international level. Neither Goebbels, Hitler, nor other Nazis mentioned the by then famous blunders by their adversaries, from underestimation of Hitler by his contemporaries to the failure to present a united opposition before and immediately after 1933. It was hardly surprising that Goebbels, having misread the source of past Nazi political successes, for all his talk of realism and difficult realities, offered a steady stream of unjustified optimism about the outcome of the war. The disaster in Stalingrad, so far from fostering reassessment on the part of Hitler, led him and Goebbels to emphasize the Nazi party's ideological roots and to blame the military leadership for the setback.

The German press responded to the disaster at Stalingrad with an evocation of the heroism of the troops, without supplying figures on the number of dead, wounded, and missing.[11] *Der Völkische Beobachter* offered few facts and a redemptive headline on page 1, "Battle of the Sixth Army in Stalingrad Ends; They Died So That Germany May Live."[12] The *Periodical Service* of February 5, 1943, set the tone for the propaganda offensive of the spring. The "undying heroism of the men of Stalingrad" would foster a spirit and power that would ensure victory. There was "only one word for editors in the coming months: Fight against Bolshevism and Jewry!" Readers must be told what Germany and the rest of Europe could expect "if they should fall victim to Bolshevism. Bolshevism is the henchman of Jewry." The consequences would include "the sterilization plans of the American Jew Kaufman," territorial fragmentation, and Bolshevization. But now "international Jewry has let its mask fall." The United States and England were both unable and unwilling to protect Europe from Bolshevism. There was "only one protection against Jewish Bolshevism's will to extermination . . . the German army." It defended "the culture and life of the European Continent." After the fateful decision that has taken place in the East [Stalingrad], the most important task of all German periodicals is to reinforce and strengthen the will of the German people and their allies to defense and victory. The essence of the Bolshevik danger must again and again be placed before the reader. Again and again, the press must show that Bolshevism would mean either extermination or lifelong suffering and enslavement . . . If Bolshevism in the Soviet Union led by the Jewish power holders succeeded in breaking the protective barrier of the German Wehrmacht in the East and the iron wall of German determination on the home front, it would repeat in far greater measure the extermination, enslavement, and immiseration of people that it has brought about in the Soviet Union. All articles that are written based on the material delivered by the *Wochendienst* [also from the Reich Press Office] must take up the theme of the threatening Jewish-Bolshevik danger. It must be shown that danger weakens only the weak. Among people who are prepared to save their lives and preserve their highest values, it is precisely this danger that awakens the powers needed to overcome the fiercest resistance. We expect that the periodicals will take these new demands into account, not only in one article but in their whole orientation and layout.[13]

In the same *Periodical Service* directive, the Reich Press Office included further anti-Semitic directives. "When the Jew Is in Power" ignored the distinction Roosevelt and Churchill had made in their Casablanca statement between the Nazi regime and the German people. Strengthening German resistance called for emphasizing the consequences of Jewish power. The more that Germans believed it to be "the firm intention of Jewry to exterminate all Germans" and accepted that the war, as Hitler had recently asserted, would leave only "the survivors and the exterminated," the more German support for the war would grow.[14] Jewry's "declaration of war" against "the European peoples" had resulted in the Nazis' taking "energetic measures" against the Jews. Periodicals were ordered to describe anti-Jewish measures as "self-preservation."[15]

The intensification of the press campaign against the Jews was evident in January. On January 14, 1943, *Der Völkische Beobachter* led with "They Won't Escape Punishment for Their Warmongering: USA Jews Must Count on a Wave of Intolerance" and on January 16 with "Rosenman Stands Behind Roosevelt: A Crown Jew on the Throne of the USA." Roosevelt was a "tool of Jewish high finance."[16] The Jews, the *VB* wrote, were coming out from behind the scenes to reveal that the "non-Jewish straw men in politics and economics only danced on the strings of Jewish wire pullers. An American victory would mean a "victory for Jewish plans for world domination . . . Rosenman speaks through Roosevelt; world Jewry speaks through the American President." On February 7, 1943, the *VB* led with "Wallace Reveals Roosevelt's Dream for the Future; The Whole World Will Be a Field for Jewish-American Exploiters. Those Who Don't Follow American Orders Will Be Bombed Mercilessly." Wallace's proposal to expand commercial passenger airline service around the world after the war was yet further proof that revealed "the plans for domination and exploitation of the world of Jewish-American imperialism Roosevelt-style."[17]

Hitler was the driving force behind the intensified propaganda offensive against the Jews. In a long speech to leaders of the government and party gathered at his East Prussian headquarters on February 8, 1943, he offered a survey of the war. He noted the extent of losses by the Soviet Union and the serious differences between the United States and England. According to the notes in Goebbels's diary entry, Hitler said, "The enemy had an advantage because it was held together by international Jewry. Jewry is the driving element in all enemy states. We have nothing comparable to juxtapose with it." Therefore, Jewry not only must be driven out of Germany but "also must be eliminated from all of Europe."[18] Hitler's message to the leaders was grim. Either Germany would dominate Europe, or it would experience "liquidation and extermination." Defeat would be possible only because of the "weakness of the people." If the Germans became weak, they "would deserve nothing other than to be obliterated." If that were to happen, he would have "no pity or sympathy for them."[19] Hitler placed the blame for all setbacks on everyone and everything but himself, finally including the Germans themselves.

In Britain and the United States during the war, harsh public criticism of Communism and the Stalin dictatorship had ended.[20] Russia was the wartime ally bearing the brunt of the war. Goebbels attributed the muting of anti-Communism by the Allies to efforts by "the Jews" to spread Communism in Europe by downplaying the threat and thus weakening Europe's powers of resistance.[21] On February 11, the lead *VB* article was titled "The Newest Burst of Jewish Hatred: They Want to Exterminate the German People Culturally and Physically; However, We Will Strike the Plutocratic and Bolshevik Sadists to the Ground."[22] This front-page article referred to "Jewish advisers" in London and Washington who not only wanted to "ruin German industry . . . but also urged that the German people must be exterminated in the literal sense of the term." The article referred to plans for firing all German teachers and professors after the war, to replace them with Jews, and for closing the universities for a long period.[23]

At his February 12 Minister's Conference, Goebbels told his staff, "Our struggle against Bolshevism must now dominate all propaganda media as the great and all-pervading propaganda theme."[24] On February 12, President Roosevelt, in a nationally broadcast speech, announced that Allied operations to drive the Nazis out of Tunisia would begin imminently and be followed by invasions of Europe to destroy Nazism and fascism. In describing the high price that would be paid in the battles to come, FDR remarked, "The amazing Russian armies in the East have been delivering overpowering blows; we must do likewise in the West."[25] The following day the article on page 1 of the *VB* was "Roosevelt Throws Europe to Bolshevism as Booty; Jews' Straw Man Bows before Moscow; We Will Give Him the Answer He Deserves."[26] As the

Casablanca declaration made clear, Roosevelt and Churchill were determined to sustain the alliance with the Soviet Union in order to defeat
Nazi Germany. That the Soviet armies would be moving westward was
above all the result of Hitler's invasion of Russia. After the tide turned
in 1943, an Anglo-American invasion from the West offered the only
realistic alternative to a fully Soviet-dominated Europe. Goebbels saw
things quite differently. In his Minister's Conference of February 17, he
stressed that German propaganda should repeat and stress "Britain and
America's betrayal of Europe."[27] The messages coming from the Propaganda Ministry and those of its Reich Press Office were coordinated
and mutually reinforcing.

All of the above themes were present in Goebbels's most famous
speech of the war, the three-hour oration "Do You Want Total War?"
("Wollt ihr den totalen Krieg?"), delivered in the Berlin Sportpalast on
February 18, 1943, and broadcast to the nation over German radio. By
September 1943, the Nazi party propaganda apparatus had distributed
fourteen million copies of the speech to all the regional *Gau* offices.[28]
Goebbels spoke from "the depths of my heart . . . with hot passion . . .
with sacred seriousness" in those weeks of "fateful importance."[29] He
said that the themes of the Nuremberg Party Rallies against Bolshevism were timely, in view of the threat to "the West, which exceeded
all previous threats." He offered three "theses." First, if the German
armies were to be defeated, Germany and the rest of Europe would fall
to Bolshevism. The goal of Bolshevism was "the world revolution of the
Jews," to be brought about through the generation of "chaos" in Europe,
followed by an "international, capitalistically camouflaged Bolshevik
tyranny." The Bolshevization of Germany would entail "the liquidation
of our whole stratum of intellectuals and leaders, and as a result the delivery of the working masses to Bolshevik-Jewish slavery."[30] Europe—
indeed, the West as a whole—was in danger. Behind the Soviet divisions
stood "Jewish liquidation commandos . . . Two thousand years of the
construction of Western humanity was in danger." It was necessary to
call the threat by its name: "international Jewry."[31]

His second thesis was that only Germany and its allies could confront the Bolshevik danger. England and the United States would certainly not stand in the way of Europe's Bolshevization:

> Jewry has so intellectually and politically penetrated the Anglo-Saxon states that they no longer even see or want to recognize the danger. In the Soviet Union they camouflage themselves as Bolsheviks, while in the Anglo-Saxon states they appear plutocratic and capitalistic. The methods of mimicry of the Jewish race are familiar. For many years, they have sought to lull their host peoples to sleep and thereby paralyze their powers of defense against their acute and life-threatening danger . . . Early on, our insight into this problem led us to understand that the cooperation between international plutocracy and international Bolshevism was not at all absurd or paradoxical. Rather, it had a deep and causal significance. Reaching across our country, superficially civilized West European Jewry shakes hands with the Jewry of the eastern ghettos. That is why Europe's life is in danger.[32]

His third thesis was that the danger was imminent. The "signs of paralysis" in the West European democracies were "heartbreaking." Jewry was doing all it could to foster this paralysis of will, just as the Jewish newspapers in Weimar had, he claimed, sought to minimize the Communist danger. Again in 1943 Jewry was demonstrating that it was "the incarnation of evil." But the Nazis would not be deterred: "If our enemies abroad raise hypocritical protests and weep crocodile tears over our measures against the Jews, they will not stop us from doing what is necessary." Germany would not "bend in the face of this Jewish threat," but instead would "immediately confront it when necessary with the complete and most radical extermination and exclusion of Jewry." The transcript records "strong applause, wild cheering, laughter."[33] As the bond between speaker and audience became ever more intense, Goebbels declared, "We will not permit the scream of international

Jewry in the whole world to divert us from the courageous and just continuation of this gigantic struggle against this world pest. *It can and must end only in victory!*" The transcript records shouts of "Heil Hitler, stormy applause, a chorus of shouts, 'German men to arms! German women to work! more applause, cheering, laughter."[34] In the midst of this bedlam, Goebbels appealed for putting an end to "false hopes and illusions" and for facing unpleasant facts in the wake of Stalingrad. The war in the East was merciless. As Hitler had said on January 30, it would "end not with winners and losers but only with survivors and the exterminated."[35] To more shouts of "Heil Hitler" and applause, Goebbels declared, "Total war is the demand of the hour"; this was because the future of Europe now depended on "our struggle in the East."[36] Now was the time for national sacrifice, deeper involvement of the whole nation in the war, a "spartan life for all, high and low, poor and rich," and increased entry of women into the workforce.[37]

The delirious bond between speaker and audience reached a climax as Goebbels posed ten rhetorical questions:

Do you believe, with the Führer and with us, in the decisive, total victory of German weapons? . . . Are you ready, with the Führer, as the phalanx of the home front behind the fighting Wehrmacht, to continue this struggle with wild determination and without wavering, through all twists of fate until victory is in our hands? . . . Are you ready . . . to work ten, twelve, if necessary fourteen and sixteen hours a day . . . to bring about victory? . . . Do you want total war, if necessary more total, more radical than we can even imagine today? . . . Do you trust the Führer? Is your readiness to follow him in all his ways and to do everything necessary to win the war absolute and unlimited? . . . Are you now ready to engage all your energy in support of the eastern front, our fighting fathers and brothers, the men and weapons that they need in order to defeat Bolshevism? . . . Do you offer a sacred oath to the front that the home front will stand with stronger, unshakable morale behind the front and will give everything for victory? . . . Do you, especially you women, want the government to ensure that every bit of labor power, including that of women, will be placed in service of the war [effort] . . . and that women in general, where possible, will step in so that men can be freed to serve at the front? . . . Do you support the most radical measures against the small circle of shirkers and profiteers who want to play during the war and use the people's suffering for their own purposes? . . . Do you agree that those who seek to avoid the war should lose their heads? . . . Do you agree that the home front should out of solidarity bear on its shoulders the heaviest burdens of the war and that they should be borne equally by high and low, and poor and rich?[38]

After each of these questions, the audience responded in a frenzied "Ja," rendered more fervent through repetition. Goebbels ended with a metaphorical and literal plea: "Now, people, rise up—and let the storm break!" This exhortation was greeted with applause and shouts of "Heil Hitler" and "Sieg Heil," followed by the singing of the "Deutschland-lied." The entire spectacle was broadcast—and rebroadcast—on German radio and included in the following week's *Wochenschau*, the weekly newsreel that Goebbels helped edit.[39] In his diary entry for the following evening, Goebbels wrote that the Sportpalast had "never seen such a turbulent scene" as at the conclusion of his speech. Surrounded as he had been by the entire cabinet and many Nazi party leaders, he thought the speech amounted to "a total cultural mobilization."[40] Hitler was very pleased.[41] Goebbels had stressed the claim that Jewry was waging a war to the death against Germany and that Germany would carry out "the most radical measures" in response. The audience response in the Sportpalast left no doubt that the regime's determination to make good on Hitler's prophecy was still popular with the Nazi faithful. Several weeks later, following a long conversation, Goebbels and Göring agreed that things had gone so far with regard to the Jews that Nazi Germany had no way out. This, however, was a good thing, because "a movement, a people, that has burned its bridges behind it fights more fiercely than do those who have the option of retreat."[42] The country would be held together thanks in part to a gangster mentality born of complicity in crime and fear of retribution.

On February 24, 1943, in the wake of the defeat of the Sixth Army at Stalingrad, Hitler declined to attend an annual celebration of the founding of the Nazi party in Munich. Instead, he sent a proclamation, which included boilerplate rehearsals of the story of the party's glory days. Two days later, the text was incorporated into the lead story on page 1 of the VB.[43] Hitler's retelling of the narrative of the Jewish conspiracy led him to repeat once more the need for a policy of mass murder. Without offering details about how he planned to do so, he assured the assembled faithful, "We will break apart and destroy the Jewish world coalition." He again assured his old comrades, "This battle will end not with the destruction of Aryan humanity, but rather with the extermination of Jewry in Europe."[44] As the war continued, National Socialist ideology would spread to other nations. Just as those who had tried to defeat the Nazis in the 1920s had instead witnessed "an explosion of National Socialist ideology in the German people as a whole," so in 1943 international Jewry would have to face the growth of anti-Semitism around the world. The war had "made the complete identity and similarity of plutocracy and Bolshevism incontrovertibly clear . . . The same alliance that we once saw between the Frankfurt stock exchange and the *Rote Fahne* in Berlin, our common enemies in the old days, manifests itself again now between the Jewish banks in New York, the Jewish-plutocratic establishment in London, and the Jews of the Kremlin in Moscow." Just as the German people had understood and then successfully battled the Jewish enemy within, so in the course of this war other peoples would come to their senses and "finally form a common front against that race which is out to exterminate them all."[45] For Hitler and the Nazi faithful, the course of the war was confirming the truth of radical anti-Semitism. Setbacks and defeats, far from causing agonizing reappraisals or second thoughts, deepened belief in the original paranoid construct.

The following week in his February 28 editorial in *Das Reich,* "Europe's Crisis," Goebbels reverted to the tone of an intellectual seeking to puzzle out a dilemma. "In order," he began, "to understand the current constellation of the war, it is necessary to understand the Jewish question." The article explained the "riddle" of the alliance between the Western governments and the Kremlin.[46] There was "only an apparent and superficial difference" between them. If one looked behind the scenes, one very quickly discovered "international Jewry, the *spiritus rector* of the whole emotional and intellectual confusion, the ferment of decomposition of states and peoples."[47] "Plutocracy and Bolshevism" differed only "in style and appearance, but not in their essence." One was "the more radical brother of the other." Their alliance was an example of "mimicry, the art of camouflage and deception," which the Jews had refined. It was now weakening Europe's will to defend itself against Bolshevism.[48]

In the next issue of *Das Reich,* Goebbels hammered away at the idea of the guiding role played by "international Jewry" in the anti-Hitler coalition. Celebration of the twenty-fifth anniversary of the Red Army in London and Allied expressions of hope for the victory of the Red Army confirmed the behind-the-scenes maneuvers of the Jews.[49] In a remark recorded in his diary several weeks later, Goebbels offered further evidence of his belief in the reality of a Jewish conspiracy that was driving events from behind the scenes, as well as of his ability to combine the conspiracy theory with tactical common sense. The Nazis should stay out of debates about Bolshevism in England and the United States, because entering into them created "the danger that the Jewish men behind the scenes of Bolshevization, along with the Anglo-Saxon states, could point to us as evidence in order to discredit anti-Bolshevik voices in England and the USA."[50]

That spring the Reich Press office directives became more central to the anti-Semitic propaganda offensive. The February 26, 1943, issue of the *Periodical Service* informed editors of the growing American influence in Iraq, Syria, and Saudi Arabia and of a plan to establish a "large Jewish state in Palestine under American leadership." Editors were urged to keep in mind that the Americans (in contrast to the British, who were concerned about Islam in colonial India) did "not have to take Islamic subjects into account." The Americans, "therefore, represent exclusively the interests of the Jews in Asia." The Americans wanted to exploit the region's wealth and "enslave the native population, a policy that corresponds to their hostility to Islam as a religion . . . In stressing the hostility of the United States to Islam, which is a consequence of Jewish domination, we must avoid giving the impression that English domination of the Near East would be better."[51]

This Nazi overture to followers of Islam was apparent on the front page of the *VB* of March 19 and 20, 1943. On the nineteenth, the Grand Mufti spoke in a Berlin mosque. The following day, at the top of page 1, the *VB* ran this article: "Appeal of Grand Mufti against Deadly Enemy of Islam—Arabs Will Fight for Their Freedom on the Side of the Axis."[52] Al-Husseini denounced the occupation of Islamic or Arab countries by "enemy oppressors" using "capitalist methods" of plunder. It was the duty of "all Muslims" to fight those who, "with the help of the Jews," aim at "the complete domination of the Holy Land." Arabs and other Muslims had "the duty to smash Jewish greed and insatiability." He said that the day of reckoning was coming, when Muslims would be freed. The *VB* report called al-Husseini "one of the outstanding personalities of the Islamic world, who has led the struggle of the Arabs against the onslaught of the Jews for many years."[53]

Though Dietrich was Hitler's channel for daily influence on the press, Hitler periodically spoke directly with Goebbels. On March 31, Hitler told him that the German press should "stress more strongly than before that Jewry is the guilty instigator of this war." Indeed, "our press must mention it again every day." Hitler added that "the Jewish question" needed to be emphasized more in Nazi propaganda aimed at England, where he thought there were anti-Semitic tendencies that were "very promising for the future." Anti-Semitism, Goebbels noted, was an "extraordinarily effective means of propaganda," one that corresponded with "the political purposes and necessities of our all-round situation."[54] Hitler gave identical orders to Dietrich. The Reich Press Office *Periodical Service* for April 2 asserted that "the press must constantly focus on the fact that Jewry is completely dominant not only in the Soviet Union but also, above all, in England and the USA. Jewry's influence on politics and the press makes it essential to haul the Jewish wire pullers out from the shadows, clearly point them out, and identify them. This should be done both in commentary and in news articles." In chilling tones, the editors were further instructed to emphasize that "Jewry as a whole comes from criminal roots . . . The criminals of all countries speak a technical language whose most important component is Hebrew. The extermination of Jewry is not a loss for humanity." Rather, it was as useful for nations as the death penalty or prison was for dealing with criminals.[55] In this confidential memo, where there was no cause for bombast and empty threats, the Reich Press Office informed periodical editors that the Jews were, at that moment, being killed and that this was "not a loss" for humanity.[56] The controlled press did not investigate to see what these foreboding words implied.

The press campaign took aim at those in the West who painted a rosy picture of the Soviet regime, such as the National Council of American-Soviet Friendship. Its chairman was Corliss Lamont, the left-leaning son of Thomas Lamont, himself the son of a Methodist-Episcopal minister and a Harvard graduate. Thomas Lamont, a longstanding senior executive of the J. P. Morgan Bank, had taken the lead in the bank's financing of Allied efforts in World War I. Following Morgan's death, he became chairman of the board, beginning in March 1943.[57] Thus Corliss Lamont stood at the top of the white, Anglo-Saxon, Protestant corporate establishment. On April 8, 1943, the *VB* described Thomas Lamont as one of "the dark men behind the scenes who pushed the wavering Wilson into the abyss of World War I," which had yielded big profits for the J. P. Morgan Bank. The young Corliss had gone to

Moscow with assistance from the Roosevelt aide Harold Ickes, "the Jew Davies," and Senator Claude Pepper, "who for a long time had emerged as a fighter for the global domination of world Jewry."[58] The *VB* then proceeded to describe this sinister mix of Jews and WASPs as follows:

> The goyim and the old USA diplomats are there to give the new plutocratic-Bolshevik firm a glamorous outer appearance and respectable representation. However, the enterprise is clearly characterized by the names Einstein, Stokowski, and Chaplin. The émigré Jewish pseudo-philosopher has made common cause with the repulsive film Jews who so far have thrived on Hollywood's swamp. Chaplin and Einstein in New York follow Eisenstein, Ehrenburg, and above all Brother Kaganovich in Moscow. The Jews are working together and hope to keep their hands on the lever of power. The American people deliver the money and weapons. The Soviet Union offers the people, because the reservoir of human life that can be sacrificed for the Jewish war is almost as inexhaustible as the gold supply of the Morgan Bank, which through the Lamonts is mobilized for the war of world Jewry. The meaning and goal of Roosevelt's war policy, which was begun years before the outbreak of the war, has never before been more shamelessly revealed to world public opinion than it has through the founding [of the National Council for American-Soviet Friendship]. Indeed, this must be labeled as a classic example of the unity of world Jewry and of its will to world domination.[59]

The article was a masterpiece of the conspiratorial mentality that lent seeming plausibility to spurious connections with a rapid-fire sequence of famous Jewish names in both the United States and the Soviet Union, which it then associated with a familiar non-Jewish name, that of the Lamonts. The piece offered no evidence that the scions of the American WASP establishment worked in the service of the Jews or that any of these persons were controlling events together. Nevertheless, the Nazi propagandists saw in the WASP-dominated National Council for American-Soviet Friendship a perfect example of the "mimicry" Goebbels had denounced. Why, after all, should wealthy bankers advocate friendship with Communists, if not for the guiding hand of "world Jewry," directing the action from behind the scenes? While the Nazi propagandists took pleasure in posing such leading questions, they did not ask why wealthy non-Jewish members of the American establishment would willingly succumb to Jews at a time when Jews were still subject to admission quotas at Corliss Lamont's alma mater, Harvard. If American Jews were unable to eliminate the Jewish quota at Harvard, where did they find the power run American foreign policy? Why would politicians as accomplished as Franklin Roosevelt or bankers as sophisticated as Thomas Lamont and his son Corliss suddenly become servants of the Jews, whose interests, the Nazis insisted, conflicted with those of non-Jewish America? By 1943, because of ideological sympathy and professional opportunism within the press corps, as well as Nazi purges and terror tactics, editors and journalists in the Nazi-controlled press did not address these questions, at least not in print.

On April 12, 1943, the German press did report on a major atrocity story—namely, the discovery of the bodies of what they claimed were 10,000 Polish officers in mass graves in the Katyn forest in Russia. In fact, 4,000 officers were missing and 1,700 bodies were found. Though many leaders in Britain and the United States initially assumed that the Nazis had killed them, it turned out much later that the Russians were indeed responsible.[60] Nazi propaganda stressed the Katyn story to attack the Soviet Union and to weaken support for it in England and the United States. In addition, it became the occasion for one of the most virulent public anti-Semitic campaigns of the war. The Nazi press claimed that "Jewish commissars" had carried out the murders. The Press Office directive asserted that the murders were evidence that "the extermination of the peoples of Europe" was now a "Jewish war aim." The directive continued that the Jews themselves would be called to account and "that finally not Europe, but Jewry would succumb to extermination."[61]

The Press Office directive of April 13 instructed editors that they must "strongly present" the "sensational discovery" of the mass grave of Polish officers who, it asserted, had been shot by the Soviets between March and May 1940. The news should be presented as "one of the most horrible events of human history."[62]

On April 14, 1943, the press directive played up the anti-Semitic dimension of the propaganda campaign. "The sensational testimony about the fact that murder commandos of the GPU were composed of Jewish commissars should be featured on the front pages of the newspapers and should be accompanied by sharp words." The Katyn murders and "the fact that they were carried out by Jews is nothing other than a confirmation of this Jewish hymn of hatred." Germany would see to it, the public should be assured: "It will be the Jews themselves who will one day be brought to account and that then finally it will be not Europe but rather Jewry that will succumb to extermination."[63] A furious Nazi propaganda campaign about the Kaytn massacre followed, stressing not only that the Soviets were responsible but also that Jews or "Jewish commissars" were the perpetrators.[64]

The *Word of the Day* directive of April 16 was no less blunt.

In several cases, the treatment of the Jewish-Bolshevik crime in Katyn is not yet accompanied by the necessary clarity about Jewish world criminality. Jewry's powerful position, which makes it possible for it to dominate Bolshevism as well as capitalism, must at every appropriate opportunity be stressed as clearly as possible to the world. This applies above all to the formulation and the headlining of news reports as well. The Jewish world conspiracy, which plotted and hatched this war and which inflamed and sowed the seeds of hatred among nations, must emerge more powerfully in the consciousness of world public opinion. Here is the point at which we must explain to the world our compelling arguments through continual emphasis.[65]

The same day the *VB* again turned the American ambassador to Moscow, Joseph Davies, into a Jew in its front-page headline: "The Jew Davies: 'We Can Trust the Soviet Union': Katyn, an Example of Judas's Blow against Europe." It described the killers of Polish officers as "Jewish commandos" who had offered an example of what "world Jewry" and its plutocratic and Soviet "agents" had in store for others. The piece quoted Western journalists expressing reluctance to criticize the Soviet Union as evidence of "how absolutely world Jewry dominates Washington and London." The *VB* article repeated the fundamental Nazi accusation. *Juda* had unleashed the war "to take revenge on the people who had stood in the way of its plans to enslave the world and who recognized Jewry as the greatest danger of our time." Fortunately, the German army was protecting Europe, in accordance with Hitler's announcement that "in this war the Jews would disappear from Europe and that it would be the Jews, not the nations of the West, that would be destroyed." The Jews would have to "atone" for the guilt that was already on their hands, a guilt made still worse by Jewish figures such as Ilya Ehrenburg and Nathan Kaufman, who called for "the extermination of all enemies."[66]

Goebbels interpreted initial foreign skepticism about the Katyn story as further evidence of Jewish power. He wrote: "One can really describe the USA as a Jewish state." He would intensify anti-Semitic propaganda, so that leaders in the enemy countries could not take the side of the Jews "without immediately being suspected by their own people of being the Jews' servant." He attributed skepticism in the Swedish press about the Katyn story to Jewish influence.[67] The *Periodical Service* instructed editors of political magazines to stress the Katyn story because it showed the world "the blood-soaked face of Bolshevism and its will for extermination in the service of the Jewish world conspiracy. It serves, above all, to clearly set forth Jewry's responsibility for these acts of murder." Rather than use the Katyn story to try to split the anti-Hitler coalition, the focus of the German press should be to point to Jews as the driving force behind the coalition, and the glue that held it together.

This in turn would strengthen domestic German support for the war in the face of a supposedly remorseless international enemy.[68]

The same issue of the *Periodical Service* included an essay entitled simply "*Juda* Wants to Murder the Peoples of Europe." The murder of the Polish officers in Katyn was "not a unique outbreak of the Jews' hatred against Poland" but "an intentional continuation of Jewish policy against all non-Jews." If Bolshevism was not defeated, the Polish officers' fate would be repeated for "all the peoples of Europe without exception." The mass murder in Katyn showed that "Jewish plans for extermination . . . of all non-Jews was not a fantasy of enemies of the Jews. Rather, they [the plans] actually exist. Where the Jews have power, they are working to realize them." The press was to stress that "Jewry of the whole world is responsible for the crime in Katyn." For good measure, the directive also instructed the editors that "Jewish ritual murder" was not a "fairy tale of opponents of the Jews" but a "hard, provable reality."[69]

On April 19, the Jews of the Warsaw Ghetto launched the first armed resistance to Nazi Germany in occupied Europe. Not a word about the uprising appeared in the German press. Instead the Anglo-American air war dominated headlines. On April 23, 1943, the *New York Times* published its first article about the ghetto revolt.[70] In his diary entry of April 25, Goebbels indicated that he was aware of fighting in the ghetto. The *VB* pressed on with its propaganda campaign about the Katyn massacre.[71] The May 6, 1943, issue of the *VB* led with "USA and England under Command of World Jewry: Plutocrats Identify with Jewish-Bolshevik Murderers."[72] On the same day, the *New York Times* ran its second story on the ghetto uprising. It reported that according to Polish sources, a battle had been raging "for seventeen days."[73] Still nothing appeared in the German press. On April 23 and April 24, the *New York Times* had published two articles about the "Katyn affair," reporting that the Red Cross would investigate Germany's charges about it.[74]

The coordinated nature of the campaign by the Nazi regime to keep Katyn in the news was apparent in Otto Dietrich's directive of April 28,

1943. "Despite repeated, urgent instructions in the 'Tagesparole,'" he noted with evident exasperation, "the fact of Jewish responsibility for the murders in Katyn has been only very weakly expressed in the text and headlines related to news reports. We call your attention to the fact that editors now have the responsibility to see that in every instance reports and headlines correspond to the procedures requested."[75] On the following day, Dietrich, who continued to be in daily contact with Hitler at his East Prussian headquarters, issued the following long directive ordering German newspapers to focus on "the Jewish face" of the murderer in Katyn.

In connection with the Katyn massacre, repeated reference must be made in headlines and captions to the Jewish-Bolshevik murder and arson. This must be done not only today and tomorrow. Rather, the deadly enemy of the world must be constantly exposed and denounced. The press will receive from the German News Agency . . . material on the Jews, which must be worked up appropriately. Furthermore, from now on it is the duty of the press to apply itself with greater intensity to the Jewish question as its permanent duty. It is not anti-Semitism when the newspapers write "London Hides Jewish-Bolshevik Murders," rather than "London Hides Bolshevik Murders." When the papers write the latter headline, they have not done enough to present Jewry's authorship. Rather, the point from now on is to build up anti-Semitism in all commentaries and articles. It is clear that one cannot draw anti-Semitism from a vacuum, but that one must have a certain basis for it, a kind of theme to which everything else can be adapted. With this in mind, the newspapers will receive a Jewish theme daily, one that should not be seized upon rigidly and unimaginatively but rather should serve only as inspiration. The newspapers here have a broad field and can themselves find the needed themes. For example, there are countless sensational stories in which the Jew is depicted as the author of a crime, which can be drawn upon here. Above all, American domestic politics offer an inexhaustible reservoir for such tales. If the papers put their staffs to work here, we will have the opportunity to see the true face, true behavior, and true Jewry depicted daily in new and varied forms. Moreover, naturally the Jew in the German press must also be presented as a political actor. In every case, it must be established that the Jews are to blame! The Jews wanted the war! Everywhere throughout the world, the Jews prepared the war against Germany! The Jew intensifies the war! The Jew profits from the war! And again and again: the Jew is guilty!

Dietrich saw an "infinitely great opportunity" to "present the true character of the Jews." There was "not a single line in the paper where this would not be possible." It was, he stressed again, "the duty of the entire German press to participate in the above-depicted anti-Semitic operation."[76] The following day, the *VB*'s page-1 headline read: "Katyn Again Reveals World Jewry, Europe Recognizes the Plot between Plutocrats and Soviet Jews, England and USA Make Pathetic Attempts to Disguise the Truth."[77]

If making reference to "Jewish-Bolshevik murderers in London" was "not anti-Semitism," then it would follow that Dietrich thought it was factually accurate, that is, good journalism, to describe the British government in such terms. Following his logic, an absence of anti-Semitic attacks would have been bad journalism because the central story of the war, from Dietrich's perspective (reflecting Hitler's), was that the Jews were the cause of the war against Germany. As noted earlier, the core accusation against the Jews was not one about physical appearance, sexual appetites, or the Jewish body, though such assaults continued in Streicher's *Der Stürmer*. Rather, it remained the primarily *political* accusation that held "international Jewry" responsible for World War II. It thus served as the key justification for mass murder of the Jewish "enemy."

The *VB* traced the source of Western skepticism to the "unscrupulous drive of the plutocratic and Bolshevik Jewish conspiracy." "No one in Europe will be deceived any longer by the Jewish wire pullers, whether their marionettes are in Moscow or in London and Washington." The May 1, 1943, issue of *Die Judenfrage* joined in with a lead article about Katyn, "Jewish-Bolshevik Blood Guilt."[78] On May 3 the party's Reich Propaganda Directorate sent rules to local officials of the NSDAP to use in speeches about the Katyn. Speakers were to stress that the Katyn story offered "striking proof" of the dangers that awaited Germany and the rest of Europe in the event of a Bolshevik victory and evidence of the "disgraceful betrayal of Europe by England and America" as a result of their political arrangement with the Soviet Union. Katyn revealed the unchanging nature of the "Bolshevik murder system" at the very time the Soviet Union was seeking to present itself to the West as Christian and democratic, according to the directorate. "Katyn will stand for all time for Jewish-Bolshevik mass murder." The directive coined a phrase, "Katynization" *(Katynierung)*. Just as the guillotine was associated with the murders of "the first revolution with Jewish origins, so *Katynierung* will become a world concept for Jewish-Bolshevik bloodthirstiness."[79] Speakers should repeat that "the Jew, Ilya Ehrenburg" had called for "the extermination of 370 million" Europeans. It was the party's task to stress the Jews' role in the Soviet Union and to use every opportunity to "stress again and again *Juda's* guilt for the war and for its frightful consequences." Katyn was a "screaming, frightening warning for Europe and the world" about the "inhumanity of a system . . . that acts only out of the criminal instinct of its Jewish instigators and slave drivers."[80]

On May 5, 1943, the party's Reich Propaganda Directorate sent another directive through the extensive organizational web of *Gau-, Kreis-,* and *Ortsgruppenleiter,* the regional and local Nazi party leaders and orators. "The Jewish Question as a Domestic and Foreign Policy Weapon," asserted that it was "dangerous and false" to allow the Jewish question to disappear from public consciousness after that issue had been "solved in Germany," because it had emerged even more powerfully abroad.[81] "For this war is a war of Jews against Germany and its allies. Just as the domestic struggle ended with the anti-Semitic revolution in Germany, so this war must end with an anti-Semitic world revolution." The directive continued as follows:

> In Germany we made the whole nation anti-Semitic. We did so by repeatedly pointing our finger at the Jews, even as they tried to camouflage themselves. Again and again, we tore the masks from their faces. The Jews often tried to divert public attention from our campaign and to focus instead on other things, because they found our impressive propaganda highly uncomfortable. So it was all the more important to stand our ground and pursue this propaganda with firmness and persistence.
>
> In the wave of meetings [to be organized by the Nazi party] in the near future, the Jewish question now must be the constant key point of all presentations. Every German must know that everything he or she must endure—the discomforts, restrictions, extra hours at work, bloody terror toward women and children, and the bloody losses on the field of battle—is to be traced back to the Jews. In every meeting, the following points must be treated:
>
> that the international Jew wanted this war, occupies the most important economic positions among all the enemy peoples and countries, and ruthlessly uses his power to drive the peoples into war; that even today, he forms public opinion in the enemy countries, owns the press, radio, and film and presents them as the voice of the people. Nevertheless, knowledge about the essence of Jewry has gained a foothold and is growing; that there is no crime in which the Jew is not involved and that abroad today, as in Germany earlier, more than half of all economic criminals, swindlers, black marketeers, and stock exchange speculators are Jews; that where the Jews do not them-

selves appear as power holders, they have bought personalities in public life who, as dependent and servile tools, do the Jews' business; that the Jews profit from the war and thus have an interest in a long war. However, scarcely a single Jew carries a weapon or earns his income by the labor of his hands; as was the case here earlier in Germany, the Jews leave fighting and labor to others; that the Jews unleashed this war as a final attempt to assert their power in the world and to strike down those who had recognized them and their intentions; that this war will end with anti-Semitic world revolution and with the extermination of Jewry throughout the world, both of which are the precondition for an enduring peace. The core sentence is this statement: The Jews are guilty of everything!

"The Jewish Question as a Domestic and Foreign Policy Weapon" concluded by drawing the recipients' attention to Goebbels's essay "The War and the Jews" and informing them that copies would be made available to "all speakers" by the Reichspropagandaleitung.[82] On May 6, the *VB* led on page 1 with "USA and England under the Command of World Jewry, Plutocrats Identify with Jewish-Bolshevik Murderers."[83] In England, "it is forbidden to talk about Katyn," and necessary to celebrate Stalin as a great man and democrat. The plutocrat in London and the Bolshevik in Moscow have become close. "The one murders and the other defends the murder." The Americans and the British all "stand under the dictatorship of world Jewry" and are involved in the same crimes.[84]

In the midst of this virulent anti-Semitic campaign, Goebbels had begun work on one of his most important anti-Semitic essays and radio address of the entire war. As he noted in his diary, he was writing "The War and the Jews," to "effectively explain the horrific role that the Jews played in this war's beginning and in its further continuation."[85] The essay was published as the standard front-page editorial in *Das Reich* of

May 9, 1943, and broadcast on the radio that week as well.[86] Goebbels expressed exasperation and surprise that there were people who were "still too naive" to understand what the war was about and what role the Jewish question played in it. The "Jewish race" and its "helpers" were waging war against "Aryan humanity as well as against Western culture and civilization." He repeated his previous claims that "Jewry wanted this war. Wherever you look in the enemy camp, be it on the plutocratic or on the Bolshevist side, you see the Jews as inspirers and agitators working behind those exponents standing in the foreground of the enemy war leadership. They [the Jews] organize the enemy war economy, develop the programs for annihilation and extermination aimed at the Axis powers," and "[form] the glue that holds the enemy coalition together." The Jews' "Old Testament threats of revenge in their newspapers and radio broadcasts" were not "mere political literature. If [the Jews] had the power to do so, they would fulfill these desires down to the last point." The Jews, had "no other goal than the annihilation and extermination of our people." Nazi Germany was the sole barrier in Jewry's path to world domination and was the "dam" protecting Europe from the "Jewish-Bolshevik danger."[87] None of Hitler's "prophetic words" had been confirmed "with such tremendous certainty and inevitability as this: if the Jews succeeded in provoking a second world war, it would end not in the annihilation of Aryan humanity but rather in the extinction of the Jewish race." This was a process that would "take time but it is no longer to be stopped." The Jews would pay not only in Germany for their "countless crimes against the happiness and peace of humanity," but "in the whole world."[88] If Germany were to lose the war, "countless millions of people in our own and other European countries . . . would be delivered without defense to the hatred and will to extermination of this devilish race."[89] Goebbels assured his thousands of readers and millions of radio listeners:

> We are moving ahead. The fulfillment of the Führer's prophecy, about which world Jewry laughed in 1939 when he made it,

stands at the end of our course of action. Even in Germany, the Jews laughed when we stood up for the first time against them. Among them laughter is now a thing of the past. They chose to wage war against us. But Jewry now understands that the war has become a war against them. When Jewry conceived of the plan of the total extermination of the German people, it thereby wrote its own death sentence. In this instance as in others, world history will also be a world court.[90]

The essay repeated and elaborated on the essential projection mechanism of Nazi propaganda: A historical actor called international Jewry had launched the World War II to exterminate the Germans. Instead, the Germans had turned the tables and were fulfilling Hitler's prophecies, that is, they were now exterminating the Jews. In this and other texts, Goebbels combined the big lie or lies—that is, that there was something called international Jewry which was directing a war against Germany; that Germany had not started the war; and that the Allies were lackeys of an unseen but all-powerful international conspiracy—with the truthful assertion that Nazi Germany was at that time murdering the Jews of Europe. Rather than indignantly deny Allied accusations about Nazi anti-Jewish atrocities, Goebbels, following Hitler's lead, presented the Nazi attack on the Jews as a justified act of self-defense, retaliation, and revenge in response to the misfortunes the Jews had inflicted and were at that moment inflicting on Germany.[91] He was pleased with the domestic and foreign reaction to the article. He was convinced that "after the question of Bolshevism," the Jewish question was "the best horse in our stable of propaganda." Anti-Semitic articles should appear in the press "every other day" and German periodicals should show "an anti-Jewish face," both of which aims would be best accomplished by promoting younger, ideologically reliable editors.[92]

In a speech to Nazi gauleiters on May 8, Hitler stressed that anti-Semitism must again, as in the early years of the party, be at the core of

Nazi "cultural offensives." He hoped that it would spread in England, especially in the Tory party. He repeated his view that the Jews dominated both Bolshevism and western plutocracy, and that the war was a matter of "extermination or of being exterminated."[93] On May 9, the *VB* led with "Signs of Growing Hostility toward the Jews, Jewish Fear in England . . . Profit Hyenas Demand Misuse of State Power." It viewed the convening of a London conference to combat anti-Semitism as evidence of its growth, which the *VB* attributed to the association of the Jews with the war.[94] Hitler told Goebbels he was satisfied with the intensification of German anti-Semitic propaganda. Goebbels told him it now constituted "70 to 80 percent" of German foreign broadcasts.[95] On May 12, as the Germans were suppressing the Warsaw Ghetto revolt, the *VB* front-page headline proclaimed, "Moscow Will Be Official Center of World Jewry"; a Jewish state in Palestine would constitute the "cornerstone of Soviet control of the Mediterranean." The Soviet Union, the paper asserted, had become supportive of Zionism because it fitted with the Kremlin's future plans in the Mediterranean.[96] On May 18, the party's Reich Propaganda Directorate sent "Twilight for the Jews All over the World!" to officials in the state and party propaganda apparatus.[97] It cited Goebbels's repetition of Hitler's prophecy in "The War and the Jews" and announced that anti-Semitism was spreading in enemy nations, including England and the United States. This development sprang from a growing understanding that "all the suffering, privations, and deprivation of this war are exclusively due to the Jews, that the war itself is the work of *Juda*."[98]

During this time, no mention of the Warsaw Ghetto revolt and its brutal suppression appeared in the German press, which concerned itself only with the alleged misdeeds of others. In the midst of the flood of Nazi Germany's anti-Semitic propaganda the *New York Times* reported that according to a representative of the World Jewish Congress, "all Jews in Warsaw's ghetto have been liquidated"—that is, the remaining 40,000 of the original 450,000 had been killed in the final battles, along with 60 Nazis.[99] On May 22, the *Times* reported that nearly 1,000

Germans had been killed or wounded in the last weeks of the Warsaw Ghetto uprising. On June 20, 1943 (on page 34), it reported that the Polish ambassador to the United States, Jan Ciechanowski, speaking of the ghetto, had told an audience of 3,000 at Carnegie Hall, "Never in the history of mankind have its chronicles registered so continuous, so methodical, so iniquitous, so barbarous, so inhuman a system of cruelty and mass extermination."[100] Meanwhile, the *VB* published denunciations on page 1 of "Jewish world politics" and "Jewish-American imperialism." As evidence of the latter it cited "the Jew Walter Lippmann's" examination of possibilities for postwar cooperation between the United States and the Soviet Union. The *VB* described Lippmann's suggestion as a further proof of an effort to establish a "Jewish world dictatorship of Wall Street and the Kremlin."[101]

On May 13, 1943, Goebbels had a long and quite remarkable conversation with Hitler. Most of it was a monologue by Hitler about the *Protocols of the Elders of Zion.* Goebbels had recently reread the *Protocols* and concluded that, contrary to his earlier view, they actually were suitable for use in "contemporary propaganda." In spring 1943 they were "as modern as the day they were first published." He was "astounded" at the remarkably thorough way in which they laid out the Jewish striving for world domination. "If the Zionist protocols are not genuine, they were created by a brilliant critic of the period." Hitler, he added, had no doubts about the origins of the infamous forgery written by the tsar's political police. "The Führer believes that the Zionist protocols are absolutely genuine." Hitler said, "No one could be so brilliant as to describe the Jewish striving for world domination as well as the Jews themselves." The Jews, he continued, did not "work from a predetermined program but according to their race instinct . . . Modern peoples had no alternative but to exterminate the Jews." Oddly, Goebbels, who had heard Hitler go on about the international Jewish conspiracy since the mid-1920s, found Hitler's comments extremely interesting, perhaps because hearing them in private underscored the intensity of Hitler views on the topic.[102]

The following evening, after learning of the German defeat in Tunis, Goebbels wrote, "Anti-Jewish propaganda must be the core of all our press activity. The Jewish question must be discussed more emphatically than ever before."[103] In the North African campaign in April and May, British, American, and some French forces defeated Rommel's army, taking 275,000 German and Italian soldiers prisoner. Only 800 escaped. The Axis had lost, in addition to its hold on parts of North Africa, two armies, vast quantities of supplies, and numerous ships and airplanes. Unity among the Allies, including the forces under General Charles de Gaulle, was enhanced, while morale in Italy plummeted over the loss of the last part of its African empire.[104] The following day, Goebbels noted in his diary, "The end of the fighting in Tunisia is very depressing." In the first five months of 1943, the "enemy has had the upper hand," striking blows in the air war over Germany, inflicting "deep wounds" on the eastern front, and imposing setbacks in North Africa. The German submarine war in the Atlantic had not achieved the promised results. Success on the eastern front, so vital to the German cause, was not attainable anytime soon. He noted that the Propaganda Ministry's reports of popular sentiment had picked up on a "rather depressed mood" due to the combined defeats at Stalingrad and now in North Africa.[105] Anti-Semitic propaganda had flourished during moments of military victory and euphoria in the summer and fall of 1941, the high tide of German expansion in 1942, as well as the period in which the tide turned after Stalingrad, in spring 1943. Now, as the fortunes of war turned against the Nazi regime, the anti-Semitic narrative continued to offer a seemingly compelling explanation. The longer Allied unity persisted and the more defeats the Allies inflicted on the German military, the more Nazi leaders saw proof that a *powerful international Jewish conspiracy* really existed and that its actions explained why Germany was suffering reversals in the war. In the view of the Nazi leadership, anti-Semitic propaganda was not a diversion from reality but an appropriate response to the actual course of events. Because the core Nazi ideological assumption about World War II was that it was a war that the Jews were waging against Germany, it followed logically that anti-Semitic propaganda should intensify in spring, summer, and fall 1943, as the tide in the war turned against the Nazi regime.

On May 17, the Reich Press Office ordered that the cultural-political sections of the papers should be more strongly defined than in the past by an anti-Semitic outlook.[106] Several days later it instructed editors that, apart from reporting on daily events, it was important to offer arguments about "the meaning and mission of the war." These lay first of all in "the war guilt of international Jewry, which via its Bolshevik and plutocratic satellites forces the nations and peoples into war in order to destroy their life force and thereby establish its international domination." Conversely, the war aims of the Axis powers were to establish peace and economic development in Europe and the world, once the economic failure of "international powers"—namely, the Allies and the Jews—was set aside.[107]

Goebbels remained deeply involved in the anti-Semitic propaganda offensive. His editorial for *Das Reich* of May 16, 1943, interpreted English skepticism about Soviet responsibility for the Katyn murders as a result of Jewish efforts to minimize the dangers of Bolshevism.[108] His speech to the Nazi faithful of June 5, 1943, in the Berlin Sportpalast focused on a denunciation of the British air war against German cities. He claimed, "The Jews above all want an invasion" of Europe; but they would not participate. In their place, British and American soldiers—that is, non-Jews—would pay the price. Despite the terrible cost of such an invasion, the Jews were pushing for it. "Churchill and Roosevelt, in any case, are only their executive organs." In response to those who were skeptical of his view that a "world cabal" was driving the enemy coalition, Goebbels asked how it was possible to explain the unity between advocates of freedom and executioners of Polish officers; religious advocates and atheists; and Bolsheviks and capitalists, other than by pointing to a "band of swindlers and cheaters who are striving for world domination and also want to subject Europe to this Jewish striving for world power." There was, in fact, no reason to wage war on

Germany other than to destroy this "last bastion" against their "treacherous Jewish-plutocratic-Bolshevik" plans. The enemy coalition was a "criminal world conspiracy," which would destroy "decent and creative humanity" unless Germany destroyed the enemy first.[109] In his diary Goebbels blamed German Jewish emigrants to England for the accuracy of Allied bombing raids on German cities, and the "Jews in the City of London" for the fact that the war was not over. A short war, he wrote, would have been bad for business. The Nazis needed to do more to inflame anti-Semitism in England. As for the uncritical Hollywood film about the Soviet Union based on Ambassador Joseph Davies's book *My Mission in Moscow,* it too was "a Jewish concoction."[110]

On May 21, 1943, Dietrich's office sent a "Special Issue against the Jews: The Goal: An Anti-Jewish Periodical Press" to editors at newspapers and periodicals. It constituted a high point in the regime's anti-Semitic press and propaganda campaign of that spring and summer.[111]

German periodicals now have a unique opportunity to resolutely lead the global struggle against the Jews. Since the Jews have acquired influence in all areas of political, economic, and cultural life in various countries in the world, every periodical can deal with this theme in its own sphere of expertise. We again repeat that the objection that the German people are already informed about the Jews and thus do not need to be further enlightened on the subject is not at all valid. Even for propaganda work within Germany, the thesis remains true that only through constant hammering away at a recognized truth will the entire people grasp and act on this truth . . . However, now the impact [of such propaganda] is even more important abroad than domestically.[112]

The directive pointed out that articles in periodicals could reach foreign audiences if they were shared with professional colleagues, friends, and family members or included in letters from Germany to recipients abroad. The credibility of such "intimate propaganda" was considerable.

"For many, what their father, brother, or friend writes to the French, Belgians, Danes, Norwegians, and Ukrainians is the truth itself." Such opinions can make their way into the foreign press and foster anti-Semitism there. Anti-Jewish propaganda would be effective only if "all German newspapers and periodicals together and simultaneously for a period of several months stress[ed] from every perspective the uncovering of the Jewish danger and the need to remove it." The directive reminded journalists of three previous issues of the *Periodical Service* and the *Deutscher Wochendienst* (German Weekly Service), which addressed these topics, respectively: "When the Jew comes to power," "Jews are criminals," and "Jewry wants to murder Europe's peoples." The special issue contained "the most important anti-Jewish themes" that had been presented previously, as well as references to "anti-Jewish writings" that, the editors assumed, could be found "in every German district library."[113]

The tone of this directive was urgent. The special anti-Jewish issue "cannot forever disappear into your safe after a one-time perusal. Rather, in the coming months the editor in chief must take it out every day. It should constantly influence his thinking about planning the next issue. We must reach a point in the coming months where there is not a single periodical page that does not in some way or another refer to the Jewish problem." Editors were to draw readers' attention to Jewish political leaders, economists, scientists, artists, bankers, and entrepreneurs, as well as firms and banks owned by Jews. The directive included clear vocabulary guidelines. When referring to such figures as Maxim Litvinov, Lazar Kaganovich, or Walter Rathenau, or such enterprises as the Rothschild bank, the Mosse publishing house, or the *New York Times,* "the text must read: the Jew Litvinov, the Jew Kaganovich, the Jew Rathenau, the Jewish Rothschild bank, the Jewish Mosse publishing house, the Jewish newspaper the *New York Times.*"[114]

For political periodicals, the service drew attention to such "leaders of U.S. politics" as Felix Frankfurter and Samuel Rosenman, and to the "Jewification of the bureaucracy" in the Soviet Union. It referred to past issues containing information on Jews in the GPU, war industries, and agriculture and Jewish commissars in the army.[115] The growth of anti-Semitism in England and the United States was to be encouraged through journals' focus on such themes as Jews shirking military service and Jews participating in black-market activities and in unfair business practices. The "journals must point out that the Jew in England and the United States is playing the role of the wire puller behind the scenes" who always works against "the host people and in favor of his racial comrades." The special issue offered an abundance of material on the United States, England, and the Soviet Union, which would "suffice for months to thoroughly flood your periodical with the anti-Jewish spirit that the press leadership now must demand from every publication. The fruit of this week's propaganda directive, to which we again give particular importance, must be manifest in every periodical that we publish: the German press must become an anti-Jewish press."[116] The issue included a section entitled "The Jews Are Guilty," which asserted that it was "the mission of all periodicals" to set aside "all sentimentality" about the Jews and to stress that "every Jew, wherever he is and whatever he does, is complicitous." None were innocent; Jews were "only more or less camouflaged."[117]

Nazism's core indictment was crystallized in a directive in this issue called "Fight World Jewry."

The course of the war had clearly shown that it was a struggle driven by world Jewry's immeasurable hatred against Aryan people as such, against their spirit, worldview, and culture. The Jewish wire pullers in London, in New York, and, not least, in Moscow planned and prepared this war with shameless campaigns of agitation to push peoples to war, so that they would take up arms against the Aryan powers of the earth. World Jewry intentionally expanded the war in hopes of winning as a result of the exhaustion of the Aryan adversary. World Jewry entered this pitiless battle in three forms: first, as a Jew; second, as a plutocrat with Jewish origins; and third, as a Jewish Bolshevik.

Its goal, evident in the Old Testament, was "Jewish world domination." Only the efforts of "the Aryan peoples" had prevented the Jews from reaching their goal. "Today Jewry again seeks world domination" through the instrument of British and American plutocrats, on the one hand, and Bolsheviks, on the other. Their seemingly different political goals camouflaged Jewish influence. The "true background of this gigantic struggle"—that is, World War II—was a "racial, ideological, political, and cultural struggle between world Jewry and Aryan humanity." Whether Jewry appeared as "London plutocrats around Churchill, the Jewish-led Soviet government, a warmonger in the form of imperialism of the first-degree Freemason Roosevelt, . . . Aryan men" would be on guard against the Jews. The former are able to recognize "the world enemy number 1 in whatever form he appears, along with his paid and tolerated stooges."[118]

On May 18, 1943, representatives of forty-five nations gathered in Hot Springs, Virginia, to attend a United Nations conference on food and agriculture. The conference was held to promote increased production of food around the world in the postwar era and to eliminate barriers to trade, transportation, and internal distribution.[119] It had nothing to do with Jewish issues. Nevertheless, on May 21 the *VB* led on page 1 with "It Could Turn Out This Way, Europe to Be Delivered to Corn Jews [*Kornjuden*]; Axis Powers Fight for Right of All Peoples to Work and Bread." Rather than to put in place the free trade principles articulated at Hot Springs, the real purpose of the conference, the *VB* maintained, was to place the "whole of the world's food supplies under the administration of the USA, England, the Bolsheviks, and China and to ration and distribute them according to a rationing system." Thus, Roosevelt's plans for eliminating hunger around the world were really "an anchoring of the political dictatorship of Wall Street Jews over the whole world."[120]

On May 25, the *VB* again attacked the Hot Springs conference in a lead headline on page 1: "International Food Bank: Jewish Plans for Exploiting the World: The People to Become the Object of Stock Exchange Speculation."[121] The *VB* described a British proposal for an international food bank to assist nations suffering from drought and food shortages as "faithful copy of the story told in the Old Testament about the great usurer Joseph." In the famous biblical tale (Gen. 41), Joseph interprets a dream of the Pharaoh to mean, "What God is about to do, he has let Pharaoh see"; therefore, the Pharaoh must store food in the seven years of good harvests to prepare for the seven years of famine that will follow. In gratitude and in acknowledgment of Joseph's foresight, the Pharaoh tells Joseph, "You shall be the one over my house! To your orders shall my people submit." In the years of famine, the Egyptians were able to survive because of the grain stored during the seven years of good harvests. It is a parable about the value of planning for the vicissitudes of nature, and one familiar to the Old Testament readers of Protestant Europe.[122] So it may have come as a bit of a surprise to Germans to read the interpretation of the story of Joseph on the front page of the *VB*:

> With the undisguised feelings of pride in his Jewish unscrupulousness and economic brutality, this national hero of the Hebrews, as the Bible shows him, hoarded corn supplies for seven years and then in the following years of drought and bad harvests economically strangled not only the Egyptian population but the neighboring peoples as well. Only he possessed the supplies for delivery and sale. He dictated the price and made sure that all the money flowed into his accounts. Then the starving people had to deliver up all their cattle. The next year he demanded all their farmland. Finally, he starved them into servitude and burdened them with eternal obligations of tribute.[123]

The *VB* described the biblical tale as "the preamble" to the proposal in Hot Springs for establishment of a world food bank.[124] The *VB* account of the biblical tale was as erroneous as its report about the Hot Springs meeting. Nothing in the original text supports either. But this distorted comparison of biblical times to those of World War II included a by-now familiar theme of Nazi propaganda: in ancient Egypt as in twentieth-century America, the Jew was the man behind the scenes and the wire puller. In ancient Egypt it was Joseph. In spring 1943, it was Bernard Baruch or Felix Frankfurter. Each gained the ear of non-Jewish political leaders and used his well-concealed power to starve and enslave the non-Jewish world. Perhaps some readers of the *VB* remembered that the original text was at odds with the Nazi reading, but by then many others would have become familiar with Nazi biblical "interpretations" along these lines.[125]

On June 2, the *VB* featured an article on page 1 called "Hunger and Chaos, Stages of Jewish World Domination, Postwar Fantasies of the Roosevelt Clique," its third headline referring to the Allies' planning for the postwar period.[126] According to the *VB* articles, American Jews were openly proclaiming that their goal was world domination. The evidence for this claim was an article by journalists Arthur Krock and Raymond Clapper in the "Jewish New York weekly magazine *Look*," which envisaged a plan for a "world government" dominated by the United States, England, and the Soviet Union. "Washington and Moscow Jewry" would be at its center. The *VB* writer assured readers that this plan was not "the phantoms of two journalists seeking a sensational story." Rather, "Krock and Clapper developed the plan in the service of Roosevelt and his Jewish men behind the scenes." The proof was that Undersecretary of State Sumner Welles had announced "exactly the same plan." In fact, Welles had called for establishment of a world court and an international police force to prevent another world war and to foster postwar economic cooperation among nations, recognition of the principle of equal sovereignty among nations, and equality of human rights.[127] For the *VB*, however, Welles's plan and the Hot Springs conference were really designed to foster "hunger, chaos, and general anarchy, so that the Jews would have the chance . . . to establish their domination."[128] Other than the facts that Krock, Clapper, and Welles had spoken about postwar plans and that a conference on food supplies after the war had taken place at Hot Springs, nothing in the *VB* articles was true. Yet this smattering of proper names and specific events was more than adequate as a way to people the Nazis' vast conspiracy theory with actors and actions.

On May 5, 1943, with the demands of war putting pressures on budgets and calling more party members into the armed forces, the party's Reich Propaganda Directorate in Berlin informed regional propaganda offices that the *Word of the Week* wall newspaper series would end.[129] That spring, however, the Propaganda Ministry distributed some of the most visually striking anti-Semitic posters of the war years. These images dispensed with the usual many lines of text in favor of simple messages and bold colors. In contrast to the *Word of the Week,* these posters showed no dateline that would associate the issue with a particular week or month or a particular set of events—and hence did not become dated. Because they featured so few words, they also could be easily translated for distribution in German-occupied Europe. "Behind the Enemy Powers: The Jew" ("Hinter den Feindmächten: Der Jude") is a remarkable visual synthesis of the Nazi conspiracy theory, depicting the anti-Hitler coalition. It shows an overweight, stereotypical Jewish man in civilian dress, wearing a gold Star of David on a gold chain and looking out from behind a curtain composed of the flags of the United States, Britain, and the Soviet Union. His placement between the American and Soviet flags underscores the Nazi argument regarding the Jewish link between the two powers. Again, the phrase *der Jude* appears in yellow.[130]

Two additional images were done by Hans Schweitzer (Mjölnir) himself. "He Bears the Guilt for the War!" ("Der ist schuld am Kriege!") offers an equally dramatic distillation of the core Nazi message. A powerful, accusing finger points downward at a cowering stereotypical Jewish man. He is dressed in civilian clothes and bent over as if trying to hide, or at least avoid, the accusing finger. The yellow Star of

David affixed to his left lapel clearly establishes his Jewish identity.[131] Schweitzer's second striking anti-Semitic image of this period was "The Jew: Instigator of the War, Prolonger of the War" ("Der Jude: Kriegsanstifter, Kriegsverlängerer"), in which a sinister-looking Jewish male looks out from behind a curtain, which, however, has been pulled aside by a muscular hand and arm.[132] A chorus of fists expressing anger and resistance appears below, and in the interval between the fists appears a landscape in flames. The image concisely conveys Nazi Germany's efforts to pull the curtain back to reveal the powers driving events. All three posters are noteworthy, in that they dispense with any presentation of stooges and accomplices, to focus exclusively on a caricatured Jewish figure. It is difficult to imagine a greater disconnect than that between the image of Jewish power conveyed in such posters and the utterly powerless and helpless state of European Jewry in Germany and occupied Europe. Although distribution figures are not available, other posters by Schweitzer disseminated around the same time appeared in editions of between 107,000 and 370,000, depending on the format.[133] Millions of people saw these posters.

In May 1943, the Soviet Union announced that it was dissolving the Comintern. Historians have demonstrated that the formal dissolution did not at all mean the end of Soviet wartime espionage.[134] The Reich Press Office directive of May 22, 1943, saw the announcement as evidence of another, familiar conspiracy. "The supposed 'dissolution' of the Third International . . . is the most recent and most brazen Jewish-Bolshevik swindle to fool the nations. Faced with the pressure of growing anti-Jewish and anti-Bolshevik awareness in all countries, Roosevelt and Churchill, as exponents of capitalist Jewry, gave Stalin the advice to undertake this genuine Jewish maneuver of deception." They did so, clearly, in order to present Bolshevism in "sheep's clothing" and thus give Stalin a free hand in Europe. Why Roosevelt and Churchill would want to give Stalin free rein in Europe or make Bolshevism appear harmless remained a mystery, which could be explained only by the deus ex machina of the Jews operating behind the scenes. The directive left little to the imagination in offering the following suggestions for headlines: "The Newest Jewish Swindle"; "Camouflaged Bolshevism"; "Bolshevism in New Masks"; "Bolshevist Camouflage of the Newest Jewish Swindle"; "New Jewish Trick"; "The Greatest Jewish Swindle"; "The Roosevelt Conspiracy"; "Churchill-Stalin, the New Jewish Liberation Tactics"; and "Bolshevism in Sheep's Clothing."[135] The following evening Goebbels's diary entry claimed that the dissolution of the Comintern was a "Jewish bluff," originating in pressure from Roosevelt and Churchill in their efforts to make Bolshevism appear harmless.[136]

The phrase "The Jewish War" appeared on occasion in Nazi propaganda, most notably in a front-page essay by the anti-Semitic propagandist Theodor Seibert in the *VB* of June 2, 1943.[137] Seibert was concerned with the issue of transmission of anti-Semitism to the successor Nazi generations. Most older National Socialists, he wrote, had joined the movement "primarily out of loathing for Jewry." By 1943, however, a large number of young people had come of age who had neither experienced the economic crises of the Weimar era nor "had any personal and direct experience of Jewry." The "purging" of the Reich after 1933 drove the Jews out of public view so suddenly that "only a year after the seizure of power it was only with great effort that one could recall a clear picture of the total Jewification of German life." This was a problem because "in January 1933, the Jew, here and abroad, began the conscious preparation of World War II, a war for the annihilation of Germany," the first state to break with "Jewish domination." In 1941, "when Roosevelt—whose enslavement to the Jews [*Judenhörigkeit*] was obvious to even the most harmless European—finally got his war," it was proof, Seibert claimed, of the Jews' role in American foreign policy.

Seibert presented the following history of "the Jewish war." It began with "mendacious atrocity campaigns" instigated by "Jewish emigrants in England, France, and the USA." Ernst Toller, Arnold Zweig, Kurt Tucholsky, and Albert Einstein, among others, "flooded the newspapers, magazines, and book publishers of the plutocratic countries with endless lies about our revolution, long before the Nuremberg Law, long before a hair on the head of the Jews in Germany had been disturbed." In the West, Jews were the leaders of the organizations "that poisoned" the public against "the new Germany." It was not the English who organized the first mass demonstrations against Germany. Rather, it was "Jews in London and Jews from Eastern Europe in New York." It was not "real English, French, and North American citizens" who organized the anti-German committees and collected signatures and money. It was, he continued, a "historical fact" that originally most people in England, France, and the United States had felt no animosity toward National Socialism. He claimed that the English had shown complete understanding for Germany's reoccupation of the Rhineland in 1936 and that the Munich agreement was met in England with "great joy" in 1938. It was the "tireless, years-long satanic agitation and defamation [of Nazi Germany] by the Anglo-American press that was either Jewified or dependent on Jewish advertising business" and by the governments in London and Washington that had created support for war against Germany following the German invasion of Poland. He did not mention that the United States had not entered the war in Europe until Hitler declared war on it in December 1941.[138]

Seibert attributed Churchill's opposition to Nazi Germany to his "intimate personal" links to Rothschild in London, Bernard Baruch in New York, and other "Jewish financial supporters and bosom friends." Churchill had "used his Jewish connections across the Atlantic to threaten the English people with Washington's anger" if they refused to support war against Germany. Before and during the war, Churchill had become linked ever more closely with "the Jewish stronghold in Roosevelt's White House." With obvious exasperation, he wrote that it was "no longer necessary to offer proof" that Roosevelt's policies were not in the American interest but instead supported "purely Jewish interests." Though the American people had no interest in war in Europe, "the goals of American imperialism" could best be advanced by "the Jews' war of revenge against Europe," which Roosevelt had "forced on the American people." The creation of the anti-Nazi coalition had been the work of "Stalin's Soviet-Jews, Litvinov, Maisky, Kaganovich, and Losovsky, who built the bridge from the Jewified Kremlin to a Downing Street dependent on the Jews, and to the Jewish White House. Only the cooperation of the Moscow, London, and Washington Jews could bring about the unnatural coalition" between the Soviet Union and the capitalist democracies. The spirit of this coalition was evident "in the GPU's mass murders as well as in the mass murder and culture devastation of the air gangsters" (*Luftgangster*) from Britain and the United States. In years to come, historians would conclude that "this second world war would never have broken out if international Jewry had not wished it to happen, prepared it systematically for years, and finally declared it, with the help of the world historical criminals Churchill and Roosevelt." Just as the responsibility of Wall Street Jews for the bloodletting of World War I had been proven, so "the day in court that Jewry fears like hell" will come, unless of course, the Jews succeeded in "destroying and burning" Europe. They now were going to "pay dearly" for their "arrogance and superiority," which had in the end left Central Europe no other choice than to fight, to prevent slavery, submission, and "a life of eternal poverty and national disgrace."[139] Seibert's tale made no distinction at all between war against the Allies and war against the Jews. In his mind, as in the minds of the Nazi leaders, it was all the same "Jewish war."

As the war stretched on, the anti-Semitic prism gave Nazi leaders hope that time was on their side. This was a reversal of Hitler's initial strategy aiming for quick victory over isolated, unprepared enemies. In May and early June, Goebbels confided to his diary that the longer the war lasted, the greater would be the number of people who would look for a scapegoat for their suffering. "In this case, the suspected scapegoat and the actual one are the same." The Jews worried: "If the war continues for a long time, their position in the enemy countries will be very dangerously undermined."[140] He had England and the United States in mind. In his editorial of June 6 in *Das Reich*, "Motorized Forces,"

Goebbels elaborated on the connection between the continuation of the war and anti-Semitism.[141] If, as the Nazis asserted, the Jews were responsible for the war, then it would make perfect sense that anti-Semitism around the world should increase, the longer the war continued. "The war has not crushed, but rather confirmed, our own view of the world."[142] As the "suspected" and the "actual" scapegoat were the same, anti-Semitism was both a useful propaganda tool and an accurate interpretation of events.

In spring 1943, the German Foreign Office published *Roosevelt's Path to War: Secret Documents of the War Policy of the President of the United States*.[143] The pamphlet covered the period from FDR's "Quarantine the Aggressors" speech in 1937 to his declaration of war on December 8, 1941. It laid the blame for the world war squarely on Roosevelt's shoulders. The supposed documentary discoveries amounted to nothing more than Roosevelt's public efforts from 1937 on to support resistance to Nazi policy, in order to deter Hitler from launching a war. For the Nazi regime, the pamphlet's value lay in giving an apparently expert interpretation of the war's origins that would focus on American striving for world dominance. It included the familiar accusation regarding "the influence of Jews," such as Felix Frankfurter, Secretary of the Treasury Henry Morgenthau, and the governor of New York, Herbert Lehman, on President Roosevelt. The Jews had "achieved their goal" when the war broke out.[144] In its press directive of July 2, the Reich Press Office told German journalists that the Foreign Ministry's pamphlet proved Roosevelt's "personal responsibility for the origins of the war," as well as the "dominant Jewish influence on American politics."[145] The lead front-page story of the July 4 issue of the *VB* featured the Foreign Ministry paper on Roosevelt's path to war: "New Documents Reinforce the Judgment: Roosevelt's War Guilt Firmly Established—'World President' as Straw Man of Jewish Warmongers."[146]

The summer of 1943 brought grim news. Mussolini had been overthrown, imprisoned, and then freed only by German paratroopers. The

Allies landed in Sicily in July. The Red Army was in the early stages of pushing the Wehrmacht westward. On August 13, Dietrich issued a remarkable press directive.

> The *Word of the Day* from the Reich press chief of August 9, 1943, again clearly pointed out that Bolshevism and capitalism are the identical Jewish world swindle, operating under different names. Nevertheless, in the treatment of Bolshevik themes the newspapers repeatedly succumb to the illusion that capitalism and Bolshevism are two different and antagonistic perspectives. In particular, communist agitation is repeatedly given a boost because the press takes Bolshevik statements seriously, as if Bolshevism really wanted to destroy capitalism. In reality, these two Jewish systems are working hand in hand with one another. Now the German press must finally put an end to this false and dangerous tendency, which sabotages the line of our policy. Editors who violate this word of the day will be held personally responsible for doing so.[147]

In his postwar account, Dietrich's aide Helmut Sündermann argued that Dietrich's directive sought to counter the impression among the German public that there was a fundamental difference between the Soviets and the West and that therefore it was possible and desirable to seek a separate peace with one side or the other. As Sündermann noted, in a postwar statement noteworthy for its unreconstructed ideological consistency, "the Jews were the element that was influential among all [the Allies]. Thus it was important from the standpoint of German war propaganda to present them at the center of the discussion, as the unifying ferment of the enemy front."[148] Goebbels admitted in his diary entry of August 8 that tensions existed between Moscow and the Western powers. Yet, like Dietrich, he intensified anti-Semitic propaganda in the hope of reducing the alleged power of the Jews in England and the United States.[149]

In June and July, the front pages of the *VB* kept up the anti-Semitic drumbeat. On June 5 the paper led with a headline declaring that the "servants of the Jews" had decided to "use bands of Negroes as terror flyers over Italy."[150] On June 18, it denounced the shipbuilder identified as "the Jew Henry Kaiser" as an example of war profiteering in the Roosevelt administration.[151] On June 22, it marked the second anniversary of the invasion of the Soviet Union. Nazi Germany and its armies to the East constituted "the West's wall of protection" that had saved Germany and the rest of Europe from domination by Bolshevism and "world Jewry."[152] On June 23, the *VB* published a speech by Alfred Rosenberg on "the world struggle and the world revolution of our time," which included a bundle of anti-American clichés under the front-page headline "Greatest Danger of World History, the Alliance between Gangsterism and Bolshevism."[153] On July 4, the *VB* featured the Foreign Office's pamphlet, "Roosevelt's Path to the War" and led with "Roosevelt's War Guilt Conclusively Proven; World President as Straw Man of the Jewish Warmongers."[154] On July 20, following the British bombing of Rome, the *VB* led with "Jews Show No Respect for Humanity's Cultural Heritage, Terror Bombers Attack Rome, New Crimes by British-American Air Gangsters." The bombing raids demonstrated "the Jewish character of this war," entailing as they did the destruction of "everything that has always been and will always be alien to the Jews."[155]

In August 1943, a memo from the Nazi party's Reich Propaganda Directorate to party officials and speakers offered a sober assessment. The party needed to counter a prevailing mood of depression. It should stress three points. First, "the Jews' will to extermination," present in the alliance of plutocracy and Bolshevism, "forces us into unconditional struggle until victory." There could be no negotiated end to the war. Second, the "genius" Germany's leadership, its occupation of the heart of Europe, the superiority of its soldiers and armaments, and the security of its agricultural supplies were grounds for confidence in the long term. And third, "the strongest . . . of our justified grounds for confidence in victory is the person of the Führer himself."[156] Yet as a directive in early

September from the party's Reich Propaganda Directorate demonstrated, stark fear at the consequences of defeat was becoming a more prominent theme in Nazi propaganda. Party officials were under strict orders not to reveal the extent of losses and destruction due to Allied bombing. Rather, they should point out that the "thousands dying under the bombing murder of the Jewish-plutocratic enemy" would become "millions under rule by the Jewish-Bolshevik enemy." Workers, farmers, children, and infants would be among those who would be "pursued like wild animals, owing to Jewish hatred and Bolshevik terror." Only German victory could prevent realization of the enemy's goal, "the extermination of Germany," along with its social achievements, economy, and culture.[157]

Nazi propagandists presented the turning of the tide in the war as confirmation of the validity of Hitler and Goebbels's warnings that the Jews were going to attempt to "exterminate" the Germans. Fear of the genocidal war aims projected onto the Jews had been a staple of the regime's wartime propaganda from the moment Hitler gave his speech of January 30, 1939. After the defeats at Stalingrad and in North Africa, Mussolini's fall, and the Allied bombing campaign against German cities, Nazi propaganda now asserted that the truth of Hitler's prophecies about Germany's extermination could be seen in the ruins of Hamburg and Cologne and in the massive destruction of German army units by the increasingly powerful Red Army. Reality appeared to lend credence to ideology. The Allies had proclaimed that they were fighting a war against the Nazi regime, party, and military forces, not the German people as a whole, but the Nazi regime did its best to convince fellow Germans that just the opposite was the case and that their only hope for survival was to fight on, to prevent extermination by Jewry's murderous hands. Radical anti-Semitism and the cultivation of mass fear would remain elements of the message that held Nazi Germany together until the Nazi regime was destroyed. As Hitler had repeatedly warned, the war would leave only survivors or the exterminated.

7 "Victory or Extermination"

In summer and fall 1943, Nazi Germany suffered further reverses in the war. Italy surrendered to the Allies on September 9, 1943. At Kursk, on the eastern front, the largest tank confrontation in military history ended in a Soviet victory. The Battle of Kursk marked the end of German offensive operations on the eastern front and prefigured the movement of the Red Army toward Germany. Less noticed but of great importance was the growing strength of the Soviet air force. A blitzkrieg in reverse began to decimate the Wehrmacht on the eastern front. Strategic interaction between the eastern and western fronts took a heavy toll on German armies. Fighting on the eastern front prevented the Germans from shifting forces to the West, while the need to defend German cities against British and American bombing reduced the airpower available to use against the Red Army.[1] German airpower steadily declined, while Allied airpower both in the West and in the East increased. The death toll among the German armed forces was grim. Before the Battle of Stalingrad, German battlefield deaths in 1942 averaged around thirty-five thousand a month. Almost four hundred thousand soldiers died in the four months from December 1942 to March 1943. The average monthly death toll from April to June was twenty-five thousand. From the Battle of Kursk in July 1943 until May 1944, German battlefield deaths averaged seventy thousand a month, that is, more than two thousand a day.[2] Though individual families knew of their losses, the Reich Press Office—indeed, the Propaganda Ministry as a whole—successfully suppressed information about the escalating death toll.

At the same time, the regime suppressed the details of the Final Solution. From summer 1943 to spring 1944, the German press carried no reports about the destruction of the Jewish ghetto in Lvov, or indeed of any ghetto in Poland, or about the completion in late June 1943 of a fifth crematorium at Auschwitz-Birkenau, which could produce 4,756 corpses every twenty-four hours. Nor was there any word about the August 1943 uprising by prisoners at Treblinka, the deportation in August 1943 of the last of 43,000 Jews from Salonika, Greece, to Auschwitz, the destruction in September 1943 of the Jewish ghettos in Minsk and Vilna, or the exhumation and burning of 100,000 bodies buried at Babi Yar, to hide traces of mass murder. No mention was made of efforts by *Sonderkommandos* in Minsk to obliterate all traces of the murder of more than 40,000 people or of the revolt in October 1943 by prisoners at Sobibor. The Nazi press ignored the establishment on October 20, 1943, of the United Nations War Crimes Commission and reported nothing about the launching on November 3 of Operation Harvest Festival, which resulted in the killing of 40,000 Jews—18,000 in one day alone—at Majdanek; the arrests of Jews in Florence, Milan, and Venice for deportation to Auschwitz; the deportation to Auschwitz on February 18, 1944, of the remnants of the Jewish community of Amsterdam; or the deportation in 147 trains between April and July 1944 of 454,551 Hungarian Jews, most of whom were murdered on arrival in the gas chambers at Auschwitz-Birkenau.[3] Total silence about these events was among the greatest "accomplishments" of the Reich Press Office and of the Propaganda Ministry. The Nazi propaganda apparatus kept the extent of the disaster that had befallen the German armed forces, as well as the details and scope of the Final Solution, entirely out of the public view. Rumors and reports spread by soldiers back from the front were no substitute for the accurate ongoing narrative that only a free and inquiring press and other independent media could offer. The absence of a free press was a crucial precondition for the implementation of the Final Solution.

Neither Dietrich nor Goebbels left a paper trail that would indicate the state of their detailed knowledge either of the Final Solution or of the real figures of German battlefield dead and wounded. Goebbels's diary entry of October 7, 1943, included a report on a meeting of Nazi gauleiters in Posen, also attended by Robert Ley, Albert Speer, Karl Dönitz, and Max Amann, among others. Himmler told those assembled: "We could solve the Jewish question for all of Europe by the end of this year." He spoke up for the most radical solution—namely, "to exterminate Jewry completely." Goebbels agreed with Himmler, saying, "We must take the responsibility" for doing so in "our time": subsequent generations would not have the Nazis' "courage and obsession" to carry it out.[4]

By October 1943, 2 to 2.5 million Jews had been murdered in the six death camps. The *Einsatzgruppen* had murdered more that 600,000 Jews in the Soviet Union, and tens of thousands more had been killed by police units, the *Ordnungspolizei,* in village and town massacres in Poland and elsewhere in Eastern Europe. Five of the six death camps had completed their task. Auschwitz-Birkenau was the only one left in operation. It is likely that what Goebbels called a "frank and unadorned picture" was Himmler's subsequently infamous speech about "the annihilation of the Jewish people," which had been delivered three days earlier to a much larger audience of SS officers in Posen, Poland.[5] Yet even then Himmler referred only to the early methods of the *Einsatzgruppen* murders and said nothing about the death camps, gas chambers, and crematoria. The evidence we have already examined suggests that high-ranking officials in the Propaganda Ministry and its Reich Press Office knew as early as fall 1941 that the German government was engaged in a program of mass murder against Europe's Jews, and that they approved of the policy. They used their control over the press, radio, and other media to fan hatred of the Jews, to offer repeated jus-tifications for murdering Jews, and to prevent any factual details about the genocide from appearing in the press. They became active acces-sories to crimes against humanity.

From late September through November 1943, the *Der Völkische Beobachter,* in another concentrated anti-Semitic propaganda campaign, published thirteen lead, front-page articles attacking the Jews and their presumed role in the war. The headlines sustained the Nazi narrative that projected onto the Allies and Jewish wire pullers the Nazis' own fanatical hatred and murderous intentions (see appendix).

The *VB*'s response to Franklin Roosevelt's expression of good wishes to American Jews on Rosh Hashanah in September 1943 illustrated how the editors placed the apparently innocuous in a sinister frame-work. Roosevelt had conveyed "my admiration of the contribution which this loyal group of our fellow-citizens has made to the nation's achieve-ments during the past year on the inexorable march toward victory."[6] The *VB* responded with the front-page headline "Roosevelt Again De-clares His Solidarity with Jewry." The *VB* saw it as proof "not of a Jew-ish contribution to the war. Rather, [Roosevelt's praise] was evidence of the contribution of the USA people to the Jewish war." The phrase "Jewish war" had moved from Seibert's signed editorial column in the spring to the news columns in the fall. Roosevelt's friendly message on the Jewish New Year confirmed that he was "an unconditional servant of the Jews" and a tool of "dark powers" in Washington and Moscow that were striving for world domination.[7] The *VB* editors avoided the simpler and truthful explanation—namely, that Franklin Roosevelt was a politician who was conveying his friendly sentiments to one of his most loyal electoral constituencies and who believed in freedom of religion.

Control over the press made it possible for the Nazi regime to prevent Germans from reading public statements by leaders of the anti-Hitler coalition concerning German atrocities. From October 18 to Novem-ber 1, 1943, the three Allied foreign ministers, Cordell Hull, Anthony Eden, and Vyacheslav Molotov, met together for the first time in Moscow.

They discussed military cooperation and planning for the postwar period. As German armies retreated, the Allies were also gathering more evidence about German war crimes. The main conference communiqué included "a solemn warning that at the time of granting an armistice to any German government those German officers and men and members of the Nazi party who have had any connection with atrocities and executions by German forces will be taken back to the countries in which their abominable crimes were committed to be charged and punished according to the laws of those countries."[8] It should be noted that an annex to the "Declaration of German Atrocities," written by Churchill and only slightly amended in Moscow, made reference to diverse crimes, such as those committed in the Soviet Union, shootings of Italian officers, executions of French, Dutch, Belgian, or Norwegian hostages and of peasants in Crete, and slaughters in Poland.[9] However, despite numerous press reports about the mass murder of the Jews by fall 1943, this declaration did *not* mention them at all, perhaps in order not to play into the hands of Nazi anti-Semitic propaganda.[10]

If so, this reticence made no difference to Nazi propagandists. On November 2, 1943, the Reich Press Office issued a fourteen-page directive about how the press should respond to the Allies' Moscow communiqué. It asserted that the unity of Germany's enemies consisted in the desire "exterminate the German people" and was to be described as "Anglo-American treason toward Europe and Anglo-American capitulation to Moscow." There was "nothing new about the atrocity propaganda," and presumably nothing true about it. The Moscow communiqué meant that the United States and England put no barriers in the way of the Bolshevization of Europe.[11] German soldiers were the "bulwark against Bolshevism" and defenders of the "culture and civilization of the West," which sought freedom from the "influence of the Anglo-American finance-Jews."[12] Even though the Moscow communiqué had made no mention of the Jews, the *Periodical Service* of November 5, 1943, asserted, "The whole spirit of the Moscow conference is exclusively that of the Jew. It is Jewish interests that are represented there."

Hence, the "fight against Jewry [was] an ever clearer and unconditional necessity for German periodical journalism."[13]

The press did not inform German readers that the Allies in Moscow had mentioned many of Nazi Germany's victims, although not the Jews. Instead, the *VB* declared: "The Plutocratic Apparatus Works for Stalin: Moscow Expands Its Demands for Power, Success of Soviet Agitation in England and USA." It asserted that "the man in the street in London and Washington" did not understand the way in which Stalin was using the Western Allies, because the ordinary person was "not clearly aware of the identity of capitalist-Bolshevik policy guaranteed by Jewry in Moscow and Washington," whose goal was the complete "Bolshevization of Europe." Even the "plutocratic apparatus," including the conservative press in Britain, was at "work for Stalin." Many Britons had still not understood that "British-American world capitalism and Moscow Bolshevism are one and the same thing."[14]

For the *VB* the results of the Moscow conference gave formal expression to the identity of the "capitalist and Bolshevik programs of extermination" and the Allies' intent to deliver Europe to Bolshevism: "It is the spirit of international Jewry that has triumphed in Moscow." Both American secretary of state Cordell Hull and British foreign minister Anthony Eden had been "agents of the world Jewry that dominates the Kremlin as much as it does the capital in Washington."[15] In propaganda aimed at the democracies, the Nazis linked anticapitalism with anti-Semitism. "Jewish capital," the *VB* proclaimed, "murders the people." It prolonged the war in order to receive greater dividends and profits, while the Axis powers were fighting for "the productive people." The "capitalist beneficiaries of the murder of nations" were prolonging the war in order to gain more war profits. Wall Street financiers and Jewish plutocrats were at war with the genuinely productive Aryan man.[16] In an address to twenty thousand young officer candidates on November 30, 1943, Hitler said that Germany had a choice: "victory or merciless annihilation." In this rare public appearance, Hitler had repeated that the goal of "the Jewish powers standing behind British politics who unleashed this war in alliance with the Soviet Union was, first of all, to exterminate Germany, in order to hand Europe over to Bolshevism." The German people and German armies were the only barrier to "our enemies' plans for extermination [of Germany], dictated by Jewish hatred."[17]

The second of the major Allied wartime conferences between Churchill, Roosevelt, and Stalin ended in Tehran on December 6, 1943. The conference communiqué underscored their agreement on "plans for the destruction of the German armed forces [and] . . . agreement as to the scope and timing of the operations which will be undertaken from the East, West and South." It expressed confidence that "no power on earth can prevent our destroying the German armies by land, their U-boats by sea, and their war plants from the air. Our attack will be relentless and unceasing."[18] The United States and Britain agreed to invade Western Europe in 1944, while Stalin agreed to enter the Pacific war against Japan after Germany was defeated. Like the Moscow statement, the communiqué from the Tehran conference said nothing about Europe's Jews. Nevertheless, the *Periodical Service* directive of December 22, 1943, responded with anti-Semitic invective and long-winded renditions of anti-Semitic histories of modern Europe. The directive mistakenly asserted that Roosevelt had invited Chiang Kai-shek to the Tehran conference. In fact, Roosevelt and Churchill had met with Chiang in Cairo just before the two of them met alone with Stalin in Tehran.[19] Though there was no meeting of the "Big Four" there, the directive described Chiang's supposed presence in Tehran as proof of the expansion of the international Jewish conspiracy to Asia. "The four appointees of world Jewry, Churchill, Roosevelt (Jewish blood and first-degree Freemason), Stalin, and Chiang Kai-shek, met in Tehran to activate their struggle for Jewry's world domination." Pointing this out was important, because "the longer the war lasts, the more our struggle against Jewry must be intensified, so that the people recognize who the truly guilty party for this war is" and how the Jews in Europe, after only a short period of emancipation, had managed to "set the whole world aflame."[20]

In his diary entry of December 12, 1943, Goebbels again expressed his hope that the spread of anti-Semitism might fracture the Allied coalition.[21] Perhaps the power of the Jews in the West would be eroded as the specter of the Red Army loomed over Europe's future. Playing up the threat of "Jewish Bolshevism," along with Roosevelt's supposed plans to "liquidate the master race in Germany," remained a key theme in Goebbels's unsuccessful efforts to fan anti-Semitism in the democracies and split the Allied coalition, as well as in his more successful endeavors to sustain support for the regime at home.[22] As the year ended, the propaganda minister looked back on 1943 as "one run of bad luck after another" and as a "nightmare" of "many blows and few successes."[23] German submarines were being driven from the Atlantic. The army on the eastern front was reeling from Red Army offensives. The Wehrmacht had been driven out of North Africa. Mussolini had been driven from power, and Italy had surrendered to the Allies. The American and British air forces were now bombing German industry and cities and gradually shooting the Luftwaffe out of the skies. Anti-Semitic propaganda had failed to split the anti-Hitler coalition or to undermine support for the war in Britain, the United States, or the Soviet Union. On the contrary, the more that news about German atrocities against the Jews and others emerged in the world press, the more determined the Allies were to fight on to unconditional surrender. Within Germany, however, the prospect of "extermination" of the Germans by "world Jewry" remained a pivotal component of Nazi propaganda until the end. Fostering stark fear was the logical consequence of radical anti-Semitism. The more the fortunes of war favored the Allies, the more the Nazi propagandists said they had been right about the Jews' enormous power and intention to exterminate the Germans.

In early 1944, despite all evidence to the contrary, Hitler and Goebbels convinced themselves that victory would be theirs if Europe rallied behind Nazi Germany in the face of Soviet forces advancing westward. Goebbels noted in his diary entry of January 22, 1944, "The closer Bolshevism moves, the more friends we will win."[24] Several days later he noted in his diary that Hitler believed German military setbacks in the East were "political victories," because the progress of the Red Army toward the West would "break open the contradictions between" the Western democracies on one side, "and the Soviets on the other." Of course, it would not be easy for "rational elements in English politics" to make their case, because "the Jews and the friends of Churchill—which generally is the same thing—have all the news media, especially the newspapers, in their hands." Dissenters could not speak out without "running the danger of being attacked in the most furious and insulting manner."[25] By late February, Goebbels committed his wishful thinking to paper when he wrote in his diary, "Harmony in the enemy camp has sunk to zero."[26]

On January 30, 1944, Hitler delivered his annual address to the nation to mark the anniversary of the Nazi accession to power. Speaking from his East Prussian field headquarters, rather than appearing in public in Berlin, he mouthed his usual attacks on England and the Jews. England's role on the Continent was finished. Either Germany or the Soviet Union would win the war, and if it was the latter, Germany would be "destroyed." In the case of a Soviet victory, England could not prevent the Bolshevization of Europe, for England had succumbed to the Jewish "plague." A Soviet victory would bring about "the complete extermination of the German nation . . . and this goal is the openly proclaimed intention of international Jewry!" Whether "the Jewish advocates of these goals sit in England or America or whether they direct from their headquarters in Moscow" was not important. German defeat would mean the end of two thousand years of "musical and material culture" in Europe. The Jews would "celebrate a second triumphal Purim festival in destroyed Europe." This disaster, however, had been prevented because Germany, since January 30, 1933, had cleansed itself of "the Jewish infection" and crushed the Bolshevik danger from within and was therefore strong enough to stop the Bolshevik threat from without. Though Jewry had lost power in Germany, it would, by unleashing a war against Germany, unintentionally help spread the ideas of National Socialism in other countries. "The world war that began in 1939 will go down in history as a gigantic repetition of the trials against the [Nazi] party in 1924." Just as the early efforts to defeat the party had been followed by the spread of Nazi ideas in Germany, so the current war would "open the people's eyes to the Jewish question and make the National Socialist answer and the measures needed for its resolution seem obviously correct and worthy of imitation."[27] Following Hitler's cue, the Reich Press Office launched another anti-Semitic barrage.

During the war, the Soviet Union sought to present itself to the West as a genuine democracy and found supporters abroad to sing its praises.[28] The daily directive of February 3, 1944, from the office of the Reich press chief responded both to Soviet assertions that it was now a federation of republics and to "the applause that the Jewish press of the whole world gives" to Soviet efforts to present itself as a democracy. The Western reaction "allows us to recognize the enormous international conspiracy of Jewry. It is the mission of the German press to present and describe this conspiracy."[29] Soviet efforts to obscure its dictatorial nature and to deny the murders in Katyn amounted to a "gigantic . . . Jewish trick. The fact that the Jewish newspapers in the whole world welcome this development allows us to recognize clearly that we are dealing here with an *enormous conspiracy of Jewry*, a Jewish conspiracy of international proportions." While it might be in England and America's interest to have one Soviet ally, rather than a multiplicity of Soviet Republics and alliance partners, Western enthusiasm for the Soviet announcement "again makes clear that the *Jewish question is the key to world history*."[30]

On February 15, 1944, the Press Office directive continued the anti-Semitic assault. "The instigator, supporter, and leader of this war is, and will remain, the international Jew [sic], that criminal race which now, as in centuries past, is to blame for the fact that the nations of the earth are arrayed against one another in war. An understanding among peoples of the earth can be hoped for only when this world pest is once and for all wiped out."[31] On March 2, the daily directive stated that "the anti-Semitic campaign must more emphatically than heretofore be placed in the foreground and made an important propaganda factor in the world struggle. . . At every opportunity the background driving forces of world Jewry, which work against the interests of the host peoples, should be nailed down . . . All the voices that give evidence of the true Jewish exterminatory intentions should be attacked and denounced. German journalists must set the goal of keeping alive in the German people the feeling for the Jewish world danger. In addition and above all, they should foster such discussion abroad . . . German correspondents abroad have a particularly important mission."[32]

Dietrich continued to intensify the anti-Semitic campaign. The press directive for March 2 stressed that "the anti-Semitic campaign must, more powerfully than to this point, be placed in the foreground as an important propagandistic factor in the world struggle. Therefore, at every opportunity, the press should focus on the effort of world Jewry operating behind the scenes, which works against the interests of its host peoples. Moreover, all voices that express the true Jewish exterminatory intentions should be noted" and denounced. German journalism must "sustain the German people's awareness of the Jewish world danger." German foreign correspondents should play an important role in fostering anti-Semitism abroad; for example, in response to a report in the *London Daily Mail* that Britain's awareness of the danger of Bolshevism had been weakened, Goebbels wrote: "The German press must stress that this [failure to grasp the danger of Bolshevism] is the result of an intensive Jewish work of subversion that has been going on for years. The Jews consciously try to put the peoples into a narcotic haze and diminish the dangers that face them, so that they then can dominate and exploit them all the more easily."[33] The following day, Goebbels and Hitler agreed that "the Jewish question has become virulent in England and the United States." They speculated that the beginning of public discussion of the Jews was "the beginning of the end of Jewish domination."[34]

In March 1944, officers of the SS from Adolf Eichmann's office arrived in Budapest to make preparations for the deportation of Hungarian Jews to Auschwitz-Birkenau. They and the Hungarian government that they had installed following their invasion and occupation of the country initiated the customary procedures of persecution. The Reich Press Office directive for April 27, 1944, ordered that reports on "the measures against the Jews" in Hungary should always be accompanied by "a detailed presentation of the crimes committed by the Jews, for the anti-Jewish measures are their consequence." It should reiterate that the Jews were "guilty." It should not only discuss the measures "the new Hungarian government" had taken against the Jews but also describe the "previous Jewification of Hungary," which had suppressed the real Hungary and made possible the advance of Bolsheviks. "The papers must also state that the Jews were Hungary's misfortune, which suppressed Hungary's genuine national character, and that it is the Jews alone who are responsible for the fact that today the Bolsheviks stand at Hungary's door . . . If this general Jewish guilt is thoroughly discussed, then the new anti-Jewish measures of the Hungarian government can be mentioned."[35] These directives were examples of effective coordination within the Nazi regime, this time between the Reich Security Main Office and the Reich Press Office in the Propaganda Ministry.

On April 1, 1944, Goebbels published "The European Narcosis," as his weekly editorial in *Das Reich*. The party's Propaganda Directorate distributed it to local leaders of the Nazi party and government. He wrote that the imminence of the Bolshevik threat would lead to a renewed will to resist among Germans and other Europeans if Jewish efforts to put Europe into a complacent trance could be thwarted. Only Germany and its armies could prevent the advent of a Bolshevik Europe, an outcome being facilitated by British and American policy. Too many in Europe ignored the impending disaster. Goebbels found the origins of this blindness in a familiar source. "The Jews are the main source of this European narcosis that is spreading through all the peoples in our part of the earth. They want to let the danger grow so great that it will be impossible to defend against it." They seek to place "the public in such a condition of paralyzing incapacity to resist" that it will passively succumb to the course of events. "We are dealing here with a worldwide conspiracy to influence public opinion," being systematically pursued in Europe's capital cities. Those who protest are shouted down by a chorus and fall silent. As a result, Europeans "peer at the danger as if they were hypnotized."[36]

It was the Nazis' "historical mission" to break this silence and Europe's paralysis over the looming Bolshevik danger. The Nazis had awakened Germany before 1933 from its narcotic state. Now it was up to Germany to sweep aside the Jewish-induced complacency regarding the Bolshevik threat. A danger from the East could give rise to a common European will, which in turn would be "the beginning of salvation."[37] Hope lay in the blend of anti-Semitism and anti-Bolshevism in England and the United States. It would, he hoped, lead to a "political crisis in England and the USA," generated by fear of "the Kremlin's drive for expansion."[38] In a speech to Nazi officials expressing confidence, despite the enemy's numerical superiority, Hitler said, "It must be the mission of [Nazi] propaganda to split the enemy coalition apart."[39] Goebbels expressed confidence that "our propaganda theses—namely, [National] socialism, anti-Bolshevism, and anti-Semitism—are slowly but surely penetrating the enemy camp. One day it will break it apart from within."[40] If it failed to do so, the Nazi leadership had an explanation ready to hand.

In 1944, while contemplating the cracks in the enemy coalition, Goebbels, Ribbentrop, and Himmler considered the prospect, dangled before their eyes by the Grand Mufti of Jerusalem, of adding to the Nazi coalition support from the Arab and Islamic world. The Grand Mufti's cooperation with the Nazis extended beyond making speeches. He urged the Foreign Ministry, as well as Adolf Eichmann, not to allow Jews from Bulgaria, Romania, and Hungary to escape to Palestine, but to send them instead to Poland. He worked with Himmler to establish an SS division of Muslims from Bosnia, appealed to the Germans to bomb Tel Aviv and Jerusalem, and received financial support from the Nazi regime in these years.[41] He also made "a very good impression" on the propaganda minister. After a long conversation with al-Husseini, Goebbels wrote in his diary of April 26, 1944, about his "absolutely Nordic appearance" and agreed that there was no "conflict of interests" between "the Arabic-Mohammedan peoples" and Nazi Germany. "The four hundred million of the Mohammedan-Arabic population are absolutely there for us to win over to our side, if only we can conduct the correct propaganda" and supply al-Husseini with the necessary paper for newspapers and magazines.[42]

On July 27, 1944, the Grand Mufti wrote to Himmler to urge him "to do what was necessary to prevent the wandering of Jews to Palestine." Doing so would be a "practical example of the allied and friendly stance" of Germany toward Arabs and Moslems.[43] In a speech of October 4, 1944, to officers and imams associated with Bosnian Moslem SS division, al-Husseini stressed that the "parallels" between National Socialism and Islam had become ever closer. These included: monotheism, defined as obedience to one spiritual, political, and military authority; an emphasis on obedience and discipline; and the celebration of battle and of labor. "As far as fighting against Jewry, Islam and National Socialism have moved very close to one another." In World War II, "a victory for the Allies would constitute a victory for Jewry, and thus a great danger for the Moslems and for Islam in general . . . Cooperation of four hundred million Moslems with their real friends, the Germans, can have a great influence on the war. It is very useful for both."[44] Not only did the Nazi regime fiercely oppose the establishment a Jewish state in Palestine and lend support to anti-Zionist Arabs, but in the positive reception it afforded al-Husseini it effected a rapprochement between Nazism and Islamic fundamentalism in its early years.

Dietrich's press directive of April 27, 1944, when the deportation of Hungarian Jews to Auschwitz was beginning, again held the Jews accountable for all the sins of the Stalin dictatorship. The papers were to stress the "sadistic regime of horror" that Bolshevism was imposing on

Eastern Europe. Anti-Jewish arguments should remain "one of the basic themes of the German press." Reports about "measures against the Jews" in Hungary must be "accompanied by extensive presentation of the crimes committed by the Jews, the consequences of which are the current measures."[45] The press was to present the "true face of Bolshevism" and the role of "the Jewish commissar." Reports about Bolshevik attacks on priests; deportations and "enslavement" of workers; "liquidation of the intelligentsia"; and separation from their wives and children of men who were then sent to Siberia—should "again and again" draw attention to "the Jewish commissar in the background." In reports about the current measures taken against the Jews by "the Hungarian government," the press should examine "the previous Jewification of Hungary, which [had] led the implementation of the anti-Jewish measures." German newspapers "must therefore establish that the Jews were Hungary's misfortune. They subordinated the true, national Hungary, and it is the Jews alone who are responsible for the fact that today the Bolsheviks are standing at Hungary's door . . . Only when and if this Jewish guilt is thoroughly discussed by the press can the new anti-Jewish measures of the Hungarian government be mentioned."[46] As the deportations continued, Dietrich's directive of May 4 cautioned, "For the time being it is not worth mentioning in the German press that the Jews of Budapest are being moved out of city neighborhoods endangered by bombing attacks."[47]

The unity of anti-Semitism and anti-Bolshevism found expression in the lead headline on the front page of the May 12, 1944, issue of the *VB*: "United with the Headquarters of the World Revolution, Moscow Becomes Official Center of World Jewry, Jewish State in Palestine Becomes Cornerstone of Soviet Control of the Mediterranean."[48] The article commented on the support for creation of a Jewish state from Rabbi Stephen Wise, a leading figure of American Reform Judaism and an outspoken foe of the Nazis. As a result of his vocal attacks on the Nazis' persecution of Jews, Wise had been a frequent target of Nazi propaganda since 1933. His support for creation of a Jewish state had emerged in response to Nazi persecution.[49] Though there is no evidence that Wise was influenced by or had any contact with Soviet officials, the *VB* invented the fiction that according to "reliable political circles in Lisbon," the Soviet ambassador to the United States had suggested to Rabbi Stephen Wise in New York that "the headquarters of world Jewry be moved from New York to Moscow." The Kremlin had shown an interest in Zionism because it coincided with Soviet aims in the Mediterranean. "Leading circles of world Jewry" were interested in "the tempting Soviet offer" for several reasons. They thought that American prospects in the war were not favorable. If the invasion of Europe failed, they "feared a deep wave of anti-Semitism in the United States," which could extend to England and "nations that up to this point had been friendly to the Jews." They also thought that only the Soviet Union had the power in the Mediterranean to bring about a Jewish state in Palestine. This rapprochement between "the headquarters of world Jewry and the headquarters of world revolution, . . . two centers of world annihilation," to form "one great power," owing to the move of the Zionists to Moscow, "belongs to the most revealing warning signs from the real background of the present." This "Bolshevization of the Mediterranean" was "a preliminary stage in the Bolshevization of the world."[50] By June 1944, when the utter lack of power and the helplessness of Europe's Jews was transparently obvious, such assertions underscored the mythic essence of Nazi ideology.

As the German armies were retreating on the eastern front and German cities were being reduced to rubble under Allied bombing, Goebbels stressed unity in the face of adversity. Two days before the Normandy invasion, he spoke to a gathering of Nazi leaders in Nuremberg. He said, "We fight simply for life, the life of our nation and our own lives."[51] In a colloquial, comradely tone, he offered an interesting rationale for refusing to offer details of the regime's plans for victory.

It would not have been very clever, if even before the seizure of power we had *completely* carried out our debate with the Jews and revealed what we intended to do to them. It was really good, it was really good and useful, that at least a part of the Jews thought, Well, things won't really be *all* that bad; they [the Nazis] talk a lot, but we'll see what they are really going to do. It was really good that they [the Jews] did not take the [Nazi party] so *seriously* as it really deserved to be taken. And it was also really good that the other political parties, the German People's Party and the Economics Party of the master baker Drewitz and the Democratic Party—*secretly* indulged this hope: Well, if we *really* can't avoid working with the Nazis, they also cook with water . . . But if we had said to them, "You will be dissolved after two-three weeks or two or three months; you won't be able to speak at all; we will make a tabula rasa of you, we intend to take power *alone* and dissolve all the other [political] parties"—if we had said that *then,* the parties probably would have put up a much stronger defense than they in actuality did.[52]

In short, it was "really good" that their opponents had underestimated the Nazis' intentions and the seriousness of their ideology. By June 1944, however, Nazi Germany had nothing to hide about what it would do in power. Yet just as Nazi propaganda suggested that history was operating behind the scenes in Moscow, London, and Washington, so Goebbels sought to reassure the party faithful by hinting that the regime had secret plans for victory that it could not reveal. The enemy, of course, sank to "Jewish tricks" and sought to make the Germans nervous about a forthcoming invasion. But it was the English, not the Germans, who suffered from "invasionitis," a clever term that evoked laughter in the audience.[53] Goebbels prided himself on his past realism about the war. "I have no cause for shame about what I said and wrote in 1939, '40, '41, '42, and '43." He was not silent about difficulties but was confident there was cause for optimism because of the presence of Hitler himself. The regime would emerge victorious from the current crisis if the party and people would "have blind faith in victory! This is

The Jewish Enemy

not only a *matter of courageous hearts* and the determination of our souls! This is a matter only of *unconditional* obedience and loyalty to our Führer!" The crowd responded with loud applause and long shouts of "Heil Hitler."[54]

On May 14, 15, and 18, in the *VB,* an extended essay by Sündermann appeared, "Stalin and the Jews."[55] He asked how it had come to pass that such an apparently unexceptional individual as Stalin had become the leader of the Soviet Union and of the Bolshevik party. Sündermann found the answer in the desires of the Jews who, he claimed, dominated the party. They were aware of the depths of anti-Semitism in Russian society. Therefore, they had sought someone like Stalin, that rare intellectual who could speak the language of the working classes. In the era of the New Economic Policy in the 1920s, the Bolsheviks had sought a way to "camouflage the fact that the Bolshevik state was not a dictatorship of the proletariat but rather one of international Jewry." When Leon Trotsky had appeared to be on the verge of becoming Lenin's successor, the Jews in the party understood that it would undermine the young government if its leading figure was a Jew, like Trotsky. Stalin, precisely because of his conflict with Trotsky, seemed to the thousands of "Moscow Jews" in the party and government the right man for the leadership position. "In the interest of the Jews and, yes, of the Soviet state . . . a full Jew must not be made into the idol of the Russian people. Lenin's successor needed to be a man who served the Jews as Lenin did but was not himself visible as a Jew!" That was why Kamenev, Zinoviev, and Kaganovich had thrown their support to Stalin as Lenin's successor. Amid the complex machinations of Soviet politics, "only one thing is certain: in all the years in which many Jews got a bullet in the head, Jewish influence on Stalin, the Jewish position in all sectors of the party and state apparatus, remained undisputed." Even as he sent his "closest friends" to their death, Stalin remained the Jews' faithful tool.[56]

For the Nazi regime, the Normandy invasion of June 6, 1944, was another example of the international Jewish conspiracy at work. The editors made this point on the front pages of the *VB* on June 22, 1944, the third anniversary of the German invasion of the Soviet Union. The lead headline stated: "Führer's Great Decision—How Jewish-Bolshevik World Conspiracy Was Thwarted; Invasion—the Path to Moscow's Goals."[57] The lead paragraph read as follows:

> For the third time we mark the day on which the German army stepped forth to defend against the Jewish-Bolshevik attack on the West. Today we know from many documentary pieces of evidence how great a danger faced the West then. Bolshevism saw the greatest chance to unleash the world revolution by overwhelming Europe. The Führer's decision exorcised this danger, and the satanic plan of the Kremlin dictator and of world Jewry was thwarted. Today the world revolution is to be realized by the [Normandy] invasion that has been undertaken on Moscow's orders and instructions. The dark driving forces of the great Jewish-Bolshevik world conspiracy against Western humanity, whose most important instrument of world revolution is the invasion, are evident in an overview of strategic and political developments.[58]

The article claimed that British and American attacks on Germany were serving the interests of the Soviet Union. Their soldiers "had fallen [in battle] for Bolshevism." At the Tehran conference, "Stalin gave the order to begin the whole endeavor" and, in so doing, "regained his original goal . . . This was the original Jewish-Bolshevik plan to bring about world revolution and the establishment of Jewish world domination: Germany was to be bled white in battle with the Western powers. The healthy *völkisch* core of these Western powers was to be so weakened that they would be unable any longer to offer any power of resistance against the Bolshevik infection. Thus, all of Europe, and finally also America, would become easy prey for Jewish Bolshevism." Stalin's original plan was undone, however, by the success of the German armies in the invasion of France in 1940. Then the Kremlin had a choice either to abandon the goals of dominating Europe and of world revolution or to enter into a war with Germany. Stalin had "ordered the march against Germany," which was thwarted by Hitler's decision "at the last minute" to attack on June 22, 1941. The *VB* article interpreted the willingness of England and the United States to invade Europe from the west in June 1944 as evidence of a renewal of the Kremlin's designs on Europe and of the craven submission of the Western democracies to Soviet wishes.[59]

Like all the lead *VB* articles that dealt with the Jews, the article was striking for the way it combined a conspiratorial thesis, lies, and considerable factual information that bore an apparent connection to the actual course of events. In addition to the falsehoods regarding the "Jewish-Bolshevik conspiracy" and the presentation of German aggression in June 1941 as a preemptive attack, the article interpreted familiar events—the Western air war, attacks on German cities, the long preparation for the Normandy invasion, Stalin's continuing plea for a second front—through the distorting prism of the conspiracy theory. The Normandy invasion in fact both shortened World War II and brought American and British forces to the center of Europe. It thus prevented the Bolshevization of Western Europe that the Nazi propaganda claimed it was intended to bring about. The article offered another example of the narrative of a conspiracy among unequal partners by denying autonomy and subjectivity to those who had it, the leaders of England and the United States, while attributing a remarkable degree of power to those who had none, the Jews.

On August 8, 1944, Goebbels delivered a long, rambling, and grim overview of the war to a meeting of Nazi party officials in Posen.[60] "The confrontation between the German National Socialist world and the Jewish-plutocratic-Bolshevistic world has reached its high point and now stands at its most serious and dramatic level." The Allied air war over Germany continued. Germany was now suffering from serious shortages of gasoline. Hopes for victory in the East had not been fulfilled. Following the attempted coup on July 20, Goebbels understood why the army that had been so successful in the years from 1939 to

1941 was experiencing such a "great military catastrophe" on the eastern front: "The middle sector of the front was led by commanders . . . who did not *want* to win."[61] "Treasonous generals" accounted for the failures in the East. Now that the traitorous clique had been uncovered, the prospects for future military success were enhanced.[62] Yet accusations of treason against military leaders did nothing to boost the public mood.

In early September, the Propaganda Ministry reported signs of deep depression and hopelessness about success in the war.[63] Adding to the gloom were the Allied air attacks on all of Germany's major and medium-sized cities—Mainz, Wiesbaden, Worms, Karlsruhe, Ludwigshafen, Mannheim, Cologne, Dusseldorf, Duisburg, and Wuppertal, as well as on the German rail network. By mid-September, Trier was coming under Allied artillery fire and Aachen had been partly evacuated. Goebbels displayed complete incomprehension of the Allies in urging Hitler on September 21 to open negotiations for a separate peace with the Soviet Union, in hopes of splitting the enemy coalition—as if Stalin would be ready to make the same deal with Hitler that he had made before millions of Soviet soldiers and civilians had died as a result of the German invasion and occupation.[64] Hitler did not take up the suggestion.

The Reich Press Office directives also sought to sustain support through vivid depictions of the consequences for Germany of Soviet victory. The *Periodical Service* of September 22, 1944, repeated the importance of the anti-Bolshevik theme, stressed that its "close link to anti-Jewish propaganda must not be forgotten," chided some economics magazines for neglecting anti-Jewish themes, and suggested that they examine "*Juda's* struggle for financial and economic domination of the world."[65] The directive of September 30, 1944, affirmed that "anti-Jewish press work" was as important as ever, but care was required in the choice of words. As the term "anti-Semitism" was appearing with great frequency in the German press, the Press Office expressed concern that "our relationships could be destroyed with non-Jewish Semites, namely the pan-Arab world that is so important for us. Hence, the press must take care to replace the words 'anti-Semitism' and 'anti-Semitic' with such expressions as 'opposition to Jews,' 'hostility to Jews,' 'anti-Judaism,' and 'antagonistic to Jews' or 'anti-Jewish.'"[66] The ministry had apparently noticed that some journalists had referred to "Jewish revenge." This tack was "not advisable," because pointing to Jewish plans for revenge could arouse "in ideologically uncertain circles the impression that this 'revenge' has been the result of what the enemy claims was our cruel behavior toward the Jews. Obviously, revenge presupposes a past injustice. Therefore, we will only speak of Jewish plans for extermination and repeatedly indicate that from the beginning Jewry was the aggressor" and that Germany responded with "a stance of life-and-death defense."[67] Nazi propaganda had repeatedly stated that the regime was intending to exterminate or was then in the process of "exterminating" the Jews. Yet it denied that it was doing anything other than responding to a war waged by "international Jewry." In so doing, it sustained the core fiction that there was no distinction between World War II and the Final Solution of the Jewish question in Europe, and that the Final Solution was a key theater of the World War II.

Summer 1944 was devastating for the German armies on both the eastern and the western fronts. From June through October, an average of more than 7,200 soldiers died every day. From the time of the invasion of Normandy to the end of October 1944, 1,082,197 German soldiers died in battle. The figures for monthly deaths are as follows: June, 182,178; July, 215,013; August, 348,960; September, 151,957; and October, 184,089. In all of 1944, 244,891 of those deaths took place on the western front, and 1,232,946 on the eastern front. Whereas German deaths between 1941 and 1943 on the western front had not exceeded 3 percent of the total from all fronts, in 1944 the figure jumped to about 14 percent. Yet even in the months following D-day, about 68.5 percent of all German battlefield deaths occurred on the eastern front, as a Soviet blitzkrieg in response devastated the retreating Wehrmacht.[68] In the West, the Allies drove the Germans out of Belgium. Charles de Gaulle declared Paris liberated on August 24, 1944.[69] Germany's air defenses had been crushed. Nazi Germany had lost control of the air over the battlefields on all fronts, as well as over its cities and industries, to the Western and Soviet air forces. The German submarine threat in the Atlantic had essentially been defeated. In October 1944, German submarines managed to sink only one merchant ship of just over 6,000 tons on all the world's oceans and had lost their bases on the French Atlantic coast. Nazi Germany's allies—Fascist Italy, Vichy France, Romania, and Bulgaria—had been driven out of the war. The alliance between the Western powers and the Soviet Union remained intact, despite the obvious tensions and differences. The French army was being reconstituted. By October 1944, fighting approached the German border on the east and the west.[70]

The last possibility for internal opposition to the Third Reich ended with the failure of the attempted coup of July 20, 1944. In the face of horrific losses, the German armies continued to fight. The population, however sullenly, lent support to the regime, while Goebbels rallied the party faithful and fellow travelers for a fight to the finish. Goebbels's delusional grasp of wartime realities was evident in a speech he delivered on October 3, 1944, to a Nazi party meeting in Aachen. American forces were fighting on the outskirts of the city. By then, about 3,700,000 German soldiers had died, countless more had been wounded, hundreds of thousands of civilians had died in bombing raids, and many of Germany's major cities stood to varying degrees in rubble. Goebbels acknowledged: "We thought military developments would take a different course than they actually have. *Nevertheless, we are not worse off today* than we were in September 1939. Given that we have been able for five years to hold off a whole world of *hate-filled enemies, without* their being able to occupy any important part of the Reich—other than small parts—well, that is the really amazing thing about this war!" A nation capable of such feats, he argued, would emerge victorious.[71]

Not missing a beat, Goebbels drew attention to the advantages of the defense. The war, he continued, had entered a new stage—namely, that of the defense of Germany itself. At this point, it was essential that the population be not only "fanatical, but fanaticized." People must understand that the war was a matter of life and death for the whole country. The supply lines for Germany's enemies were becoming longer, while Germany's became shorter. The natural benefits of the defense would come into play as the war moved closer to Germany. He pointed to the response of the Soviet Union in 1941 as a source of hope. Just as Soviet resistance had intensified as Germany penetrated deeper into Russia, so in 1945 German resistance would strengthen as the war came into German territory. Further, he stressed that the Anglo-American forces were no better than the Soviets. Both would "establish a terror regime on German soil." In any case, he "knew" that Germany would win the war, both because of new weapons from German arsenals and because the enemies were now "making the same mistakes that we made earlier"—that is, extending supply lines in the process of invading other countries.[72] Yet Germany was going to win the war. If it failed to do so, the consequences for the entire German people would be catastrophic. Despite this bold speech, Goebbels's diary entries of fall 1944 reflected the gloom that had settled on the German leadership in the face of night- and daytime bombing by the American and British air forces, the resulting rise in the civilian death toll, the destruction of German industry and infrastructure, and the continuing advance by the Red Army in the East. By November 1944, 1,200 British and American bombers were flying over Germany every day. Goebbels acknowledged that the bombings had a devastating impact on German morale.[73]

In the midst of this gloom, on January 21, 1945, Goebbels published his last lead editorial in *Das Reich* devoted exclusively to the Jews, "The Glue of the Enemy Coalition: The Origin of the World's Misfortune."[74] The essay was both an outburst of rage and hatred and an explanation of how and why the war had reached to its current point. His themes, language, and syntax were numbingly familiar: "[It is] not possible to understand this war, if we do not always keep in mind the fact that international Jewry is the motor behind all the perverse activity by which our united enemies lie to the world and attempt to control humanity from the shadows. It [Jewry] forms, so to speak, the cement that holds the enemy coalition firmly together, despite the striking clash of ideologies and interests among its members." Capitalism and Bolshevism had "the same Jewish roots." International Jewry had various methods with which "it oppresse[d] and dominate[d] nations." It controlled public opinion in "all the enemy and . . . most of the neutral countries" where criticism of the Jews was "taboo." Germany had broken the power of the Jews, but they in turn had "mobilized the whole world against us." All Russian, English, and American soldiers were mercenaries of "this world conspiracy of a parasitic race" and were certainly not fighting for their country's national interests. The day, he predicted, would "not be far off on which the peoples of Europe, indeed of the whole world, will break into an outcry: The Jews are guilty for all this misfortune! Therefore, they must soon and fundamentally be brought to account."[75] The Jews' efforts to avoid this accusation, to argue that the Nazis were simply looking for a scapegoat, would fail. The evidence of their guilt was too obvious.

> Who drives the Russians, English, and Americans into the fire, and sacrifices masses of foreign lives in a hopeless struggle against the German people? The Jews! In their newspapers and radio broadcasts, they sing the songs of war, while the peoples they have misled are led to the slaughter. Who invents new programs of hatred and extermination against us, and in so doing makes this war into an awful act of horrendous self-slaughter and self-annihilation of Europe's life, its economy, education, and culture? The Jews! Who invented, implemented, and jealously watches over the repulsive alliance between England and the USA on the one hand, and Bolshevism on the other? Who justifies this perverse political situation with a cynical hypocrisy and fear? . . . Jews, only the Jews! The are named Morgenthau and Lehmann and stand in the so-called Brain Trust behind

Roosevelt. Melchett and Sassoon serve as Churchill's financial supporters. They are called Kaganovich and Ehrenburg and are Stalin's trendsetters and intellectual guides. Wherever you look, you see Jews.[76]

This was all "the truth" that could "no longer be denied." The Jews had erred in coming out into the open at that point. "Not Europe, but the Jews themselves will perish" and, as a result, "the source of the world's" —not only Germany's—"misfortune" be "buried under rubble."[77]

In the last months of the war, Nazi propaganda remained a torrent of repetition. In preparation for reporting on the Yalta Conference, the press directive of February 2, 1945, simply referred to "the Jewish coalition of our enemies," which was stated to have achieved no successes nor shaken the Reich nor paralyzed the power of the German people.[78] Yet more than 450,000 German soldiers died in battle in January 1945 alone, while civilians continued to perish under Allied bombing of German cities. Now Hitler's dire predictions of national extermination may have seemed to many in Germany like simply a statement about the actual unfolding apocalypse.[79] German propaganda countered Allied efforts to distinguish between the Nazi government and the German people by pointing to the sinister fate the enemy had in store for all Germans. Only continued obedience to Hitler could stave off the "bloodthirsty arbitrariness of the plutocratic-Bolshevik criminal clique." Several days later, the Press Office directive instructed journalists to make clear that "plutocracy and Bolshevism, USA imperialism and Bolshevik world domination, would mean permanent war and that peace would come only with their defeat."[80]

Meanwhile the communiqué from the Allies' Yalta Conference in February 1945 reasserted Allied unity and determination to defeat Nazi Germany. The text included statements regarding the occupation and control of Germany, reparations, formation of the United Nations, Poland and Yugoslavia, and a liberated Europe. It was the sections regarding Germany itself that preoccupied the Nazi Propaganda Ministry. "Nazi

Germany," the Allies bluntly asserted, "is doomed. The German people will only make the cost of their defeat heavier to themselves by attempting to continue hopeless resistance." The communiqué was quite specific about which Germans had the most to worry about:

> It is our inflexible purpose to destroy German militarism and Nazism and to ensure that Germany will never again be able to disturb the peace of the world. We are determined to disarm and disband all German armed forces; break up for all time the German General Staff that has repeatedly contrived the resurgence of German militarism; remove or destroy all German military equipment; eliminate or control all German industry that could be used for military production; bring all war criminals to just and swift punishment and exact reparation in kind for the destruction wrought by the Germans; wipe out the Nazi party, Nazi laws, organizations and institutions; remove all Nazi and militarist influences from public office and from the cultural and economic life of the German people and to take in harmony such other measures in Germany as may be necessary to the future peace and safety of the world. It is not our purpose to destroy the people of Germany, but only when Nazism and Militarism have been extirpated will there be hope for a decent life for Germans, and a place for them in the comity of nations.[81]

Despite the clarity with which the Yalta communiqué stated that the Nazi regime and party and their associated organizations, *not* the German people as a whole, were to be destroyed, Nazi propagandists maintained that just the opposite was the case. The February 16, 1945, *Periodical Service* directive turned to *Mein Kampf* to explain the results of the Yalta Conference and to refute the notion that the Allies were going to make distinctions among the Germans. The Jews, Hitler had written, would exterminate the national intelligentsia and enslave nations. This, the directive claimed, was "the program of extermination from Yalta." The "intent to bring about the total extermination of the German people" was the enemy's war aim. Defeat meant disarmament, deindustrialization, forced deportations, "extermination of the whole national leadership stratum—that is, our whole intelligentsia in all strata and professions." The options facing the Germans were not victory or defeat but "victory or extermination."[82] Other than "unconditional recognition of all the facts created by Stalin and the deliverance of Europe to Bolshevism" by Britain and the United States, the "shared will for extermination of the German people" was the only element agreed on by Stalin, Churchill, and Roosevelt. However, "this mania for extermination by the plutocratic-Bolshevik enemies under shared Jewish leadership" would not weaken German resistance. Rather, it would strengthen it. The German people knew what was in store for them in case of defeat. "The national leadership of National Socialist Germany is not a narrow, limited, self-enclosed caste. Rather, it reaches down to its soldiers, workers, farmers, skilled workers, civil servants, and intellectuals. Whatever or whoever is left after extermination by the Bolshevik bullet in the back of the head will be deported at the will of the war criminals in Yalta to Bolshevik forced-labor camps in Siberia." Indeed, "all the suffering and dangers of the war are minor when compared to the fate that the enemies plan for Germany in a Bolshevik 'peace.'" In order to survive, Germans had only one option, that of continued resistance, in contrast to what the directive called the failure of the home front in 1918–1919. On the same day, the *VB* dutifully ran the following lead story on page 1: "Germany Only Counterweight against Moscow: Yalta, a Death for Europe; German Assessments of Roosevelt's and Churchill's Capitulation to Stalin Confirmed."[83]

As Hitler rejected any talk of surrender, and all possibilities of internal opposition were gone, the Nazi propagandists rallied the nation to fight on in a war in which German defeat was almost certainly only a matter of time. The Red Army liberated Auschwitz-Birkenau on January 27, 1945, and Budapest on February 13. American forces crossed the Rhine on March 7. The toll on the German armed forces and on civilians in the last months of the war was horrific: 1.4 million German soldiers died in battle between January 1, 1945, and the end of the war on May 8; more than 370,000 died in the last five weeks of the war.[84] More than 500,000 German and Russian soldiers and German civilians died in the Battle of Berlin alone, in the last three weeks of the war.[85] At the same time, thousands of Jews were dying on death marches, and about 25,000 German civilians were killed in a British air raid on Dresden on February 13–14.[86] In the midst of this apocalypse of death and destruction, Sündermann, in a *VB* front-page editorial on March 22, 1945, repeated the prediction of national extermination in the event of defeat. A victory of the enemy coalition would "not only exterminate and obliterate the existence of the Reich. It must also lead to the enslavement and thus the extermination of all creative and productive parts of our people."[87] Now "fanatical resistance" on all fronts was essential, in order to open splits in the enemy coalition. The "untenable nature of the Jewish apparatus" in which British and American soldiers were fighting for the Bolshevization of Europe, and then of the whole world, was clear. Germany's "unconditional resistance" to the West would shatter an alliance "whose only real foundation lay in Jewish hate plans directed against the German people."[88] On the one hand, Sündermann wrote that the only thing holding the anti-Hitler alliance together was the Jews. Yet precisely because that was the case, "fanatical resistance," and hence deaths of non-Jewish British and American soldiers, made sense, for it increased pressure to stop this Jewish war.

On February 28, 1945, Goebbels gave a nationally broadcast radio address to bolster morale, denounce the enemies to the east and the west, and offer an explanation of why Nazi Germany had suffered such serious setbacks.[89]

We are not ashamed of our setbacks in this gigantic struggle. They were possible only because the European West and the plutocratically led USA gave the Soviet military backing on the flanks and tied our hands, with which we are still today trying to strike

Bolshevism to the ground. The plutocrats' plans for blood-soaked hatred and revenge against the Reich and against the German people are no less serious than those of the Soviets . . . It will be the eternal shame and disgrace of this century that in the moment of its greatest threat from the East, Europe was shamefully left in the lurch and abandoned by the Western countries. Indeed, these nations sank so low that they even encouraged the storm from inner Asia and at the same time tried to break apart the last protective dam on which it could have been stopped. In any case, we expected nothing else. Through years of systematic labor of disintegration and subversion, international Jewry so poisoned public opinion in these countries that they were no longer capable of thinking—not to mention acting—for themselves.[90]

To the end, Goebbels never wavered from the deluded but internally consistent anti-Semitic explanation for why Nazi Germany was about to lose the war: it had been betrayed and abandoned, one might say "stabbed in the back" by the Western Allies, who had succumbed to Jewish domination. In the minds of the Nazi leaders, World War II ended as World War I had, with noble Germany betrayed. This time, though, betrayal did not come from within, as in 1918–1919, but from abroad, at the hands of the Western, Jewish plutocracies. Goebbels argued, in effect, that Jewish power and policy making in London and Washington had prevented Nazi Germany from winning the war. In February 1945, the propaganda minister held the Jews responsible for the Third Reich's impending defeat. As the chroniclers of the death marches of spring 1945 have recalled in recent years, "revenge" continued up to the very end against the relentless and soon-to-be-victorious foe.[91]

On April 4 one of the last directives from the Reich Press Office ordered that the entire press and all propaganda were to "exclusively serve the purpose" of raising morale and the spirit of resistance on the military front and the home front.[92] Every direct or indirect means that fostered the goal was to be encouraged. Everything that undermined it was to be avoided. The "main mission of the press and radio" was to stress the identity of the "infamous goals and the same devilish plans for extermination of the German people" held by the enemies in the West and the East. The press needed to make clear that if the Germans were to cease fighting now, "Churchill, Roosevelt—just as much as Stalin"— would "mercilessly implement their plans for extermination" of the Germans.[93] The press was to foster unity between the regime and the people, and between the battlefield and the home front. In mid-April, in the midst of these appeals for unity, Dietrich resigned his position as Reich press chief.

Hitler committed suicide with a gunshot to the head in his bunker in Berlin on April 30, 1945. On April 29 he had written his "Political Testament."[94] The war he had started was now clearly lost, as was his connection to military realities. Red Army artillery shells were landing within hundreds of yards of his bunker. As he had his whole life, Hitler placed blame for Germany's setbacks everywhere but on himself. "It is not true that I or anyone else in Germany wanted war in 1939. It was desired and launched exclusively by those international statesmen who either were of Jewish origin or worked for Jewish interests." He had made "too many arms reduction proposals" to assume responsibility for the war. From the ruins of Germany's cities "hatred against the people ultimately responsible will be repeatedly renewed, the people whom we have to thank for everything: international Jewry and its helpers!" The "truly guilty party of this murderous battle is Jewry!"[95]

Goebbels had delivered his last public speech on the evening of April 19, 1945. Hitler, he said, was responsible for the fact that Germany—and indeed Europe and all of the West—with its "culture and civilization" still existed.[96] He claimed that "the perverse coalition between plutocracy and Bolshevism was breaking apart." He then offered a striking blend of religious and secular themes. As the enemy armies stormed the Reich, he said, "international Jewry froths at the mouth as the driver behind the scenes. It does not want peace until it has realized its satanic goal of the destruction of the world. It seeks that goal in vain.

As he has so often in the past when he stood before the door of power over all peoples, God will again push Lucifer back into the abyss from which he came." Hitler, a man of "secular greatness" was God's instrument for doing so. Had it not been for him, Europe would have already succumbed to Bolshevism. In the spirit of "Germanic loyal obedience," Goebbels appealed for loyalty to Hitler. Twelve days later, on May 1, 1945, with tens of thousands dying in the Battle of Berlin raging above Hitler's bunker, Goebbels concluded that life without Hitler was not worth living. His wife Magda poisoned their six children. Then she and Goebbels committed suicide by taking cyanide pills.[97]

Hitler's testament repeated the obsessional narrative that had guided his policy toward the Jews. "I have left no doubt that if the peoples of Europe were again [as in World War I] treated like a block of shares on the stock exchange of these international money and finance conspirators, then this people would be called to account, the ones who are the truly guilty ones for this murderous struggle: Jewry! I left no one in doubt that this time millions of adult men would not die and hundreds of thousands of women and children burn in the cities and die under bombardment without the really guilty party's having to pay for his guilt, albeit by more humane means." Hitler repeated the familiar mix of blunt assertion, regarding his intent to commit mass murder, and absence of factual detail about its implementation. He concluded as follows: "Above all, I command the leadership and followers of the nation carefully to uphold the racial laws and to engage in pitiless resistance against the world poisoner of all peoples, international Jewry."[98] To the end, he persisted in the paranoid logic of innocence, irresponsibility, and projection.

Hitler, Goebbels, Dietrich, and other officials in the Nazi regime, both inside and outside the Propaganda Ministry, had either repeated threats to murder European Jewry or recast them in their own terms during the entire period of World War II in Europe. Hitler had first voiced his murderous prophecy on January 1, 1939, eight months before he started the war. He and his associates gave vent to it following the invasion of the Soviet Union in June 1941, and as the Final Solution began in summer and fall 1941. They did so again as the extermination camps went into operation in 1942, as the tide of war turned against Nazi Germany in winter and spring 1943, and in the two following years, as the war eventually came home to Germany. The paranoid vision that flowed from Hitler's pen on April 29, 1945, of an international Jewish conspiracy waging aggressive and genocidal war against an innocent Nazi Germany had been the central element in the text and imagery of the Nazi regime's anti-Semitic propaganda from the beginning to the end of World War II and the Holocaust.

Conclusion

When Hitler and his accomplices took the leap from persecution to mass murder in the midst of World War II, they said they did so in retaliation against the international Jewish conspiracy they held responsible for starting and escalating a war of extermination against Germany. Europe's longest hatred, anti-Semitism, resulted in the mass murder of European Jewry in part, as I have shown, because the leaders of the Nazi regime interpreted the events of World War II through the distorted prism of this paranoid narrative. Reversing cause and effect, Nazi propaganda projected the subjectivity of a regime racing toward war and mass murder onto its defenseless victims. In so doing, the Nazi leaders publicly asserted that the connection between the war and the policy of mass murder was one of necessity, of cause and effect, rather than of coincidence of timing and geography or of opportunity seized when offered. Projection and paranoia were the handmaidens of aggression and genocide. The translation of abstract ideological postulates into a story of ongoing events—into news—made those fundamental Nazi convictions accessible to a mass audience. In a cascade of self-fulfilling prophecies, Hitler's nightmare of encirclement became reality, as he invaded one country after another and thereby caused an unlikely alliance to be forged between the Soviet Union and the Western democracies. In the summer and fall of 1941, when victory appeared within reach, and in 1942 and 1943, when stalemate gave way to setback, the paranoid vision appeared to merge with the actual course of events. Rather than acknowledge the consequences of his own decisions and actions, Hitler, with the assistance of his spokesmen in the Propaganda Ministry, infused Nazi propaganda with an internally consistent narrative that had nothing at all to do with the political or military realities of the era.

This analysis requires rethinking the meaning of the familiar phrase "the war against the Jews."[1] For the Nazi leadership and many millions of its followers, there were not two distinct events, World War II on the one hand and the Final Solution on the other. Rather, the war against the Jews was in their minds synonymous with World War II—that is, the war against the leading powers of the anti-Hitler coalition, Great Britain, the Soviet Union, and the United States. These were accomplices and puppets of the Jewish wire pullers operating behind the scenes, according to the Nazis. In private conversations and in speeches broadcast to millions, they asserted that Jewry was the driving force of World War II. They attributed seemingly unlimited autonomy, subjectivity, and power to the Jews, while denying these attributes to the political leaders of the most powerful nations in the world at that time, notably Winston Churchill, Franklin D. Roosevelt, and Joseph Stalin.[2] As the Allies waged war against Nazi Germany, the Nazis insisted that the Jews would pay for it. When Soviet tanks and American and British bombers rained death and destruction on the armies and cities of the Third Reich, the Nazi propaganda machine interpreted the Allied attacks as Jewry's unprovoked assault and to constitute tangible evidence that international Jewry was indeed in the process of trying to exterminate the Germans.

The radical anti-Semitism that accompanied and justified the Holocaust described the Jews first and foremost as a racially constituted *political* subject. To be sure, radical anti-Semitism had been preceded by a despicable but nongenocidal traditional anti-Semitism that had largely shaped the Nazi policies of anti-Jewish persecution from 1933 to 1941. They included purges from the professions; theft of property and large-scale economic impoverishment; ghettoization and apartheid enforced by the Nuremberg Laws of 1935; racial pseudoscience, with its comparative measurements of the brain, nose, and ears; fantasies of "Aryan" beauty and Jewish ugliness; the pogrom of November 1938; and arrests, imprisonment, and random violence. Yet these measures, as horrific as they were, did not lead to a policy of mass murder. The core ideological justification for the Holocaust lay in the depiction of Jewry as constituting a powerful international anti-German conspiracy that was the driving force behind the scenes of the world war. Nazi propaganda during the war and the Holocaust brought the conspiracy theory in *The Protocols of the Elders of Zion* into the middle of Europe's twentieth century and peopled that conspiracy with names and faces from the contemporary political scene in Moscow, London, and Washington.

With the paranoid logic of a war said to be waged by Jewry against Germany, and with the detailed day-to-day and week-to-week chronicle of events that appeared to flow from it, the Nazi leadership embedded the most extraordinary statements expressing its determination to exterminate and annihilate Europe's Jews within a seemingly ordinary and normal narrative of attack and counterattack in war. The denial of the uniqueness of the Final Solution was part of its implementation, because it was not an act of war in the sense that the term had been understood in Europe for centuries, but instead a mass slaughter of innocents. The interweaving of the extraordinary language of genocide with the more ordinary and conventional narrative of warfare was a central feature of Nazism's anti-Semitic propaganda. That is why, in the Nazi imagination, there was no such thing as an innocent Jew. As the Jews had started and escalated the war, it made perfect sense, within the framework of this internally consistent yet irrational "delirious discourse," that murderous hatred of the Jewish people as a whole should intensify as the war was extended, escalated, and eventually brought home to Germany.[3] So it was that as the utter defenselessness of European Jewry was manifested in the death camps, Nazi propaganda attempted to instill terror in the hearts and minds of millions of Germans, through predictions of Jewry's intent to exterminate them all. As Goebbels put it, the Jews were guilty and deserved to be punished. In this way, the Nazis presented the most extraordinary of historical events—indeed, one that was unique—the Holocaust, as an ordinary consequence of the logic of war.

During World War II anyone in Nazi Germany who regularly read a newspaper, listened to the radio, or walked past the Nazi political posters between 1941 and 1943 knew of the threats and boasts of the Nazi regime about intentions to exterminate European Jews, followed by public assertions that it was implementing that policy. Claims of ignorance regarding the murderous intentions and assertions of making good on such threats defy the evidence, logic, and common sense. With confidence we can say that millions and millions of Germans were told on many occasions that the Jews had begun a war to exterminate the Germans, but that the Nazi regime was exterminating the Jews instead.

The evidence indicates that when Hitler, Goebbels, and Dietrich used the words *Vernichtung* (extermination) and *Ausrottung* (annihilation), the inhabitants of Nazi Germany understood that those words referred to a policy of mass murder. As was mentioned in Chapter 1, this assessment represents a revision of the conventional wisdom, associated with George Orwell, on the role of euphemism and plain speech in this totalitarian dictatorship. When the Nazis referred to the extermination and annihilation of the Jews, they were not speaking euphemistically, nor were the terms euphemisms in German political culture at the time. The Nazis said exactly what they meant, and the meaning was clearly conveyed to millions of people. In contrast to past militaristic uses, such as Clausewitz's *Vernichtungsschlacht* or the extermination of enemy armies advocated by General Falkenhayn at Verdun in World War I, Hitler, Goebbels, and others used the term *Vernichtung* to refer to the mass murder of a whole people, not whole armies.[4] When the Nazis talked about Jewish plans to exterminate or annihilate the Germans, they meant that the Jews were going to engage in mass murder, not merely defeat the German armed forces. To German ears and eyes, the Nazi pronouncements about turning the tables and exterminating the Jews in Europe were extraordinary assertions, in the history of German militarism. These threats of mass murder were hiding in plain sight.

The evidence also indicates that the Nazis combined blunt speech about their general intentions with suppression of any facts or details regarding the Final Solution. They did so for both practical and ideological reasons. Preserving secrecy in the midst of war reduced the likelihood of attacks on the death camps by Allied air forces. Given that the Nazi leaders believed that Jewish wire pullers in London, Moscow, and Washington were controlling policy, accurate accounts in the press of the murders by *Einsatzgruppen* and *Ordnungspolizei,* gas chambers, and crematoria would have increased foreign pressure to put an end to the genocide. Public reaction to the November pogrom of 1938 led the Nazi leadership to conclude that only moderate, rather than genocidal, anti-Semitism had support in German society beyond the confines of the Nazi party. Support for discrimination and deportation would not necessarily extend to mass murder. Factual reporting about the mass murder was also incompatible with both the myth of Hitler as a defender of Western civilization and the account of a powerful Jewry at war with Nazi Germany. The Nazis presented Hitler as a heroic moral leader who was battling against powerful, evil enemies on all sides. The truth about the genocide of the Jews would have revealed him to be instead a criminal of unprecedented dimensions and would also have shattered the fabrications about the power of the Jews. If the Jews were so powerful, why were they *powerless* to prevent their own extermination? Details about the death camps would have taken Hitler's threats of extermination and annihilation of the Jewish enemy out of the logic of war and placed them squarely within the realm of crime. The propaganda narrative that made no distinction between the war against the Allies and policy towards the Jews would have collapsed, as it became obvious that the often-declared extermination of the Jews had nothing to do with war understood as a clash of armed states and everything to do with the slaughter of innocent civilians, as its primary aim, not as a means to some other end. The interweaving of extraordinary discourse of extermination and the more ordinary language of war would have become impossible. Conversely, for some of those who believed that the vast conspiracy existed, presentation of the facts would have been terrifying for the opposite reason. If the Jews were so powerful, what sense would it make to enrage them further with news reports about the Final Solution? The mixture of blunt speech and suppression of the facts was adequate to consolidate a "covenant of gangsters," while offering to the silent, indifferent, and uncurious majority a fig leaf of plausible deniability.

The Nazis' contemporaries had great difficulty, as have subsequent historians, understanding the full dimensions of fanaticism in power. Karl Bracher's insightful comment that the history of Nazism was also the history of its underestimation remains important.[5] Since the formulation of the concept of ideology during the French Revolution, political sophistication in modern politics has meant looking beyond manifest statements for their latent or real meaning and viewing ideas as instruments used for other purposes. This rationalist bias prevented observers across the political spectrum from seeing Nazi anti-Semitic propaganda as anything more than a revolting bundle of rationalizations opportunistically seized upon by base and evil men. Despite the vast literature on Nazi Germany, World War II, and the Holocaust, the rationalist bias about human motivation has persisted, reinforced by the positivism of the social sciences and challenges to intellectual and cultural history within the discipline of history. Resistance to grasping the power and impact of nonrational and irrational currents in Nazi Germany has been considerable.

Yet Hitler, Goebbels, Dietrich, and their staffs were accomplished liars, as well as men immersed in the paranoid logic of a conspiracy theory that was, from the beginning, refuted by even the most elementary confrontation with fact. The Nazi leadership pushed to the extreme the widespread human capacity for delusion and belief in illusions. The assumption that these men did not believe these fantasies relies on an optimistic view of the power of human rationality, justified neither by the events of modern history nor by our now widespread awareness of the role of nonrational forces in human experience. The weight of evidence leads to the conclusion that members of the Nazi leadership viewed the world in the way that they said they did, and supplied a narrative of events that seemed to offer an iron-clad explanation of them as well as justification for uniting ideology and practice in war and mass murder.

From the diplomacy of expansion in the 1930s to the wars of aggression begun between 1939 and 1941 and then the Holocaust, Hitler's policies drove events forward. In these same years, Nazi propaganda asserted that precisely the opposite was the case, and that Nazi Germany was merely responding to threats and actual attacks launched against it by others. Nazi propaganda presented more paranoia than grandiosity, more assertions of outraged innocence than blueprints for Aryan world domination. This is true even of the infamous prophecy of January 30, 1939, by Hitler. Knowing he was planning to unleash a war as soon as possible, he ordered his propagandists to assert that exactly the opposite was taking place—namely, that international Jewry was about to launch and implement a war of extermination against Germany and the Germans. For the Nazi leaders, the coming of the war Hitler had started appeared to confirm the validity of their paranoid anti-Semitism and to radicalize the consequences of this centuries-old hatred to an unprecedented degree.

Hitler's violation of the elementary logic of chronology and cause and effect was so flagrant that it was and remains tempting to view his assertions as cynical tools that would work to convince only the most naive of fanatics. Mutually contradictory though they were, grandiose visions of world domination by a master race coexisted with the paranoia of the righteously indignant innocent victim. If sheer repetition, in public and private contexts, can be taken as proof of belief, then it appears that Hitler, Goebbels, Dietrich, their staffs, and an undetermined percentage of German listeners and readers believed that an international Jewish conspiracy was the driving force behind the anti-Hitler coalition in World War II. If they regarded this aspect of their own propaganda with cynicism, they did not leave much trace of that skepticism behind. Yet the sources point to the presence of true believers. They certainly acted as if the Final Solution was Nazi Germany's punishment of the Jews, whom the Nazis found guilty of starting and prolonging World War II. Sincerity of belief was a secondary matter. As E. H. Gombrich put it, the myth of an all-powerful, enveloping conspiracy "becomes self-confirming. Once you are entrapped in this illusionary universe it will become reality for if you fight everybody, everybody will fight you, and the less mercy you show, the more you commit your side to a fight to the finish. When you have been caught in this vicious circle there really is no escape."[6]

So it was that Hitler and Goebbels wasted each other's time with late-night ruminations about the truth of the *Protocols of the Elders of Zion*. They were indeed totalitarians and fanatics. The possession of power, rather than moderating Hitler and Goebbels's views as they collided with recalcitrant realities, only fed the radicalism of these two men, as they sought to make events conform to their ideologically driven "prophecies." Though they detested the universalist and humanist core of the European Enlightenment, they called their own institution the Ministry of *Public Enlightenment* and Propaganda. Heirs to an age of suspicion of all ideologies, they were modernists of a crackpot sort who believed they had discovered the real truth lurking hidden behind the scenes. They believed that they understood the way the world really worked better than did the masses mired in contingency and trapped by common sense. It is sobering to note that both Goebbels and Dietrich had doctorates from prestigious German universities. The staffs of the Reich Press Office and of the Propaganda Ministry were filled with highly educated people. They constituted a community of anti-Semitic intellectuals bound together by the books, journals, and newspapers they all read. They received the recognition intellectuals

seek. Their books and essays were published in large editions, distributed widely, reviewed favorably in newspapers and magazines, and presumably read by many people. These propagandists were not the most
brilliant or creative minds of their generation, but neither were they the
most stupid and mediocre. An enormous amount of intelligence and
talent in Nazi Germany went to waste in the production and diffusion
of its anti-Semitic propaganda.

Much has been written about conflicts within the Nazi regime. Yet
this study of wartime propaganda reveals cooperation among different
and at times antagonistic institutions. As the tense relations between
Goebbels and Dietrich indicate, high-ranking officials engaged in turf
battles—in their case over who would control the press. But they also
cooperated with great effectiveness in pursuit of a common goal. Dietrich's press directives brought the work of Goebbels's writers to the attention of three thousand newspaper and periodical editors on a regular
basis. Goebbels's propagandists elaborated on press directives conveyed
at the daily and weekly press conferences of the Reich Press Office.
The massive hierarchy of the Nazi party and its activist membership
disseminated the regime's propaganda.

Examination of the institutional mechanisms of Nazi propaganda
calls for revision of ideas about who played a key role in some of its aspects. Joseph Goebbels's enormous celebrity, his voluminous published
work, and his remarkable diary have all influenced scholarship about Nazi
propaganda. Whereas the minister of propaganda was obviously a key
figure, he did not control daily and periodical journalism in the Third
Reich to the extent that is often thought to be the case. Adolf Hitler did,
or rather Hitler did so via Otto Dietrich and the Reich Press Office.
Hitler's and Dietrich's key role in the shaping of the wartime narrative in
the press was thoroughly examined at the Ministries Trial in Nuremberg
after the war. Once both Hitler and Goebbels were dead, it was understandable that Dietrich's defense lawyer would present his client as an
unimportant cog in the bureaucracy by comparison with the celebrated

maestro of propaganda, Goebbels. In the course of the trial, however, American prosecutors introduced into evidence press directives that German journalists August Brammer and Theodore Oberheitmann had kept hidden during the war. The Oberheitmann file of wartime directives was vital to the conviction of Dietrich for crimes against humanity as a result of his role in the regime's anti-Semitic propaganda campaigns.[7] In the next half century, though several historians examined the contents of the Oberheitmann file and the directives of the Press Office *Periodical Service,* the role of Hitler, Dietrich, and the Reich Press Office directives in elaborating the Nazi regime's anti-Semitic narrative and shaping the German press remained on the margins of much of the scholarship on Nazi propaganda. The directives show clearly the way radical anti-Semitism shaped the news in Nazi Germany and illustrate how Hitler was able, through Dietrich and the Reich Press Office bureaucracy, to exert constant pressure on the German press. As we have seen, the directives are essential in order to understand how radical anti-Semitism shaped the news in Nazi Germany and how the regime was able to exert a regular impact on the German press.[8]

In their judgment of April 14, 1949, the judges in the Ministries Trial in Nuremberg took issue with commentators who minimized the significance of "these press and periodical directives." Though the court recognized that Goebbels was able at times to influence the ministry's press directives, Dietrich's role was central. The directives "were not mere political polemics, . . . aimless expressions of anti-Semitism, and they were not designed only to unite the German people in the war effort. Their clear and expressed purpose was to enrage Germans against Jews, to justify measures taken and to be taken against them, and to subdue any doubts which might arise as to the justice of measures of racial persecution to which the Jews were to be subjected." The court found that in issuing them, "Dietrich consciously implemented, and by furnishing excuses and justifications, participated in, the crimes against humanity regarding Jews," and it thus found him guilty. The judgment marked the first time since the development of mass communications that a decision maker had been held accountable for the use of the press to incite hatred linked to genocide.[9]

The weekly wall newspapers called the *Word of the Week* are another crucial piece of visual evidence. Despite the importance of these ubiquitous intrusions into the everyday life in Nazi Germany, they do not figure at all in major works about the regime. They constitute a chapter in the history of "reactionary modernism," a blend of modern technology with political reaction that was one component of Nazi ideology.[10] The aesthetic sensibility on display in the posters was traditional, indeed reactionary, by comparison with the cultural modernism of artistic movements such as Expressionism, the Bauhaus, and Dada. Yet the posters made use of the technology of mass reproduction to disseminate their multicolored political messages to a broad audience. On the one hand, anti-Semitic visual propaganda depersonalized the Jews by reducing them to archetypes of "the Jew." On the other, the *Word of the Week* featured mass-produced photographs of such actual personages as Bernard Baruch and Maxim Litvinov, in the attempt to put names and faces to the vast conspiracy. For a mass audience that had no other reliable and readily accessible source of information about the outside world, such photos and the seemingly accurate detailed information that accompanied them must have lent plausibility to the conspiracy theory. About a third of the time from 1940 to early 1943, the wall newspapers featured the narrative of radical anti-Semitism and its murderous implications. The messages stared out at the mass public for a week at a time in tens of thousands of places German pedestrians were likely to pass in the course of the day. We do not know what people in Nazi Germany made of the wall newspapers with the headlines "They Will Stop Laughing!!!" or "The Jewish Conspiracy." We do know that people saw them.

The question of Zionism and Jews in Palestine was a secondary issue in the period of World War II and the Holocaust, but its aftereffects are still with us. Although the regime did allow Jewish emigration to Palestine between 1933 and 1939 and though some officials thought that Germany could be emptied of Jews through deportation, this was not Hitler's view. The conspiracy theory and associated fears of a "Jewish Vatican" based in Palestine sparked opposition to the idea of a Jewish state in Palestine or anywhere else. Nazi support for some Jewish emigration to Palestine did not conflict with Hitler's view that the Zionist project was one component of international Jewry's drive for world domination and must be opposed on that basis. During World War II this deep structure of Nazi ideology converged with strategic arguments concerning the importance of gaining Arab, and eventually pan-Islamic, support for the war in the Mediterranean. This conjuncture led to a historically significant meeting of minds between Nazism and radical fundamentalist Islam. Through the Grand Mufti of Jerusalem, Nazism's message was diffused to the Arab and the rest of the Islamic world. From the Grand Mufti's perspective, international Jewry not only won the world war but won another victory in 1948 with the establishment of the state of Israel. In the ideological documents of fundamentalist Islam in recent decades, the replacement of history's contingencies and complexities persists, as do the seemingly absolute clarity and simplicity of a paranoid conspiracy theory focused on actions attributed to international Jewry. Examination of the impact of Nazism on the Arab and Muslim world is still in its early stages. Regrettably, however, the themes of this study have a contemporary echo in the terrorism that is one manifestation of Islamic fundamentalism.

The material presented here does not resolve the issue of what most Germans knew or thought about the Holocaust, how they responded to the radical anti-Semitic discourse and images churned out by Nazi propaganda, or how widespread radical anti-Semitism was in the Third Reich. The beginning of wisdom in these matters is a certain restraint and much less certainty regarding what "ordinary Germans" made of Nazi propaganda. We do know that only one protest took place against deportation of Jews, and that was by non-Jewish wives of Jewish husbands. We know that the home front never collapsed as the German troops fought to the very last hours, even while suffering almost unimaginable casualties, and that in the year after the war, the Allied occupation authorities had sufficient evidence to arrest almost 100,000 people on charges of war crimes and crimes against humanity.[11] Beyond these facts, skepticism is in order about assertions regarding what most Germans in Nazi Germany really believed, because the evidence is insufficient to support assertions on that score. The evidence from the period is fragmentary, anecdotal, not based on representative samples of the population, and tainted by the mode of collection and its reporting by Nazi security services. The postwar record is subject to the distorting influences of memory and political self-interest.[12] David Bankier, who has revealed a good deal concerning what most Germans knew about the death camps, has examined rumors about shootings and gassing conveyed by soldiers returning from the eastern front, and reports of Allied radio broadcasts. He writes that "clearly, there was no scarcity of information" and that there is "no doubt that those who wished to know had the means at their disposal to acquire such knowledge."[13] Yet what they could "know" was fragmentary and not an adequate substitute for accurate and reliable journalism, which the Nazi regime had destroyed. Bankier's own research indicates that hard facts were scarce and that it was doubtful that those who wished to know had the ability to grasp the dimensions and methods of the Final Solution. Martin Broszat's detailed studies of Bavaria under the Nazis reveal the spread of disillusionment and cynicism about Hitler and the Nazis after the defeat at Stalingrad.[14] Yet however disillusioned and cynical they may have been, the German armies fought to the bitter end.

Ian Kershaw, who has examined messages from the Nazi regime and their reception from below has concluded that the "vast majority of Germans" had "no more than minimal interest" in the fate of the Jews.[15] Though the extent of awareness about the death camps "will never be known," it was doubtful that even rumors about Auschwitz-Birkenau as an extermination center were widely circulated in Germany. The "very secrecy of the 'Final Solution' demonstrates more clearly than anything else the fact that the Nazi leadership felt it could not rely on popular backing for its extermination policy." In any case, mass support for genocide was unnecessary. The "latent anti-Semitism and apathy" of the population was sufficient to "allow the increasingly criminal 'dynamic' hatred of the Nazi regime the autonomy it needed to set in motion the Holocaust."[16] Although we cannot resolve the issue of what most Germans knew and believed, the present work does explore, in greater detail than has been the case before, what those caught up in the regime's "dynamic hatred" believed about the Jews during the period of the Holocaust. The most plausible reading of the evidence is that a fanatical, but not small, minority embedded in or hovering around the front organizations of the Nazi party adopted the anti-Semitic narrative described here, and that these fanatics were surrounded by a society in which milder forms of anti-Semitism had become commonplace.

By the time Hitler committed suicide, he was perhaps clinically insane. Yet as the original writers about totalitarianism understood so well, mental illness was not the key to understanding the Nazi regime and the Holocaust. Many emotionally well-adjusted, well-educated, highly competent, professionally accomplished people working in the Nazi regime and Nazi party adopted an ideological outlook—radical anti-Semitism—that bore no relation at all to the actual course of events. In varying forms and in most radical variants, these adherents celebrated the active efforts of the Nazi regime to seize the initiative and start a second world war at a time and place of Hitler's choosing, while simultaneously claiming that they and this same Hitler were innocent victims of a vast Jewish network of power. In the first decade of the twenty-first century the demented discourse of radical anti-Semitism and totalitarianism has returned in different idioms and cultural contexts. It would be complacent to assume that variants on the narrative explored in this work will not play a part in the future as well. The insight that history is not the product of conspiracy and that political events are full of contingency is an antidote that, though often taken for granted, is yet among the most important a historian can offer to this most lethal of all ideological poisons.

Appendix
List of Abbreviations
Notes
Acknowledgments
Bibliography
Bibliographical Essay
Index

Appendix: The Anti-Semitic Campaigns of the Nazi Regime as Reflected in Lead Front-Page Stories in *Der Völkische Beobachter*

There were two anti-Semitic front-page lead stories in *Der Völkische Beobachter* in 1939, none in 1940, seventeen in 1941, four in 1942, fifty in 1943, ten in 1944, and two in spring 1945. Four periods accounted for most of the front-page stories: July–August 1941 (seven), April–July 1943 (twenty-six), October–November 1943 (thirteen), and May–June 1944 (nine).

1939

Jan. 5, "62,000 Jews in State Bureaucracy of USA."

Jan 31, "The Führer before the First Reichstag of Greater Germany, 'We Fight an Enormous Fight; We Will Win This Battle'—Prophetic Warning to Jewry."

1941

Feb. 5, "Churchill Promises Germany As Booty to Jews, Solidarity with World Parasite Again Announced."

Mar. 18, "Who Governs the 'Democracies'? Blood Guilt of Capitalism in Jewish-Anglo-Saxon Form."

Mar. 29 (Alfred Rosenberg), "The Jewish Question As a World Problem."

July 10, "Bolshevism Reveals Its Jewish Face: Litvinov-Finkelstein Comes Out from Behind the Scenes."

July 12, "The Summit of Jewish Shamelessness: Bolsheviks' Crimes Attributed to Our Army—Battlefield Hyenas in Role of 'Liberators.'"

July 13, "Jewry [*Juda*] Floods England with Soviet Lies; British Made Stupid by Moscow's False Reports."

July 15, "London Commits Itself to Rescue of Bolshevism; Moscow Pact Shows Plutocrats and Soviets Arm in Arm against Europe; Sober Neutrals Grasp True War Situation."

July 23, "Roosevelt Primary Tool of Jewish Freemasonry; Sensational Document Reveals Connection of the Warmonger with International Clique of Masons; Source of Roosevelt's Hebraic Hatred against Reich."

July 24, "Enormous Jewish Extermination Program [*Vernichtungsprogramm*]: Roosevelt Demands Sterilization of German People; German People to Be Exterminated within Two Generations."

Aug. 10, "Jewish World Domination on Point of USA Bayonets; Roosevelt's Navy Secretary Announces 'New Program.'"

Aug. 19, "Roosevelt's Goal Is World Domination by Jews—the Program: Control over Both Hemispheres, Arms Monopoly of English-Speaking People, and Lash of Hunger against Europe."

Sept. 14, "Germany's Cities to Be Depopulated; Roosevelt Adviser Demands Destruction of Our Economy."

Oct. 10, "The Military End of Bolshevism: The Eastern Campaign Has Been Decided; Timoshenko and Voroshilov Army Groups Surrounded; Budjenny Army Group Dissolving—Incomparable Masterstroke of Strategy."

Oct. 27, "They Are Digging Their Own Grave: Jewish Warmongers Seal Jewry's [*Judas*] Fate; Their Crimes Receive Deserved Punishment; Antonescu Rejects Impudent Complaints of Romanian Jews."

Oct. 29, "Roosevelt Outdoes Himself: Most Recent Emergence of His Jewish Gangster Fantasy; Germany Wants to Divide South America and Abolish All Religions."

Nov. 7, "Litvinov-Finkelstein Sent to Roosevelt As Jewish Adviser: Stalin Hopes for Activation of American Help for Soviet Union."

Nov. 12, "The Jewish Enemy."

1942

Feb. 20, "Declaring War Aims Is Supposed to Stress Confidence in Victory; Vansittart Dreams of Germany's Complete Extermination; Churchill Promises Galician Jews 'Free Austria.'"

Aug. 24 (Joseph Goebbels), "Prisoner of the Kremlin" (South German edition).

Aug. 29, "Informative French Document: USA Stands under Jews' Thumb; Already in 1926, Government and Congress Obeyed Jewish Commands."

Sept. 13, "Roosevelt and His Jews: Baruch Becomes U.S. Economic Dictator—Man Who Twice Drove America into War, Speculator, Tribute Hyena, Secret President."

Sept. 24, "Comintern Plan for Bolshevization of U.S. Negroes, Roosevelt As Moscow's Pace-Setter."

Nov. 18, "Roosevelt's Fifth Column: The Jews' Role in North Africa; in Moscow's Synagogues They Give Jahweh's Blessings to Stalin."

1943

Jan. 14, "They Won't Escape Punishment for Their Warmongering: USA Jews Must Count on Wave of Intolerance."

Jan. 16, "Rosenman Stands behind Roosevelt: A Crown Jew on Throne of USA; USA President Unquestionably Tool of Jewish High Finance."

Feb. 7, "Wallace Reveals Roosevelt's Dream for Future: Whole World Will Be Field for Jewish-American Exploiters. Those

Who Don't Follow American Orders Will Be Bombed Mercilessly."

Feb. 11, "Most Recent Burst of Jewish Hatred: They Want to Exterminate the German People Culturally and Physically; However, We Will Strike the Plutocratic and Bolshevik Sadists to the Ground."

Feb. 14, "Stalin's Agents at Work, Roosevelt Throws Europe to Bolshevism As Booty; Jews' Straw Man Bows before Moscow, We Will Give Him the Answer He Deserves."

Feb. 20, "First Echo of Our Answer to Goebbels's Questions: Passionate Agreement of Our People Is Important, Strong Echo in Entire World."

Feb. 24, "These Plans Will Undermine Eastern Front; USA Completely Agrees with Bolshevization of Europe; Stalin Will Trample Balkans and Hungary."

Feb. 26, "Twenty-five Years Ago, I Predicted Victory of Party; Today I Prophesy the Victory of Germans: Führer's Address to His Old Party Comrades."

Mar. 20, "Appeal of Grand Mufti against Deadly Enemy of Islam: Arabs Will Fight for Their Freedom on the Side of the Axis."

Mar. 23, "Europe Understood the Führer: Merciless Battle against the Bolshevik World Enemy; Continent Determines Its Fate According to Its Own Law."

Apr. 11, "Again, Seven Jews Appointed as Soviet Generals: Jewish Plutocracy Threatens with Anger of Bolshevik Racial Comrades."

Apr. 15, "Why Stalin Is Silent about Poland: The Secret of Katyn —A Polish Delegation Visits Site of Bolshevik Mass Murder."

Apr. 16, "The Jew Davies: 'We Can Trust Soviet Union'; Katyn— an Example of Jewry's Blow at Europe; Where Are the 500,000 Polish Soldiers Who Fell into Soviets' Hands, 12,000 Captured Polish Officers Assassinated by Jewish Commandos?"

Apr. 18, "The Gangster from New York."

Apr. 30, "Katyn Again Reveals World Jewry; Europe Recognizes Conspiracy of Plutocrats and Soviet Jews; England and USA Make Pitiful Efforts at Concealment."

May 3, "England Knuckles Under to Kremlin Jews; Cynical Abandonment of Poland in Light of European Press."

May 6, "USA and England under Orders from World Jewry: Plutocrats Identify with Jewish-Bolshevik Murderers."

May 9, "Signs of Growing Hostility to Jews; Jewish Fear in England; Screams for Help from Courts; Profit Hyenas Demand Misuse of State Power."

May 12, "United with Main Headquarters of World Revolution, Moscow Will Be Official Center of World Jewry; Jewish State As Cornerstone of Soviet Control of Mediterranean."

May 12, "40,000 Polish Jews Released As Soviet Agitators; Bullets in the Skull for 12,000 Officers, Death By Starvation for 1.5 Million, Passports and Train Tickets for the Jews" (South German edition).

May 13, "Letter of an English Sailor, 'On the Day on which There Are No More Jews in the World'; Belated Recognition in Great Britain."

May 21, "It Could Turn Out This Way: Europe to Be Delivered to Corn Jews; Axis Powers Fight for Right of All Peoples to Work and Bread."

May 25, "International Agricultural Bank, Jewish Plans for World Exploitation: Daily Bread of Nations to Become Object of Stock Exchange Speculation."

June 2, "Hunger and Chaos as First Stages of Jewish World Domination, Postwar Fantasies of Roosevelt Clique."

June 2 (Theodor Seibert), "The Jewish War."

June 2, "Murder 'in the Spirit of Freedom': London Admits Terror As Principle; Churchill's House Organ Admits to Gangster Methods of Air War" (South German edition).

June 5, "Negro Bands to Be Used As Terror Flyers over Italy—
Ineradicable Disgrace in Conduct of War by Servants of the
Jews."

June 18 (Alfred Rosenberg), "The World Parasite."

June 22, "Two Years of War against Bolshevism: The West's Protection Wall Stands—Uncompromising Struggle to Defeat Europe's
Deadly Enemy."

June 23, "Financial Scandal in Roosevelt's America: Armaments
Hyenas Make Enormous Profits—the Jewish Business."

June 24, "Greatest Danger in World History, Alliance between
Gangsterism and Bolshevism; Alfred Rosenberg Describes
Great Struggle of Our Time" (South German edition).

July 4, "New Documents Confirm Judgment: Roosevelt's War
Guilt Irrefutably Proven—'World President' As Front Man of
Jewish Warmongers."

July 18, "North Africa, Colony of Roosevelt-Jews."

July 20, "Jews Show No Respect for Humanity's Cultural Trea-
sures: Terror Bombs Strike Rome; New Crimes of British-
American Air Gangsters."

July 23, "Why Not Annex Like Texas? England and the Empire to
Become American: *Chicago Daily Tribune* Uncovers Plan for
Jewish World Republic."

July 24, "Jewish-American Imperialism Operating at Full Tilt: New
Evidence of Arrogance and Greed."

July 26, "The USA's Dream of World Domination: Portugal's
Colonies Also to Become American Booty; New York Jews
Strive for 'Internationalization' of All Colonial Territories."

Aug. 20 (Helmut Sündermann), "Our Enemy's War Aims."

Oct. 1, "Roosevelt Again Declares Solidarity with Jewry [*Juda*];
Growing Criticism of American Jews to Be Stifled."

Oct. 6, "Jewry Presents the Change: Palestine, Egypt, and Iraq to
Become Jewish-American Colonies."

Oct. 9, "Adolf Hitler: 'This War Will End with a Great German

Victory'; Meeting of Reich Leaders and Gauleiters; Displays Fighting Determination of German Nation."

Oct. 11, "England As Policeman for World Jewry: British Military Power to Establish Order and Security in Palestine."

Oct. 13, "Unified Jewish Direction behind Plans for Extermination—Simultaneous Dreams in Moscow and Washington."

Oct. 26, "Anglo-Americans Abandon West to Moscow; Small Nations Receive No Protection against Soviets from USA and Great Britain."

Oct. 30, "Plutocratic Apparatus Works for Stalin; Moscow Expands Its Claims to Power: Success of Soviet Agitation in England and USA."

Oct. 31, "USA President Confirms It: Europe to be Delivered to Bolshevism; Hull and Eden Executive Organs of World Jewry."

Nov. 1, "Bolsheviks Agitate among North American People; Jews Appeal for Cooperation with Soviets."

Nov. 5, "Roosevelt Suffers Blow: Alarming Impact of Gubernatorial Elections in USA, Advance of Republicans against Democratic Clique in White House."

Nov. 16, "Why Jewish Capital Murders the Peoples: Dividends Prolong War; Axis Fights for Productive Man."

Nov. 27, "Establishment of Jewish Bank for Plundering World: All Nations of the Earth to be Beaten with Chains of Gold."

Nov. 30, "What the Führer Demands of German Officers: Courage, Hardness, and Political Fanaticism, Victory or Merciless Extermination—There Is No Third Option; Adolf Hitler Spoke to 20,000 Officer Candidates."

Dec. 21, "USA Jew Confirms Betrayal of Small Nations: Baltic States and Poland to Become Bolshevik Dominions."

1944

June 10, "Jewish Business with Invasion."

June 22, "Führer's Great Decision: How Jewish-Bolshevik World

Conspiracy Was Thwarted; Invasion—the Path to Moscow's Goal."

1945

Feb. 13, "Kremlin to Dominate Europe, Stalin Has Freedom of Action."

Mar. 22 (Helmut Sündermann), "Our Stance and the Enemy Coalition."

Mar. 23, "Jewish Occupiers in Cologne, Programmatic Appointment to the Anglo-American Occupation Authorities."

Apr. 14 (Eugen Mandler), "Enemy Cooperation."

Note: There were two overlapping editions of *Der Völkische Beobachter*. Unless indicated otherwise, these headlines are from the North German edition (Berlin), rather than from the South German edition (Munich).

Abbreviations

BAK, SO	Bundesarchiv Koblenz, Sammlung Oberheitmann
BDC	Berlin Document Center
IMT	*Trials of War Criminals before the Nuerenberg Military Tribunals*
NARA	United States National Archives and Records Administration
NWCT	Nuremberg War Crimes Trials
RG	Records Group
USHMMA	United States Holocaust Memorial Museum Archive
VIdRMVP	Vertrauliche Informationen des Reichsministeriums für Volksmeinung und Propaganda

Notes

1. The Jews, the War, and the Holocaust

1. Max Domarus, ed., *Hitler: Reden und Proklamation, 1932–1945,* 2 vols. (Neustadt: Schmidt, 1972), p. 1058.

2. Victor Klemperer, entry for July 20, 1944, in *I Will Bear Witness, 1942–1945,* trans. Martin Chalmers (New York: Knopf, 2000), p. 335; Victor Klemperer, *Tagebücher, 1944* (Berlin: Aufbau Verlag, 1995), p. 85.

3. E. H. Gombrich, *Myth and Reality in German War-Time Broadcasts* (London: Athlone, 1970), p. 18.

4. See Norman Cohn, *Warrant for Genocide: The Myth of the Jewish World Conspiracy and the Protocols of the Elders of Zion* (New York: Harper and Row, 1967).

5. Saul Friedlander, *Nazi Germany and the Jews,* vol. 1, *The Years of Persecution, 1933–1939* (New York: HarperCollins, 1997), pp. 73–113.

6. Ian Kershaw, *Hitler, 1889–1936: Hubris* (New York: Norton, 1999), p. 151.

7. Adolf Hitler, "München, 6 April 1920: Diskussionsbeitrag auf einer NSDAP-Versammlung," in Eberhard Jäckel and Axel Kuhn, *Hitler: Sämtliche Aufzeichnungen, 1905–1924* (Stuttgart: Deutsche Verlagsanstalt, 1980), pp. 119–120.

8. See Reginald H. Phelps, "Hitlers 'grundlegende' Rede über den Antisemitismus," *Vierteljahrshefte für Zeitgeschichte* 16 (1968): 417; Jäckel and Kuhn, *Hitler,* pp. 184–204. See also the discussion of the speech in Eberhard Jäckel, *Hitler's World View: A Blueprint for Power,* trans. Herbert Arnold (Cambridge, Mass.: Harvard University Press, 1981), pp. 50–52.

9. Adolf Hitler, *Mein Kampf,* trans. Ralph Mannheim (Boston: Houghton Mifflin, 1971 [1925]), p. 679.

10. For a representative example of Hitler's denunciations of "Jewish domination," see Adolf Hitler, document 237, "29. February 1928, Rede auf NSDAP-Versammlung in München," in Bärbel Dusik, ed., *Hitler: Reden, Schriften, Anordnung, Februar 1925 bis Januar 1933,* vol. 2, *Juli 1926–Mai 1928* (Munich: Sauer; Institut für Zeitgeschichte, 1992), pp. 681–716.

11. On the Transfer Agreement, see Francis R. Nicosia, *The Third Reich and the Palestine Question,* 2nd ed. (New Brunswick, N.J.: Transaction, 1999); "Zionism and Palestine in Anti-Semitic Thought in Imperial Germany," *Studies in Zionism* 13, no. 2 (1992): 115–131; "Ein nützlicher Feind: Zionismus im Nationalsozialistischen Deutschland, 1933–1939," *Vierteljahrshefte für Zeitgeschichte* 37, no. 3 (1989): 367–400; "Zionism in National Socialist Jewish Policy in Germany, 1933–39," *Journal of Modern History* 50, no. 4 (1978): 1253–1282; Friedlander, *Nazi Germany and the Jews,* pp. 62–63.

12. For a balanced assessment of the mixture of fanaticism and calculation in Hitler's public denunciations of the Jews up to 1939, see Friedlander, *Nazi Germany and the Jews,* pp. 73–113.

13. On Hitler's worldview and its relation to his foreign policy, see Jäckel, *Hitler's World View,* and Gerhard Weinberg, ed., *Hitler's Second Book: The Unpublished Sequel to Mein Kampf by Adolf Hitler,* trans. Krista Smith (New York: Enigma, 2003). On Nazi preparations for war with the United States, see Norman Goda, *Tomorrow the World: Hitler, Northwest Africa, and the Path toward America* (College Station, Tex.: Texas A&M University Press, 1998). On the translation of racist ideology into race war on the eastern front, see Omer Bartov, *Hitler's Army: Soldiers, Nazis, and War in the Third Reich* (New York: Oxford University Press, 1991); *The Eastern Front, 1941–1945: German Troops and the Barbarization of Warfare,* 2nd ed. (London: Palgrave Macmillan, 2001); Jürgen Förster, "Securing 'Living Space,'" in *The Attack on the Soviet Union,* vol. 4 of Horst Boog, et al., eds., *Germany and the Second World War* (New York: Oxford University Press, 1998); Ulrich Herbert, ed., *National Socialist Extermination Policies: Contemporary German Perspectives and Controversies* (New York: Berghahn, 2000); Andreas Hillgruber, *Hitlers Strategie: Politik und Kriegsführung, 1940–1941* (Munich: Bernard & Graefe, 1982 [1965]); Hillgruber, *Germany and the Two World Wars,* trans. William C. Kirby (Cambridge, Mass.: Harvard University Press, 1981).

14. Norman Rich, *Hitler's War Aims: Ideology, the Nazi State, and the Course of Expansion* (New York: Norton, 1973).

15. As Gerhard Weinberg has written: "Once Germany had by her rapid rearmament gained a head start over her neighbors, the sooner she struck,

the greater the chances for success. The longer war was postponed, the more likely it would be that rearmament programs inaugurated by others in response to the menace from Germany would catch up with and surpass that of the Third Reich. Lacking in her original borders the economic resources for the continued replacement of one set of weapons by more modern ones, Germany could either strike while she had the advantage over others or see the balance of strength shift to her potential adversaries." Weinberg, *The Foreign Policy of Hitler's Germany: Starting World War II, 1937–1939* (Chicago: University of Chicago Press, 1980), p. 663. For his reconstruction of the factor of time in Hitler's march toward war, see Weinberg, *Foreign Policy of Hitler's Germany,* chaps. 10–13. See also Weinberg, *Germany, Hitler, and World War II* (New York: Cambridge University Press, 1995), chaps. 3, 5, 8, 11–13, 15–17; Williamson Murray, *The Change in the European Balance of Power, 1938–1939: The Path to Ruin* (Princeton, N.J.: Princeton University Press, 1984).

16. For the text of the January 30, 1939, speech and the repetitions of and variations in the prophecy on January 30, 1941, January 30, 1942, February 15, 1942, September 30, 1942, November 8, 1942, and February 24, 1943, see Domarus, *Hitler: Reden und Proklamationen,* 2:1058, 1663–1664, 1843, 1920, 1937, 1992.

17. The concluding chapter of Hitler's *Second Book,* written in 1928 but not published until 1961, offered a summary of the kind of anti-Semitic narrative of "Jewish domination" over world affairs that emerged in Nazi propaganda during World War II. See Weinberg, *Hitler's Second Book,* pp. 229–234.

18. The coexistence of such contradictory motivations is a familiar theme of psychoanalysis. See Sigmund Freud, *Beyond the Pleasure Principle* and *Civilization and Its Discontents,* in Peter Gay, ed., *The Freud Reader* (New York: Norton, 1989), pp. 594–626, 722–772.

19. Max Horkheimer and Theodor Adorno, *The Dialectic of Enlightenment,* trans. John Cumming (New York: Herder and Herder, 1972 [1944]), p. 187.

20. On historians and narrative, see David Carr, *Time, Narrative, and History* (Bloomington: University of Indiana Press, 1986); Paul Ricoeur, *Time and Narrative,* trans. Kathleen McLaughlin and David Pellauer (Chicago: University of Chicago Press, 1984–1988); Hayden White, *Metahistory: The Historical Imagination in Nineteenth-Century Europe* (Baltimore, Md.: Johns Hopkins University Press, 1973).

21. On paranoia and Nazi wartime propaganda, see Gombrich, *Myth and Reality in German War-Time Broadcasts.* On paranoid politics among the Jacobins during the French Revolution, see François Furet, *Interpreting the*

French Revolution, trans. Elbourg Forster (New York: Cambridge University Press, 1981); on paranoid politics in the United States, see Richard Hofstadter, *The Paranoid Style in American Politics and Other Essays* (New York: Knopf, 1965; repr. Cambridge, Mass.: Harvard University Press, 1996); for a discussion of anti-Semitism and paranoia, see Horkheimer and Adorno, *The Dialectic of Enlightenment,* pp. 187–200.

22. On delirious discourse, see Michel Foucault, *Madness and Civilization: A History of Insanity in the Age of Reason* (New York: Random House, 1965).

23. George L. Mosse, *The Crisis of German Ideology: Intellectual Origins of the Third Reich* (New York: Grosset and Dunlap, 1964; New York: Howard Fertig, 1999); and *Towards the Final Solution: A History of European Racism* (Madison: University of Wisconsin Press, 1985 [1978]); John Weiss, *The Ideology of Death: Why the Holocaust Happened in Germany* (Chicago: Ivan R. Dee, 1996). On the era of persecution, see Friedlander, *The Years of Persecution.*

24. On the formation of such a consensus, see Jehuda Bauer, *Rethinking the Holocaust* (New Haven, Conn.: Yale University Press, 2001), pp. 104–105. See also Robert Gellately, *Backing Hitler* (New York: Oxford University Press, 2000); Ian Kershaw, *Hitler, 1936–1945: Nemesis* (New York: Norton, 2000).

25. George Mosse, *The Fascist Revolution: Toward a General Theory of Fascism* (New York: Howard Fertig, 1999), p. 66.

26. This was also a methodological problem in Daniel Goldhagen's much-discussed *Hitler's Willing Executioners: Ordinary Germans and the Holocaust* (New York: Knopf, 1996).

27. The earliest study is the wartime work of Derrick Sington and Arthur Weidenfeld, *The Goebbels Experiment: A Study of the Nazi Propaganda Machine* (New Haven, Conn.: Yale University Press, 1943). Postwar works on the propaganda effort as a whole, as well as on the role of anti-Semitism, include Caesar Aronsfeld, *The Text of the Holocaust: A Study of the Nazis' Extermination Propaganda, 1919–1945* (Marblehead, Mass.: Michah Publications, 1985); Aronsfeld, "Perish Judah! Extermination Propaganda," in *Patterns of Prejudice* 12, no. 5 (September–October 1978), 17–26; Ernest Bramsted, *Goebbels and National Socialist Propaganda, 1925–1945* (East Lansing: Michigan State University Press, 1965); Jay Baird, *The Mythical World of Nazi War Propaganda, 1939–1945* (Minneapolis: University of Minnesota Press, 1974); Gombrich, *Myth and Reality in German War-Time Broadcasts;* Alexander Hardy, *Hitler's Secret Weapon: The "Managed" Press and Propaganda Machine of Nazi Germany* (New York: Vantage, 1967);

Robert Herzstein, *The War That Hitler Won: The Most Infamous Propaganda Campaign in History* (New York: Putnam's Sons, 1978); Jürgen Hagemann, *Die Presselenkung im Dritten Reich* (Bonn: Bouvier, 1970); Peter Longerich, *Propagandisten im Krieg: Die Presseabteilung des Auswärtigen Amtes unter Ribbentrop* (Munich: Oldenbourg, 1987); Ralf Georg Reuth, *Goebbels: Eine Biographie* (Munich: Piper Verlag, 1995); David Welch, *Nazi Propaganda: The Power and the Limitations* (London: Croom Helm, 1983).

28. A valuable initial study of anti-Semitic wartime visual propaganda is Jürgen Bernatzky, "'Juden-Läuse-Flecktyphus': Der nationalsozialistischen Antisemitismus im Spiegel des politischen Plakats," in Günther B. Ginzel, ed., *Antisemitismus: Erscheinungsformen der Judenfeindschaft gestern und heute* (Bielefeld: Verlag Wissenschaft und Politik, 1991), pp. 389–417. On Nazi weekly wartime wall newspapers, see Franz-Josef Heyen, *Parole der Woche: Eine Wandzeitung im Dritten Reich, 1936–1945* (Munich: Deutscher Taschenbuch Verlag, 1983).

29. Lucy Dawidowicz, *The War against the Jews, 1933–1945* (New York: Holt, Rinehart and Winston, 1975).

30. See, for example, Bartov, *Hitler's Army;* Richard Breitman, *The Architect of Genocide: Himmler and the Final Solution* (New York: Knopf, 1991); Christopher Browning, *The Path to Genocide* (New York: Cambridge University Press, 1992); Browning, *Nazi Policy, Jewish Workers, German Killers* (New York: Cambridge University Press, 2000); Philipp Burrin, *Hitler and the Jews: The Genesis of the Holocaust,* trans. Percy Southgate (London: Edward Arnold, 1994); Asher Cohen, Yehoyakim Cochavi, and Yoav Gelber, eds., *The Shoah and the War* (New York: Peter Lang, 1992); Jürgen Förster, "Das nationalsozialistische Herrschaftssystem und der Krieg gegen die Sowjetunion," in Peter Jahn and Reinhard Rürup, eds., *Erobern und Vernichten: Der Krieg gegen die Sowjetunion, 1941–1945* (Berlin: Argon, 1991); Förster, "Complicity or Entanglement: Wehrmacht, War, and Holocaust," in Michael Berenbaum and Abraham J. Peck, eds., *The Holocaust and History: The Known, the Unknown, the Disputed and the Reexamined* (Washington, D.C., United States Holocaust Memorial Museum; and Bloomington: Indiana University Press, 1998), pp. 266–283; Jeffrey Herf, "The Nazi Extermination Camps and the Ally to the East: Could the Red Army and Air Force Have Stopped or Slowed the Final Solution?" *Kritika: Explorations in Russian and Eurasian History* 4, no. 4 (Fall 2003), 913–930; Gerhard Weinberg, *A World at Arms: A Global History of World War II* (New York: Cambridge University Press, 1994).

31. The German historian Karl Bracher has referred to this issue as "the problem of underestimation." See Karl Bracher, "The Role of Hitler: Perspectives

of Interpretation," in Walter Laqueur, ed., *Fascism: A Reader's Guide* (Berkeley: University of California Press, 1976), pp. 211–225.

32. The classic texts are George Orwell, "Politics and the English Language," in Sonia Orwell and Ian Angus, eds., *George Orwell: The Collected Essays, Journalism and Letters of George Orwell,* vol. 4, *In Front of Your Nose, 1945–1950* (New York: Harcourt, Brace Jovanovich, 1968), pp. 136, 127–140; and, of course, Orwell's *1984.* For a recent elaboration of the role of euphemism in the language of the Final Solution, see Berel Lang, *Act and Idea in the Nazi Genocide* (Chicago: University of Chicago Press, 1990).

33. Other terms include "special handling" *(Sonderbehandlung)* and "deportation to the east." See s.v. "Endlösung der Judenfrage," and "Sonderbehandlung," Cornelia Schmitz-Bering, *Vokabular des National-Sozialismus* (Berlin: de Gruyter, 1998), pp. 174–176, 584–587. In his recent discussion of terms such as "Final Solution" *(Endlösung)* and others associated with the Holocaust, Berel Lang has restated Orwell's approach in pointing to "the blatant disparity between the normal connotation of the word and its reference" in Nazi vocabulary and of "'language rules' explicitly designed to conceal literal meaning." See Lang, *Act and Idea,* p. 88.

34. Hannah Arendt, *The Origins of Totalitarianism* (Cleveland: Meridian, 1958), p. 343. In his less well-known works of the late 1970s and mid-1980s, Aronsfeld developed this point further. See Caesar Aronsfeld, "Perish Judah! Extermination Propaganda," pp. 17–26; and Aronsfeld, *Text of the Holocaust.*

35. "Extermination" and "annihilation" in this work are thus translations of *Vernichtung* and *Ausrottung,* respectively. Except for very well-known works or in an effort to ease identification of particular images presented here, I have not included German-language titles of books and essays in the text. The original German-language titles appear in the notes. For example, *Die Parole der Woche* is rendered as *Word of the Week, Zeitschriften-Dienst* as *Periodical Service,* and *Parole des Tages* as *Word of the Day.* In cases where a German word does not translate easily into English, I have included the German term in parentheses in the text.

36. German historians have played a major role in encouraging us to think about the history of concepts and how the meanings of the same word evolve over time and in context, but we do not yet have an adequate history of the meanings of *Vernichtung* and *Ausrottung.* See Rinehart Koselleck, *Futures Past: On the Semantics of Historical Time,* trans. Keith Tribe (Cambridge, Mass.: MIT Press, 1985); *The Practice of Conceptual History: Timing History, Tracing Concepts,* trans. Todd Samuel Presner (Stanford, Calif.: Stanford University Press, 2002); Otto Brunner and Werner Conze, eds.,

Geschichtliche Grundbegriffe: Historisches Lexikon zur politisch-sozialen Sprache in Deutschland (Stuttgart: Klett, 1972–1997); Melvin Richter, *The History of Social and Political Concepts: A Critical Introduction* (New York: Oxford University Press, 1995).

37. Hannah Arendt, in *The Origins of Totalitarianism,* drew possible links between colonialism and racism in Africa on the one hand and racism and anti-Semitism in Europe on the other. On Germany's war in southwest Africa, see Jürgen Zimmerer, *Deutsche Herrschaft über Afrikaner: Staatliche Machtanspruch und Wirklichkeit im kolonialen Namibia* (Münster: Lit, 2001); and Zimmerer with Joachim Zeller, *Völkermord in Deutsch-Südwestafrika: Der Kolonialkrieg (1904–1908) in Namibia und seine Folgen* (Berlin: Links, 2003). On implications for German policy in Eastern Europe, see Wendy Lauer, *Nazi Empire-Building and the Holocaust in Ukraine* (Chapel Hill: University of North Carolina Press, 2005).

38. For extraordinary research and analysis, see John Horne and Alan Kramer, *German Atrocities 1914: A History of Denial* (New Haven, Conn.: Yale University Press, 2001).

39. The issue of the linguistic and political continuity and the break between the traditions of German militarism in World War I and on the eastern front in World War II is the subject of some excellent scholarly literature. See, for instance, Jehuda L. Wallach, *The Dogma of the Battle of Annihilation: The Theories of Clausewitz and Schlieffen and Their Impact on the German Conduct of Two World Wars* (Westport, Conn.: Greenwood, 1986); Hillgruber, *Germany and the Two World Wars;* Hillgruber, *Hitlers Strategie;* Förster, "Securing 'Living Space'"; Fritz Fischer, *Germany's Aims in the First World War* (New York: Norton, 1967). Fischer and Hillgruber famously disagreed about issues of continuity and a break in modern German history. Yet a comparison of Fischer's analysis of the traditional and successful integration of means and ends on the eastern front in World War I with Hillgruber's pathbreaking analysis of the racist war of extermination on the eastern front in World War II clearly illustrates how the ideology and policy of the Nazi regime changed the nature of war.

40. On the use of the term "ordinary" to describe Germans involved in the Final Solution, see Christopher Browning, *Ordinary Men: Reserve Police Battalion 101 and the Final Solution in Poland* (New York: HarperCollins, 1992); Goldhagen, *Hitler's Willing Executioners* (whose subtitle is "Ordinary Germans and the Holocaust").

41. On the daily press conferences, see Hardy, *Hitler's Secret Weapon;* Reuth, *Goebbels;* and Bramsted, *Goebbels and National Socialist Propaganda.*

Notes to pages 14–18

42. On the daily operations of the Reich Press Office and on the conflict between Dietrich and Goebbels, see the "Judgment" of Otto Dietrich in his trial at Nuremberg in April 1949, in "XV. Judgment," *Trials of War Criminals before the Nuerenberg Military Tribunals under Control Council Law no. 10,* vol. 14, Nuremberg, October 1946–April 1949 (Washington, D.C.: U.S. Government Printing Office, 1950), pp. 565–576. On the phrase "working towards the Führer," see Kershaw, *Hitler,* 2:527–591.

43. On the *Wochenschau,* see Ulrike Bartels, *Die Wochenschau im Dritten Reich: Entwicklung und Funktion eines Massenmediums unter besonderer Berücksichtigung völkischer-nationaler Inhalte* (Frankfurt am Main: Lang, 2004).

44. On the role of the German Labor Front, organizations of physicians and hotel owners, and Nazi party propagandists in the regional and local distribution of the *Parole der Woche,* see "An Parteigenossen Adami," Berlin, May 17, 1940, Bundesarchiv Berlin (henceforth BA Berlin), NS 18, Reichspropagandaleitung, folder 1401, pp. 7–26.

45. The key source has been the reports of the Sicherheitsdienst. See Heinz Boberach, ed., *Meldungen aus dem Reich: Die geheimen Lageberichte des Sicherheitsdienstes der SS, 1938–1945,* 17 vols. (Herrsching: Pawlak, 1984). For reports by Social Democratic agents in the 1930s, see *Deutschland-Berichte der Sozialdemokratische Partei Deutschlands* (Frankfurt am Main: Verlag Petra Nettelbeck, 1980).

46. On the multiple components of traditions, see Thomas Nipperdey's important "neo-Rankean" reflections in *Nachdenken über die deutsche Geschichte: Essays* (Munich: Verlag C. H. Beck, 1986).

2. Building the Anti-Semitic Consensus

1. As the focus of this work is on propaganda used in narrating events as they unfolded, I shall not examine one important component of anti-Semitic propaganda—namely, feature films such as *Der ewige Jude* and *Jud Süss.* A systematic study of the weekly newsreel the *Wochenschau,* though of great importance for the subject, is beyond the scope of this work. See Ulrike Bartels, *Die Wochenschau im Dritten Reich: Entwicklung und Funktion eines Massenmediums unter besonderer Berücksichtigung völkischer-nationaler Inhalte* (Frankfurt am Main: Lang, 2004).

2. Norbert Frei and Johannes Schmitz, *Journalismus im Dritten Reich* (Munich: Verlag C. H. Beck, 1999), pp. 17, 25–28.

3. Ralf Georg Reuth, *Goebbels,* trans. Krishna Winston (New York: Harvest, 1993), pp. 174–175; Frei and Schmitz, *Journalismus im Dritten Reich,* p. 22. The Nazis allowed one of the leading liberal papers of the Weimar era, the

Frankfurter Zeitung, to continue publishing until the end of August 1943. See Günther Gillessen, *Auf verlorenem Posten: Die Frankfurter Zeitung im Dritten Reich* (Berlin: Wolf Jobst Siedler Verlag, 1986).

4. On the Editorial Control Law, see Alexander Hardy, *Hitler's Secret Weapon: The "Managed" Press and Propaganda Machine of Nazi Germany* (New York: Vantage, 1967). For the text of the law in English translation, see appendix 4, pp. 267–278.

5. Reuth, *Goebbels* (trans.), p. 176.

6. "Amann, Max," in Walther Killy, ed., *Deutsche Biographische Enzyklopädie (DBE),* vol. 1 (Munich: Sauer, 1995); "Amann, Max," in Wolfgang Benz, Hermann Graml, and Hermann Weiß, eds., *Enzyklopädie des Nationalsozialismus* (Munich: Deutscher Taschenbuch Verlag, 1987), p. 819; Frei and Schmitz, *Journalismus im Dritten Reich,* p. 212. In 1941 Amann became an *Obergruppenführer* in the SS. In 1948, he was convicted of war crimes and sentenced to ten years in prison.

7. Michael Kater, "Figure 1: Growth of Nazi Party Membership, 1919–1945," in *The Nazi Party: A Social Profile of Members and Leaders, 1919–1945* (Cambridge, Mass.: Harvard University Press, 1983), p. 262.

8. Robert Ley, *Das Organisationsbuch der NSDAP,* 3rd ed. (Munich: Franz Eher Verlag, 1937), p. 97.

9. Robert Ley, "Gaue der NSDAP," in Ley, *Organisationsbuch der NSDAP,* pp. 84–85.

10. "Anschriftenverzeichis der Reichspropagandaämter, Stand vom 1. Mai 1939," *Nachrichtenblatt des Reichsministeriums für Volksaufklärung und Propaganda,* no. 10 (June 1, 1939): 1–4, in Berlin Document Center (henceforth BDC) Microfilms, United States National Archives and Records Administration (henceforth NARA), A3345-B 0060, 0225–0027.

11. Ley, "Gaue der NSDAP," p. 84.

12. "Reichskarte der NSDAP mit Gauenteilung," in Ley, *Organisationsbuch der NSDAP,* p. 85.

13. See Heinz Boberach, ed., *Meldungen aus dem Reich: Die geheimen Lageberichte des Sicherheitsdienstes der SS, 1938–1945,* 17 vols. (Herrsching: Pawlak, 1984).

14. Reuth, *Goebbels* (trans.), pp. 37–39.

15. *Nachrichtenblatt des Reichsministeriums für Volksaufklärung und Propaganda,* no. 8 (May 3, 1939): 49, in BDC Microfilms, NARA, A3345-B 0061, 564, 577, 590, 606, and 622.

16. The figures for expenditures in Reichmarks are as follows: 1937, 43,825,000; 1938, 54,800,000; 1940, 54,857,800; 1941, 74,912,550; 1942,

84,611,050. The ministry reported budget surpluses in these years, due in part to income from sales of government-authorized radios and compulsory fees to use them. See "Vorwort zu Haushalt des Reichsministeriums für Volksaufklärung und Propaganda" for the years 1937, 1938, 1939, 1940, 1941, and 1942, in *Nachrichtenblatt des Reichsministeriums für Volksaufklärung und Propaganda,* BDC Microfilms, NARA, A3345-B 0060, 0217.

17. Joseph Goebbels, "Parole im neuen Staat," in *Revolution der Deutschen: 14 Jahre Nationalsozialismus* (Oldenburg: Gerhard Stalling, 1933), p. 150.

18. "Der Reichspropagandaleiter der NSDAP," in Ley, *Organisationsbuch der NSDAP,* p. 297.

19. "Die Reichspropagandaleitung der NSDAP," *Unser Wille und Weg* 6 (1936): 6–10. See also "Die Reichspropagandaleiter und Propagandaleiter der NSDAP," in Ley, *Organisationsbuch der NSDAP,* p. 297.

20. See Angelika Heider, "Das *Reich,*" in Benz, Graml, and Weiß, *Enzyklopädie des Nationalsozialismus,* p. 663; and Carin Kessemeier, *Der Leitartikler Goebbels in den NS-Organen "Der Angriff" und "Das Reich"* (Münster: Verlag C. J. Fahle, 1967), pp. 136–137. On the founding of *Das Reich,* see also Ralf Georg Reuth, *Goebbels: Eine Biographie* (Munich: Piper Verlag, 1995), pp. 447–449; and Jay Baird, *The Mythical World of Nazi Propaganda, 1939–1945* (Minneapolis: University of Minnesota Press, 1974), p. 25.

21. On wage rates in Germany, see Gerhard Bry, *Wages in Germany, 1871–1945* (Princeton, N.J.: Princeton University Press, 1960), p. 331.

22. Ibid., pp. 141–142.

23. For a full listing of titles of Goebbels's editorials, see Kessemeier, *Der Leitartikler Goebbels.*

24. On Dietrich and the Ministries Trial, see Hardy, *Hitler's Secret Weapon.*

25. Whereas Goebbels merits an entry in *The Holocaust Encyclopedia,* for example, there is none for Dietrich.

26. "Judgment," *Trials of War Criminals before the Nuerenberg Military Tribunals* (IMT), 14: 565–576. Emphasis in the original.

27. See Otto Dietrich, *Mit Hitler an die Macht: Persönliche Erlebnisse mit meinem Führer* (Berlin: Franz Eher Verlag, 1934); Dietrich, *Die philosophischen Grundlagen des Nationalsozialismus: Ein Ruf zu den Waffen deutschen Geistes* (Breslau: Hirt, 1935); Dietrich, *Nationalsozialistische Pressepolitik: Vortrag gehalten am 7. März 1938 in Berlin auf dem Empfangsabend des Außenpolitischen Amtes im Hotel Adlon vor Mitgliedern des diplomatischen Korps und Vertretern der ausländischen Presse* (Berlin: Junker & Dunnhaupt, 1938); Dietrich, *Revolution des Denkens* (Dortmund: Westfalen-Verlag, 1939); Dietrich, *Die geistigen Grundlagen der neuen Europa* (Berlin: Franz Eher Verlag, 1941); Dietrich, *12 Jahre mit Hitler* (Munich: Isar Verlag, 1955).

28. See "Dietrich, Otto," in Killy, *DBE* 1:537; Hardy, *Hitler's Secret Weapon,* pp. 50–51.

29. Affidavit of Paul Karl Schmidt, document NG-3590, affirmed by oral testimony (transcript pp. 1370–13890) before the tribunal, document book 12, A, case no. 11, Nuremberg War Crimes Trials (henceforth NWCT), cited in Hardy, *Hitler's Secret Weapon,* p. 66.

30. Affidavit of Karl August Brammer, document NG-3070, affirmed by oral testimony (starting on transcript p. l435) before the tribunal, document book 12, A, case no. 11, NWCT, cited in Hardy, *Hitler's Secret Weapon,* pp. 38–40.

31. Hardy, *Hitler's Secret Weapon,* pp. 33–47, 51.

32. See testimony of Hans Gensert, "Daily Press Directive–extract Brammer Material," vol. 4, document NG-4472, prosecution exhibit 884, document book 12, B, case no. 11, NWCT; and document NG-4477, prosecution exhibit 886, cited in Hardy, *Hitler's Secret Weapon,* p. 45.

33. Baird, *Mythical World,* p. 28.

34. RMVP, T-70, roll 3, 3505763, NA.

35. For an interesting discussion, drawing on the files and interviews with former officials in the ministry, of the Goebbels-Dietrich conflict, see Baird, *Mythical World,* pp. 28–31.

36. Robert Wistrich, "Rosenberg, Alfred," in Walther Killy and Rudolf Vierhaus, eds., DBE (Munich: Saur, 1998) 8:391; Frei and Schmitz, *Journalismus im Dritten Reich,* pp. 99–100. Rosenberg was convicted of war crimes and crimes against humanity by the International Military Tribunal in Nuremberg and executed in autumn 1946.

37. Another Nazi organ deserves mention but will not be the subject of analysis here. *Das Schwarze Korps,* edited by Gunter d'Alquen, was a weekly organ of the SS, begun in 1935, with an initial circulation of 70,000, which reached 500,000 in 1937 and 750,000 by 1944, when it was the second-largest political weekly in Germany, after *Das Reich.* See Frei and Schmitz, *Journalismus im Dritten Reich,* pp. 101–104.

38. Robert Wistrich, "Weiß, Wilhelm," in Killy and Vierhaus, DBE (Munich: Saur, 1999), 10:411. Weiß was interned after the war and convicted by Allied occupation courts, sentenced to three years in a labor camp, loss of 30 percent of his property, and ten years' ban on employment as a journalist. See Wilhelm Weiß, *Krieg im Westen* (Munich: Franz Eher Verlag, 1941).

39. "Aufgaben und Tätigkeit der Anti-Komintern," in Antisemitische Aktion und Antikomintern, Berlin, October 5, 1942, BAK, R-55–373, RMVP, pp. 77–79.

40. Eberhard Taubert, "Notiz für Herrn Schippert in Angelegenheit Etat der Antisemitischen Aktion," November 24, 1939, BAK, R-55–841, RMVP,

p. 15. On Taubert, see Baird, *Mythical World;* Taubert had received a doctorate in law from the University of Heidelberg in 1930.

41. "Prüfungsbericht, 4. Dezember 1940," in Antisemitische Aktion und Antikomintern, BAK, R-55–373, RMVP, pp. 3–8.

42. Antisemitische Aktion und Antikomintern, 1942–1944, BAK, R-55–373, RMVP, p. 71; also microfilm, United States Holocaust Memorial Museum Archive (henceforth USHMMA), 14.029M, R-55.

43. From February 1937 to December 1939, it was published by the Institut zum Studium der Judenfrage under the title *Mitteilungen über die Judenfrage* (Reports on the Jewish Question). In June 1940 the name was changed to *Die Judenfrage in Politik, Recht, Kultur und Wirtschaft* (The Jewish Question in Politics, Law, Culture, and the Economy). Beginning in January 1940, it was published by the above-mentioned office of Antisemitische Aktion until December 1943, when it ceased publication, owing to wartime shortages of paper and of young male staff members. In the spring of 1942, in accord with linguistic changes necessitated by efforts to appeal to the Arab world, its name was changed to Anti-Jewish Action (Antijüdische Aktion). See *Die Judenfrage in Politik, Recht, Kultur und Wirtschaft,* Library of Congress microfilm 39477.

44. "Zur Einführung," *Mitteilungen über die Judenfrage* 1, no. 1 (February 1, 1937): 1.

45. See Bartels, *Die Wochenschau im Dritten Reich.*

46. On the wall newspaper, see Franz-Josef Heyen, *Parole der Woche: Eine Wandzeitung im Dritten Reich, 1936–1943* (Munich: Deutscher Taschenbuch Verlag, 1983); on anti-Semitism and Nazi political posters, see Jürgen Bernatzky, "'Juden-Läuse-Flecktyphus': Der nationalsozialistische Anti-Semitismus im Spiegel des politischen Plakats," in Günther B. Ginzel, ed., *Anti-Semitismus: Erscheinungsformen der Judenfeindschaft gestern und heute* (Bielefeld: Verlag Wissenschaft und Politik, 1991), pp. 389–417.

47. "Bestand an Kraftwagen," and "Bestand an Krafträdern," *Statistisches Jahrbuch für das Deutsche Reich, 1941–1942* (Berlin: Statistisches Reichsamt, 1942), p. 109.

48. "Personenverkehr der Straßenbahnen in Großstädten," *Statistisches Jahrbuch,* p. 110.

49. On Schweitzer, see Peter Paret, "God's Hammer," in *German Encounters with Modernism, 1840–1945* (New York: Cambridge University Press, 2001), pp. 202–228; Hans Schweitzer (Mjölnir), "Meine Arbeit–mein Ziel," *Unser Wille und Weg* 6, no. 9 (September 1936): 286–287.

50. "*Die Parole der Woche,* Folge 10, 4.–10. Juni 1936, Parteiamtliche

Wandzeitung der NSDAP," *Unser Wille und Weg,* June 1936, pp. 4–10. See also *"Die Parole der Woche," Unser Wille und Weg,* January 1940, pp. 6–8; "Die Arbeit der Partei-Propaganda im Kriege," *Unser Wille und Weg* 11, no. 1 (January 1941): 1–12; "The Work of Party Propaganda in War," German Propaganda Archive, *http://www.calvin.edu/academic/cas/gpa/warprop.htm.*

51. "Die Parole der Woche, . . . Parteiamtliche Wandzeitung der NSDAP."

52. As one historian has noted, the Nazi propagandists understood the advantages the widely distributed wall newspaper had over other forms of propaganda. "A pamphlet or newspaper could be thrown away unread, the radio turned off, political meetings not attended, and the same with the cinema. But everyone at some time or another walked in the streets. The poster could not be avoided." Heyen, *Parole der Woche,* p. 17.

53. The figures are based on the holdings of the Landeshauptarchiv Koblenz, Bestand 712 (Plakate), Wandzeitung *Parole der Woche,* NSDAP, Reichspropagandaleitung, Munich. This collection covers the years 1940–1942.

54. Joseph Goebbels, "Richtlinien für die Durchführung der Propaganda der NSDAP," September 23, 1939, NARA, T81, roll 84, RG 242 (Records of the National Socialist German Labor Party), pp. 95624–95633.

55. Ibid., pp. 95626–95627.

56. Ibid., pp. 95627–95628. Goebbels also stressed the importance of the weekly radio broadcasts "The Party Speaks—the People Listen."

57. "An Parteigenossen Adami," Berlin, May 17, 1940, BA Berlin, NS 18, Reichspropagandaleitung, folder 1401, pp. 7–26. See also Wandzeitung *Parole der Woche,* ibid., pp. 1–30.

58. "An Parteigenossen Adami," pp. 7–26. As the memo does not disclose the duration of the orders and as many *Gaue* are not mentioned, it is not possible to extrapolate from this document to assertions about how many *Wandzeitungen* were distributed on average each week in Germany, Austria, and the Sudetenland. On April 11, 1940, the "physician's chambers" *(Ärztekammer)* alone all over Germany ordered 29,720 *Wandzeitungen* from the RPL. Presumably, the posters were hung in doctors' offices and hospitals. The regional chambers with the numbers each ordered included Bavaria, 2,500; Schlesia, 2,500; Berlin, 2,750; Sudentenland, 1,500; Westphalia, 2,500; Baden, 1,100; Danube and the Alps (Vienna), 3,700; Frankfurt am Main, 800; and Bremen, 250. Wandzeitung *Parole der Woche,* BA Berlin, NS 18, Reichspropagandaleitung, folder 1401, pp. 1–30.

59. Erwin Schockel, *Das politische Plakat: Eine psychologische Betrachtung,* 2nd ed. (Munich: Zentralverlag der NSDAP, Franz Eher Verlag, 1939).

60. Ibid., pp. 239–240.

61. Friedrich Madebach, *Das Kampfplakat: Aufgabe, Wesen und Gesetzmäßigkeit des Politischen Plakats, nachgewiesen an den Plakaten der Kampfjahre von 1918–1933* (Frankfurt am Main: Verlag Moritz Diesterweg, 1941).

62. Before 1933, in Berlin alone, there were 3,063 poster areas to rent, and more were set up by the Nazi party. Ibid., p. 2.

63. Ibid., pp. 12–14.

64. "Sie müssen Plakate der Reichspropagandaleitung . . . ," in *Unser Wille und Weg* 10, no. 4 (April 1940): 60.

65. "Propaganda in Zahlen," in *Unser Wille und Weg,* January 1941, p. 1.

66. As an article in 1941 indicated, the Reich Propaganda Directorate sent detailed instructions to local party members about how to run a meeting: flags and speaker were to be on the stage; the room had to be large enough for the crowd; they were to remember to invite women; introductions were to be short; interruption with applause was permitted; the speech was to be kept to an hour; the meeting was to end with a march and music. See "Wie führe ich eine öffentliche Versammlung durch?" in *Unser Wille und Weg* 11, no. 4 (April 1941): 44–46.

67. This summary draws on the following: Abraham Barkai, "Die Juden als sozio-ökonomische Minderheitsgruppe in der Weimarer Republik," in Walter Grab and Julius H. Schoeps, eds., *Juden in der Weimarer Republik* (Stuttgart: Burg Verlag, 1986), pp. 330–346; Esra Bennathan, "Die demographische und wirtschaftliche Struktur der Juden," in Werner E. Mosse, ed., *Entscheidungsjahr 1932: Zur Judenfrage in der Endphase der Weimarer Republik,* 2nd ed. (Tübingen: Mohr, 1966); Donald L. Niewyk, *The Jews in Weimar Germany* (New Brunswick, N.J.: Transaction, 2001). See also the following, all in *The Leo Baeck Yearbook* 36 (1991), pp. 171–217: Konrad Jarausch, "Jewish Lawyers in Germany, 1848–1938: The Disintegration of a Profession"; Geoffrey Cocks, "Partners and Pariahs: Jews and Medicine in Modern German Society"; Fritz K. Ringer, "Academics in Germany: German and Jew, Some Preliminary Remarks"; "The German Professionals and Their Jewish Colleagues: Comments on the Papers of Konrad Jarausch, Geoffrey Cocks, and Fritz K. Ringer."

68. See Barkai, "Die Juden als sozio-ökonomische Minderheitsgruppe," pp. 330–331; Bennathan, "Die demographische und wirtschaftliche Struktur der Juden," pp. 94–95; Niewyk, *Jews in Weimar Germany,* p. 12.

69. Figures cited by Jarausch, "Jewish Lawyers in Germany," p. 177.

70. Figures taken from Niewyk, *Jews in Weimar Germany,* pp. 13–15.

71. Figures taken from "Die jüdischen Erwerbspersonen Deutschlands nach ihren hauptsächlichen Berufen am 16. Juni 1933," *Statistik des*

Deutschen Reichs, vol. 451/5, cited in Bennathan, "Die demographische und wirtschaftliche Struktur der Juden," pp. 111–112.

72. E. G. Lowenthal, "Die Juden im öffentlichen Leben," in Mosse, *Entscheidungsjahre 1932,* pp. 57–58.

73. Barkai, "Die Juden als sozio-ökonomische Minderheitsgruppe," p. 337.

74. Jarausch, "Jewish Lawyers in Germany," p. 177.

75. See Saul Friedlander, *Nazi Germany and the Jews,* vol. 1, *The Years of Persecution, 1933–1939* (New York: HarperCollins, 1997), pp. 27–31.

76. Ibid., p. 62.

77. On *Der Angriff,* see: "Der Angriff" in Benz, Graml, and Weiß, *Enzyklopädie des Nationalsozialismus,* p. 362; Reuth, *Goebbels,* pp. 124–129; Kessemeier, *Der Leitartikler Goebbels,* pp. 47–84; Joseph Goebbels, *Der Angriff: Aufsätze aus der Kampfzeit* (Munich: Zentralverlag der NSDAP, 1935).

78. Joseph Goebbels, "Warum Angriff," *Der Angriff* (July 4, 1927), pp. 98–99.

79. Joseph Goebbels, "Heil Moskau," *Der Angriff* (November 21, 1927), pp. 236–238.

80. Joseph Goebbels, "Der Jude," *Der Angriff* (January 21, 1928), pp. 323–324.

81. Joseph Goebbels, "Der Weltfeind," *Der Angriff* (March 19, 1928), pp. 333–334.

82. Ibid., pp. 334–335.

83. He offered one of his most extensive catalogues of "Jewish domination" of world politics in his never-published book written in 1928. See Gerhard L. Weinberg, ed., *Hitler's Second Book: The Unpublished Sequel to Mein Kampf by Adolf Hitler,* trans. Krista Smith (New York: Enigma, 2003), esp. pp. 229–234.

84. Adolf Hitler, as cited in Max Domarus, *Hitler: Reden und Proklamationen, 1932–1945,* vol. 1, *Triumph, 1932–1938* (Neustadt: Schmidt, 1962), pp. 251–252.

85. Ibid. Joseph Goebbels, "Wider die Greuelhetze des Weltjudentums," in Goebbels, *Revolution der Deutschen: 14 Jahre Nationalsozialismus* (Oldenburg: Gerhard Stalling, 1933), pp. 155, 157, 158–160.

86. On the mixed public reaction, see Friedlander, *Nazi Germany and the Jews,* pp. 21–24.

87. On the Nazi view of the United States, see the comprehensive study by Philipp Gassert, *Amerika im Dritten Reich: Ideologie, Propaganda und Volksmeinung, 1933–1945* (Stuttgart: Franz Steiner Verlag, 1997).

88. "Die Juden in Neuyork: Eine amerikanische Tragödie," *Der Völkische Beobachter* (henceforth *VB*) (January 12, 1937).

89. "Neuyorks jüdischer Oberbürgermeister als politischer Gangster," *VB* (March 15, 1937).

90. Joseph Goebbels, *Rassenfrage und Weltpropaganda* (Beher & Mann, 1934). For a transcription of the speech at the Nuremberg Party Rally, see Goebbels (September 2, 1933), "Ansprache auf dem Nürnberger Reichsparteitag über Rassenfrage und Weltpropaganda," in Walter Roller and Susanne Höschel, eds., *Judenverfolgung und jüdisches Leben unter den Bedingungen der nationalsozialistischen Gewaltherrschaft,* vol. 1, *Tondokumente und Rundfunksendungen, 1930–1946* (Potsdam: Verlag für Berlin-Brandenburg), pp. 8, 25–28.

91. Goebbels, "Ansprache auf dem Nürnberger Reichsparteitag," September 2, 1933, p. 27.

92. On the visual impact and symbolism of the Nuremberg rallies, see Peter Reichel, *Der schöne Schein des Dritten Reiches: Faszination und Gewalt des Faschismus* (Munich: Carl Hanser Verlag, 1991); George Mosse, *The Nationalization of the Masses: Political Symbolism and Mass Movements in Germany from the Napoleonic Wars through the Third Reich* (New York: Howard Fertig, 1975).

93. Domarus, *Hitler,* 1:536–37.

94. Joseph Goebbels, "Rede des Reichsministers Dr. Goebbels auf dem Nürnberger Parteitag am 13. September 1935 gegen den Bolschewismus," in Axel Friedrichs, ed., *Dokumente der deutschen Politik,* vol. 3, *Deutschlands Weg zur Freiheit, 1935* (Berlin: Junker & Dunnhaupt, 1937), pp. 3–20. See also Joseph Goebbels, *Kommunismus ohne Maske* (Munich: Zentralverlag der NSDAP, 1935).

95. Goebbels, "Rede des Reichsministers Dr. Goebbels auf dem Nürnberger Parteitag am 13. September 1935," pp. 4–5.

96. Ibid., pp. 6, 14–15.

97. Goebbels, "Rede des Reichsministers Dr. Goebbels auf dem Nürnberger Parteitag am 13. September 1935," pp. 19, 5.

98. Ibid., pp. 6, 11. Goebbels here uses the German phrases *Vernichtung der Völker und Staaten* and *Ausrottung* to refer to the possible fate of the bourgeois world.

99. Ibid., pp. 14–15. Goebbels referred to "die Hintermänner dieser Weltvergiftung."

100. Goebbels, "Rede des Reichsministers Dr. Goebbels auf dem Nürnberger Parteitag am 13. September 1935," p. 19.

101. Adolf Hitler (September 9, 1936), "Ansprache auf der 'Kulturtagung' des Reichsparteitages der NSDAP in Nürnberg," in Roller and Höschel, *Judenverfolgung und jüdisches Leben,* 1:62–64.

102. Joseph Goebbels, "Rede des Reichsministers Dr. Goebbels auf dem Parteikongress in Nürnberg über die 'Weltgefahr des Bolschewismsus' vom 10. September 1936," in Friedrichs, *Dokumente der deutschen Politik,* vol. 4, *Deutschlands Aufstieg zur Grossmacht* (Berlin: Junker & Dunnhaupt, 1939), pp. 53–77; quotations on pp. 54, 58, 76. On Jews in the Soviet Union in the Stalin era, see Zvi Gitelman, *A Century of Ambivalence: The Jews of Russia and the Soviet Union* (New York: Schocken, 1988).

103. Hitler (September 3, 1937), "Ansprache auf dem Reichsparteitag der NSDAP in Nürnberg," in Roller and Höschel, *Judenverfolgung und jüdisches Leben,* 1:95–98.

104. DNB Rundruf, November 7, 1938, cited in Ernest Bramsted, *Goebbels and National Socialist Propaganda, 1925–1945* (East Lansing: Michigan State University Press, 1965), p. 385.

105. For accounts of the pogrom, see Bramsted, *Goebbels and National Socialist Propaganda,* pp. 383–387; Ian Kershaw, *Hitler, 1936–1945: Nemesis* (New York: Norton, 2000), pp. 136–143; Reuth, *Goebbels* (trans.), pp. 240–242; Hermann Graml, *Reichskristallnacht: Antisemitismus und Judenverfolgung im Dritten Reich* (Munich: Deutscher Taschenbuch Verlag, 1988); and Hermann Graml, *Antisemitism in the Third Reich,* trans. Tim Kirk (Oxford: Blackwell, 1992), pt. 1, 6:180.

106. Joseph Goebbels, *Die Tagebücher von Joseph Goebbels (TBJG),* ed. Elke Fröhlich (Munich: Sauer, 1994), entry for November 10, 1938, I/6, p. 180.

107. Bramsted, *Goebbels and National Socialist Propaganda,* pp. 384–385.

108. Joseph Goebbels, "Der Fall Grünspan," *VB* (November 12, 1938).

109. Report of the Supreme Party Court to Göring of February 13, 1939, in IMT, 32:27.

110. Reuth, *Goebbels* (trans.), pp. 240–241.

111. Joseph Goebbels (November 25, 1938), "Ansprache auf der 5. Jahrestagung der Reichskulturkammer und der NS-Gemeinschaft 'Kraft durch Freude' im Opernhaus zu Berlin," in Roller and Höschel, *Judenverfolgung und jüdisches Leben,* 1:122–124; quotations on p. 123.

112. See Gerhard Weinberg, "Undoing Munich, October 1938–March 1939," in *The Foreign Policy of Hitler's Germany: Starting World War II, 1937–1939* (Chicago: University of Chicago Press, 1980), pp. 465–534.

113. Adolf Hitler, "Geheimrede vor der deutschen Presse (November 10, 1938)," in Domarus, *Hitler,* 1:973–977; quotation on p. 977.

114. Gassert, *Amerika im Dritten Reich,* pp. 209–213.

115. Ibid., pp. 222–229.

116. Ibid., pp. 230–231. See also Jeffrey Herf, *Reactionary Modernism:*

Technology, Culture, and Politics in Weimar and the Third Reich (New York: Cambridge University Press, 1984); Mary Nolan, *Visions of Modernity: American Business and the Modernization of Germany* (New York: Oxford University Press, 1994).

117. See the excellent discussion in Gassert, *Amerika im Dritten Reich,* pp. 238–246.

118. Ibid., pp. 252–257.

119. See William Shirer, *Berlin Diary* (New York: Knopf, 1941), pp. 165–166.

120. See Jutta Sywottek, *Mobilmachung für den totalen Krieg: Die propagandistische Vorbereitung der deutschen Bevölkerung auf den Zweiten Weltkrieg* (Opladen: Westdeutscher Verlag, 1976).

121. Gassert, *Amerika im Dritten Reich,* p. 260.

122. Rundererlaß des Auswärtigen Amtes, Akten zur deutschen auswärtigen Politik, January 1939, D/V, no. 664, 25. Cited in Gassert, *Amerika im Dritten Reich,* p. 260.

123. See Robert Dallek, *Franklin Delano Roosevelt and American Foreign Policy, 1932–1945* (New York: Oxford University Press, 1979), p. 179.

124. "Die Hebräerplakette für F.D. Roosevelt," *VB* (January 4, 1939); "USA. unter jüdischer Diktatur" *VB* (May 5, 1939).

125. Adolf Hitler (September 13, 1937), "Ansprache auf dem Reichsparteitag der NSDAP in Nürnberg," in Roller and Höschel, *Judenverfolgung und jüdisches Leben,* 1:98.

126. Adolf Hitler (September 6, 1938), "Ansprache auf dem Reichsparteitag der NSDAP in Nürnberg," in Roller and Höschel, *Judenverfolgung und jüdisches Leben,* 1:113.

127. On the anti-Semitic consensus, see Jehuda Bauer, *Rethinking the Holocaust* (New Haven, Conn.: Yale University Press, 2001), pp. 104–105. On the scope and nature of anti-Semitism in German society during the Nazi era, see David Bankier, ed., *Probing the Depths of German Anti-Semitism: German Society and the Persecution of the Jews, 1933–1941* (New York: Berghahn, 2000).

3. "International Jewry" and the Origins of World War II

1. Max Domarus, ed., *Hitler: Reden und Proklamationen,* vol. 2, *Untergang, 1939–1945* (Neustadt: Schmidt, 1962), pp. 1055–1066; quotations on p. 1055. Hitler used the term *Vernichtung,* or "annihilation," of the Jewish race in Europe.

2. Ibid., p. 1058.

3. "30. Januar 1939," ibid., p. 1058; "30. Januar 1941," p. 1663; "30. Januar 1942," pp. 1828–1829; "15. Februar 1942," p. 1843; "30. September

1942," p. 1920; "8. November 1942," p. 1937; "24. Februar 1943," pp. 1991–1992. For radio transcripts of these and other Nazi propaganda attacks on the Jews that were broadcast on German radio, see Walter Roller and Susanne Höschel, eds., *Judenverfolgung und jüdisches Leben unter den Bedingungen der nationalsozialistischen Gewaltherrschaft,* vol. 1, *Tondokumente und Rundfunksendungen, 1930–1946* (Potsdam: Verlag für Berlin-Brandenburg, 1996), pp. 141–142, 165–166, 216–217, 219. Hitler's statements of February 15, 1942, and February 24, 1943, were read by aides to Nazi officials in Munich.

4. Rudolf Urban, "Judenherrschaft in Mitteleuropa beendet," *Die Judenfrage* 3, nos. 11–12 (March 21, 1939): 1–3.

5. Joseph Goebbels, "Wer will den Krieg?" in *Die Zeit ohne Beispiel: Reden und Aufsätze aus den Jahren 1939/40/41* (Munich: Zentralverlag der NSDAP, 1941), pp. 93, 94–95.

6. Goebbels, "Die Einkreiser," ibid., pp. 144–149.

7. Goebbels, "Nochmals: Die Einkreiser," ibid., pp. 150–156.

8. See Gerhard Weinberg, *A World at Arms: A Global History of World War II* (New York: Cambridge University Press, 1994).

9. On Stalin's ideologically induced miscalculations associated with the nonaggression pact, see Gerhard Weinberg, *Germany, Hitler, and World War II: Essays in Modern German and World History* (New York: Cambridge University Press, 1995).

10. From the extensive literature, see Alexander Nekrich and Mikhail Heller, *Utopia in Power: A History of the Soviet Union from 1917 to the Present,* trans. Phyllis B. Carlos (New York: Summit, 1986), pp. 316–370; François Furet, *The Passing of an Illusion,* trans. Deborah Furet (Chicago: Chicago University Press, 1999); Nicholas Werth, "A State against the People: Violence, Repression, and Terror in the Soviet Union," in Stephanie Courtois, ed., *The Black Book of Communism* (Cambridge, Mass.: Harvard University Press, 1999), pp. 33–268.

11. Winston Churchill, *The Gathering Storm* (Boston: Houghton Mifflin, 1948), pp. 366–367.

12. Arkady Vaksburg, *Stalin against the Jews,* trans. Antonina W. Bouis (New York: Vintage, 1995), pp. 80–102; Arno Lustiger, *Rotbuch: Stalin und die Juden* (Berlin: Aufbau Verlag, 1998).

13. See Weinberg, *A World at Arms.*

14. Some examples: Weinberg, *A World at Arms;* Weinberg, *The Foreign Policy of Hitler's Germany,* vol. 2, *Starting World War II, 1937–1939* (Chicago: University of Chicago Press, 1980); Churchill, *The Gathering Storm;* Robert Dallek, *Franklin Delano Roosevelt and American Foreign Policy, 1932–1945*

(New York: Oxford University Press, 1979); Ian Kershaw, *Hitler, 1936–1945: Nemesis* (New York: Norton, 2000); Telford Taylor, *Munich: The Price of Peace* (Garden City, N.Y.: Doubleday, 1979); Andreas Hillgruber, *Hitlers Strategie: Politik und Kriegführung, 1940–1941* (Munich: Bernard & Graefe, 1982 [1965]).

15. Vertrauliche Informationen des Reichsministeriums für Volksmeinung und Propaganda (henceforth VIdRMVP) V.I. 188/39, August 22, 1939, Zeitgeschichtliche Sammlung (henceforth ZSg.) 109/2, Bundesarchiv Koblenz, Sammlung Oberheitmann ([Oberheitmann Collection], henceforth BAK, SO). Also see Ralf Reuth, *Goebbels: Eine Biographie* (Munich: Piper Verlag, 1995), pp. 418–422.

16. Kershaw, *Hitler,* 2:221; Alan Bullock, *Hitler: A Study in Tyranny* (New York: Harper and Row, rev. ed. 1960), pp. 488–489.

17. Domarus, *Hitler,* 2:1315.

18. VIdRMVP, S.I. 212/39, September 1, 1939, ZSg. 109/3, BAK, SO.

19. On the Nazi fabrications that accompanied Germany's invasion of Poland, see Norman Davies, *God's Playground: A History of Poland* (New York: Columbia University Press, 1982).

20. "Für alle Zeitschriften! Zusätzliche Anweisung des Reichsministeriums für Volksaufklärung und Propaganda," *Zeitschriften-Dienst,* September 1, 1939. For Hitler's speech of September 1, 1939, see Domarus, *Hitler,* 2: 1312–1317.

21. Hitler, speech of September 3, 1939, ibid., 1342.

22. "Judas Kriegshetze in England," *Zeitschriften-Dienst,* directive 816, September 23, 1939, p. 7.

23. "Die Polenpropaganda–eine Gefahr!" *Zeitschriften-Dienst* 26, no. 1085 (October 23, 1939): 26.

24. "Aussprache unter Uns: Polen, Juden und Zigeuner," *Zeitschriften-Dienst* 27, no. 1134 (November 3, 1939): 18.

25. "Die Arbeit der Partei-Propaganda im Kriege," *Unser Wille und Weg* 11, no. 1 (January 1941): n.p.

26. Ibid., 7–10.

27. VIdRMVP, S.I. 213/39, "Reichspressechef Dr. Dietrich vor der deutschen Presse am 3. September 1939," September 2, 1939, ZSg. 109/3, BAK, SO.

28. VIdRMVP, "Richtlinien für die Behandlung vertraulicher Mitteilungen der Presseabteilung der Reichsregierung," n.d., ZSg. 109/12, BAK, SO.

29. VIdRMVP, V.I. 199/39, September 6, 1939, ZSg. 109/3, BAK, SO.

30. VIdRVMP, V.I. 217/39, September 25, 1939, ZSg. 109/3, BAK, SO. Emphasis in the original. In an effort to erode public support for English policy,

several language-use directives in December 1939 defined the war against England as an "antiplutocratic" struggle to "destroy English capitalism" by raising the slogan of "people's socialism or plutocracy." "Plutocracy," referring to democracy perverted by financial domination by the Jews, replaced "democracy" and even "capitalism" as the appropriate term to use in reference to the United States and England. It evoked the anticapitalist and antibourgeois themes that characterized National *Socialist* propaganda against England and the United States. VIdRMVP, V.I. 291/39, December 20, 1939, ZSg. 109/6, BAK, SO.

31. Wolff Heinrichsdorff, "Die jüdische Entscheidung: Die Juden auf Englands Seite," *Die Judenfrage* 3, nos. 36–37 (September 18, 1939): 1. The use of the words *Juda* and *Alljudas* became common in Nazi anti-Semitic language. They evoked a link between the Jews and Judas Iscariot, whom the New Testament depicts as having betrayed Jesus.

32. Ibid. For a reminder of the party's anti-Semitic outlook in the same journal, see Walter Tießler, "Die Partei im neuen Kampfabschnitt gegen Judentum und Freimaurerei," in *Unser Wille und Weg* 9, no. 10 (October 1939): 236–237. In 1940, Tießler became the director of the Reichspropagandaleitung. See "Tießler, Walter," in Ernst Klee, *Das Personenlexikon zum Dritten Reich: Wer war was vor und nach 1945* (Frankfurt am Main: Fischer Verlag, 2003), p. 626.

33. Bernard Wasserstein, *Britain and the Jews of Europe, 1939–1945* (New York: Oxford University Press, 1988), pp. 345, 348–357.

34. "Themen der Zeit: Die Juden in England," *Zeitschriften-Dienst,* no. 1040 (October 23, 1939): 7.

35. Ibid.

36. Peter Aldag, *Juden erobern England and Juden beherrschen England*, vols. 1 and 2 of *Juden in England* (Berlin: Nordland-Verlag, 1939); Jens Lornsen, *Britannien: Hinterland des Weltjudentums* (Berlin: Junker & Dunnhaupt, 1940).

37. Domarus, *Hitler,* 2:1442.

38. VIdRMVP, V.I. 6/40, January 8, 1940, ZSg. 109/7, BAK, SO. On Hore-Belisha, on the need to offer anti-Semitic themes in the German press, and for recommendations for further reading about England sent out by the Propaganda Ministry in January 1940, see VIdRMVP, V.I. 11/40, January 13, 1940, ZSg. 109/7, BAK, SO; "Bücher: Auseinandersetzung mit England," *Zeitschriften-Dienst* 39, no. 1661 (January 19, 1940). Among authors listed were Hermann Wanderscheck, Otto Kriegk, Adolf Rein, Peter Aldag, and the English author and fascist sympathizer Wyndham Lewis, whose book *The Mystery of John Bull* had been translated and published in Germany in 1939 as *Der mysteriöse John Bull* (Essen: Essener Verlagsanstalt, 1939).

39. "Es will das Reich fallen, um das deutsche Volk zu vernichten." Goebbels, speech of February 28, 1940, "Gelobt sei, was hart macht: Rede auf der Großkundgebung in Münster, i.W.," in *Die Zeit ohne Beispiel,* pp. 243–271; quotations on pp. 249, 252–253.

40. "So würde sie keinen Augenblick zögern, das deutsche Volk in seiner Gesamtheit zu vernichten." Ibid., p. 253.

41. Ibid., pp. 256, 270. On the transformation of the meaning of "fanaticism" from its pejorative connotations linked to an attack on reason, see Victor Klemperer, *The Language of the Third Reich, LTI, Lingua, Tertii, Imperii: Notes of a Philologist* (London: Athlone, 2000).

42. See Goebbels, speech of June 16, 1940, "Die Zeit ohne Beispiel," in *Die Zeit ohne Beispiel,* pp. 289–300.

43. See Peter Novick, *The Holocaust in American Life* (Boston: Houghton Mifflin, 1999); and Saul Friedlander, *Prelude to Downfall: Hitler and the United States, 1939–1941* (New York: Knopf, 1967).

44. On plutocracy and Jewry, see "Das Lichtbild im Kriegseinsatz," in *Unser Wille und Weg,* April 1940, p. 58.

45. For Goebbels's suggestions about fanning hatred of France, see "May 30, 1940," in *The Secret Conferences of Dr. Goebbels,* Willi A. Boelcke, ed. (New York: Dutton, 1970), p. 47; "June 12, 1940," ibid., p. 52; and "June 25, 1940," ibid., p. 61.

46. "Die Juden, Frankreichs Totengräber," *Zeitschriften-Dienst,* July 26, 1940, p. 6.

47. Ibid., pp. 6–8. See Heinz Ballensiefern, *Juden in Frankreich* (Berlin: Nordland Verlag, 1939); Edouard Drumont, *Das verjudete Frankreich* (Paris: 1889); Walter Franck, *Nationalismus und Demokratie in Frankreich der dritten Republik* (Hamburg: Hanseatischer Verlag 1933); Georges Bernanos, *Edouard Drumont* (Paris: Grasset, 1931); Paul Gerard, *Le Juif–notre maître* (Paris, n.d.); Paul Ferdonnet, *La guerre juive* (Paris: Editions Baudinière, 1938). The directive brought the *Weltdienst* in Frankfurt am Main, as well as Antijüdische Aktion in Berlin, to the editors' attention.

48. "Die Glosse: Der ewige Ahasver," *Zeitschriften-Dienst* 57, no. 2906 (August 7, 1940): 9.

49. On Hitler's strategy, see Weinberg, *Germany, Hitler, and World War II*; Hillgruber, *Hitlers Strategie.*

50. Gerhard Weinberg, ed., *Hitler's Second Book: The Unpublished Sequel to Mein Kampf by Adolf Hitler,* trans. Krista Smith (New York: Enigma, 2003), pp. 172, 174.

51. Goebbels, "Von der Gottähnlichkeit der Engländer," in *Die Zeit ohne Beispiel,* pp. 301–304; quotation on p. 304.

52. "July 24, 1940," in Boelcke, *The Secret Conferences of Dr. Goebbels,* p. 70.

53. "Themen der Zeit: Juden beherrschen England," directive 3004 (August 16, 1940), p. 6.

54. The transformation of "Jew" into "Jewification" *(Verjudung)* or the verb "to Jewify" *(verjuden)* preceded Nazism and had roots in nineteenth-century anti-Semitic literature. In her study of Nazi vocabulary, Cornelia Schmidt-Berning cites such word use in works by Richard Wagner (1850), Wilhelm Marr (1879), and Eugen Duhring (1881). The term had become common enough in German to be included in the 1929 edition of the authoritative German dictionary the *Duden,* which in 1929, 1934, and 1941, which defined it as Jewish influence, domination, and infiltration by a "Jewish essence," owing to a high percentage of Jews in the population, professions, political parties, and so on. The entry for *Verjudung* was deleted in the 1947 edition and subsequent editions. See Cornelia Schmidt-Berning, *Das Vokabular des Nationalsozialismus* (Berlin: Walter de Gruyter, 1998), pp. 630–632; and Steven E. Aschheim, "'The Jew Within': The Myth of 'Judaization' in Germany," in *Culture and Catastrophe: German and Jewish Confrontations with National Socialism and Other Crises* (New York: New York University Press, 1996), pp. 45–68.

55. "Themen der Zeit: Die englisch-jüdische Allianz," *Zeitschriften-Dienst,* directive 950 (October 14, 1940): 6. Wolf Meyer-Christian, *Die englisch-jüdische Allianz: Werden und Wirken der kapitalistischen Weltherrschaft* (Berlin: Niebelungen Verlag, 1940).

56. "Schriftum," *Zeitschriften-Dienst* 69, no. 3004 (August 16, 1940): 7. The recommended works included Jens Lornsen, *Britannien, Hinterland des Weltjudentums* (Britain: Hinterland of World Jewry) (Berlin: Junker & Dünnhaupt, 1940); Peter Aldag, *Juden beherrschen England* (Jews Dominate England) and *Juden erobern England* (Jews Conquer England) (Berlin: Nordland Verlag, 1939); Heinz Krieger, *England und die Judenfrage in Geschichte und Gegenwart* (England and the Jewish Question in History and the Present) (Frankfurt am Main: Verlag Moritz Diesterweg, 1938); W. Ziegler, *Über die englische Demokratie* (Berlin: Deutscher Verlag, 1940).

57. VIdRMVP, V.I. 152/40, May 2, 1940, ZSg. 109/13, BAK, SO.

58. "Themen der Zeit: Die englisch-jüdische Allianz," p. 6. A series of essays on the English-Jewish alliance published from October to December 1939 served as the basis of a book by the same title, *Die englisch-jüdische Allianz,* published the following year in *Mitteilungen über die Judenfrage,* then still put out by the Institut zum Studium der Judenfrage. See Wolf Meyer-Christian, "Die englisch-jüdische Allianz, 2: Orientpolitik nach jüdischem Befehl,"

Mitteilungen über die Judenfrage; 3, no. 40–41 (October 17, 1939): 1–3; "Die englisch-jüdische Allianz, 3: Disraeli, 'Engländer,' 'Christ'–Zionist Weizmann, Balfour und Lloyd George," ibid., no. 42–43, pp. 3–6; "Die englisch-jüdische Allianz, 6: Die Macht der Vier, der Gangster als Vizekönig–der Giftgas Jude–Entartete Oberschicht," ibid., no. 50–51, pp. 4–6.

59. "Die englisch-jüdische Allianz," 3504, in *Zeitschriften-Dienst* (November 8, 1940). On anti-Semitic "scholarship" during the Nazi era, see the classic study by Max Weinreich, *Hitler's Professors: The Part of Scholarship in Hitler's Crimes against the Jewish People* (New Haven, Conn.: Yale University Press, 1999 [1946]).

60. "Die englisch-jüdische Allianz," 3504, pp. 10, 11.

61. Ibid., pp. 18, 78.

62. Ibid., p. 200.

63. The literature on Sombart is extensive. See Jeffrey Herf, *Reactionary Modernism: Technology, Culture, and Politics in Weimar and the Third Reich* (New York: Cambridge University Press, 1984), pp. 130–151; Friedrich Lenger, *Werner Sombart: Eine Biographie* (Munich: Verlag C. H. Beck, 1994); and Jerry Z. Muller, *The Mind and the Market: Capitalism in Modern European Thought* (New York: Knopf, 2003).

64. Meyer-Christian, *Die englisch-jüdische Allianz,* pp. 207–208.

65. In his diary entry of March 7, 1942, Goebbels noted with dismay the support for the Jews in the British House of Lords. It was "astonishing how much the English people, above all the upper classes, have become Jewified *(verjudet)* and scarcely have an English character anymore." This development was due to the fact that "the upper ten thousand have been so Jewishly infected through marriages to Jews that they are scarcely any longer able to think as English people." Ibid., p. 457.

66. Ibid., p. 89.

67. Ibid., p. 141.

68. Ibid., pp. 142–145.

69. Ibid., pp. 185, 188.

70. On the Nazi regime and Zionism, see Francis R. Nicosia, *The Third Reich and the Palestine Question,* 2nd ed. (New Brunswick, N.J.: Transaction, 1999); Nicosia, "Zionism and Palestine in Anti-Semitic Thought in Imperial Germany," *Studies in Zionism* 13, no. 2 (1992): 115–131; Nicosia, "Ein Nützlicher Feind: Zionismus im Nationalsozialistischen Deutschland, 1933–1939," *Vierteljahrshefte für Zeitgeschichte* 37, no. 3 (1989): 367–400; and Nicosia, "Zionism in National Socialist Jewish Policy in Germany, 1933–39," *Journal of Modern History* 50, no. 4 (1978): 1253–1282.

71. On the Haavarah agreement, see Nicosia, *The Third Reich and the*

Palestine Question; Leni Yahil, *The Holocaust: The Fate of European Jewry* (New York: Oxford University Press, 1991), pp. 100–104.

72. Adolf Hitler, *Mein Kampf,* trans. Ralph Mannheim (Boston: Houghton Mifflin, 1971 [1943]), pp. 324–325.

73. Alfred Rosenberg, *Schriften aus den Jahren 1917–1921* (Munich: Hoheneichen Verlag, 1943). See, in particular, Rosenberg's discussions of the Jews and the Freemasons, Zionism, and Jewish world rule and its consequences. See also the Nazi publication of the *Protocols of the Elders of Zion* with Rosenberg's foreword and introduction: Alfred Rosenberg, *Die Protokolle der Weisen von Zion und die jüdische Weltpolitik,* 4th ed. (Munich: Deutscher Volksverlag, 1933). By the time this fourth edition came out, the press had published twenty-five thousand copies.

74. Alfred Rosenberg, *Der Staatsfeindliche Zionismus* (Munich: Zentralverlag der NSDAP, Franz Eher Verlag, 1938), p. 86.

75. For some examples of the propaganda and of press directives drawing attention to it, see works by Hermann Erich Seifert (Heinrich Hest): *Weltjuda ohne Maske,* vol. 2, *Palästina: Judenstaat? England als Handlanger des Weltjudentums* (Berlin: Joh. Kasper, 1939); *Der Aufbruch in der arabischen Welt* (Berlin: Zentralverlag der NSDAP, Franz Eher Verlag, 1941); "Der Kampf um die Scholle Palästina, Das Geld des Weltjudentums kauft den besten Boden auf," *Die Judenfrage* 3, no. 7 (February 16, 1940): 1–2; and "Bucher: Juden, Engländer, Araber," *Zeitschriften-Dienst* 17, no. 656 (August 26, 1939): 18.

76. Giselher Wirsing, *Engländer, Juden, Araber in Palästina* (Jena: Eugen Diederichs Verlag, 1939).

77. Ibid., p. 120.

78. "Antisemitismus" in *Zeitschriften-Dienst* 6, no. 222 (June 13, 1939).

79. VIdRMVP, V.I., 215/44, September 30, 1944, ZSg. 109/51, BAK, SO.

80. On the defeat of Hitler's initial strategy for victory, see Winston Churchill, *History of the Second World War,* vol. 2, *Their Finest Hour* (Boston: Houghton Mifflin, 1983 [1949]); Warren F. Kimball, *Churchill and Roosevelt: The Complete Correspondence* (Princeton, N.J.: Princeton University Press, 1984); Hillgruber, *Hitlers Strategie;* John Lukacs, *The Duel: Hitler vs. Churchill* (New York: Ticknor and Fields, 1991); Weinberg, *Germany, Hitler, and World War II.*

81. Joseph Goebbels, *Die Tagebücher von Joseph Goebbels (TBJG),* ed. Elke Fröhlich (Munich: Sauer, 1994), entry for December 12, 1940, I/9, p. 48.

82. For Goebbels's denunciation of Churchill on January 4, 1941, see "England und seine Plutokraten," in *Die Zeit ohne Beispiel,* pp. 359, 362, 389.

83. "Churchill verspricht den Juden Deutschland als Raubgut, Solidarität der Weltschamarotzer erneut befundet," *VB,* February 5, 1941, p. 1.

84. Adolf Hitler, speech of January 30, 1941, in Domarus, *Hitler,* 2:1663–1664. See also Adolf Hitler (January 1, 1941), "Kundgebung im Berliner Sportpalast zum 8. Jahrestag der nationalsozialistischen Machtergreifung," in Roller and Höschel, *Judenverfolgung und jüdisches Leben,* 1:165–166. These paragraphs were featured on the front page of *Die Judenfrage,* then published by the office of Antisemitische Aktion. See "Der Führer sprach: Aus dem Rede im Sportpalast vom 30. Januar 1941," *Die Judenfrage* 5, no. 2 (February 10, 1941): 1.

85. "When Hitler Threatens," *New York Times,* January 31, 1941, p. 18.

86. Goebbels, "Im richtigen Augenblick," *Die Zeit ohne Beispiel,* 396–400.

87. Ibid., p. 359.

88. Goebbels, speech of March 30, 1941, "Britannia Rules the Waves," ibid., pp. 441–445; quotation on p. 444.

89. The 2,035,000 Jews in New York City constituted almost 28 percent of its population. The figures for the Bronx, Brooklyn, and Manhattan, respectively, were: 592,185, or 43.57 percent; 974,765, or 36.64 percent; and 351,037 or 18.64 percent. See Harry Schneiderman and the American Jewish Committee, *The American Jewish Yearbook 5702* (1941–1942) (Philadelphia: Jewish Publication Society of America, 1941), 43:654–659.

90. Ibid., 43:584, 586.

91. On Hull, Stimson, and Morgenthau, see Dallek, *Franklin Delano Roosevelt and American Foreign Policy.* On anti-Semitism and the American military, see Joseph Bendersky, *The 'Jewish Threat': Anti-Semitic Politics of the U.S. Army* (New York: Basic, 2000).

92. Novick, *The Holocaust in American Life.*

93. On American political and military strategy in the Battle of the Atlantic before the United States had formally entered World War II, see William L. Langer and S. Everett Gleason, *Undeclared War, 1940–1941* (New York: Harper, 1953). On Roosevelt's focus on preventing Britain's defeat, see his correspondence with Winston Churchill of summer 1940, Warren Kimball, ed., *Churchill and Roosevelt: Their Complete Correspondence,* vol. 1 (Princeton, N.J.: Princeton University Press, 1987).

94. Henry L. Feingold, *A Time for Searching: Entering the Mainstream, 1920–1945* (Baltimore, Md.: Johns Hopkins University Press, 1992), pp. 71, 130.

95. See Marcia Graham Synnott, *The Half-Opened Door: Discrimination and Admissions at Harvard, Yale, and Princeton, 1900–1970* (Westport, Conn.: Greenwood, 1979).

96. Jerold S. Auerbach, *Unequal Justice: Lawyers and Social Change in Modern America* (New York: Oxford University Press, 1976), pp. 128–129.

97. "Jews in America," *Fortune* 13, no. 2 (February 1936): 130, 131, 141. The editors concluded that the Jews would have numerous allies in opposing fascism and Nazism. Yet the assessment concluded on a note that revealed the continuing anxiety in the American establishment about the recent advances made by American Jews. "The first condition of their [the Jews'] success will be the quieting of Jewish apprehensiveness and the consequent elimination of the aggressive and occasionally provocative Jewish defensive measures which the country has recently and anxiously observed" (p. 141).

98. See Neil Baldwin, *Henry Ford and the Jews: The Mass Production of Hate* (New York: Public Affairs, 2001). For a thorough examination of the Nazi view of the United States, see Philipp Gassert, *Amerika im Dritten Reich: Ideologie, Volksmeinung und Propaganda, 1933–1945* (Stuttgart: Steiner, 1997).

99. See Scott A. Berg, *Lindbergh* (New York: Putnam, 1998).

100. Charles Herbert Stember and others, *Jews in the Mind of America* (New York: Basic, 1966), pp. 114–116, 120–121. By June 1962, those answering yes had declined dramatically, to 17 percent.

101. Ibid., p. 128. As is true of other measures of anti-Semitism, the perception of Jews as a menace declined dramatically, such that by 1960 only 5 percent of Americans viewed Jews in this way.

102. See David S. Wyman, *The Abandonment of the Jews: America and the Holocaust, 1941–1945* (New York: New Press, 1998 [1984]).

103. Alfred Rosenberg, "Die Judenfrage als Weltproblem," *Weltkampf: Die Judenfrage in Geschichte und Gegenwart*, pp. 64–72; also in *VB*, March 29, 1941, pp. 1–2; also see the radio transcript of the speech, Alfred Rosenberg (March 28, 1941), "Rundfunkvortrag in Berlin im Anschluß an die erste Arbeitstagung des 'Instituts zur Erforschung der Judenfrage' in Frankfurt am Main über 'Die Judenfrage als Weltproblem,'" in Roller and Höschel, *Judenverfolgung und jüdisches Leben*, 1:181–187.

104. Ibid., p. 68.

105. Theodor Seibert, *Das amerikanische Rätsel: Die Kriegspolitik der USA in der Ära Roosevelt* (The American Riddle: The War Policy of the USA in the Roosevelt Era) (Berlin: Franz Eher Verlag, 1941). For similar works that followed, see Hans Schadewaldt, *Was will Roosevelt?* (Dusseldorf: Völkischer Verlag, 1941); Johann von Leers, *Kräfte hinter Roosevelt* (Berlin: Theodor Fritsch Verlag, 1942); Wolfgang Ispert, *Roosevelts Angriff auf Europa* (The Hague: Schriftenreihe der Forschungstelle Volk und Raum, 1944).

106. Seibert, *Das amerikanische Rätsel,* pp. 6–7.

107. Ibid., pp. 56–57.

108. Ibid., pp. 63–63.

109. Goebbels, speech of May 25, 1941, "Aus dem Lande der unbegrenzten Möglichkeiten," in *Die Zeit ohne Beispiel,* pp. 486–491.

110. Ibid., p. 491.

111. Goebbels, "Botschaft aus USA," speech of May 29, 1941, in *Die Zeit ohne Beispiel,* pp. 492–496.

112. Goebbels, entry for May 30, 1941, *TBJG,* I/9, p. 342.

113. "Das Hauptthema: Juden in den USA!" *Zeitschriften-Dienst* 109 (May 30, 1941): 4–6; and "Themen der Zeit: Juden in USA!" *Zeitschriften-Dienst* 110 (June 6, 1941): 6–9.

114. *"Das Hauptthema: Juden in den USA!"* *Zeitschriften-Dienst* 109 (May 30, 1941): 4.

115. Ibid.

116. Ibid., pp. 5–6.

117. "Themen der Zeit: Juden in USA!" *Zeitschriften-Dienst* 110, no. 4676 (June 6, 1941): 6–9. From the offices of Anti-Semitische Aktion and the Archiv des Reichsministeriums für Volksaufklärung und Propaganda.

118. Ibid. Emphasis in the original.

119. Goebbels, entry for April 28, 1941, *TBJG,* I/9, p. 276.

120. Entry for May 25, 1941, ibid., p. 334.

121. Entry for June 7, 1941, ibid., p. 357.

122. Entry for June 8, 1941, ibid., p. 359.

123. Entry for June 4, 1941, ibid., p. 353.

124. Entry for June 6, 1941, ibid., p. 355.

125. Entry for June 16, 1941, ibid., pp. 377–379.

126. Entry for June 20, 1941, ibid., pp. 389–390.

127. Domarus, *Hitler,* 2:1726.

4. At War against the Alliance of Bolshevism and Plutocracy

1. Mikhail Heller and Alexander M. Nekrich, *Utopia in Power: The History of the Soviet Union, 1917 to the Present,* trans. Phyllis B. Carlos (New York: Summit, 1986), pp. 353–354. The authors calculated that during those seventeen months, the Soviet Union supplied Germany with 865,000 tons of oil, 140 tons of manganese ore, 14,000 tons of copper, 3,000 tons of nickel, 101,000 tons of raw cotton, over 1 million tons of lumber, 11,000 tons of flax, 26,000 tons of chrome ore, 15,000 tons of asbestos, 184,000 tons of phosphates, 6,019 pounds (2,736 kilograms) of platinum, and 1,462,000 tons of grain. In addition, the Soviet Union purchased raw materials for Germany in

the Far East, the Middle East, and Latin America and shipped great quantities of rubber bought by Japan to Germany on the Trans-Siberian Railway. Heller and Nekrich surmise, "It is entirely possible that without this help Germany would not have been able to go to war with the USSR."

2. Ibid., p. 364.

3. Willi A. Boelcke, ed., *"Wollt Ihr den totalen Krieg?" Die Geheimen Goebbels-Konferenzen, 1939–1943* (Munich: Deutscher Taschenbuch Verlag, 1969), p. 236; see English translation, Willi A. Boelcke, ed., *The Secret Conferences of Dr. Goebbels: The Nazi Propaganda War, 1939–1943*, trans. Ewald Osers (New York: Dutton, 1970), p. 176.

4. The evening before the invasion, Churchill famously commented, "If Hitler invaded Hell, I would make at least a favorable reference to the Devil in the House of Commons." Cited in Winston Churchill, *The Second World War*, vol. 3, *The Grand Alliance* (Boston: Houghton Mifflin, 1950), p. 370. Also see Jeffrey Herf, "If Hitler Invaded Hell: Distinguishing between Nazism and Communism during World War II, the Cold War and since the Fall of European Communism," in Helmut Dubiel and Gabriel Motzkin, eds., *The Lesser Evil: Moral Approaches to Genocide* (London: Routledge, 2004), pp. 182–195.

5. "Speech of June 22, 1941," cited in Churchill, *The Grand Alliance*, 3:371.

6. Boelcke, *"Wollt Ihr den totalen Krieg?"* pp. 372–373.

7. Ibid., June 24, 1941, p. 399.

8. Ibid., June 25, 1941, p. 404.

9. Ibid., July 7, 1941, p. 430.

10. Presse-Rundschreiben 2/98/41, VIdRMVP, June 25, 1941, Reichspropagandaamt Berlin, R55/1387 BAK, p. 55.

11. Joseph Goebbels, "Die alte Front," June 26, 1941, in Joseph Goebbels, *Die Zeit ohne Beispiel: Reden und Aufsätze aus den Jahren 1939/40/41* (Munich: Zentralverlag der NSDAP, 1941), p. 508.

12. Ibid., p. 511.

13. Benjamin Pinkus, *The Jews of the Soviet Union: The History of a National Minority* (New York: Cambridge University Press, 1988), p. 77.

14. Ibid, pp. 78–79.

15. Ibid., p. 80.

16. Ibid., pp. 82–83. In the 1920s, Jews constituted 4.57 percent of the Red Army High Command.

17. See Amir Weiner, *Making Sense of War: The Second World War and the Fate of the Bolshevik Revolution* (Princeton, N.J.: Princeton University Press, 2001); and Jeffrey Herf, "The Extermination Camps and the Ally to the East:

Could the Red Army and Air Force Have Stopped or Slowed the Final Solution?" *Kritika* 4, no. 4 (Fall 2003): 913–930.

18. "Schiffbruch der 'proletarischen Kultur': Die weltanschauliche Auseinandersetzung mit der Sowjet-Union," *Zeitschriften-Dienst* 113, no. 4797 (June 27, 1941): 4–5. See *Warum Krieg mit Stalin? Das Rotbuch der Anti-Komintern* (Berlin: Nibelungen Verlag, 1941). Wilfred Bade was the head of the *Periodical Service* throughout the war.

19. Ibid.

20. R55/1387 BAK, p. 67.

21. Presse-Rundschreiben, 2, 103, VIdRMVP, June 25, 1941, Reichspropagandaamt Berlin; W. F., "*Warum Krieg mit Stalin? Das Rotbuch der Anti-Komintern,*" *Die Judenfrage in Politik, Recht, Kultur und Wirtschaft* 5, no. 11–12 (August 1, 1941): 1.

22. Adolf Hitler, "Aufruf des Führers," cited in *Warum Krieg mit Stalin?* p. 6.

23. Ibid., p. 14. Emphasis in the original.

24. Ibid., p. 15.

25. "Die Juden in der Sowjetunion," pp. 57–73.

26. Ibid., pp. 18.

27. *Aufklärungs- und Redner-Informationsmaterial der Reichspropagandaleitung der NSDAP, Deutschland zum Endkampf mit dem jüdisch-bolschewistischen Mordsystem angetreten* (Munich: Zentralverlag der NSDAP, 1941), in NARA, T81, roll 672, RPL 52, 5480200.

28. Ibid., pp. 5, 6.

29. Ibid., 7.

30. Ibid., p. 21.

31. Ibid., pp. 21–22.

32. Ibid.

33. Ibid., p. 22. Emphasis in the original.

34. Ibid., pp. 23–24.

35. "Sie sind gerichtet!!!" (July 23, 1941) Bestand (collection) 712 (Plakate), Wandzeitung (Posters, wall newspaper) *Parole der Woche,* published by the NSDAP, Reichspropagandaleitung, Munich, no. 1692, Folge (series) 30, Landeshauptarchiv Koblenz.

36. "Das ist der jüdische Bolschewismus . . ." (July 30, 1941), ibid., Folge 31.

37. "Blasts Appeasers: President Denounces 'Deeper Sabotage' than Bombs," *New York Times,* July 5, 1941, p. 1.

38. "Roosevelt Tells Kalinen We Back Russian People," *New York Times,* July 12, 1941, p. 3.

39. Robert Dallek, *Franklin Delano Roosevelt and American Foreign Policy, 1932–1945* (New York: Oxford University Press, 1979), pp. 278–281.

40. Joseph Goebbels, "Der Schleier fällt," July 6, 1941, in *Die Zeit ohne Beispiel,* pp. 520–525.

41. Ibid., p. 523.

42. Ibid., p. 524. On the *Ordnungspolizei* and what British intelligence was learning from their radio transmissions, see Richard Breitman, *Official Secrets: What the Nazis Planned, What the British and Americans Knew* (New York: Hill and Wang, 1998), chaps. 2–6.

43. Joseph Goebbels, *Die Tagebücher von Joseph Goebbels (TBJG),* ed. Elke Fröhlich (Munich: Sauer, 1994), entry for July 7, 1941, II/1, pp. 36–38.

44. On this see Steven M. Miner, *Stalin's Holy War: Religion, Nationalism and Alliance Politics, 1941–1945* (Chapel Hill: University of North Carolina Press, 2003).

45. Goebbels, entry for July 10, 1941, *TBJG,* II/1, p. 42.

46. Entry for July 10, 1941, ibid., p. 44.

47. "Der Bolschewismus enthüllt sein jüdisches Gesicht, Litvinov-Finkelstein tritt hinter der Kulisse hervor," *VB,* July 10, 1941, p. 1.

48. On what the British knew and conveyed about the murders by the *Einsatzgruppen* and the *Ordnungspolizei,* see Richard Breitman, *Official Secrets.*

49. Goebbels, entry for July 11, 1941, *TBJG,* I/1, p. 49.

50. Ibid., p. 49.

51. Entry for August 1, 1941, ibid., pp. 157–158.

52. Entry for September 17, 1941, ibid., p. 436. On Lozovsky, his wartime role, and his postwar trial and execution, see Joshua Rubenstein and Vladimir P. Naumov, eds., *Stalin's Secret Pogrom: The Postwar Inquisition of the Jewish Anti-Fascist Committee* (New Haven, Conn.: Yale University Press, 2001), pp. 218–220. "His favorite pastime was to disprove German claims and call them 'just some more lies out of the gossip factory,'" p. 220.

53. Goebbels, entry for July 14, 1941, *TBJG,* II/1, p. 35.

54. Ibid.

55. "Zur Lage," *Zeitschriften-Dienst* 117, no. 4961 (July 25, 1941), p. 1. A week later, the *Periodical Service* denounced "Roosevelt and his Jews," asserting that FDR was a Freemason, an affiliation that supposedly proved his "dependence on world Jewry." See "Zur Lage," *Zeitschriften-Dienst* 117, no. 4961 (July 25, 1941): 1.

56. "Roosevelt Hauptwerkzeug der jüdischen Freimauerei, Sensationelles Dokument enthüllt die Zusammenhänge der Kriegstreiber mit dem internationalen Maurerklüngel," *VB,* July 23, 1941, p. 1.

57. Ibid.

58. Reichspropagandaamt Berlin, Presse-Rundschreiben 2/107/41, VIdR-MVP, July 24, 1941, R55/1387, BAK, p. 73.

59. Joseph Goebbels, "Mimikry," July 20, 1941, in *Die Zeit ohne Beispiel,* pp. 526–531.

60. Ibid., p. 526.

61. Ibid., p. 527.

62. Ibid., pp. 527–528.

63. By August, 1941, Goebbels was claiming that the Kremlin's plan to attack Germany was so obvious that it needed "no further proof." See Joseph Goebbels, "Um die Entscheidung," August 3, 1941, in *Die Zeit ohne Beispiel,* pp. 537–542. For the by now standard scholarly refutation of the preventive war thesis, see Horst Boog et al., eds., *Germany and the Second World War,* vol. 4, *The Attack on the Soviet Union,* trans. Dean S. McMurray, Ewald Osers, and Louise Wilmott (New York: Oxford University Press, 1998).

64. Ibid., p. 529.

65. Ibid., p. 530.

66. Ibid., pp. 530–531.

67. Hans Diebow, *Die Juden in USA* (Berlin: Zentralverlag der NSDAP, Franz Eher Verlag, 1941).

68. Ibid., p. 8.

69. Ibid., p. 57. See W. Ross Yates, "Charles Michael Schwab," in John A. Garraty and Mark C. Carnes, eds., *American National Biography* (New York: Oxford University Press, 1999), pp. 465–467.

70. Hans Diebow, *Die Juden in USA,* pp. 6, 10, 61, and 62. Diebow also deployed the unflattering photo as a instrument of ridicule and humiliation. He juxtaposed a photo of LaGuardia pursing his lips and that of an ape. A photo of an unsmiling, serious Felix Frankfurter, described by an unnamed source as "the most influential individual" in the United States, could be viewed as rather foreboding. Diebow might also take perfectly harmless photos—for example, of two women enjoying dinner at a restaurant or in evening dress—to make pejorative comments about Jews in "the land of milk and honey" or adorned with silk, gold, and pearls. A man smiling with his right arm raised, originally seen celebrating Herbert Lehman's election, reappeared in a poster announcing, "USA Radio is 90 percent Jewified," the companion piece to another poster, featuring a man with stereotypically Jewish features who is counting money, which asserts: "USA Finances are 98 percent Jewified."

71. "Die Juden haben den Krieg gewollt!" BAK, Plakaten, 003–020–023.

72. Ibid.

73. "Roosevelts Ziel ist die Weltherrschaft der Juden," *VB,* August 19, 1941, p. 1.

74. "Ein ungeheurerliches jüdisches Vernichtungsprogramm, Roosevelt fordert Sterilisierung des deutschen Volkes, binnen zwei Generationen soll das deutsche Volk ausgerottet sein," *VB*, July 24, 1941, p. 1.

75. Ibid.

76. On the uses of Kaufman's book in Nazi propaganda, see Wolfgang Benz, "Judenvernichtung aus Notwehr? Die Legenden um Theodore N. Kaufman," *Vierteljahrshefte für Zeitgeschichte* 29, no. 4 (1981): 615–630. See Theodore Nathan Kaufman, *Germany Must Perish!* (Newark, N.J.: Argyle, 1941). Goebbels left off the author's less obviously Jewish-sounding first name.

77. On this see Benz, "Judenvernichtung aus Notwehr," pp. 627–629.

78. Goebbels, entry for July 24, 1941, *TBJG*, II/1, pp. 116–117.

79. Entry for August 3, 1941, ibid., pp. 168–169. In his diary entry of August 13, Goebbels wrote of his decision to publish the book in parts, accompanied with appropriate commentary "from our side." Entry for August 13, 1941, ibid., p. 225. See also the Goebbels diary entry in which he writes that "the book by the American Jew Nathan Kaufman" was published "in millions of copies . . . The book has been in the hands of the German people for some time and has been devoured by all sectors of society. It has been extraordinarily useful for us domestically. It is impossible to imagine a better illustration of the desires and goals of the other side. The book could not have been more helpful to us if it had been written by a member of the Propaganda Ministry." Entry for October 22, 1941, ibid., p. 155.

80. Ibid., p. 271.

81. See "Wolfgang Diewerge," in Ernst Klee, *Das Personenlexikon zum Dritten Reich, Wer war was vor und nach 1945* (Frankfurt am Main: Fischer, 2003), p. 111. After 1945 and 1949, Diewerge was one of the ex-Nazis active in the Free Democratic Party until their efforts were uncovered and disrupted by British occupation forces. On this see Norbert Frei, *Adenauer's Germany and the Nazi Past,* trans. Joel Golb (New York: Columbia University Press, 2001), pp. 277–302.

82. Goebbels, *TBJG*, entry for August 29, 1941, II/1, pp. 168–169.

83. "Judas satanischer Mordplan," *Zeitschriften-Dienst* 123, no. 5283 (September 5, 1941).

84. Wolfgang Diewerge, *Das Kriegsziel der Weltplutokratie: Dokumentarische Veröffentlichung zu dem Buch des Präsidenten der amerikanischen Friedensgesellschaft Theodore Nathan Kaufman, Deutschland muß sterben, "Germany must perish"* (Berlin: Zentralverlag der NSDAP, Franz Eher Verlag, 1941).

85. Ibid., p. 5.

86. On forced sterilization in Nazi Germany, see Gisela Bock, *Zwangssterilisation im Nationalsozialismus: Studien zur Rassenpolitik und Frauenpolitik* (Opladen: Westdeutscher Verlag, 1986); and Dieter Kuntz and Susan Bachrach, eds., *Deadly Medicine: Creating the Master Race* (Chapel Hill: University of North Carolina Press, 2004).

87. Ibid., p. 9. Wolfgang Benz writes that neo-Nazi and radical right-wing figures after 1945, including Paul Rassinier, Erich Kern, and most prominently Adolf Eichmann, referred to "the Kaufman plan" as if it were an expression of American policy. On this, see Benz, "Judenvernichtung aus Notwehr," pp. 623–626. In his posthumously published memoirs Eichmann wrote: "Kaufman intended to bring about the complete extermination of our people by total sterilization . . . If this plan was intended as a provocation, then one can only say that the Jews accomplished their goal. For it is probable that in our highest leadership circles, the Kaufman plan served as a stimulating factor for (our) own extermination plans." Rudolf Aschenauer, ed., *Ich, Adolf Eichmann: Ein historischer Zeugenbericht* (Leoni am Starnberger See: Druffel Verlag, 1980), pp. 177–178.

88. Ibid., p. 25.

89. Ibid., p. 14.

90. Ibid., p. 32.

91. Hans Diebow, *Die Juden in USA* (Berlin: Zentralverlag der NSDAP, Franz Eher Verlag, 1941).

92. Ibid., p. 11.

93. "Immer das gleiche Ziel: Deutschland muss vernichtet werden" (October 10, 1941), no. 1724, Folge 40; also see "Der Jude Kaufman übertrumpft" (August 8, 1942), Bestand 712 (Plakate) Wandzeitung *Parole der Woche* no. 1758; Bestand 712 (Plakate), Folge 35, Wandzeitung *Parole der Woche,* Landeshauptarchiv Koblenz.

94. "Kampf dem Weltjudentum!" *Zeitschriften-Dienst* 119, no. 5046 (August 8, 1941): 3–4; see also *Deutscher Wochendienst* 8840 (May 21, 1943): 9.

95. Ibid., p. 5. The following week the service published a primer on racial distinctions between Jews and Aryans. See "Hauptthema: Kampf den Weltjudentum! Rasse, Bauerntum Kultur und Wirtschaft," *Zeitschriften-Dienst,* August 15, 1941, pp. 4–7. On September 24, 1941, the Nazi regime released the anti-Semitic film *Jud Süss.* On the same day, Goebbels told his Minister's Conference that the press should address the "fundamental" issues about the Aryan and Jewish world discussed in the film. "24. September 1940," Boelcke, "*Wollt Ihr den totalen Krieg?*" p. 139. In his essay in *Das Reich* of July 27, 1941, Goebbels repeated his assertions about the role of

the "Jews in the city [of London] and the Jews in the Kremlin." See Joseph Goebbels, "Die Deutschen vor der Front!" July 27, 1941, in Goebbels, *Die Zeit ohne Beispiel,* pp. 532–536.

96. Goebbels, *TBJG,* entry for August 20, 1941, II/1, p. 278. In the entry for August 26, 1941, ibid., pp. 311–312, Goebbels again emphasizes his determination to take to measures against the Jews, despite "resistance," and to proceed with publication of the Kaufman book.

97. Entry for August 12, 1941, ibid., p. 218.

98. Entry for September 24, 1941, ibid., II/2, pp. 480–481.

99. Entry for October 19, 1941, ibid., p. 142.

100. Entry for October 24, 1941, ibid., p. 168.

101. Entry for August 25, 1941, ibid., 1:307.

102. Entry for September 14, 1941, ibid., pp. 415–416. In the first week of October 1941, Goebbels wrote, "That would be too bad if Lindbergh were thus deprived of the possibility to engage in political activity. In America, he has performed extraordinary service for us." Entry for October 5, 1941, ibid., II/2, p. 76.

103. September 14, 1941, ibid., p. 418.

104. "Auszug aus dem 'Oberheitmann Material,'" pp. 200–201, in U.S. Nuerenberg War Crimes Trials, *United States of America v. Ernst von Weizsäcker et al.,* October 28, 1941, in NARA, RG 238, War Crimes Records Collection, M 897, roll 34, NG 3800, vol. 9, V.I. 283/41, "Tagesparole des Reichspressechefs," doc. 4703.

105. Ibid.

106. Peter Aldag, "Weltherrschaftspläne," *Die Judenfrage* 5, no. 19 (October 28, 1941): 213–214.

107. "Das militärische Ende des Bolschewismus, Der Ostfeldzug ist entschieden, Heeresgruppen Timoschenko und Woroschilow eingeschlossen, Heeresgruppe Budjenny in Auflösung, Unvergleichliches Meisterstück der Strategie," *VB,* October 10, 1941, p. 1.

108. Gü (pseudonym), "Die Kriegsschuld des Juden," *Die Judenfrage* 5, no. 18 (October 15, 1941): 1–3.

109. Goebbels, *TBJG,* entry for October 9, 1941, II/2, p. 81.

110. Adolf Hitler (November 8, 1941), "Ansprache im Münchener Löwenbräukeller zur Erinnerung an den Marsch auf die Feldherrnhalle 1923," in Walter Roller and Susanne Höschel, eds., *Judenverfolgung und jüdisches Leben unter den Bedingungen der nationalsozialistischen Gewaltherrschaft,* vol. 1, *Tondokumente und Rundfunksendungen, 1930–1946* (Potsdam: Verlag für Berlin-Brandenburg, 1996), pp. 199–200. This text is based on the

transcript of the radio broadcast. See also Max Domarus, ed., *Hitler: Reden und Proklamationen,* vol. 2, *Untergang, 1939–1945* (Neustadt: Schmidt, 1963), pp. 1772–1773.

111. Ibid., p. 200.

112. Ibid.

113. Richard Breitman, *Architect of Genocide: Himmler and the Final Solution* (Hanover, N.H: University of New England Press, 1992) dates the crucial decisions to spring 1941, whereas Christopher Browning in *The Path to Genocide: Essays on Launching the Final Solution* (New York: Cambridge University Press, 1992) argues that Hitler made them in late summer.

114. On the emergence of a genocidal consensus, see Yehuda Bauer, *Rethinking the Holocaust* (New Haven, Conn.: Yale University Press, 2001).

115. Goebbels, *TBJG,* entry for November 2, 1941, II/2, pp. 199–200.

116. Joseph Goebbels, "Die Juden sind Schuld!" November 16, 1941, in Joseph Goebbels, *Das eherne Herz: Reden und Aufsätze aus den Jahren 1941/42* (Munich: Zentralverlag der NSDAP, 1943), pp. 85–91.

117. Joseph Goebbels, "Die Juden sind Schuld!" November 16, 1941, Goebbels, *Das eherne Herz,* pp. 85–91; quotation on p. 85.

118. Ibid., p. 88. The German reads in part: "Das Weltjudentum hat in der Anzettelung dieses Krieges die ihm zur Verfügung stehenden Kräfte vollkommen falsch eingeschätzt, und es erleidet nun einen allmählichen Vernichtungsprozess, den es uns zugedacht hätte und auch bedenkenlos an uns vollstrecken liesse, wenn es dazu die Macht besässe. Es geht jetzt nach seinem eigenen Gesetz: 'Auge um Auge, Zahn um Zahn!' zugrunde."

119. Ibid., p. 91.

120. "Goebbels Spurs Abuse for Jews," *New York Times,* November 14, 1941, p. 11. The *Times* article referred to the "forthcoming Sunday issue of the Propaganda Minister's weekly, *Das Reich.*" The article accurately summarized Goebbels's essay, except that it did not translate his reference to a "gradual process of extermination" that the Jews were "now" enduring.

121. Goebbels, *TBJG,* entry for November 17, 1941, II/2, p. 304.

122. VIdRVMP, V.I. 316/41 (1. Erg. [first addendum]), December 1, 1941, ZSg. 109/28, BAK, SO.

123. "Dr. Goebbels vor der Deutschen Akademie," *Deutsche Allgemeine Zeitung,* December 2, 1941, p. 1. The Propaganda Ministry soon published the text as a separate pamphlet with the title *Das eherne Herz* (The Iron Heart). See Joseph Goebbels, *"Das eherne Herz": Rede vor der Deutschen Akademie* (Munich: Zentralverlag der NSDAP, 1942). On Goebbels's pleasure over the reception of the speech, see Goebbels, diary entries for December 2 and 3, 1941, *TBJG,* II/2, pp. 416, 442. See also "Dr. Goebbels vor

den Deutschen Academie, 'Wir können, müssen und werden siegen,'" *Deutsche Allgemeine Zeitung,* December 2, 1941, pp. 1–2. Writing in his diary that evening, Goebbels believed that he had "succeeded in bringing these circles certainly closer to the state and [making them] more devoted to the war than was the case before." Entry for December 2, 1941, *TBJG,* II/2, p. 416.

124. Goebbels, *Das eherne Herz,* p. 5.
125. Ibid., p. 21.
126. "Die nationale Intelligenz und die geistige Führung auszurotten." Ibid., p. 23.
127. Ibid., pp. 28–30.
128. Ibid., pp. 34–35.
129. Ibid., pp. 35–36.
130. Ibid., p. 37. The German reads: "die Judenfrage endgültig zu lösen."
131. Ibid., p. 41. The German reads: "vernichtet, ausgerottet und ausgelöscht werden muß."
132. Goebbels, entry for December 2, 1941, *TBJG,* II/2, p. 417.
133. Ibid., p. 420.
134. Entry for December 9, 1941, ibid., p. 444.
135. VIdRMVP, 322/41, December 8, 1941, ZSg. 109/28, BAK, SO.
136. Ibid.
137. "Das jüdische Komplott" (December 10, 1941), Imperial War Museum, London, Department of Art, PST 8357; also available in Bestand 712 (Plakate) Wandzeitung *Parole der Woche,* no. 1709, Folge 50 (1941), Landeshauptarchiv Koblenz.
138. In an anti-Semitic collection of photos he published in 1937, Hans Diebow displayed a photo of Ivan Maisky and Maxim Litvinov in London and referred to the latter as Litvinov-Wallach-Finkelstein. See Hans Diebow, *Der ewige Jude: 265 Bilddokumente, gesammelt von Dr. Hans Diebow* (Munich: Zentralverlag der NSDAP, Franz Eher Verlag, 1937), p. 119.
139. Domarus, *Hitler,* 2:1793–1811; for the instruction to print the text in the press, see VIdRMVP, 326/41, December 12, 1941, ZSg. 109/28, BAK, SO.
140. Domarus, *Hitler,* 2:1801. The Propaganda Ministry's press directive of December 12 stressed that Roosevelt should be denounced "again and again" as the man responsible for the expansion of the war. See VIdRMVP, 326/41, December 12, 1941, ZSg. 109/28, BAK, SO.
141. Ibid., p. 1803.
142. Ibid., p. 1804.
143. Ibid., p. 1808.
144. Ibid.
145. Ibid., p. 1810.

146. See Ian Kershaw, *Hitler, 1936–1945: Nemesis* (New York: Norton, 2000), pp. 448–449.

147. Goebbels, entry for December 13, 1941, *TBJG*, II/2, pp. 498–499.

148. Gü, "Japans Kampf gegen das Weltjudentum," *Die Judentum* 5, no. 22 (December 24, 1941): 245–247.

149. Ibid., pp. 245–246.

150. Ibid., p. 247.

151. Johann von Leers, *Kräfte hinter Roosevelt* (Berlin: Theodor Fritsch Verlag, 1941). Von Leers was one of the most prolific of the Nazi anti-Semitic propagandists. See, for example, his *14 Jahre Judenrepublik: Die Geschichte eines Rassenkampfes* (Berlin-Schöneberg: NS Druck und Verlag, 1933); *Der Verbrechernatur der Juden* (Berlin: Hochmuth, 1944); *Geschichte auf rassischer Grundlage* (Leipzig: Reclam, 1934); *Juden sehen dich an* (Berlin-Schöneberg; NS Druck und Verlag, 1930–1939).

152. Von Leers, *Kräfte hinter Roosevelt*, pp. 80–82.

153. Ibid., p. 109.

154. Goebbels, entry for December 31, 1941, *TBJG*, II/2, p. 610.

5. Propaganda in the Shadow of the Death Camps

1. About a third had some anti-Semitic content. Twelve appeared from January to July 1942 alone. See the poster collection in the Landeshauptarchiv Koblenz: Bestand 712 (Plakate) Wandzeitung *Parole der Woche,* published by the NSDAP, Reichspropagandaleitung, Munich, Landeshauptarchiv Koblenz.

2. VIdRMVP 33/42, January 7, 1942, ZSg. 109/30, BAK, SO.

3. Leni Yahil, *The Holocaust: The Fate of European Jewry,* trans. Ina Friedman and Haya Galai (New York: Oxford University Press, 1990), p. 294.

4. Ibid., pp. 378–385.

5. Judith Tydnor Baumel, "Extermination Camps," in Walter Laqueur, ed., *The Holocaust Encyclopedia* (New Haven, Conn.: Yale University Press, 2001), pp. 174–179.

6. On journalism during the Nazi years, see Norbert Frei and Johannes Schmitz, *Journalismus im Dritten Reich* (Munich: Verlag C. H. Beck, 1999); Günther Galician, *Auf verlorenem Posten: Die Frankfurter Zeitung im Dritten Reich* (Berlin: Siedler Verlag, 1986); Alexander Hardy, *Hitler's Secret Weapon: The Managed Press in Nazi Germany* (New York: Vantage, 1967).

7. Rüdiger Övermann, *Deutsche militärische Verluste im Zweiten Weltkrieg* (Munich: Oldenbourg, 2000), pp. 238–239.

8. Joseph Goebbels, *Die Tagebücher von Joseph Goebbels (TBJG),* ed. Elke Fröhlich (Munich: Sauer, 1994), entry for March 6, 1942, II/3, p. 422.

9. Max Domarus, *Hitler: Reden und Proklamationen, 1932–1945,* vol. 2, *Untergang,* 1939–1945 (Neustadt: Schmidt, 1963), pp. 1820–1821. At his January 13, 1942, Minister's Conference, Goebbels ordered: "In the future there are to be no more references to Anglo-Saxons, but only to Anglo-American plutocracy. The concept 'Anglo-Saxon' suggests too much their German descent and is not at the present moment suitable as a concept for our enemies." Willi G. Boelcke, ed., *The Secret Conferences of Dr. Goebbels: The Nazi Propaganda War, 1939–1943,* trans. Ewald Osers (New York: Dutton, 1970), p. 202; see also, Willi G. Boelcke, ed., *"Wollt Ihr den totalen Krieg?":* *Die geheimen Goebbels-Konferenzen, 1939–1943* (Munich: Deutsche Taschenbuch Verlag, 1969), p. 270.

10. Ibid., p. 1821.

11. Joseph Goebbels, "Wir bauen eine Brücke," January 11, 1942, in *Das eherne Herz: Reden und Aufsätze aus den Jahren 1941–42* (Munich: Zentralverlag der NSDAP, 1943), pp. 172, 174. The first print run of the book was 50,000 copies. Goebbels repeated the argument on February 15, 1942, in "Blick über die Weltlage," and on May 17, 1942, in "Die Ostfront," ibid., pp. 209–214, 316–321.

12. "Sie haben den Krieg gewollt!!" (January 14, 1942) Bestand 712 (Plakate) Wandzeitung *Parole der Woche,* no. 1790, Folge (series) 3, Landeshauptarchiv Koblenz.

13. Goebbels, entry for January 20, 1942, *TBJG,* II/3, p. 154.

14. Goebbels, "Wandlung der Seelen," January 25, 1942, in *Das eherne Herz,* pp. 190–191.

15. "Churchills Verrat an Europa" (January 28, 1942), Bestand 712 (Plakate), Wandzeitung *Parole der Woche,* no. 1813, Folge 5, Landeshauptarchiv Koblenz.

16. Ibid. Goebbels referred to a "jüdisch-bolschewistischen Ausrottungskrieg."

17. Boelcke, *The Secret Conferences of Dr. Goebbels,* p. 215. In his diary entries in late February 1942, Goebbels described Cripps as "our best propagandist" and "Stalin's messenger in London," whose "participation in the [Churchill] government is really priceless. German propaganda should set aside an additional honorarium for him." Goebbels, entries for February 20 and 25, *TBJG,* II/3, pp. 335, 373–374.

18. Goebbels, "Der Gefangene des Kreml," *VB,* August 24, 1942, p. 1.

19. "Juden Komplott gegen Europa" (1942), Imperial War Museum, London, Department of Art, PST 8359.

20. Hitler, speech of January 30, 1942, in Domarus, *Hitler,* 2:1828–1829.

21. Goebbels, entry for January 31, 1942, *TBJG,* II/3, p. 228.

22. Entry for February 15, 1942, ibid., pp. 320–321.

23. Ibid.

24. "Das Ziel der Kriegsverbrecher" (February 11, 1942), Bestand 712 (Plakate), Wandzeitung *Parole der Woche,* no. 1794, Folge 7, Landeshauptarchiv Koblenz.

25. "Hoover Plan Rejection a Blunder, Says Official," *Washington Post,* May 20, 1941, p. 4.

26. "Das Ziel der Kriegsverbrecher."

27. Ibid.

28. Goebbels, entry for March 6, 1942, *TBJG,* II/3, pp. 425–426.

29. Entry for March 7, 1942, ibid., p. 431–432.

30. Hitler, speech of March 15, 1942, in Domarus, *Hitler,* 2:1849; see also Adolf Hitler (March 15, 1942), "Ansprache im Berliner Zeughaus anläßlich des Heldengedenktages," in Walter Roller and Susanne Höschel, eds., *Judenverfolgung und jüdisches Leben unter den Bedingungen der nationalsozialistischen Gewaltherrschaft,* vol. 1, *Tondokumente und Rundfunksendungen, 1930–1946* (Potsdam: Verlag für Berlin-Brandenburg, 1996) p. 207.

31. Hitler, speech of March 15, 1942, in Domarus, *Hitler,* 2:1849.

32. Goebbels, entry for March 16, 1942, *TBJG,* II/3, pp. 431–432.

33. Entry for March 20, 1942, ibid., p. 513.

34. Entry for March 27, 1942, ibid., II/2, pp. 431–432.

35. Entry for March 29, 1942, ibid., p. 576.

36. For additional diary entries in April and May 1941 that mention "the realization of the Führer's prophecy," "paying a high price," and other euphemisms for mass murder, see the entry for April 21, 1942, *TBJG,* II/3, p. 378; and the entries for April 27, 1942, ibid., II/4, p. 160; May 11, 1942, ibid., p. 272; and May 24, 1942, ibid., p. 355.

37. Entry for April 24, 1942, ibid., II/3, p. 160.

38. The literature on Nazi racial pseudoscience is extensive. See, for example, George Mosse, *Toward the Final Solution: A History of European Racism* (Madison: University of Wisconsin Press, 1985); Benno Muller-Hill, *Murderous Science: Elimination by Scientific Selection of Jews, Gypsies, and Others in Germany, 1933–1945* (Plain View, N.Y.: Cold Spring Harbor Laboratory Press, 1998); Ute Deichmann, *Biologists under Hitler* (Cambridge, Mass.: Harvard University Press, 1996); Michael Burleigh and Wolfgang Wipperman, *The Racial State: Germany, 1933–1945* (New York: Cambridge University Press, 1991); Susan Bachrach, ed., *Deadly Medicine: Creating the Master Race* (Washington, D.C.: United States Holocaust Memorial Museum, 2004; Chapel Hill: University of North Carolina Press, 2004).

39. "Die Katze lässt das Mausen nicht!" (July 1, 1942), Bestand 712

(Plakate), Wandzeitung *Parole der Woche,* no. 1704, Folge 27, Landeshauptarchiv Koblenz.

40. See Ian Kershaw, *Hitler, 1936–1945: Nemesis* (New York: Norton, 2000), pp. 510–511; Daniel T. Brigham, "Hitler Now Looks to 'Next Winter'; Gets New Power over His Officials; R.A.F. Blasts Rostock, Skoda Plant," *New York Times,* April 27, 1942, p. 1; "Excerpts from Reichsfuehrer Adolf Hitler's Review of the War before the German Reichstag," *New York Times,* April 27, 1942, p. 4. The *Times* excerpt conveyed the general sense of Hitler's attack on the Jews but left out some of its most inflammatory passages.

41. Hitler, speech of April 26, 1942, in Domarus, *Hitler,* 2:1866–1867.

42. Ibid., 2:1866–1867; see also, "Der Führer sprach," *Die Judenfrage* 6, no. 10 (May 15, 1942): 1. Emphasis in the original.

43. On Wilson's diplomacy as an effort to establish a democratic, noncommunist bulwark *against* the Soviet Union and Communist revolution in Europe, see Arno J. Mayer, *Politics and Diplomacy of Peacemaking: Containment and Counterrevolution at Versailles, 1918–1919* (New York: Harcourt, 1967).

44. Hitler, speech of April 26, 1942, in Domarus, *Hitler,* 2:1868.

45. Ibid., p. 1869.

46. "Die Drahtzieher! Es sind nur Juden!" (May 27, 1942), Imperial War Museum, London, Department of Art, PST 8355; also available in Bestand 712 (Plakate), Wandzeitung *Parole der Woche,* no. 1800, Folge 22, Landeshauptarchiv Koblenz.

47. Ibid.

48. "Ley, Robert," in Ernst Klee, ed., *Das Personenlexikon zum Dritten Reich: Wer war was vor und nach 1945* (Frankfurt am Main: Fischer, 2003), p. 370.

49. Robert Ley (May 10, 1939), "Ansprache auf der Konstituierenden Sitzung der Gauarbeitskammer," in Roller and Höschel, *Judenverfolgung und jüdisches Leben,* 1:151.

50. Robert Ley (end of 1939), "Ansprache vor deutschen Arbeitern in Lodz," ibid., p. 158.

51. Robert Ley (September 3, 1941), "Ansprache in Troisdorf anläßlich der erstmaligen Verleihung von Kriegsverdienstkreuzern an Frauen," ibid., p. 189.

52. Robert Ley (February 6, 1942), "Schulungsappell der politischen und wirtschaftlichen Unterführer des Hauses Siemens im Berliner Sportpalast," ibid., pp. 206–207.

53. Robert Ley (May 10, 1942), "Ansprache auf einer gemeinsamen Kundgebung der NSDAP und der NSB in Heerlen," ibid., p. 210. In his speeches, Ley repeatedly used the German verbs *ausrotten* and *vernichten.*

54. See Richard Overy, "The Means to Victory: Bombers and Bombing," in *Why the Allies Won* (New York: Norton, 1995), pp. 101–133; Mary Nolan, "Air Wars, Memory Wars," *Central European History* 38, no. 1 (2005): 7–40; and Thomas Childers, "*Facilis descensus averni est:* The Allied Bombing Campaign of Germany and the Issue of German Suffering," *Central European History* 38, no. 1 (2005): 75–105.

55. Hans-Ulrich Thamer, *Verführung und Gewalt: Deutschland, 1933–1945* (Berlin: Siedler Verlag, 1986), p. 751.

56. Goebbels, "Der Luft- und Nervenkrieg," June 14, 1942, in *Das eherne Herz,* pp. 344–350.

57. "Der Mann, der den Bombenkrieg gegen die Zivilbevölkerung erfunden hat," Bestand 712 (Plakate), Wandzeitung *Parole der Woche,* no. 1770, Folge 43, Landeshauptarchiv Koblenz.

58. "Nazis to Kill Jews in Reprisal for British Raids," *Washington Post,* June 14, 1942, p. 12; "Nazis Blame Jews for Big Bombings," *New York Times,* June 14, 1942, p. 7.

59. Goebbels, "Die sogennante russische Seele," July 19, 1942, in *Das eherne Herz,* pp. 402–403.

60. Ibid., p. 404.

61. See Gerhard Weinberg, *A World at Arms: A Global History of World War II* (New York: Cambridge University Press, 1994), pp. 348–363.

62. See Bernard Wasserstein, *Britain and the Jews of Europe, 1939–1945* (New York: Oxford University Press, 1988), pp. 17–39.

63. Goebbels, entry for May 28, 1942, *TBJG,* II/4, p. 384.

64. Klaus Gensicke, *Der Mufti von Jerusalem, Amin el-Husseini und die Nationalsozialisten* (Frankfurt am Main: Verlag Peter Lang, 1988). On their contact, beginning in 1937, see pp. 45–55. For a very early and quite detailed account of al-Husseini's cooperation with the Nazis, see Simon Wiesenthal, *Großmufti–Großagent der Achse* (Salzburg: Ried Verlag, 1946).

65. Amin al Husseini, "Nr. 18a; Rundfunkerklärung 'an das ägyptische Volk,'" July 2, 1942, in Gerhard Höpp, ed., *Mufti-Papiere: Briefe, Memoranden, Reden und Aufrufe Amin al-Husainis aus dem Exil, 1940–1945* (Berlin: Klaus Schwarz Verlag, 2001), pp. 45–46. Al-Husseini's name is spelled a variety of ways in German sources.

66. Goebbels, entry for May 28, 1942, *TBJG,* II/5, pp. 274–275.

67. "Die islamische Welt als Kulturfaktor," *Zeitschriften-Dienst* 175/44, no. 7514 (September 11, 1942): 2.

68. Ibid.

69. "Abschrift: Entspricht dem von Dr. Dietrich und Dr. Goebbels unter-

schriebenen Original," 1936–1944, NARA, T70, RG 242, Records of the National Socialist German Labor Party, roll 3, pp. 3505763–3505766.

70. Ibid.

71. "Ein weitblickender Engländer," Bestand 712 (Plakate), Wandzeitung *Parole der Woche,* no. 1722, Folge 33, Landeshauptarchiv Koblenz. Emphasis in the original.

72. "Der Jude Kaufman übertrumpft!" (August 19, 1942), Bestand 712 (Plakate), Wandzeitung *Parole der Woche,* no. 1758, Folge 34, Landeshauptarchiv Koblenz. Emphasis in the original.

73. "Roosevelt und seine Juden: Baruch wird USA.-Wirtschaftsdiktator," *VB,* September 13, 1942, p. 1.

74. "Nation-Wide Gasoline Curb Pledged Soon by Roosevelt after Baruch Asks Action," *New York Times,* September 11, 1942, pp. 1, 14; see also "The Rubber Inquiry," *New York Times,* August 7, 1942, p. 16. The Baruch Committee recommendations included a speed limit of thirty-five miles an hour and a reduction in the average annual mileage limit per car from 6,700 to 5,000 miles.

75. See David S. Wyman, *The World Reacts to the Holocaust* (Baltimore, Md.: Johns Hopkins University Press, 1996).

76. On the image of the United States in Nazi Germany, see Philipp Gassert, *Amerika im Dritten Reich: Ideologie, Propaganda und Volksmeinung, 1933–1945* (Stuttgart: Franz Steiner Verlag, 1997).

77. "Die Maske Fällt!" (September 30, 1942), Imperial War Museum, Department of Art, PST 8361; also in Bestand 712 (Plakate), Wandzeitung *Parole der Woche,* no. 1787, Folge 40, Landeshauptarchiv Koblenz.

78. Ibid. Emphasis in the original.

79. Hitler, speech of September 30, 1942, in Domarus, *Hitler,* 2:1915.

80. On the context of the speech, see Kershaw, *Hitler,* 2:535–536.

81. Hitler, speech of September 30, 1942, in Domarus, *Hitler,* 2:1920. See also Adolf Hitler (September 30, 1942), "Ansprache auf einer Kundgebung im Berliner Sportpalast zur Eröffnung des Kriegswinterwerks," in Roller and Höschel, *Judenverfolgung und jüdisches Leben,* 1:216–217. The editors of the October 1 issue of *Die Judenfrage* put this quotation on the front page. See "Der Führer sprach," *Die Judenfrage* 6, no. 19 (October 1, 1943): 1.

82. "Das Lachen wird ihnen vergehen!!!" Wandzeitung *Parole der Woche,* NSDAP, Reichspropagandaleitung, Hoover Institution Archives, poster collection, GE 3848.

83. Hermann Göring (October 4, 1942), "Ansprache auf einer Feier zum Erntedankfest im Berliner Sportpalast," Roller and Höschel, *Jüdenverfolgung und jüdisches Leben,* 1:217.

84. Ibid.

85. Adolf Hitler (November 8, 1942), "Ansprache im Münchener Löwenbräukeller anläßlich einer Gedenkfeier zum Marsch auf die Feldherrnhalle, 1923," in Roller and Höschel, *Judenverfolgung und jüdisches Leben*, 1:219.

86. "Themen der Zeit, Roosevelts Kriegsziel," *Zeitschriften-Dienst* 184/53, no. 7859 (November 13, 1942).

87. Weinberg, *A World at Arms*, pp. 360–363.

88. "Gangstertum und Judentum in den USA," *Zeitschriften-Dienst* 185, no. 54 (November 20, 1942): 7899.

89. "Wer ist am Kriege schuld?" *Parole der Woche*, November 18–24, 1942. Institut für Zeitungsforschung, Stadt Dortmund, *Parole der Woche: Parteiamtliche Wandzeitung der NSDAP*, Folge 29/22.

90. Ibid. Emphasis in the original.

91. Amin al-Husseini, speech no. 45a, "Rundfunkrede an die Nordafrikaner," November 25–26, 1942, in Höpp, *Mufti-Papiere*, p. 115.

92. Amin al Husseini, "Nr. 42: Rundfunkrede an die Araber" ("Märtyrerrede"), November 11, 1942, ibid., p. 103.

93. Ibid., p. 104.

94. Ibid.

95. Ibid., pp. 104–105.

96. "Senate, House Join in Palestine Plea: 63 Senators, 181 Representatives Assail Mass Murder of Jews by Germany," *New York Times*, December 5, 1942, p. 9.

97. "11 Allies Condemn Nazi War on Jews, United Nations Issue [*sic*] Joint Declaration of Protest on 'Cold Blooded Extermination,'" *New York Times*, December 18, 1942, p. 1.

98. "Nazi Retribution Widened by Eden; He Warns German People of Responsibility If Cruelties to Jews Are Continued; MPs Stand in Silence," *New York Times*, December 18, 1942, p. 10.

99. See Wasserstein, *Britain and the Jews of Europe*, p. 174.

100. Goebbels, entry for December 9, 1942, *TBJG*, II/6, p. 415.

101. Entry for December 12, 1942, ibid., p. 434.

102. Boelcke, *The Secret Conferences of Dr. Goebbels*, p. 308; Boelcke, *"Wollt Ihr den totalen Krieg?"* pp. 409–410.

103. Goebbels, entry for December 13, 1942, *TBJG*, II/6, pp. 438–439.

104. Entry for December 14, 1942, ibid., pp. 445–446.

105. Boelcke, *The Secret Conferences of Dr. Goebbels*, pp. 308–309; Boelcke, *"Wollt Ihr den totalen Krieg?"* p. 410. In the next evening's diary entry Goebbels noted that the Propaganda Ministry would thus create a "propaganda campaign similar to what the English were doing with the Jewish

question. I assume that the English will then quickly lose interest in continuing to talk to us in this tone about the Jewish question." Goebbels, entry for December 15, 1942, *TBJG*, II/6, p. 449.

106. Boelcke, *The Secret Conferences of Dr. Goebbels,* p. 309; Boelcke, *"Wollt Ihr den totalen Krieg?"* p. 411.

107. Goebbels, December 17, 1942, *TBJG*, II/6, p. 461.

108. Entry for December 19, 1942, ibid., p. 472.

109. Klaus Gensicke, *Der Mufti von Jerusalem*, pp. 134–139.

110. Cited ibid., p. 155.

111. Amin al-Husseini, "Nr. 55: Rede zur Eröffnung des Islamischen Zentral-Instituts in Berlin, 18.12.1942," in Höpp, *Mufti-Papiere*, pp. 123–126.

112. Ibid., p. 124.

113. Ibid., pp. 125–126.

114. VIdRMVP, 323/42, December 17, 1942, ZSg. 109/40, BAK, SO.

115. "Das 'Nachkriegs-Programm' des Zionismus," *Die Judenfrage* 6, no. 24 (December 15, 1942): 1–2.

116. Johann von Leers, "Judentum und Islam als Gegensätze," *Die Judenfrage* 6, no. 24 (December 24, 1942): 275–278.

117. Ibid., p. 278.

118. Goebbels, entry for December 31, 1942, *TBJG*, II/6, p. 534.

6. *"The Jews Are Guilty of Everything"*

1. See Martin Gilbert, *The Macmillan Atlas of the Holocaust* (New York: Da Capo, 1982), pp. 142–58; and Leni Yahil, *The Holocaust: The Fate of European Jewry* (New York: Oxford University Press, 1990), pp. 404–414.

2. Max Domarus, ed., *Hitler: Reden und Proklamationen, 1932–1945,* vol. 2, Untergang, 1939–1945 (Neustadt: Schmidt, 1963), p. 1967.

3. Hitler, speech of January 1, 1943, in Domarus, *Hitler,* 2:1970–1971.

4. Horst Seemann, "Roosevelt gegen Europa," *Die Judenfrage* 7, no. 1 (January 1, 1943): 3–5.

5. "Samuel Irving Rosenman, der wahre Präsident der USA," *Die Judenfrage* 7, no. 3 (February 1, 1943): 32–33.

6. "Draft Statement to the Press," Casablanca Conference, January 22, 1943, *Foreign Relations of the United States: The Conferences at Washington, 1941–1942, and Casablanca, 1943* (Washington, D.C.: U.S. Government Printing Office, 1958), pp. 834–835.

7. Joseph Goebbels, *Die Tagebücher von Joseph Goebbels (TBJG)*, ed. Elke Fröhlich (Munich: Sauer, 1994), entry for January 25, 1943, II/7, pp. 189–190.

8. "Zur Lage," *Zeitschriften-Dienst* no. 195/64 (January 29, 1943); Goebbels, entry for January 29, 1943, *TBJG*, II/7, p. 219.

9. Domarus, *Hitler,* 2:1978.

10. Joseph Goebbels, "Führer befiehl, wir folgen: Rede zum zehnten Jahrestag der Machtübernahme" (January 30, 1943), in Goebbels, *Der steile Aufstieg: Reden und Aufsätze aus den Jahren 1942/43,* 2nd ed. (Munich: Zentralverlag der NSDAP, 1944), pp. 138–150. The print run was 55,000 copies.

11. On all fronts, the Wehrmacht suffered 83,792 deaths in December 1942 and 185,376 in January 1943, the bulk of them due to the encirclement and defeat at Stalingrad. See Rüdiger Overmans, *Deutsche militärische Verluste im Zweiten Weltkrieg* (Munich: Oldenbourg, 2000), p. 238.

12. "Sie starben, damit Deutschland lebe," *VB,* February 4, 1943, p. 1.

13. "Die Kampfparole," *Zeitschriften-Dienst* 196/65, no. 8312 (February 5, 1943): 1. The text referred to the "Vernichtungswillen des jüdischen Bolschewismus" and the alternative of "entweder Vernichtung oder lebenslange Verelendung und Versklavung." These documents were also used in preparation for the Ministries Trial after the war. See "Die Kampfparole" (February 5, 1943) *Deutscher Wochendienst* directive 8312, U.S. Nuerenberg War Crimes Trials, *United States of America v. Ernst von Weizsäcker et al.,* case 11, November 4, 1947, in NARA, RG 238, War Crimes Records Collection, M 897, roll 34, doc. 4714, prosecution exhibit 1265.

14. "Wenn der Jude an der Macht ist," *Zeitschriften-Dienst* 196/65, no. 8314 (February 5, 1943).

15. "Europa wehrt die Juden ab," *Zeitschriften-Dienst* 196/65, no. 8312 (February 5, 1943).

16. "Sie entgehen der Sühne für ihre Kriegshetze nicht, USA.-Juden müssen mit einer Welle der Intoleranz rechnen," *VB,* January 14, 1943, p. 1; "Hinter Roosevelt steckt Rosenman: Ein Erzjude auf dem Thron der USA.," *VB,* January 16, 1943, p. 1.

17. "Wallace verrät Roosevelts Zukunftsträume; Die ganze Welt ein Feld jüdisch-amerikanischer Ausbeuter; Wer den USA.-Befehlen nicht nachkommt, soll erbarmungslos bombardiert werden," *VB,* February 7, 1943, p. 1.

18. Goebbels, entry for February 8, 1943, *TBJG,* II/7, p. 295.

19. Ibid., p. 296. Hitler used the nouns *Liquidierung* and *Ausrottung* and the verb *ausgelöscht* to refer to the fate of Germany if it lost the war.

20. On the impact of the war on perceptions of the Soviet Union in the West, see François Furet, *the Passing of an Illusion: The Idea of Communism in the Twentieth Century,* trans. Deborah Furet (Chicago: University of Chicago Press, 1999).

21. Goebbels, entry for February 9, 1943, *TBJG,* II/7, p. 304. See also entry for February 10, 1943, ibid., p. 312.

22. "Die neueste Ausgeburt jüdischen Hasses, Sie wollen das deutsche Volk geistig und körperlich vernichten, Wir werden die plutokratischen und bolschewistischen Sadisten zu Boden schlagen," *VB*, February 11, 1943, p. 1.

23. Ibid.

24. Boelcke, ed., *Secret Conferences of Dr. Goebbels*, p. 330.

25. "Hard Blows in '43; Roosevelt Promises 'Bad News' for Nazis, Italians and the Japanese," *New York Times*, February 13, 1943, p. 1.

26. "Roosevelt wirft Europa dem Bolschewismus als Beute hin; Judas Strohmann macht Kotau vor Moskau–Wir werden ihm die gebührende Antwort geben," *VB*, February 14, 1943, p. 1.

27. Boelcke, *Secret Conferences of Dr. Goebbels*, p. 333.

28. Joseph Goebbels, "Nr. 17., 18.2.43—Berlin, Sportpalast—Kundgebung des Gaues Berlin der NSDAP," in *Reden, 1939–1945* (Munich: Wilhelm Heyne Verlag, 1972) 2:172–208. This text draws on the radio transcript. See also Joseph Goebbels, "Nun, Volk steh auf, und Sturm brich los!" in Goebbels, *Der steile Aufstieg*, pp. 167–204; Günter Moltmann, "Goebbels Rede zum Totalen Krieg am 18. February 1943," *Vierteljahreshefte fur Zeitgeschichte*, 1964; and Iring Fetscher's comphrehensive discussion in *Joseph Goebbels im Berliner Sportpalast 1943: "Wollt ihr den totalen Krieg?"* (Hamburg: Europäische Verlagsanstalt, 1998). On the distribution of the fourteen million copies to regional *Gau* propaganda offices, see Reichspropagandaleitung, Berlin, Meldung (announcement) no. 3002, Hauptamt, Propaganda, September 10, 1943, BA Berlin, Reichspropagandaleitung, NS 18, folder 848, p. 80.

29. Goebbels, "Nr. 17, 18.2.43–Berlin Sportpalast," p. 173.

30. Ibid., p. 177.

31. Ibid., pp. 178–179.

32. Ibid., p. 181.

33. Ibid., pp. 182–183. Goebbels referred to the "vollkommener und radikalster Ausrott[ung], [Aus]schaltung des Judentums."

34. Ibid., p. 183. Emphasis in the original.

35. Ibid.

36. Ibid., pp. 185–186.

37. Ibid., pp. 195–199.

38. Ibid., pp. 204–206.

39. Ibid., p. 208.

40. Goebbels, entry for February 19, 1943, *TBJG*, II/7, p. 373.

41. "Leidenschaftliche Zustimmung unseres Volkes bedeutsam; Starker Widerhall in aller Welt," *VB*, February 20, 1943, p. 1.

42. Goebbels, entry for March 2, 1943, *TBJG*, II/7, p. 454.

43. "Vor 25 Jahren verkündete ich den Sieg der Partei, Heute prophezeie ich den Sieg der Deutschen, Ansprache des Führers an seine alten Parteigenossen . . . ," *VB*, February 26, 1943, p. 1.

44. Domarus, *Hitler,* 2:1991–1992.

45. Ibid., p. 1992. On its front page, *Die Judenfrage* excerpted this passage, which concluded with Hitler's prediction, "We will break and smash the power of the Jewish world coalition" on the path to victory. "Worte des Führers, aus der Proklamation des Führers zur Parteigründungsfeier in München am 24. Februar 1943," *Die Judenfrage* 7, no. 6 (March 15, 1943): 1.

46. Joseph Goebbels, "Die Krise Europas," in Goebbels, *Der steile Aufstieg,* p. 205.

47. Ibid., p. 206.

48. Ibid., pp. 207–208.

49. Joseph Goebbels, "Damals und Heute," in Goebbels, *Der steile Aufstieg,* pp. 214–217.

50. Goebbels, entry for March 3, 1943, *TBJG,* II/7, p. 526.

51. "Die Briten–Helfer des Bolschewismus," and "USA auch in Vorderasien," *Zeitschriften-Dienst* 199/68, nos. 8433 and 8435 (February 26, 1943): 2.

52. "Aufruf des Großmufti gegen die Todfeinde des Islams, Araber werden für ihre Freiheit an der Seite der Achse kämpfen," *VB*, March 20, 1943, p. 1.

53. Ibid.

54. Goebbels, entry for March 31, 1943, TBJG, II/7, p. 676. In his postwar memoir, Helmut Sündermann, Dietrich's chief of staff in Berlin, wrote that anti-Semitism was important for Hitler "above all" as a component of his "war propaganda struggle with the enemies in the East and West." This was why, Sündermann continued, "during the last two years of the war he repeatedly pushed German journalists to put the international impact of Jewry at the center of their commentaries and headlines." Sündermann, *Tagesparolen: Deutsche Presseanweisungen, 1939–1945: Hitlers Propaganda und Kriegsführung* (Leoni am Starnberger See: Druffel-Verlag, 1973), p. 259.

55. "Juden sind Verbrecher," *Zeitschriften-Dienst* 204/73, no. 8615 (April 2, 1943): 2.

56. The following week, the *Periodical Service* offered yet more themes for editors to pursue: "Jews in the war economy"; "Europe defends itself against the Jews"; "When the Jews are in power"; "Jews in French North Africa"; "Japan's struggle against Jewry"; "Jews in South America"; "Jews and plutocrats in the English aristocracy"; "Jews in culture"; "Jews in the economy"; "The influence of Jewry in the world press." See "Zur Lage," *Zeitschriften-Dienst* 205/74, no. 8648 (April 9, 1943): 1.

57. See "Davies's 'Mission' Praised at Rally, *New York Times,* May 21, 1943, p. 4; "Lamont Succeeds to Morgan's Post," *New York Times,* March 18, 1943, p. 27. For a telling example of the wartime mood, see comments by the acting American secretary of state, Edward Stettinius, Soviet ambassador Andrei Gromyko, and the earl of Halifax, British ambassador, at a rally of the National Council of American-Soviet Friendship in Madison Square Garden, "Excerpts of Speeches at Soviet Friendship Rally," *New York Times,* November 17, 1944, p. 6.

58. Joseph Davies was American ambassador to the Soviet Union in 1937–38. The 1940 edition of *The American Jewish Yearbook* included a listing of Jews who had served or were then serving as American ambassador. Davies's name is not on the list. See "Jews in the Diplomatic Service of the United States," in Harry Schneiderman, ed., *American Jewish Yearbook 5701,* vol. 42, *October 3, 1940, to September 21, 1941* (Philadelphia: Jewish Publication Society of America, 1940), pp. 585–586.

59. "Der jüdische Krieg," *VB,* April 8, 1943, p. 1.

60. Peter Calvocaressi and Guy Wynt, *Total War: Causes and Courses of the Second World War* (New York: Penguin, 1972), p. 344.

61. VIdRMVP 94/43 (1. Erg. [first addendum]), ZSg. 109/42, BAK, SO.

62. "Tagesparole des Reichspressechefs," April 13, 1943, cited in Sündermann, *Tagesparolen,* p. 246. Also see "Die jüdische Brücke," *VB,* April 8, 1943, p. 1.

63. Joseph Goebbels, "Tagesparole," April 14, 1943, in Sündermann, *Tagesparolen,* p. 253.

64. The *VB* ran a lead article titled "The Secret of Katyn": "Das Geheimnis von Katyn," *VB,* April 15, 1943, p. 1.

65. VIdRMVP 96/43, April 14, 1943, ZSg. 109/42, BAK, SO; see also Goebbels, "Tagesparole," April 14, 1943.

66. "Der Jude Davies: 'Wir können der Sowjetunion trauen': Katyn–ein Beispiel für Judas Anschlag auf Europa," *VB,* April 16, 1943, p. 1.

67. Goebbels, entry for April 17, 1943, *TBJG,* II/8, pp. 115, 124.

68. "Zur Lage," *Zeitschriften-Dienst* 207/76, no. 8710 (April 22, 1943): 1.

69. "Der Jüdische Ritualmord," *Zeitschriften-Dienst* 207/76, no. 8713 (April 22, 1943).

70. "Warsaw's Ghetto Fights Deportation; Tanks Reported Used in Battle to Oust 35,000 Jews," *New York Times,* April 23, 1943, p. 9.

71. "England vor den Kremljuden zu Kreuz gebrochen," *VB,* May 3, 1943, p. 1.

72. "USA. und England unter dem Befehl des Weltjudentums, Plutokraten identifizieren sich mit den jüdisch-bolschewistischen Mördern," *VB,* May 6, 1943, p. 1.

73. "Battle Is Reported in Warsaw's Ghetto," *New York Times*, May 7, 1943, p. 7.

74. "Red Cross Decision Made on 'Massacre,'" *New York Times*, April 23, 1943, p. 3; "Massacre Inquiry Depends on Soviet," *New York Times*, April 24, 1943, p. 4.

75. VIdRMVP, V.I. 155/43 (1. Erg.), April 28, 1943, ZSg. 109/42, BAK, SO; also cited in "Tagesparole," April 28, 1943, in Sündermann, *Tagesparolen*, p. 254.

76. VIdRMVP 106/43 (1. Erg.), April 29, 1943, ZSg. 109/42, BAK, SO; VIdRMVP 106/43 (Erg.), April 29, 1943, in War Crimes Records Collection, U.S. Nuerenberg War Crimes Trials, *United States of America v. Ernst von Weizsäcker et al.*, case 11, November 4, 1947, in NARA, RG 238, War Crimes Records Collection, M 897, roll 34, doc. 4705, prosecution exhibit 1270. Copy from "Oberheitmann Material," NG 3800, vol. 12, pp. 67–68. For a further directive that stressed the Jewish links to the Katyn massacres, see VIdRMVP, V.I. 109/43, May 3, 1943, ZSg. 109/42, BAK, SO.

77. "Katyn entlarvt erneut das Weltjudentum, Europa erkennt das Komplott der Plutokraten und Sowjetjuden, England und USA. machen jämmerliche Verschleierungsversuche," *VB*, April 30, 1943, p. 1.

78. "Jüdisch-bolschewistische Blutschuld," *Die Judenfrage* 7, no. 9 (May 1, 1943): 1–2.

79. "Katyn!" Redner Schnellinformation, Lieferung 56, NSDAP Reichspropagandaleitung, Hauptamt Propaganda, Amt: Rednerwesen, May 3, 1943, NARA, Captured German Documents, T-81, roll 683, pp. 4721681–4721684. The German here reads: "Zum Weltbegriff jüdisch-bolschewistischen Blutrausches."

80. Ibid., pp. 4721682, 4721684. On the same day, the *VB*'s front-page lead was "England Knuckles Under to Kremlin Jews; Cynical Abandonment of Poland in Light of the European Press." See "England vor den Kremljuden zu Kreuz gekrochen, Die zynische Preisgabe Polens im Lichte der europäischen Presse," *VB*, May 3, 1943, p. 1.

81. "Die Judenfrage als innen- und außenpolitisches Kampfmittel," Redner-Schnellinformation, NSDAP. Reichspropagandaleitung, Hauptamt Propaganda, Amt: Rednerwesen, May 5, 1943, NARA, Captured German Documents, T-81, roll 683, pp. 4721685–4721686.

82. Ibid.

83. "USA. und England unter dem Befehl des Weltjudentums, Plutokraten identifizieren sich mit den jüdisch-bolschewistischen Mördern," *VB*, May 6, 1943, p. 1.

84. Ibid.

85. Goebbels, entry for April 27, 1943, *TBJG*, II/8, p. 173.

86. Joseph Goebbels, "Der Krieg und die Juden," in *Der steile Aufstieg,* pp. 263–270.

87. Ibid., pp. 263–264.

88. Ibid., p. 266.

89. Ibid., pp. 269–270.

90. Ibid., p. 270.

91. The story in the *New York Times* ran on page 34. See "Goebbels Turns Fire on 'Jewish Problem,'" *New York Times,* May 9, 1943, p. 34.

92. Goebbels, entry for May 10, 1943, *TBJG*, II/8, p. 255.

93. Ibid., p. 237.

94. "Im Zeichen wachsender Judenfeindlichkeit, Jüdische Angst schreit in England nach dem Büttel, Profithyänen verlangen Mißbrauch der Staatsgewalt," *VB,* May 9, 1943, p. 1.

95. Goebbels, entry for May 10, 1943, *TBJG*, II/8, p. 261.

96. "Moskau wird offizielles Zentrum des Weltjudentums, Judenstaat Palästina als Eckstein der Sowjetkontrolle im Mittelmeer," *VB,* May 12, 1943, p. 1.

97. "Judendämmerung in aller Welt," Redner-Schnellinformation, Lieferung 60, NSDAP, Reichspropagandaleitung, Hauptamt Propaganda, Amt: Rednerwesen, NARA, Captured German Records, T-81, roll 683, pp. 4721687–4721690.

98. "All Warsaw Jews Held 'Liquidated,'" *New York Times,* May 15, 1943, p. 6.

99. Ibid.

100. "Jews' Last Stand Felled 1,000 Nazis," *New York Times,* May 22, 1943, p. 4; "35,000 Slain Jews Honored at Rally," *New York Times,* June 20, 1943, p. 34.

101. "Jüdisch-amerikanischer Imperialismus läuft auf Hochtouren," *VB,* July 24, 1943, p. 1.

102. Goebbels, entry for May 13, 1943, *TBJG*, II/8, pp. 287–288, 291.

103. Ibid., pp. 294–295. In his postwar retrospective on the Propaganda Ministry during the war, Dietrich's chief of staff Helmut Sündermann sought to place all the responsibility for the anti-Semitic directives on Hitler, of course, and Goebbels. Sündermann wrote that "in the press directives in those days [spring 1943] one finds again and again an effort to bring the anti-Jewish thesis more into the headlines. Hitler wanted this to happen and Goebbels demanded it with special emphasis." Sündermann, *Tagesparolen,* pp. 254–255. So too, however, did Dietrich and Sündermann.

104. See Gerhard Weinberg, *A World at Arms: A Global History of World War II* (New York: Cambridge University Press, 1994), pp. 445–447.

105. Goebbels, entry for May 14, 1943, *TBJG,* II/8, p. 297.

106. VIdRMVP 117/43, May 17, 1943, ZSg. 109/42, BAK, SO.

107. Ibid., 125/43, May 21, 1943.

108. Joseph Goebbels, "Das große Wagnis," in Goebbels, *Der steile Aufstieg,* pp. 271–278.

109. Joseph Goebbels, "Überwundene Winterkrise," ibid., pp. 298–299; quotation on p. 298. For another assertion of links between Jews and the air war, see M. F. L., "Der Luftterror und die Juden," *Die Judenfrage* 7, no. 9 (May 1, 1943), pp. 143–144.

110. Goebbels, entry for May 19, 1943, *TBJG,* II/8, pp. 323–324.

111. "Anti-Juden-Sondernummer: Das Ziel: Eine antijüdische Zeitschriftenpresse," *Deutscher Wochendienst,* May 21, 1943, nos. 8838–8846, War Crimes Records Collection, U.S. Nuerenberg War Crimes Trials, *United States of America v. Ernst von Weizsäcker et al.,* case 11, in NARA, RG 238, War Crimes Records Collection, M 897, roll 34, NG 4716, prosecution exhibit 1276, pp. 1–13. The issue was introduced in evidence for the prosecution at Otto Dietrich's trial in Nuremberg.

112. Ibid., p. 1.

113. Ibid. The issues are no. 196, with directive 8314, "Wenn der Jude an der Macht ist"; no. 204, directive 8615, "Die Juden sind Verbrecher"; and no. 207, directive 8712, "Juda will Europas Völker morden."

114. Ibid., p. 2.

115. Ibid.

116. Ibid., p. 5.

117. "Die Juden sind schuld!" *Deutscher Wochendienst* no. 8839 (May 21, 1943): 5.

118. "Kampf dem Weltjudentum," ibid., p. 9.

119. "Roosevelt Urges Food Parley Waive Tariffs for Health; Asks World Agriculture Rise to Meet Nutritional Needs without Trade Barriers; Part of Four Freedoms," *New York Times,* May 19, 1943, p. 1.

120. "Das könnte ihnen so passen, Europa soll amerikanischen Kornjuden ausgeliefert werden, Dreierpaktmächte erkämpfen für alle Völker das Recht auf Arbeit und Brot," *VB,* May 21, 1943, p. 1.

121. "Internationale Lebensmittelbank, Jüdischer Weltausbeutungsplan, Das tägliche Brot der Völker soll Objekt der Börsenspekulation werden," *VB,* May 25, 1943, p. 1.

122. "Genesis, 41," *The Five Books of Moses,* ed. and trans. Everett Fox (New York: Schocken, 1983), pp. 192–199. Thomas Mann, in American

exile during the war, was writing the fourth volume of *Joseph and His Brothers*, titled *Joseph the Provider*. See *Joseph und seine Brüder, Der vierte Roman, Joseph der Ernäher* (Stockholm: Berman-Fischer, 1943). For the complete English translation, see Thomas Mann, *Joseph and His Brothers* (London: Penguin, 1978).

123. "Internationale Lebensmittelbank," p. 1.

124. Ibid.

125. Susannah Heschel, *Transforming Jesus from Jew to Aryan: Protestant Theologians in Nazi Germany* (Tucson: University of Arizona Press, 1995).

126. "Hunger und Chaos Vorstufen der jüdischen Weltherrschaft, Nachkriegsphantasien der Roosevelt-Clique," *VB*, June 2, 1943, p. 1.

127. "World Peace Aims Mapped by Welles; Court and Police Force Will Be Essential, He Tells North Carolina Negro College," *New York Times,* June 1, 1943, p. 8.

128. "Hunger und Chaos Vorstufen der jüdischen Weltherrschaft," p. 1.

129. On the cancellation of the *Parole der Woche* see Reichspropagandaleitung Berlin, Meldung no. 3009, "An alle Gaupropagandaleitungen, betrifft: Parteiamtliche Wandzeitung: *Die Parole der Woche,*" May 5, 1943, BA Berlin, NS 18, Reichspropagandaleitung, folder 848, p. 105.

130. "Hinter den Feindmächten: Der Jude," BAK, Plakatensammlung (poster collection), no. 003–20–021.

131. Hans Schweitzer, "Der ist schuld am Kriege!" BAK, Plakatensammlung, no. 003–020–020.

132. "Der Jude: Kriegsanstifter, Kriegsverlängerer," (1943) BAK, Plakatensammlung, no. 003–020–022.

133. "Victory or Bolshevism," by Hans Schweitzer, was distributed in March 1943. The Reichspropagandaleitung printed 107,840 copies measuring 84 x 118.9 centimeters, and 373,745 copies measuring 84.1 x 59.4 centimeters. The figures for distribution of the two sizes of the poster in some prominent cities and areas follow: Berlin, 25,000 and 55,000, respectively; Hessen (with the *Gau* office in Frankfurt am Main), 3,000 and 5,000; Munich, 2,160 and 4,315; Upper Silesia, 10,000 and 50,000; Sachsen (with the *Gau* office in Dresden), 1,200 and 31,270; and North Westphalia (*Gau* office in Münster), 1,500 and 7,450. "Rundspruch nr. 6 an alle Gaupropagandaleiter, betrifft: Plakat no. 35, Sieg oder Bolshewismus," March 1, 1943, BA Berlin, NS 18, Reichspropagandaleitung, folder 848, p. 141.

134. On this point, see Adam Ulam, *Stalin: The Man and His Era* (New York: Viking, 1973), p. 585; and Ulam, *Expansion and Coexistence: The History of Soviet Foreign Policy, 1917–1967* (New York: Praeger, 1974). The dissolution of the Comintern did not bring Soviet espionage to an end in the

United States and Britain. Of the growing scholarly works on the subject, see especially Harvey Klehr, John Earl Haynes, and Kyrill M. Anderson, *The Soviet World of American Communism* (New Haven, Conn.: Yale University Press, 1998); and Ronald Radosh and Joyce Milton, *The Rosenberg File: A Search for the Truth* (New York: Holt, Rinehart and Winston, 1983).

135. VIdRMVP, V.I. 126/43, May 22, 1943, ZSg. 109/42, BAK, SO.

136. Goebbels, entry for May 23, 1943, *TBJG*, II/8, p. 351.

137. Theodor Seibert, "Der jüdische Krieg," *VB* (Munich edition), June 2, 1943, p. 1; also see Theodor Seibert, *Das amerikanische Rätsel: Die Kriegspolitik der USA in der Ära Roosevelt* (Berlin: Franz Eher Verlag, 1941). In the same issue of the *VB*, the lead news article, "Hunger and Chaos: First Steps of Jewish World Domination, Postwar Fantasies of the Roosevelt Clique," stressed an anti-Semitic message. "Hunger und Chaos Vorstufen der jüdischen Weltherrschaft: Nachkriegsphantasien der Roosevelt-Clique," June 2, 1943, p. 1.

138. Ibid.

139. Ibid.

140. Goebbels, entry for May 23, 1943, *TBJG*, II/8, p. 350.

141. Joseph Goebbels, "Die motorischen Kräfte," in Goebbels, *Der steile Aufstieg*, pp. 307–314.

142. Ibid., pp. 310–311.

143. *Roosevelts Weg in den Krieg: Geheimdokumente zur Kriegspolitik des Präsidenten der Vereinigten Staaten* (Berlin: Deutscher Verlag, 1943). The editors of *Die Judenfrage* brought the pamphlet to the attention of their readers. See "Die Kriegsschuld Roosevelts und der Juden: Zu den neuesten amtlichen Veröffentlichungen," *Die Judenfrage* 7, no. 14 (July 15, 1943): 225–228.

144. *Roosevelts Weg in den Krieg*, p. 12.

145. VIdRMVP, V.I. 160/43 (1. Erg.), July 2, 1943, ZSg. 109/43, BAK, SO; see also the directive of July 3, 1943, with similar instructions, V.I. 161/43. *Roosevelts Weg in den Krieg* made only rather brief comments about the Jews. The Propaganda Ministry's take on the text underscored the degree to which it was focusing on anti-Semitic dimensions of the Nazi narrative.

146. "Neue Dokumente erhärten das Urteil: Die Kriegsschuld Roosevelts steht unwiderleglich fest, Der 'Weltpräsident' als Strohmann der jüdischen Kriegshetzer," *VB*, July 4, 1943, p. 1.

147. Sündermann, *Tagesparolen*, pp. 255–256.

148. Sündermann, *Tagesparolen*, p. 256.

149. Goebbels, entry for August 7, 1943, *TBJG*, II/9, p. 232.

150. "Negerverbände sollen als Terrorflieger über Italien eingesetzt werden, Unauslöschliche Schande in der Kriegführung der Judenknecht," *VB,* June 5, 1943, p. 1.
151. "Schieberskandale in Roosevelt-Amerika, Rüstungshyänen schanzen sich Riesenprofite zu, Das große jüdische Geschäft," *VB,* June 18, 1943, p. 1.
152. "Zwei Jahre Krieg gegen den Bolschewismus, Der Schutzwall des Abendlandes steht, Kompromißloser Kampf bis zur Niederringung der Todfeinde Europas," *VB,* June 22, 1943, p. 1.
153. "Größte Gefahr der Weltgeschichte, Das Bündnis zwischen Gangstertum und Bolschewismus, Alfred Rosenberg zeichnet das große Ringen unserer Zeit," *VB,* June 23, 1943, p. 1.
154. "Neue Dokumente erhärten das Urteil."
155. "Juden kennen keine Scheu vor den Kulturgütern der Mensheit, Terrorbomber griffen Rom an, Neues Verbrechen britisch-amerikanischer Luftgangster," *VB,* July 20, 1943, p. 1. See also "Warum nicht eingliedern wie Texas? England und das Empire sollen amerikanisch werden, 'Chicago Daily Tribune' enthüllt den Plan der jüdischen Weltrepublik," *VB,* July 23, 1943, p. 1; "Der USA. Weltherrschaftstraum, Auch Portugals Kolonien Ziel amerikanischer Raubgier, Die Neuyorker Juden erstreben 'Internationalisierung' aller Kolonialländer," *VB,* July 26, 1943, p. 1.
156. "Die Monatsparole," Redner-Schnellinformation, Lieferung 64, NSDAP Reichspropagandaleitung, Hautpamt: Propaganda, Amt: Rednerwesen, August, 1943, NARA, Captured German Records, T-81, roll 683, pp. 4721712–4721714.
157. "Ohne Sieg kein Wiederaufbau, Zur Luftkriegslage," Redner-Schnellinformation, Lieferung 67, NSDAP Reichspropagandaleitung, Hauptamt Propaganda, Amt: Rednerwesen, September 1943, NARA, Captured German Records, T-81, roll 683, pp. 4721726–4721727.

7. *"Victory or Extermination"*

1. On the interaction of the fronts and the course of the war on land and sea and in the air, see Gerhard Weinberg, *A World at Arms: A Global History of World War II* (New York: Cambridge University Press, 1994), pp. 593–609; and Richard Overy, *How the Allies Won* (New York: Norton, 1995).
2. Rüdiger Övermanns, *Deutsche militärische Verluste im Zweiten Weltkrieg* (Munich: Oldenbourg, 2000), pp. 238–239.
3. Chronology drawn from Rinat-ya Gorodnzik Robinson, "Chronology," in Walter Laqueur, ed., *The Holocaust Encyclopedia* (New Haven, Conn.: Yale University Press, 2001), pp. xxxii–xxxiv.

4. Joseph Goebbels, *Die Tagebücher von Joseph Goebbels (TBJG)*, ed. Elke Fröhlich (Munich: Sauer, 1994), Joseph Goebbels, entry for October 7, 1943, II/10, p. 72.

5. For the text of Himmler's Posen speech, see "Himmler's Summation, October 4, 1943," in Lucy S. Dawidowicz, ed., *A Holocaust Reader* (West Orange, N.J.: Behrman House, 1976), pp. 130–140. Also see Richard Breitman, *The Architect of Genocide: Himmler and the Final Solution* (New York: Knopf, 1991), pp. 242–243.

6. "Jewish New Year to Begin Tonight," *New York Times*, September 29, 1943, p. 15.

7. "Roosevelt erklärt sich erneut mit Juda solidarisch," *VB*, October 11, 1943, p. 1.

8. "Anglo-Soviet-American Communiqué on the Conference in Moscow of the Three Foreign Secretaries," *Foreign Relations of the United States* (henceforth *FRUS*), *Diplomatic Papers*, 1943, vol. 1, *General* (Washington, D.C.: U.S. Government Printing Office, 1963), pp. 743–744.

9. "Annex 10: Declaration on German Atrocities," ibid., pp. 768–769.

10. See "War-Crime Trials Settled by Allies," *New York Times*, November 2, 1943, p. 12.

11. VIdRMVP 269/43, November 3, 1943, ZSg. 109/46, BAK, SO.

12. VIdRMVP 279/43, November 14, 1943, ZSg. 109/46, BAK, SO.

13. *"Die Parole der Woche,"* *Zeitschriften-Dienst* 235/104, no. 9570 (November 5, 1943): 1.

14. "Der plutokratische Apparat arbeitet für Stalin: Moskau erweitert seine Machtansprüche: Erfolg der Sowjetagitation in England und USA.," *VB*, October 30, 1943, p. 1.

15. "Der USA.-Präsident bestätigt: Europa soll dem Bolschewismus ausgeliefert werden: Hull und Eden Vollzugsorgane des Weltjudentums," *VB*, October 31, 1943, p. 1.

16. "Wofür das jüdische Kapital die Völker mordet: Die Dividenden verlängern den Krieg, Die Dreierpaktmächte im Kampf für die schaffenden Menschen," *VB*, November 16, 1943, p. 1.

17. "Was der Führer vom deutschen Offizier fordert: Mut, Härte und politischen Fanatismus, Sieg oder unbarmherzige Vernichtung–ein Drittes gibt es nicht: Adolf Hitler sprach zu 20,000 Offiziersanwärtern," *VB*, November 30, 1943, p. 1.

18. "Declaration of the Three Powers," Tehran Conference, December 6, 1943, *FRUS, Diplomatic Papers, The Conferences at Cairo and Tehran, 1943*, pp. 640–641.

19. James B. Reston, "Allies Achieve Unity for War and Peace," *New York Times*, December 5, 1943, p. E3.

20. "Das Hauptthema für alle Zeitschriften: Die Judenemanzipation, Das größte Unheil des 19. Jahrhunderts," *Deutscher Wochendienst* 242/112, no. 9746 (December 22, 1943).

21. Goebbels, entry for December 12, 1943, *TBJG*, II/10, pp. 432–433.

22. Entry for December 26, 1943, ibid., p. 550.

23. Entries for December 28, 1943, and December 31, 1943, ibid., pp. 560–563, 576.

24. Entry for January 22, 1944, ibid., II/11, p. 136.

25. Entry for January 25, 1944, ibid., pp. 157, 161.

26. Entry for February 28, 1944, ibid., p. 359.

27. Max Domarus, *Hitler: Reden und Proklamationen*, vol. 2 *Untergang, 1939–1945* (Neustadt: Schmidt, 1963), pp. 2083–2085.

28. On this ideological incorporation into the ranks of the democracies, see chapters 8 and 9 in François Furet, *The Passing of an Illusion: The Idea of Communism in the Twentieth Century*, trans. Deborah Furet (Chicago: University of Chicago Press, 1999).

29. "Tagesparole des Reichspressechefs," February 3, 1944, p. 2, in U.S. Nuerenberg War Crimes Trials Records Collection, *United States of America v. Ernst von Weizäcker et al.*, case 12, December 20, 1947–April 14, 1949, in NARA, RG 238, War Crimes Records Collection, M 897, roll 34, Prosecution Exhibits NG 3408, 1275. See, for example, "Die Juden in der Wissenschaft," *Zeitschriften-Dienst*, 248/117, no. 9864 (February 4, 1944): 5–11; "Das Ostjudentum: Reservoir des Weltjudentums," *Deutscher Wochendienst*, 240/109, no. 9706 (December 10, 1943): 5–8. Such articles included bibliographies of relevant works and thus served to link the regime's anti-Semitic think tanks and university-based academics with a broader reading public.

30. "Tagesparole des Reichspressechefs," February 3, 1944, p. 2. Emphasis in the original.

31. Cited in "Opening Statement for the Prosecution," *Trials of War Criminals before the Nuerenberg Military Tribunals under Control Council Law no. 10*, vol. 12, Nuremberg, October 1946–April 1949 (Washington, D.C.: U.S. Government Printing Office, 1949), p. 204.

32. VIdRMVP 54/44, March 2, 1944, ZSg. 109/48, BAK, SO; "Tagesparole," March 2, 1944, Helmut Sündermann, *Tagesparolen: Deutsche Presseanweisungen, 1939–1945: Hitlers Propaganda und Kriegsführung* (Leoni am Starnberger See: Druffel-Verlag, 1973), p. 258. Also in U.S.

Nuerenberg War Crimes Trials Records Collection, *United States of America v. Ernst von Weizäcker et al.*, case 12, December 20, 1947–April 14, 1949, in NARA, RG 238, War Crimes Records Collection, M 897, roll 34, Prosecution Exhibits NG 3410, 1277.

33. "Tagesparole des Reichspressechefs," March 2, 1944, in U.S. Nuerenberg War Crimes Trials Records Collection, *United States of America v. Ernst von Weizäcker et al.*, case 12, December 20, 1947–April 14, 1949, in NARA, RG 238, War Crimes Records Collection, M 897, roll 34, Prosecution Exhibits NG 3410, 1277.

34. Goebbels, entry for March 4, 1944, *TBJG*, II/11, p. 399.

35. "Tagesparole des Reichspressechefs," April 27, 1944, U.S. Nuerenberg War Crimes Trials Records Collection, *United States of America v. Ernst von Weizäcker et al.*, case 12, December 20, 1947–April 14, 1949, in NARA, RG 238, War Crimes Records Collection, M 897, roll 34, Prosecution Exhibits NG 3412, 1279.

36. Joseph Goebbels, "Die europäische Narkose," *Das Reich,* April 1, 1944; also see NSDAP, Reichspropagandaleitung, Sonderlieferung no. 13/44, "Die europäische Narkose," March 29, 1944, NARA, T-81, roll 683, 4721756–4721759.

37. Ibid., pp. 4721758–4721759. On the same day, Goebbels saw "positive political effects" of Soviet advances in southeastern Europe, in the form of a "wave of fear of Bolshevization," especially in France. See Goebbels, entry for April 1, 1944, *TBJG*, II/12, p. 34.

38. Goebbels, entry for April 3, 1944, *TBJG*, ibid., p. 45.

39. Entry for April 18, 1944, ibid., pp. 138–139.

40. Ibid., p. 139.

41. Klaus Gensicke, *Der Mufti von Jerusalem, Amin el-Husseini und die Nationalsozialisten* (Frankfurt am Main: Verlag Peter Lang, 1988). On the Bosnian and Muslim SS volunteer division, see pp. 167–212.

42. Entry for April 26, 1944, *TBJG*, II/2, pp. 188–189.

43. Amin al-Husainis, "Nr. 101: An Himmler, 27.7.1944," in Gerhard Höpp, ed., *Mufti-Papiere: Briefe, Memoranden, Reden und Aufrufe Amin al-Husainis aus dem Exil, 1940–1945* (Berlin: Klaus Schwarz Verlag, 2001), p. 216.

44. Amin al-Hussainis, "Nr. 104: Rede vor den Imamen der bosnischen SS-Division, 4.10.1944," in Höpp, *Mufti-Papiere*, pp. 219–222.

45. "Tagesparole des Reichspressechefs," April 27, 1944.

46. Ibid., p. 232.

47. VIdRMVP, V.I. 84/44, May 4, 1944, ZSg. 109/49, BAK, SO; also in "Tagesparole des Reichspressechefs," May 4, 1944, U.S. Nuerenberg War

Crimes Trials, *United States of America v. Ernst von Weizsäcker et al.*, case 11, NARA, RG 238, War Crimes Records Collection, M 897, roll 34, NG 3413, prosecution exhibit 1280.

48. "Mit dem Hauptquartier der Weltrevolution vereinigt, Moskau wird offizielles Zentrum des Weltjudentums, Judenstaat Palästina als Eckstein der Sowjetkontrolle im Mittelmeer," *VB*, May 12, 1944, p. 1.

49. On Wise, see Melvin I. Urofsky, *A Voice That Spoke for Justice: The Life and Times of Stephen S. Wise* (Albany: State University of New York Press, 1982); and Stephen Wise, *Challenging Years: The Autobiography of Stephen Wise* (New York; Putnam, 1949).

50. "Mit dem Hauptquartier der Weltrevolution vereinigt." Dietrich wrote in a press directive of June 1, 1944, "We will smash the enemy's onslaught, and as a result the whole Jewish house of cards will be both militarily and politically destroyed." "Tagesparole des Reichspressechefs," V.I. 107/44, June 1, 1944, U.S. Nuerenberg War Crimes Trials, *United States of America v. Ernst von Weizsäcker et al.*, case 11, NARA, RG 238, War Crimes Records Collection, M 897, roll 34, NG 4706, prosecution exhibit 1281.

51. Joseph Goebbels, "Nr. 26, 4.6.44—Nürnberg, Adolf-Hitler-Platz (Hauptmarkt)–Großkundgebung anläßlich des Kreistages des Kreises Nürnberg-Stadt der NSDAP" in *1939–1945,* vol. 2 of Helmut Heiber, ed., *Goebbels-Reden* (Dusseldorf: Droste Verlag, 1972), p. 324.

52. Ibid., pp. 330–331. Emphasis in the original.

53. Ibid., pp. 334–335.

54. Ibid., pp. 340–341.

55. Helmut Sündermann, "Stalin und die Juden: Notizen zu einem weltpolitischen Tatbestand," appeared as follows: Part 1, *VB*, May 14, 1944, p. 3; Part 2, *VB*, May 15, 1944, p. 3; Part 3, *VB*, May 16, 1944, p. 3. May 14, 15, and 16, 1944, p. 3.

56. Sündermann, "Stalin und die Juden: Notizen zu einem weltpolitischen Tatbestand: Part 3," *VB*, May 16, 1944, p. 3.

57. "Der große Entschluß des Führers, Wie die jüdisch-bolschewistische Weltverschwörung vereitelt wurde, Invasion–der Weg zum Ziel Moskaus," *VB*, June 22, 1944, p. 1.

58. Ibid. Emphasis in the original.

59. Ibid.

60. Joseph Goebbels, "Nr. 28, 3.8.44–Posen, Schloß–Tagung der Reichsleiter, Gauleiter und Verbändeführer der NSDAP," in Heiber, *Goebbels-Reden,* 2:361–404.

61. Ibid., pp. 365–366.

62. Ibid., p. 394. On Hitler's view of treason and betrayal in the military as an explanation for wartime setbacks, see Ian Kershaw, *Hitler, 1936–1945: Nemesis* (New York: Norton, 2000).

63. Goebbels, entry for September 1, 1944, *TBJG,* II/13, p. 378.

64. Entry for September 21, 1944, ibid., pp. 536–542.

65. "Parole der Woche," *Zeitschriften-Dienst,* September 22, 1944, A692, p. 2.

66. VIdRMVP, V.I. 215/44, September 30, 1944, ZSg. 109/51, BAK, SO.

67. Ibid.

68. The total for German battlefield deaths on all fronts in 1944 was about 1.8 million. Again, the figures are drawn from Övermanns, *Deutsche militärische Verluste,* pp. 238–239, 266.

69. On the liberation, see Julian Jackson, *France: The Dark Years, 1940–1944* (New York: Oxford University Press, 2001), pp. 561–567.

70. This summary draws on Weinberg, *A World at Arms,* pp. 750–753.

71. Joseph Goebbels, "Nr. 29, 3.10.44–Köln, Werkhalle eines Industriebetriebs–Kundgebung des Gaues Köln–Aachen der NSDAP," in Heiber, *Goebbels-Reden,* 2:407. Emphasis in the original.

72. Ibid., pp. 424, 428.

73. Goebbels, entry for November 3, 1944, *TBJG,* II/14, pp. 164, 166.

74. Joseph Goebbels, "Der Kitt der Feindkoalition: Die Urheber des Unglücks der Welt," *Das Reich,* January 21, 1945, pp. 1–2. A sarcastic, distorted article about Samuel Rosenman amplified the anti-Semitic focus of the front page. See "Samuel Rosenman," *Das Reich,* January 21, 1945, p. 1.

75. Goebbels, "Der Kitt der Feindkoalition," pp. 1, 2.

76. Ibid.

77. Ibid.

78. VidRVMP, V.I. 27/45, February 2, 1945, ZSg. 109/54, BAK, SO.

79. See Övermanns, *Deutsche Militärische Verluste,* pp. 238–239.

80. VIdRMVP, V.I. 31/45, February 2, 1945, ZSg. 109/54, BAK, SO.

81. "Communiqué Issued at the End of the Conference," February 11, 1945, *FRUS, Diplomatic Papers, The Conferences at Malta and Yalta, 1945* (Washington, D.C.: U.S. Government Printing Office, 1955), pp. 970–971.

82. "Zur Lage," *Zeitschriften-Dienst,* 301/171, February 19, 1945, pp. 1–2.

83. "Das Vernichtungsprogramm von Jalta," *Zeitschriften-Dienst,* 302/171, February 19, 1945, pp. 2–3.

84. Övermanns, *Deutsche Militärische Verluste,* pp. 238–239.

85. John Erickson, *The Road to Berlin* (Boulder, Colo.: Westview, 1983), p. 622.

86. For a discussion of the Dresden figures, see Richard Evans in *Lying about Hitler: History, Holocaust, and the David Irving Trial* (New York: Perseus, 2001), pp. 174–177.

87. Helmut Sündermann, "Unser Halten und die Feindkoalition," *VB*, March 22, 1945, p. 1. See also Sündermann, *Tagesparolen*; and "Helmut Sündermann," in Ernst Klee, *Das Personenlexikon zum Dritten Reich: Wer war was vor und nach 1945* (Frankfurt am Main: Fischer Verlag, 2003), p. 615.

88. Sündermann, "Unser Halten und die Feindkoalition," p. 1. The *VB* article claimed that Yalta represented the completion of the "Bolshevik world revolution" combined with an "extermination plan" (*Vernichtungsplan*) aimed at Germany that would bring about the "extinction or obliteration (*Auslöschung*) of the German people." Therefore, the Yalta declaration should only strengthen the nation's will to resist. Yalta signaled "world revolution through the Western powers." It was now clear, the *VB* declared, that "without Germany the West would be lost" to Bolshevik murder and plunder. See "Deutschland einziges Gegengewicht gegen Moskau, Jalta–das Todesurteil Europas, Die deutschen Feststellungen über Roosevelts und Churchills Kapitulation vor Stalin allgemein bestätigt," *VB*, February 16, 1945, p. 1; see also "Kreml soll Europa beherrschen: Stalin hat alle Freiheit des Handelns," *VB*, February 12, 1945, p. 1.

89. Joseph Goebbels, "Nr. 30, 28.2.45–Rundfunkansprache," in Heiber, *Goebbels-Reden* 2:429–446.

90. Ibid., p. 433.

91. On the death marches, see Robert Gellately, *Backing Hitler* (New York: Oxford, 2001); and Daniel Goldhagen, *Hitler's Willing Executioners* (New York: Knopf, 1996).

92. Goebbels, entry for April 4, 1945, *TBJG*, II/15, pp. 675–677.

93. Ibid.

94. See the classic account in H. R. Trevor-Roper, *The Last Days of Hitler* (New York: Collier, 1962), pp. 225–265; and more recently, Kershaw, *Hitler*, 2:820–828.

95. Domarus, *Hitler*, 2:2236.

96. Joseph Goebbels, "Nr. 31, 19.4.45–Rundfunkansprache am Vorabend von Hitlers 56. Geburtstag," in Heiber, *Goebbels-Reden*, 2:448.

97. On Goebbels's end, see Rolf Reuth, *Goebbels: Eine Biographie* (Munich: Piper, 1995), pp. 613–614; English trans., Reuth, *Goebbels* (New York; Harcourt, 1994), pp. 362–363.

98. Ibid., pp. 2236–2237, 2239.

Conclusion

1. Lucy Dawidowicz, *The War against the Jews, 1933–1945* (New York: Holt, Rinehart and Winston, 1975).

2. "Subjectivity" in this context refers to the ability of a political actor to influence events, as opposed to being influenced by other persons, factors, or events.

3. On "delirious discourse," see Michel Foucault, *Madness and Civilization,* trans. Richard Howard (New York: Random House, 1965), pp. 86–96.

4. On the radicalization of the application of the terms *Vernichtung* and *Vernichtungskrieg* from Clausewitz to Verdun in World War I and then to the Nazi war on the eastern front in World War II, see Jan Phillip Reemtsma, "Die Idee des Vernichtungskrieges: Clausewitz, Ludendorff, Hitler," in Hannes Heer and Klaus Naumann, eds. *Vernichtungskrieg: Verbrechen der Wehrmacht, 1941–1944* (Hamburg: Hamburger Edition, 1995), pp. 377–401.

5. Karl Bracher, *The German Dictatorship,* trans. Jean Steinberg (New York: Praeger, 1970); and "The Role of Hitler: Perspectives of Interpretation," in Walter Laqueur, ed. *Fascism: A Reader's Guide* (Berkeley and Los Angeles: University of California Press, 1976), pp. 211–225.

6. E. H. Gombrich, *Myth and Reality in German War-Time Broadcasts* (London: Athlone, 1970), p. 23.

7. On the origins of the Brammer and Oberheitmann files, see Alexander Hardy, *Hitler's Secret Weapon: The "Managed" Press and Propaganda Machine of Nazi Germany* (New York: Vantage, 1967).

8. See, for example, Ernest Bramsted, *Goebbels and National Socialist Propaganda, 1925–1945* (East Lansing: Michigan State University Press, 1965); Jay Baird, *The Mythical World of Nazi War Propaganda, 1939–1945* (Minneapolis: University of Minnesota Press, 1974); and Robert Edwin Herzstein, *The War That Hitler Won: Goebbels and the Nazi Media Campaign,* 2nd rev. ed. (New York: Paragon House, 1987 [1978]). As noted previously, the most extensive previous study of the Dietrich trial and the anti-Semitic dimensions of the press directives is Alexander Hardy, *Hitler's Secret Weapon: The 'Managed' Press and Propaganda Machine of Nazi Germany* (New York; Vantage, 1967).

9. "XV. Judgment," Trials of War Criminals before the Nuerenberg Military Tribunals under Control Council Law No. 10, vol. 14, Nuremberg, October 1946–April 1949 (Washington, D.C.: U.S. Government Printing Office, 1950), p. 576. Following decisions by the U.S. High Commission in

Germany, Dietrich was released from prison in August 1950, after serving only one year of a seven-year sentence. He had been in prison since 1945. See "Flick, Steel Baron, and Seven Other Nazis Convicted of War Crimes Will Be Freed," *New York Times,* August 17, 1950, p. 9; and "Ex-Hitler Press Chief Flees Questioners as 19 Nazi Criminals Are Freed from Jail," *New York Times,* August 26, 1950, p. 7.

10. Jeffrey Herf, *Reactionary Modernism: Technology, Culture, and Politics in Weimar and the Third Reich* (New York: Cambridge University Press, 1984).

11. On the Berlin protest, see Nathan Stoltzfus, *Resistance of the Heart: Intermarriage and the Rosenstrasse Protest in Nazi Germany* (New York: Norton, 1996). According to one remarkable recent study, more than 1.5 million deaths occurred from January to May 8, 1945. See Rüdiger Overmanns, *Deutsche Militärische Verluste im Zweiten Weltkrieg* (Munich: Oldenbourg, 1999). On the postwar indictments, see Jeffrey Herf, *Divided Memory: The Nazi Past in the Two Germanys* (Cambridge, Mass.: Harvard University Press, 1997).

12. The key source has been the reports of the Sicherheitsdienst. See Heinz Boberach, ed., *Meldungen aus dem Reich: Die geheimen Lageberichte des Sicherheitsdienstes der SS, 1938–1945,* 17 vols. (Herrsching: Pawlak, 1984). For reports by Social Democratic agents in the 1930s, see *Deutschland-Berichte der Sozialdemokratische Partei Deutschlands* (Frankfurt am Main: Verlag Petra Nettelbeck, 1980).

13. David Bankier, *The Germans and the Final Solution: Public Opinion under Nazism* (Oxford: Blackwell, 1992), p. 115; David Bankier, ed., *Probing the Depths of German Antisemitism: German Society and the Persecution of the Jews, 1933–1941* (New York: Berghahn, 2000; Jerusalem: Yad Vashem and the Leo Baeck Institute, 2000).

14. Martin Broszat, Klaus Dietmar Henke, and Hans Woller, eds., *Von Stalingrad zur Währungsreform: Zur Sozialgeschichte des Umbruchs in Deutschland, 1943–1948* (Munich: Oldenbourg, 1988); Martin Broszat and Elke Fröhlich, *Alltag und Widerstand: Bayern in Nationalsozialismus* (Munich: Piper, 1987). On Broszat and the analysis of anti-Semitism and the Holocaust, see Nicholas Berg, *Der Holocaust und die westdeutschen Historiker: Erforschung und Erinnerung* (Göttingen: Wallstein, 2003).

15. See Ian Kershaw, *Hitler, 1889–1936: Hubris* (New York: Norton, 1999); *Hitler, 1936–1945: Nemesis* (New York: Norton, 2000); *The Hitler Myth: Image and Reality in the Third Reich* (Oxford: Oxford University Press,

1987); and *Popular Opinion and Political Dissent in the Third Reich: Bavaria, 1933–1945* (Oxford: Oxford University Press, 1983). Also see Marlis G. Steinert, *Hitler's War and the Germans: Public Mood and Attitude during the Second World War,* trans. Thomas E. J. de Witt (Athens: Ohio University Press, 1977). On the diffusion of anti-Semitism in the German army fighting on the eastern front, see Omer Bartov, *Hitler's Army: Soldiers, Nazis, and War in the Third Reich* (New York: Oxford University Press, 1991).

16. Kershaw, *Popular Opinion and Political Dissent,* pp. 359–372. On the rumors, see Lawrence Stokes, "The German People and the Destruction of the European Jews," *Central European History* 6, no. 2 (1973): 167–191; and Bankier, *The Germans and the Final Solution.*

Acknowledgments

With pleasure, I acknowledge the people and institutions that supported the research and writing of this book.

Ludger Kühnhardt, co-director of the Center for European Integration Studies at the University of Bonn, supported a fellowship there in summer 1998, when work on the project began. Hartmut Lehman, director of the Max Planck Institute for History in Göttingen, Germany, made possible a summer research fellowship there in 1999. Bruce Steiner, chair of the Department of History at Ohio University in Athens, granted me a leave of absence in the spring quarter of 2000. I am especially grateful to him, and to Norman Goda, Alonzo Hamby, Steven Miner, and other fine colleagues and friends in Athens for making my years there such good ones. Anita Shapira, then director of the Yitzhak Rabin Center for Israel Studies, invited me to spend spring 2000 as a Fellow at the Center. There, I had the good fortune to share ideas with a stimulating group of Israeli scholars, and to draw on the collections of Nazi-era materials in the Wiener Library, now housed at the University of Tel Aviv's Sourasky Library. At the University of Maryland in College Park, whose History Department I joined in fall 2000, colleagues and students have shared valuable comments. James Harris, dean of the College of Arts and Humanities, and John Lampe, then chair of the Department of History, supported my leave for research in the spring semester of 2002 and 2004. A grant from the university's Graduate Record Board, which had the support of our department's current chair, Gary Gerstle, made possible the full-color reproduction of the Nazi-era posters and wall newspapers in this book.

Fellowships at the Center for Advanced Holocaust Studies at the United States Holocaust Memorial Museum in spring 2004, and at the Woodrow Wilson International Center for Scholars, also in Washington, D.C., in fall 2004 offered time, excellent resources, and helpful staff that were of great assistance to me as I finished writing the manuscript. Both institutions demonstrate that scholarship is valued and encouraged in this city of politicians, journalists, policy advisers, lawyers, and bureaucrats. Lee Hamilton, the director of the Wilson Center, deserves the thanks of many scholars for convincing politicians that basic research in the humanities and social sciences is well worth supporting. The library staff of the Wilson Center library was particularly helpful. At the Holocaust Museum, Sharon Muller in the photo archive offered valuable suggestions about the visual dimensions of Nazi propaganda.

A special thank-you to the archivists in Germany at the Bundesarchiv Koblenz; the Landeshauptarchiv Koblenz; the Institut für Zeitungsforschung in Dortmund; and the Bayerisches Hauptstaatsarchiv. All offered valuable assistance as I did research into the posters and wall newspapers produced by the Nazi regime. The same goes for the staff at the Imperial War Museum in London and the Hoover Institution Archives in Stanford, California. The Center for Research Libraries in Chicago made it possible to read through original editions of *Der Völkische Beobachter*. The Bundesarchiv Koblenz quickly responded to requests for microfilm. The staff of the United States National Archives and Record Administration, situated adjacent to the University of Maryland campus, eased access to its own impressive microfilm collections dealing with the Nazi era. Two of my graduate students provided assistance. Christina Morina gathered important files from archives and libraries in Berlin, while Nicholas Schlosser offered timely assistance at the Library of Congress in Washington.

Comments and questions from colleagues too numerous to mention, in response to presentations about the work in progress, offered much food for thought as the manuscript evolved. Thanks to colleagues and participants in the German Study Group at the Minda de Gunzberg Center for European Studies, Harvard University; New York Area Intellectual and Cultural History Seminar, Graduate Center, City University of New York; the conference "Convergence and Divergence in Historical Perspective: Anti-Semitism and Anti-Zionism" at Brandeis University; the Simon Dubnow Institute for Jewish History, University of Leipzig, Germany; the International Research Center in the Cultural Sciences, Vienna, Austria; participants at the conference "Nazi Berlin," at Dartmouth College; Washington-area German historians; commentators and panelists at the German Studies Association conferences in 2001, 2003, and 2005; Central European University, Budapest, Hungary; the Department of History, the Meyerhoff Center for Jewish Studies, and the Center for Historical Studies, University of Maryland, College Park; participants at the conference "The Lesser Evil" at New York University; participants in seminars at the United States Holocaust Memorial Museum, Washington, D.C.; and the Woodrow Wilson International Center for Scholars, Washington, D.C.; participants at a conference on totalitarianism at Stanford University in fall 2004, and at "Lessons and Legacies," a conference at Brown University, also in fall 2004.

Parts of the work in progress appeared as "'The Jewish War': Goebbels and the Anti-Semitic Campaigns of the Nazi Propaganda Ministry" in *Holocaust and Genocide Studies* 19, no. 1 (Spring 2005):51–80; and as "'Der Krieg und die Juden'—Die narrativen Strukturen von Goebbels' antisemitischer Propaganda," in Jorg Echternkamp, ed., *Das Deutsche Reich und der Zweite Weltkrieg,* vol. 9, book 2: *Die deutsche Kriegsgesellschaft, 1939–1945* (Munich: Deutsche Verlagsanstalt, 2005). Thanks go to the respective editors who offered comments. The Boston psychologist John Wechter drew my attention to psychoanalytic clinical findings regarding the simultaneous occurrence of grandiosity and paranoia.

At Harvard University Press, thanks are due to the probing and helpful comments from the readers of the manuscript, to my manuscript editor for her careful reading, probing questions, and helpful suggestions and to Rachel Weinstein and then Fabienne François, who guided the text through the press. I extend special thanks to my excellent editor Joyce Seltzer. Her fine judgment and valuable remarks have helped make the manuscript more accessible to a general audience, while it retains its value for my fellow scholars.

As has been the case for many years, I have been extremely fortunate to benefit from the insights, probing questions, encouragement, and love of a very fine historian, my wife, Sonya Michel.

Bibliography

Archives

Bundesarchiv Berlin
NS 18 Reichspropagandaleitung der NSDAP
NS 42 Reichspressechef der NSDAP/Reichspressestelle: 1. Dr.
Otto Dietrich
Bundesarchiv Koblenz, Sammlung Oberheitmann, "Vertrauliche
Informationen" des Reichsministeriums für Volksaufklärung
und Propaganda für die Presse, Zeitgeschichtliche Sammlung
(ZSg.) 109, July 1939–March 1945
United States Holocaust Memorial Museum, Washington, D.C.
R-55 373, microfilm Reichsministerium für Volksaufklärung
und Propaganda (RMVP)
United States National Archives and Records Administration
(NARA)
T81 Records of the National Socialist German Labor Party,
rolls 22, 67, 84, 683
70 Record Group (RG) 242, Records of the Reich Ministry for
Propaganda, 1936–1944
RG 238, War Crimes Records Collection, U.S. Nuerenberg

War Crimes Trials, *United States of America v. Ernst von Weizsäcker, et al.*, case 11, December 20, 1947–April 14, 1949, M 897, microfilm reels 9, 34 (Prosecution Exhibits 1211–1365), 137 (Otto Dietrich), 152
NARA microfilm, Berlin Document Center, A3345-B 060 *Nachrichtenblatt des Reichsministeriums für Volksaufklärung und Propaganda,* 1937
RG 226, OSS station files, Washington and field station files, Washington-MO Propa 1–3, nn3–226–85–3 A-1, box 101, entry 139

Selected Primary Documents

Boberach, Heinz, ed. *Meldungen aus dem Reich: Die geheimen Lageberichte des Sicherheitsdienstes der SS, 1938–1945,* vols. 1–15. Herrsching: Pawlek Verlag, 1984.

Boelcke, Willi A., ed. *Kriegspropaganda, 1939–1941: Geheime Ministerkonferenzen im Reichspropagandaministerium.* Stuttgart: Deutsche Verlags-Anstalt, 1966.

———. *"Wollt Ihr den totalen Krieg?" Die Geheimen Goebbels-Konferenzen, 1939–1943.* Munich: Deutscher Taschenbuch Verlag, 1969.

———. *The Secret Conferences of Dr. Goebbels: The Nazi Propaganda War, 1939–1943,* trans. Ewald Osers. New York: Dutton, 1970.

Deutscher Wochendienst, December 1943–March 1944.

Diebow, Hans. *Die Juden in USA.* Berlin: Zentralverlag der NSDAP, Franz Eher Verlag, 1941.

Dietrich, Otto. *Mit Hitler in die Macht: Persönliche Erlebnisse mit meinem Führer.* Berlin: Franz Eher, 1934.

———. *Die philosophischen Grundlagen des Nationalsozialismus, ein Ruf zu den Waffen deutschen Geistes.* Breslau: Hirt, 1935.

———. *Nationalsozialistische Presse Politik: Vortrag gehalten am 7. März 1938 in Berlin auf dem Empfangsabend des Aussenpolitischen Amtes im Hotel Adlon vor Mitgliedern des Diplomatischen*

Korps und Vertretern der auslandischen Presse. Berlin: Junker und Dunnhaupt, 1938.

———. *Revolution des Denkens*. Dortmund-Leipzig: Westfalen-Verlag, 1939.

———. *Die geistigen Grundlagen der neuen Europa*. Berlin: Franz Eher Verlag, 1941.

———. *12 Jahre mit Hitler*. Munich: Isar Verlag, 1955.

Diewerge, Wolfgang. *Das Kriegsziel der Weltplutokratie: Dokumentarische Veröffentlichung zu dem Buch des Präsidenten der amerikanischen Friedensgesellschaft Theodore Nathan Kaufman, Deutschland muß sterben 'Germany must perish.'* Berlin: Zentralverlag der NSDAP, Franz Eher Verlag, 1941.

Domarus, Max, ed. *Hitler: Reden und Proklamationen, 1932–1945*. Vol. 2, *Untergang*. Neustadt: Schmidt, 1963.

Foreign Relations of the United States (FRUS) Diplomatic Papers. *The Conferences at Malta and Yalta, 1945*. Washington, D.C.: U.S. Government Printing Office, 1955.

———. *The Conferences at Cairo and Tehran, 1943*. Washington, D.C.: U.S. Government Printing Office, 1961.

———. *1943*. Vol. 1, *General*. Washington, D.C.: U.S. Government Printing Office, 1963.

———. *The Conferences at Washington, 1941–1942, and Casablanca, 1943*. Washington, D.C.: U.S. Government Printing Office, 1968.

Friedrichs, Axel. *Dokumente der deutschen Politik*. Vol. 3, *Deutschlands Weg zur Freiheit, 1935*. Berlin: Junker and Dunnhaupt, 1937.

———. *Dokumente der Deutschen Politik*. Vol. 4, *Deutschlands Aufstieg zur Grossmacht*. Berlin: Junker and Dunnhaupt, 1939.

Fröhlich, Elke, ed., with the Institut für Zeitgeschichte, Munich, and the Bundesarchiv. *Die Tagebücher von Joseph Goebbels: Samtliche Fragmente*. Munich: Saur, 1987–2001. Part 1, *1923–1941*, 9 vols; part 2, *1941–1945*, 15 vols.

Goebbels, Joseph, *Kommunismus ohne Maske*. Munich: Zentralverlag der NSDAP, 1935.

———. *Die Zeit ohne Beispiel: Reden und Aufsätze aus den Jahren 1939/40/41*. Munich: Zentralverlag der NSDAP Eher Verlag, 1941.

———. *Das eherne Herz: Reden und Aufsätze aus den Jahren 1941–42*. Munich: Zentralverlag der NSDAP, 1943.

———. *Der steile Aufstieg: Reden und Aufsätze aus den Jahren 1942–43*, 2nd ed. Munich: Zentralverlag der NSDAP, 1944.

———. "Die europäishe Narkose," *Das Reich*, April 1, 1944.

———. "Der Kitt der Feindkoalition: Die Urheber des Unglücks der Welt," *Das Reich*, no. 3, January 21, 1945.

Hardy, Alexander. *Hitler's Secret Weapon: The "Managed" Press and Propaganda Machine of Nazi Germany*. New York: Vantage, 1967.

Heiber, Helmut, ed. *Goebbels-Reden, 1939–1945*, Vol. 2. Munich: Wilhelm Heyne Verlag, 1972.

Höpp, Gerhard, ed. *Mufti-Papiere: Briefe, Memoranden, Reden und Aufrufe Amin al Husainis aus dem Exil, 1940–1945*. Berlin: Klaus Schwarz Verlag, 2001.

Leers, Johann von. *Kräfte hinter Roosevelt*. Berlin: Theodor Fritsch Verlag, 1941.

Ley, Robert, Reichsorganisationsleiter der NSDAP, *Das Organisationsbuch der NSDAP*. Munich: Franz Eher Verlag, 1937 and 1943.

Meyer-Christian, Wolf. *Die englisch-jüdische Allianz: Werden und Wirken der kapitalistischen Weltherrschaft*. Berlin: Niebelungen Verlag, 1940.

Roller, Walter, and Susanne Höschel, eds. *Judenverfolgung und jüdisches Leben unter den Bedingungen der nationalsozialistischen Gewaltherrschaft*. Vol. 1, *Tondokumente und Rundfunksendungen, 1930–1946*. Potsdam: Verlag Berlin-Brandenburg, 1996.

Statistisches Jahrbuch für das Deutsche Reich, 1941–1942. Berlin: Statistisches Reichsamt, 1942.

Sündermann, Helmut. *Tagesparolen: Deutsche Presseanweisungen, 1939–1945, Hitlers Propaganda und Kriegsführung.* Leoni am Starnberger See: Druffel Verlag, 1973.

Toepser-Ziegert, Gabriele. *NS-Presseanweisungen der Vorkriegszeit.* Munich and New York, 1984–1988.

Trials of War Criminals before the Nuerenberg Military Tribunals under Control Council Law No. 10, vols. 12 and 14, Nuremberg, October 1946–April 1949 (Washington, D.C.: U.S. Government Printing Office, 1950).

Zeitschriften-Dienst, June 1939–August 1944, Reichspresseamt des Reichsministeriums für Volksaufklärung und Propaganda.

Visual Materials

Bayerisches Hauptstaatsarchiv, Munich

Bundesarchiv, Koblenz

Department of Art, Imperial War Museum, London

Hoover Institution Archives, Stanford, California

Institut für Zeitungsforschung der Stadt Dortmund, Germany

Landeshauptarchiv Koblenz, Germany (*Die Parole der Woche,* 1940–1942)

United States Holocaust Memorial Museum, Photo Archives, Washington, D.C.

Journals and Newspapers

Deutsche Allgemeine Zeitung (1941)

Judenfrage in Politik, Recht, Kultur und Wirtschaft, Die (1940–1943), Ministry for Public Enlightenment and Propaganda, Library of Congress microfilm 39477

Mitteilungen über die Judenfrage (1937–1939). Ministry for Public Enlightenment and Propaganda, Library of Congress microfilm 39477

New York Times

Reich, Das, 1940–1945

Unser Wille und Weg: Monatsblätter der Reichspropagandaleitung der NSDAP (1931–1941)
Völkische Beobachter, Der, 1939–1945
Washington Post

Bibliographical Essay

Intellectual and cultural history, and the related endeavor of the history of political culture, assume that the most important documents are, in the case of Nazi Germany, those which millions of people read, heard, or saw. Through interlibrary loan, which thanks to the wonders of the Internet has transformed national research collections into a public good available to widely dispersed scholars, all this published material—books, speeches, articles in the daily and periodical press—is available in research libraries in the United States, Europe, and Israel in the original paper form or on microfilm. In addition, two underutilized sources played a key role in my research for this work.

First, the Oberheitmann file, which includes all the wartime press directives of the Reich Press Office and which was first brought to light by the American prosecutors of Otto Dietrich at the Nuremberg Ministries Trial, has received a rather modest amount of attention, in view of its importance, especially for Nazi anti-Semitic propaganda during the war. The use of the file in the original trial is apparent in the court transcripts held in the National Archives of the United States; the complete original lies in the Bundesarchiv (federal archive) in Koblenz, Germany. The Center for Advanced Holocaust Studies at the United States Holocaust Memorial Museum now possesses a copy on microfilm. Any study of Nazi propaganda during the war must take into account this comprehensive collection dealing with all of its themes, not only the Jewish issue. Second, the Landeshauptarchiv (Main State Archive) in Koblenz has the most complete collection of *Parole der Woche (Word of the Week)*, the Nazi wall newspaper of 1937–1943. It too, until now, has been greatly underutilized. Readers will note the considerable use made in this work of Goebbels's diaries, first published in full in Germany in the 1980s and 1990s. A large variety of English translations of Nazi propaganda texts and some visual images can be found in Calvin College's online German Propaganda Archive at *http://www.calvin.edu/academic/cas/gpa/*.

In view of the extensive scholarship on Nazi Germany and the Holocaust, it is surprising to note that this work is the first archive-based study to deal in depth with the role of anti-Semitism in the regime's propaganda. The impressive scholarship on the organization and major themes of the Reich Ministry for Public Enlightenment and Propaganda (RMVP) includes, in chronological order: Derrick Sington and Arthur Weidenfeld, *The Goebbels Experiment: A Study of the Nazi Propaganda Machine* (1943); Oron J. Hale, *The Captive Press in the Third Reich* (1964); Ernest Bramsted, *Goebbels and National Socialist Propaganda, 1925–1945* (1965); Carin Kessemeier, *Der Leitartikler Goebbels in den NS-Organen "Der Angriff" and "Das Reich"* (1967); Jürgen Hagemann, *Die Presselenkung im Dritten Reich* (1970); Jay Baird, *The Mythical World of Nazi War Propaganda, 1939–1945* (1974); Julia Sywottek, *Mobilmachung für den totalen Krieg: Die propagandistische Vorbereitung der deutschen Bevölkerung auf den Zweiten Weltkrieg* (1976); Robert Herzstein, *The War That Hitler Won: The Most Infamous Propaganda Campaign in History* (1978); David Welch, *Nazi Propaganda: The Power and the Limitations* (1983); Caesar Aronsfeld, *The Text of the Holocaust: A Study of the Nazis' Extermination Propaganda, 1919–1945* (1985); Peter Longerich, *Propagandisten im Krieg: Die Presseabteilung des Auswärtigen Amtes unter Ribbentrop* (1987); Iring Fetscher, *Joseph Goebbels im Berliner Sportpalast, 1943: "Wollt Ihr den totalen Kreig?"* (1998); Norbert Frei and Johannes Schmitz, *Journalismus im Dritten Reich* (1999). Ralf Georg

Reuth's *Goebbels,* published in 1990 in German and in 1993 in English, draws on extensive research to present a comprehensive view of Goebbels's political views and actions, his behavior in office behind the scenes, and his private life, such as it was. On Goebbels's view of the Jews, see Christian T. Barth, *Goebbels und die Juden* (2003). Ernst Piper's *Alfred Rosenberg: Hitlers Chefideologe* (Munich: Blessing Verlag, 2005) underscores Rosenberg's importance to the regime's anti-Semitic propaganda, from its think tanks to the pages of *Der Völkische Beobachter.*

Although other institutions, such as the SS, the Foreign Office, and the military, also produced propaganda, the RMVP and the staffs of Goebbels and Dietrich supplied the core of the ongoing Nazi narrative presented to both the German and the foreign audiences. One of the most interesting, yet oddly overlooked, assessments, which contains crucial material about the Reich Press Office, is Alexander Hardy, *Hitler's Secret Weapon: The "Managed" Press and Propaganda Machine of Nazi Germany* (1967). Hardy was one of the American prosecutors of Otto Dietrich at his postwar trial in Nuremberg, in the course of which the prosecution team introduced into evidence the daily and weekly confidential press directives on which I have drawn in this work. E. H. Gombrich, *Myth and Reality in German War-Time Broadcasts* (1970), clearly and succinctly offered insights—which the evidence and argument of this work reinforce—into the paranoid nature of the Nazi narrative.

While the famous anti-Semitic films such as *Jud Süss* and *Der ewige Jude* have received attention, Nazi poster propaganda has been less often examined. Franz-Josef Heyen, *Parole der Woche: Eine Wandzeitung im Dritten Reich, 1936–1943* (1983), offers a brief account of the basic facts of the wall newspaper. Jürgen Bernatzky examines anti-Semitic themes in Nazi posters in his essay "'Juden-Läuse-Flecktyphus': Der nationalsozialistische Antisemitismus im Spiegel des politischen Plakats," in Gunter B. Ginzel, ed., *Anti-Semitismus: Erscheinungsformen der Judenfeindschaft gestern und heute* (1991). Ruth Mellinkoff, *Outcasts: Signs of Otherness in Northern European Art of the Late Middle Ages* (1993), examines the long-standing historical connections between the color yellow and negative views of Jews. Peter Paret offers an astute assessment of Hans Schweitzer in "God's Hammer," in *German Encounters with Modernism, 1840–1945* (2001). Ulrike Bartels, *Die Wochenschau im Dritten Reich: Entwicklung und Funktion eines Massenmediums unter besonderer Berücksichtigung völkischer-nationaler Inhalte* (2004) is a pioneering work in the study of the regime's weekly newsreel, but much remains to be done in examining the view of the war it presented.

Hannah Arendt's classic study of totalitarianism struck the first, loudest, and most influential blow in favor of taking the fanaticism of Nazi ideology seriously. George Orwell's wartime essays on Nazism, though they took a different tack, remain an important point of departure. For a recent philosophical assessment, see Berel Lang, *Act and Idea in the Nazi Genocide* (1990). The works of Fritz Stern and George Mosse form an intrinsic part of any intellectual and cultural history of the Nazi regime. Norman Cohn, *Warrant for Genocide* (1967), a study of the *Protocols of the Elders of Zion,* remains essential reading for work on Nazi propaganda. Karl Dietrich Bracher, *The German Dictatorship* (1970), the first German history to incorporate the work of Jewish refugee scholars on anti-Semitism, remains an excellent analysis of the intersection of ideas, institutions, and politics in Nazi Germany. Ian Kershaw's two-volume *Hitler* (1999, 2000) superbly integrates insights from social, political, and intellectual history. It draws on and expands an important scholarly examination of the relation between Nazi myths and the response to them among the German elites and general public. From the vast scholarship on anti-Semitism, several recent works have been particularly helpful. Robert Wistrich, *Antisemitism: The Longest Hatred* (1991), puts the genocide of 1941–1945 into a broader time frame. Susannah Heschel, *Transforming Jesus from Jew to Aryan: Protestant Theologians in Nazi Germany* (1995), explores the interaction of Nazi and traditional Christian anti-Jewish motifs. Steven E. Aschheim, *Culture and Catastrophe: German and Jewish Confrontations with National Socialism and Other Crises* (1996), includes an insightful essay about "Judaization" *(Verjudung),* a theme that was prominent in Nazi propaganda. Wolfgang Benz, author of many works on anti-Semitism, carefully explores the story of Wolfgang Diewerge's German version of Nathan Kaufman's *Germany Must Perish!* "Judenvernichtung aus Notwehr? Die Legenden um Theodore N. Kaufman," *Vierteljahrshefte für Zeitgeschichte* 29, no. 4 (1981): 615–630. A recent important synthetic work that incorporated Austria and Austrian Catholicism into a story usually monopolized by Luther and his successors is John Weiss, *The Ideology of Death: Why the Holocaust Happened in Germany* (1996). For the Grand Mufti's contribution to Nazi anti-Semitic propaganda, see Simon Wiesenthal, *Großmufti–Großagent der Achse* (Salzburg: Ried Verlag, 1946), and Klaus Gensicke, *Der Mufti von Jerusalem, Amin al-Husseini und die Nationalsozialisten* (Frankfurt am Main: Verlag Peter Lang, 1988). On Nazi ideology and policy toward Zionism and Palestine in the 1930s, see Francis R. Nicosia's valuable *The Third Reich and the Palestine Question,* 2nd ed. (1999). On anti-Semitic intellectuals, see Alan Steinweis's trenchant *Studying the Jew: Scholarly Antisemitism in Nazi Germany* (2006).

In the past decade, historians have greatly advanced our knowledge about the decision that led to the Holocaust. See, in particular, Richard Breitman, *The Architect of Genocide: Himmler and the Final Solution* (1991), and Christopher Browning, *Paths to Genocide* (1992), *Nazi Policy, Jewish Workers, German Killers* (2000), and *The Origins of the Final Solution: The Evolution of Nazi Jewish Policy, September 1939–March 1942* (2004), as well as Phillipe Burrin, *Hitler and the Jews: The Genesis of the Holocaust* (1994). On the relation between Hitler's policies regarding the Jews and those of the Allies, see Shlomo Aronson, *Hitler, the Allies and the Jews* (New York: Cambridge University Press, 2004) and Uwe Dietrich Adam, *Judenpolitik im Dritten Reich* (1972).

On the chronology, ideological roots, implementation, and basic facts of the Holocaust, see Walter Laqueur, ed., and Judith Tydnor Baumel, associate ed., *The Holocaust Encyclopedia,* (2001); Lucy Dawidowicz, *The War against the Jews, 1933–1945* (1975); and Leni Yahil, *The Holocaust: The Fate of European Jewry* (Hebrew ed., 1987; English ed., 1990). On the crucial yet underexamined geography of the Holocaust, see Martin Gilbert's important work *The Macmillan Atlas of the Holocaust*

(1982). One of the first efforts to examine the connection between the war and the Holocaust is Asher Cohen, Yehoyakim Cochavi, and Yoav Gelber, eds., *The Shoah and the War* (1992). Gerhard Weinberg's remarkable body of work on Hitler's diplomacy and military strategy is indispensable for the scholar and serious general reader. Either audience would do well to begin with *Germany, Hitler and World War II* (1995). In *The Foreign Policy of Hitler's Germany: Starting World War II, 1937–1939* (1980), Weinberg offers a powerful and detailed account of time and strategy in Nazi policy before and after the Munich agreement. Weinberg's *World at Arms: A Global History of World War II* (1994) is essential reading for scholars and the serious general reader. In *How the Allies Won* (1995), Richard Overy (like Weinberg) reintroduces contingency into the history of an event that in retrospect at times has seemed like a foregone conclusion. For an understanding of Hitler's ideology and strategy, see Weinberg's edition of *Hitler's Second Book: The Unpublished Sequel to Mein Kampf by Adolf Hitler* (2003), Kershaw's biography, Weinberg's *The Foreign Policy of Hitler's Germany*, and Eberhard Jäckel's succinct yet important *Hitler's World View: A Blueprint for Power* (1981; German ed., 1969). Andreas Hillgruber was the pioneer among German historians who demonstrated how radical anti-Semitism fused with visions of Lebensraum and violent anticommunism to produce a policy of race war and mass murder on the eastern front. His unfortunate involvement in the *Historikerstreit* of the 1980s has, for a younger generation of scholars, obscured his important contributions. His *Hitlers Strategie: Politik und Kriegführung, 1940–1941* (1982 [1965]), and *Germany and the Two World Wars* (1982; German ed., 1967) are required reading for understanding the impact of ideology on policy. Jürgen Förster, "Operation Barbarossa in Historical Perspective," in *The Attack on the Soviet Union,* vol. 4 of *Germany and the Second World War* (1998; German ed., 1996), pp. 1245–1255, adds to understanding of this issue. Omer Bartov has examined the question of the diffusion of ideology among the ranks of the German army on the eastern front in *Hitler's Army: Soldiers, Nazis, and War in the Third Reich* (1991). Wendy Lauer draws on more recently opened archives in *Nazi Empire-Building and the Holocaust in Ukraine* (2005). On the idea of a "war of extermination" in German military thinking, see Isabel V. Hull, *Absolute Destruction: Military Culture and the Practices of War in Imperial Germany* (2005); Jan Phillip Reemtsma, "Die Idee des Vernichtungskrieges: Clausewitz, Ludendorff, Hitler," in Hannes Heer and Klaus Naumann, eds., *Vernichtungskrieg: Verbrechen der Wehrmacht, 1941–1944* (1995), pp. 377–401; and Jehuda L. Wallach, *The Dogma of the Battle of Annihilation: The Theories of Clausewitz and Schlieffen and Their Impact on the German Conduct of Two World Wars* (1986). On continuities and breaks with the experience of World War I, see Hillgruber, as well as the important study by John Horne and Alan Kramer, *German Atrocities, 1914: A History of Denial* (2001). Rüdiger Övermanns, *Deutsche militärische Verluste im Zweiten Weltkrieg* (2000), amounts to a very significant advance in our knowledge of where, when, and how many deaths took place in the Nazi armies.

The scholarship on the impact and reception of Nazi ideology has struggled to draw plausible conclusions on the basis of anecdotal, unrepresentative, and unscientifically chosen samples. More caution is called for, especially following the outpouring in response to Daniel Goldhagen's arguments in *Hitler's Willing Executioners* (1996), which, provocative as they were, in my view extrapolated well beyond what the evidence could bear. On the response of German elites in the 1930s, see Saul Friedlander's subtle and important analysis in *Nazi Germany and the Jews*, vol. 1, *The Years of Persecution, 1933–1939* (1997); Jehuda Bauer, *Rethinking the Holocaust* (2001); and Robert Gellately, *Backing Hitler* (2001). The German historian Michael Wild's *Generation des Unbedingten: Das Führungskorps des Reichssicherheitshauptamtes* (2003) offers a fascinating portrait of the path from the radical right of the 1920s universities to the leadership of the SS and Reich Security Main Office. A comparable study of the trajectory of journalists and propagandists in the government ministries remains to be done. In *The Other God That Failed: Hans Freyer and the Deradicalization of German Conservatism*

(1987), Jerry Z. Muller offers an excellent example of one elite intellectual's path into and–very quietly–out of Nazi ideology and politics. Steven P. Remy, *The Heidelberg Myth: The Nazification and Denazification of a German University* (2002), offers a sobering study of politics and culture at Heidelberg University, where Goebbels completed his doctorate in 1921. On the ideas and institutions that diffused racism and anti-Semitism in Nazi Germany in the 1930s, see Claudia Koonz, *The Nazi Conscience* (2003). On elite and popular responses to Nazi anti-Jewish policies, see David Bankier, *The Germans and the Final Solution: Public Opinion under Nazism* (1992), and his valuable edited collection *Probing the Depths of German Anti-Semitism: German Society and the Persecution of the Jews, 1933–1941* (2000). On German society during World War II, see the comprehensive essay collection edited by Jorg Echternkamp, *Das deutsche Reich und der zweite Weltkrieg*, vol. 9/2, *Die deutsche Kriegsgesellschaft, 1939 bis 1945* (2004); and Marlis G. Steinert, *Hitler's War and the Germans: Public Mood and Attitude during the Second World War* (1977; German ed., 1970). In addition to Kershaw's biography of Hitler, see his *Popular Opinion and Political Dissent in the Third Reich: Bavaria, 1933–1945* (1983). On the mix of belief, cynicism, "resistance," and withdrawal, see Martin Broszat and Elke Fröhlich, *Alltag und Widerstand: Bayern in Nationalsozialismus* (1987), and Martin Broszat, Klaus Dietmar Henke, and Hans Woller, eds., *Von Stalingrad zur Währungsreform: Zur Sozialgeschichte des Umbruchs in Deutschland, 1943–1948* (1988). Yet see also Nicholas Berg's important critical history of West German historiography of the Nazi period, *Der Holocaust und die westdeutschen Historiker: Erforschung und Erinnerung* (2003).

American and British intelligence services compiled much material on the Nazi regime; see Richard Breitman, *Official Secrets: What the Nazis Planned, What the British and Americans Knew* (1998); and Richard Breitman, et al., *U.S. Intelligence and the Nazis* (2005). More work remains to be done on how the United States and Britain, and especially the Soviet Union, interpreted Nazi propaganda. Alexander

Nekrich and Mikhail Heller, *Utopia in Power: A History of the Soviet Union from 1917 to the Present* (1986), powerfully depicts Stalin's misjudgments of 1941. Amir Weiner, *Making Sense of War: The Second World War and the Fate of the Bolshevik Revolution* (2001), assesses the place that the fate of the Jews held in wartime Communist ideology. On Jews in the Soviet Union during this period, see Benjamin Pinkus, *The Jews of the Soviet Union: The History of a National Minority* (1988); and on the purges of the 1930s, see Nicholas Werth, "A State against the People: Violence, Repression, and Terror in the Soviet Union," in Stephanie Courtois, ed., *The Black Book of Communism* (1999), pp. 33–268. On Nazi propaganda about the United States, see the comprehensive study by Philipp Gassert, *Amerika im Dritten Reich: Ideologie, Propaganda und Volksmeinung, 1933–1945* (1997). On anti-Semitism and the situation of Jews in American life during this period, see Jerold S. Auerbach, *Unequal Justice: Lawyers and Social Change in Modern America* (1976); Neil Baldwin, *Henry Ford and the Jews: The Mass Production of Hate* (2001); Scott A. Berg, *Lindbergh* (1998); Henry L. Feingold, *A Time for Searching: Entering the Mainstream, 1920–1945* (1992); and Marcia Graham Synott, *The Half-Opened Door: Discrimination and Admissions at Harvard, Yale, and Princeton, 1900–1970* (1979). In *The Holocaust in American Life* (1999), Peter Novick offers acute judgments about the American official and public responses to news of the Holocaust. Charles Herbert Stember, ed., *Jews in the Mind of America* (1966), provides very interesting results from public opinion research, a new endeavor at the time of the book's publication. On the Roosevelt administration's response to Hitler and the Holocaust, see Robert Dallek, *Franklin D. Roosevelt and American Foreign Policy, 1932–1945* (1979). On the British response, see, in addition to Winston Churchill's multivolume history of the war and Martin Gilbert's multivolume biography of Churchill, Bernard Wasserstein, *Britain and the Jews of Europe, 1939–1945* (1988).

Now-standard reference works on the members of the Nazi regime, and in some cases on their postwar fate, are Wolfgang Benz, Hermann

Graml, and Hermann Weiß, eds., *Enzyklopädie des Nationalsozialismus* (1997); and Ernst Klee, *Das Personenlexikon zum Dritten Reich: Wer war was vor und nach 1945* (2003). On the vocabulary of Nazism, see the classic study by Victor Klemperer, *The Language of the Third Reich, LTI, Lingua Tertii Imperii: Notes of a Philologist* (2000; German ed., 1949), and more recently Cornelia Schmidt-Berning, *Das Vokabular des Nationalsozialismus* (1998). Also see Klemperer's perceptive Nazi-era diaries *I Will Bear Witness, 1942–1945*, (German ed., 1991; English ed., 2000). For a standard German biographical encyclopedia, see Walther Killy, ed., *Deutsche Biographische Enzyklopädie*, (1995).

In my thinking about narrative and ideology I remain indebted to works by social theorists from Alexis de Tocquevillle and Max Weber to Daniel Bell and Clifford Geertz, and to the work of such historians as Karl Bracher, François Furet, George Mosse, Thomas Nipperdey, and Fritz Stern. This work is an effort to build on and develop the history of ideas and politics they did so much to advance. For helpful reflections on break and continuity in cultural traditions, see Michael Andre Bernstein, *Foregone Conclusions: Against Apocalyptic History* (1984). David Carr offers helpful insights in *Time, Narrative, and History* (1986). Michel Foucault, *Madness and Civilization: A History of Insanity in the Age of Reason* (1965), brilliantly captured the madness and logic of "delirious discourse." Max Horkheimer and Theodor Adorno's *Dialectic of Enlightenment* (1944) contained very acute insights into the link between fascism and paranoia, albeit within a generalizing analysis of modernity that conflicts with my views about historical specificity. Richard Hofstadter, *The Paranoid Style in American Politics and Other Essays* (1965), is important reading for historians of political fanaticism in modern history. Joseph Goebbels and Nazi propaganda have been a subject of interest since I described him as a reactionary modernist in my *Reactionary Modernism: Technology, Culture and Politics in Weimar and the Third Reich* (1984).

Index

Plutocracy (*continued*)
256, 260, 261; alleged to be in
conspiracy with Bolshevism, 100,
105, 106, 166, 187, 193, 196,
197; war aim of, 113–114. *See
also* Churchill, Winston; England;
Jews; Roosevelt, Franklin D.;
United States
Pogrom of November 9, 1938, 4,
44–46, 268
Poland, 31, 56, 58, 59, 61, 65, 90,
121, 139–140, 149, 154,
171–172, 174–175, 177, 179,
184, 204, 223, 243, 256, 284,
285, 287; propaganda and German invasion in 1939, 51, 56–58,
64; date of invasion and Hitler's
prophecy, 77; Katyn story,
201–207; death camps in,
232–233, 235
Posters: "He Bears Guilt for the War,"
222; "Behind the Enemy Powers:
The Jew," 222; "The Jew: Instigator and Prolonger of the War,"
223. *See also Word of the Week
(Parole der Woche)*
Press directives (*Presseanweisungen*),
Reich Press Office, 13, 24, 35,
57, 60, 71, 138, 183, 192, 242,
271, 272, 273; Hitler's role,
24–26; "on Jews in England," 58,
62–63, 70–72; general attacks on
the Jews, 58, 189–190, 196, 197,
207–209, 215–219, 257–258; secrecy, 60, 62; book recommendations, 63–64; on Jews in France,
68; language rules, 76, 160, 217,
251–252; on Jews in USA,
84–88; on Franklin D. Roosevelt,
85–86, 118, 128; on war with

Soviet Union, 95–97, 99; on "international Jewry" and Allies,
96–97, 105–106; claim Jews
planned to exterminate Germans,
112, 229–230, 240–241; nonre-
porting of Final Solution, 138,
232–234, 245; on Arabs and
Islamic world, 159–160, 180,
197–198; on Katyn campaign,
201–207; on Jews and Soviet
Union, 223–224, 240; on identity
of Bolshevism and capitalism,
228; claim Allies planned to exterminate Germans, 235; on Allies'
Moscow communiqué, 235–236;
Jewish question as "key to world
history," 240–241; on Hungarian
Jewry, 242–245. *See also* Dietrich,
Otto; Goebbels, Joseph; Hitler,
Adolf; *Periodical Service
(Zeitschriftendienst);* Reich Press
Office; *Völkische Beobachter, der;
Word of the Day (Parole des Tages)*
Projection, 37, 40, 57, 88, 92, 113,
133, 172, 211, 262, 264. *See also*
Anti-Semitism; Paranoia
Protocols of the Elders of Zion, 71, 81,
86, 213, 266, 271
Public opinion in Nazi Germany,
276–277
Puritans and Puritanism in England,
63–64, 71–73. *See also* Aldag,
Peter; Meyer-Christian, Wolf

Radical anti-Semitism, 6–10, 13,
49, 150–152, 206, 230, 265,
273–275, 277. *See also* Anti-
Semitism
Rath, Ernst von, 44
Rathenau, Walter, 154